*Living the* ~~Faith~~

# Living the Tarot

*Applying an ancient oracle to the
challenges of modern life*

---

## Amber Jayanti

**Wordsworth Reference**

This edition first published in 2000 by Wordsworth Editions Limited
Cumberland House, Crib Street, Ware, Hertfordshire SG12 9ET

ISBN 1 84022 513 0

Wordsworth® is a registered trademark of
Wordsworth Editions Ltd

Typeset by Antony Gray
Printed and bound in Great Britain by
Mackays of Chatham plc, Chatham, Kent

*Dedication*

In loving memory of my teachers, Paul Foster Case,
Ann Davies and Baba Muktananda, who helped
launch me on my journey home. To the
builders of the Adytum for their years
of selfless service and dedication to
sharing the light of truth. For my
dearest friend, Bernard, for
his love and support.
With special thanks to
Joseph Nolen, who has inspired
me with his unique brand of humour,
wisdom and understanding. And, of course,
to my students, without whom this book would
not have been possible.

# Contents

**PART FOUR**
*The Gateway of Adulthood*

**PART FIVE**
*The Gateway of Wisdom*

# *Foreword*

This book is important for two reasons First, the subject, which is the Tarot, and second, the motivation of the author, which can obscure or elevate the importance of the subject.

In a world filled with the delusions of appearance, the Tarot is a window into reality. It is marvellous beyond any written doctrine because it is wordless. It is expressed in the universal language of images that all understand without the distortion of a *written or spoken* language whose words have slightly different meanings for each reader. The images in the *true* Tarot are liberating in their effect as they present the reality behind appearance which is the search of all aspirants. That revelation was the purpose behind the creation of the Tarot, but like some other great gifts of redemption, its name and its purpose have been besmirched through the superstitious fear of those who believe that the existence of another Path of Return threatens the veracity of their own. But to those of open mind and perception, the gift of the Tarot is ever there. A word of warning, however – literally hundreds of versions of the Tarot have been 'invented and interpreted' by many who have only artistic qualifications to support their efforts. The Tarot is so profound that its images can be presented with spiritual accuracy only by an advanced Adept of the Western Mystery Tradition. The *true* Tarot decks that have been published by authentic Mystery Schools, such as the Order of the Golden Dawn of England with the Rider deck, and the Builders of the Adytum of the US with the Case deck, are *true* in that they most closely approximate the unpublished Tarot of the Inner School, the Spiritual Hierarchy of the world. The Case deck is used in this book and I consider it the very best available.

I well remember my first good look at a Tarot deck. It aroused a tremendous desire to see *behind* each card for the meaning I sensed was there. And why were they called Tarot 'Keys'? I found out much later that they are so called because a key unlocks something that was closed and allows entry into what was previously unknown. The

Tarot is the easiest gateway to the Great Mysteries of Life – Who, What, Where and Whence. I would add 'How' to that ancient group of questions. Hence, the Tarot is a major part of the basic curriculum of the highest level of the Western Mystery Schools such as Builders of the Adytum.

We are all students of life and some of the more advanced among us are perfecting their knowledge of life through teaching. A real teacher in any subject is one who brings enthusiasm, joy and humour to his instruction, besides a thorough knowledge of the field he teaches. Amber Jayanti is such a teacher. The common danger in teaching a subject like the Tarot is that of becoming a 'Guru', especially in one's own mind. Amber presents her subject with such vulnerability that she completely avoids this sticky, ego-elevating trap. Also, if a subject like the Tarot is presented as either *very occult* or 'super holy', the learning process is debilitated. Amber has a very wholesome, natural approach to the Tarot that dispels the phony mystery and superstition that surrounds the subject and makes it as workable as a cooking recipe. No bell, book and candle here!

In times of personal as well as national and world crisis, which we are certainly experiencing at present, individuals look for spiritual security with an intensity commensurate with the crisis they feel is upon them. Some return to the fundamentalism of their childhood where all you had to do was *believe* to be saved; understanding was unnecessary. Consequently, we are seeing a tremendous resurgence of religious fundamentalism in the world, which is presenting a political problem in certain countries. Paradoxically, because of the same pressures, other individuals seek a deeper understanding of themselves and the hidden processes of life in order to find peace with the reality of *what is*. These conditions are producing a great wave of searchers for reality known as spiritual aspirants. 'When Life desires, Life also answers.' *Living the Tarot* is one of the answers.

REVEREND JOSEPH NOLEN
*Laguna Beach, California*

# Introduction

Amber Jayanti's *Living the Tarot* follows in the hermetic and magical tradition of the Order of the Golden Dawn, and Paul Foster Case's Builders of the Adytum (B.O.T.A.). These organisations teach the 'Ageless Wisdom' as encoded in the mystical body of the knowledge known as the Qabalah, and as pictured in the 22 Major Arcana cards of the Tarot. The word 'arcana' comes from 'ark', which means box or container. Each of these 22 cards contains or represents an entire 'book' of knowledge, an encyclopaedic treatise on the education of the personality, intellect and soul. Together, the Major Arcana cards describe the journey of the individual on the road to self-realisation. In the Ageless Wisdom teachings, this is the knowledge of the Self as One with Source. It is said that much of this wisdom cannot be passed on through books and writing alone, for it requires not only knowledge, but also practice. Spiritual truth is ineffable; true wisdom passes only from teacher to student because it must be experienced through the senses, and transferred from heart to heart.

I feel Amber Jayanti has come as close as is possible in a book to giving the reader the chance to work with a teacher attuned to the heart of Tarot. Like many others have done before her, she provides basic meanings for the symbols and interpretations of the cards. But Jayanti uniquely includes vital links that are usually missing: How can you find the relevance to your own life of the static two-dimensional symbols on the cards? How can you begin to recognise when these seemingly simple symbols have taken on a living form and are activated by an everyday occurrence? How do you know what actions are immature and which show wisdom in confronting life's pitfalls, blocks and limitations? By relating stories from her own life and those of her students, Amber demonstrates problem-solving action you can take. Unlike traditional stories, these examples are tangible and contemporary. They represent the kind of situations in which insight and loving guidance are helpful and appreciated.

'In order to be satisfied that I know a Tarot card,' says Amber

Jayanti, 'I need to feel or experience it in my everyday life.' She describes how she chose the Tarot to accompany and guide her on the path to self-realisation. Reflecting her own potentials and limitations, the Tarot showed her the stages along her path. Chronicling her personal journey, Amber tells how at each crossroad and rough spot she would turn to the Tarot images with such basic questions as: 'What am I not seeing or not understanding in this situation? What am I here to learn?' Again and again Amber found a message in the card she was studying or a card she drew from the deck for assistance. The guidance she found in the cards helped to clear a way for action, break through a negative pattern or yield a new understanding of herself and others.

Amber explains: 'For example, if I began feeling drawn into an emotional cyclone, I sought out my friend the Tarot for some first aid.' Thus the Tarot is a means of immediate assistance, a kind of readily available 'therapy', useful in fulfilling a specific need or achieving a definite purpose. Once fixed in your mind's eye, it is always there showing you how to best handle the situation. Perhaps it suggests compassion for someone else. Perhaps you recognise it as an oft-repeated problem. Through the symbolic information on the cards, the Tarot recommends appropriate possible actions or, just as importantly, attitudes. Perhaps you hear an inner voice speaking through a figure on the card, reminding you of a present lesson and how to use it opportunely. Whatever its form, there is always guidance for deconditioning the automatic reactions of the ego, and for accessing the wisdom of the essential Self.

Having found the Tarot helpful in her life, Amber Jayanti began teaching it to others. Her Tarot classes are the core of the living aspect of this book. *Living the Tarot* is filled with people from all walks of life who have found that the Tarot is a source of 'first aid' and inspiration. Now you can become a participant in these classes. At your own pace – daily, weekly, monthly – you accompany Amber on an exploratory trek through the cards. The presence of her other students is a tangible part of the experience. You learn, as they do, to use this ancient tool for self-knowledge in order to understand and change the events in your life. In their experiences, you will find echoes of your own daily confrontations and challenges. As you work out the lessons of each card, you will discover what limitations and opportunities each card proposes. As you recognise where you are stuck in behavioural patterns that are no longer appropriate, you will find the Tarot pointing to new ways of perceiving your immediate circumstances. These fresh perspectives open up the world of choice, bringing the exhilaration of freedom.

Unlike most other books on the Tarot that teach the Ageless Wisdom, this book is not arcane or 'occult'. There is no need here to hide the truth of the teachings, or to mask it from the uninitiated. The intention of the practices given here is to help you examine your life, discovering both the helpfulness and limitations of your desires, motivations and actions. This results in a process of *dehabituation* or *deconditioning*, of removing control from the externally oriented ego and investing it directly in your essential Self. By committing yourself to thus elevate your own soul, you elevate every other being, as all souls are a part of the One Soul.

The 'Suggestions for Application and Integration' following each card tell you how to fill your mind, heart and memory, as well as all your bodily senses, with the qualities and characteristics of that particular archetypal energy in yourself. In so doing, there is no room left for anything else. This experience produces a unity of word, thought and action – a concentration of intellect, emotion and physical experience that is the key to understanding the essence of each energy. This opens you to new perceptions and fresh choices, where before you saw only the rut of a well-worn path.

If you are already familiar with the Tarot and, like me, lack the patience for a consecutive program of study, then, when you need assistance, simply open the book at random to any page – a form of divination called 'bibliomancy'. That card will supply you with the precise advice needed for the moment. You can also draw a Major Arcana card from any Tarot deck to answer a specific question and, by reading the lessons and stories of that card, find practical suggestions for your problem. Likewise, for each birthday, anniversary and year of your life, there are particular Major Arcana cards, determined numerologically, that can help you find the personal meaning and significance of those times. To do this, add together the month, day and year of any date of interest, and then reduce the sum, to discover the appropriate Tarot card. For example, to find the card that indicates your own lessons for any given year, add your birth month and day to the year you want to know about. For myself, this would be:

$$
\begin{array}{rl}
10 & \text{(Month)} \\
14 & \text{(Day)} \\
+1992 & \text{(Year)} \\
\hline
2016 & = 2 + 0 + 1 + 6 = 9 = \text{The Hermit}
\end{array}
$$

When this answer is reduced to a number that is 22 or below, I can read about the corresponding Tarot card for insights into my major growth issues for that entire year.

The 22 Major Arcana cards of the Tarot represent the essence or archetypal energies that exist within each human being. They describe your 'fate' in that you are destined to face and explore them, each in your own individual way. They are the psychic building blocks from which each event, whether inner or outer, is constructed. Each of these schemata affords you infinite potential for expression. The activation of any of them presents you with the opportunity to use its potential, and to discover the 'meaning' behind your experiences. To know and use all 22 archetypal energies at their highest level of functioning can be considered the purpose of life here on earth. When your mind and heart respond only to the highest level of spirit, you become complete and whole. Amber Jayanti shows you how to use the Tarot cards as signposts along this spiritual path, as guides to achieving your individual purpose. When you are consistently expressing the energies of each card at the level of Wisdom (described by Amber as the 'Gateway of Wisdom'), then you have arrived at Enlightenment. For most of us, this is a goal not yet realised. You are here in physical form to learn the significance of these energies by encountering and grappling with them so that they may be lived, not as a reaction to old behaviours and memories, but for themselves, in the fresh now, and with a practical application of their skills and opportunities.

MARY KATHERINE GREER
*San Francisco, California*

# *Preface*

By the time you read these words, I shall be nearly fifty years old. For more than half my life I have been living, studying, consulting with and teaching the Tarot and Qabalah.[1] Like most of us, I was raised in a dysfunctional family. But 'dysfunctional' is only a contemporary label for the human condition. In generations before dysfunction was identified as such, people began travelling spiritual paths in an effort to alleviate personal pain and heal themselves of life's traumas. In an effort to transcend the wounds of my childhood, I sought spiritual practice. Initially, my attraction to the Tarot was to help me to 'magically' separate from my pain and leave the troubles of this world behind by ascending to a higher plane.

The Tarot, however, became a tool through which I learned that in order to transcend the physical, I first had to transform it. The Tarot made me aware that I needed to recall, examine and in some instances re-experience certain deep-seated issues and patterns in a conscious, feeling type of way in order to resolve my difficulties. From this came great mental and emotional relief, as well as the spontaneous alteration of numerous obsolete habit patterns. The Tarot's imagery then helped to reinforce these changes and taught me how to continue transforming other worn-out ways of thinking and feeling. From this, I have become increasingly able to perceive myself, others and the world from a more objective point of view via

---

1 The Tarot is rooted in the teachings of the ancient mystery school tradition known as the Qabalah. When spelled with the letter Q, the word Qabalah refers to Universal Qabalah. As I know it, Universal Qabalah is a body of esoteric and practical wisdom that blends Judeo-Christian mysticism (Kabbalah and Cabala) with the teachings of other disciplines – the Hermetic arts and sciences such as tarot, astrology, alchemy, numerology and sacred geometry, Buddhism, Hinduism, Sufism and Shamanism. Universal Qabalah is a nonracist, nonsexist and nonhomophobic system that bridges the inner traditions of the East and West. Qabalah is not limited to or associated with any particular religious denomination.

the Tarot's eyes. The Tarot, like any true spiritual tradition, is a means through which an individual may harmonise his/her life with the cosmic order. The Tarot has taught me that this world is a very spiritual and magical place.

Magic occurs when one ceases to survive and starts to thrive! Because so many of us grew up in dysfunctional, or perfectly imperfect, human families, we were not adequately prepared for adult life. We grew into adult 'survivors', who after becoming aware of our pain, have sought to re-educate/re-parent ourselves in order to do more than merely get by. Consequently, many have turned childhood adversity and trauma into opportunities to grow wiser, more compassionate and better able to thrive.

We, as individuals and as a collective consciousness, are slowly becoming equipped with the skills we *ideally* should have been taught as children – a working knowledge of the universal and natural laws and principles with which to navigate through life successfully. But it is not an ideal world, and our parents are as perfectly imperfect as ourselves. Blaming our parents for our failings is too often an impulse existing in Western culture. We can choose either to remain stuck in blame or accept that we have come into the physical world to learn our spiritual lessons and that our parents are an integral part of this package. Until the time that we are *all* enlightened, there will continue to be imperfections and human frailty (a.k.a. dysfunction) present in both child-rearing and life. This book addresses how the Tarot has, and is, fostering this transformation in myself and others. It is about how the Tarot may be used as a powerful practical tool to guide us through the process of transforming our attitudes, actions, ourselves and our lives.

Now I hear you asking, 'How, out of all the spiritual paths, did you pick the Tarot?' My religious upbringing was an unusual combination of Orthodox and Reformed Judaism. As a young teenager, I would sit with my more intellectual friends and discuss the existence or nonexistence of a Superior consciousness. I had several intense spiritual experiences during childhood, but was unable to articulate or truly identify them as such. I recall going to the synagogue and praying fervently to personally experience God or the Most High. However, the Most High was not evident in such forms in either my own religious upbringing or in those of my friends, some of whom were churchgoers. Besides the fact that sexism ran rampant, "God the Father, or Lord", the emphasis always seemed to be on how much money a family donated to the temple/

church, how much better one group was than another, or on what new fashion should be worn to religious services.

My hunger eventually led to an expansion of my mind through some guided LSD experiences in the mid-1960s, wherein I encountered brief glimpses of the divinity within all. Not long afterwards, I set eyes on the Tarot. I guess you might say that the Tarot picked me. From the first moment, I was drawn to it as to a dear old friend. When an acquaintance told me that the Tarot leads to a direct and lasting knowledge of divinity, I was committed. But because I had been warned on several occasions that buying Tarot cards for yourself was unlucky, I waited to be given them. Of course, I was overjoyed when my best friend gave me *The Tarot of Marseilles* for Christmas in 1967. Since then, after much thought, I have decided that buying cards for yourself is fine, because with each new deck you make a gift to your own spiritual nature within – your Higher Self. I later learned that the literal translation for the word *Qabalah*, the ancient esoteric mystery school tradition upon which the Tarot is founded, was a gift that is passed from mouth to ear down through the generations. I then realised that the modern idea of gift-giving is a distorted interpretation of the fact that certain spiritual teachings are gifts that cannot be purchased, but only passed down from one's inner teacher when the student is ready to receive them.

The Magical Tradition of Tarot and Qabalah study is perhaps the most unrecognised and discredited of spiritual traditions. Through my Tarot studies, I have learned that magic is not pulling pigeons from a coat sleeve, or casting spells to bring back a lost love. It is the ability to derive extraordinary understanding out of the ordinary. It is knowing how to shift the shape of our thoughts, feelings, attitudes, and life situations. Magic is the practice of transforming our lives via the desire to wilfully apply the universal and natural laws and principles to everyday situations. It is about employing your personality – its gifts and liabilities – as a means to change into your divine Self and as a vehicle for transforming this planet into Paradise. In other words, whether we are cognisant of it or not, we all can be magicians living magical lives!

After beginning my studies, the Tarot and I became almost inseparable. Occasionally, I even slept with certain cards under my pillow, hoping to learn their secrets through my dreams. I spent hours meditating on their imagery and devoured every book on the Tarot I could find. The most significant of these books were two by Paul Foster Case; *The Tarot: A Key to the Wisdom of the Ages*, and

*The Book of Tokens: 22 Meditations on the Ageless Wisdom.* Paul Foster Case was formerly the head of the Order of the Golden Dawn, the first publicly accessible group in the Western Mystery School Tradition in over 1,600 years. Members included Dion Fortune, William Butler Yeats, Israel Regardie, Eliphas Levi, Moina and Macgregor Mathers, Aleister Crowley, Lady Freda Harris (creator of the Thoth Deck), Arthur Edward Waite and Pamela Coleman Smith (creator of the Rider-Waite Deck), to name just a few.

An important door had opened for me. My interest and study were intense, so much so that early in my studies, when I lived and worked in a busy communal-type household in San Francisco's Haight-Ashbury – then the heart and soul of the spiritual and metaphysical renaissance – I'd hide out in the bathroom with my cards and books, as it was often the only place where I would be undisturbed. My interest in the Tarot was further spurred by my involvement in the so called 'counter-culture'. I was attracted to this movement because it was anti-war, peace- and love-oriented, and it acknowledged and gave meaning to reincarnation, psychic phenomena and spiritual experiences. These were things I had known about from early childhood, yet lacked external points of reference for. It is exciting to note that some of what was then considered 'counter-culture' is now slowly becoming part of the mainstream culture.

In the spring of 1968, I learned about Paul Foster Case's school for Tarot and Qabalah study, Builders of the Adytum[2] (B.O.T.A.), based in Los Angeles. I immediately began taking both his and his successor's, Ann Davies, correspondence courses. Although Paul Foster Case died nearly fifty years ago, and Ann Davies passed on in the 1970s, the school is still alive and busy, mailing its carefully planned lessons in Tarot and the Qabalah to students all over the world. Through this work, I learned that the Tarot is a pictorial representation of the Qabalah, an esoteric mystery school tradition.

One of the most common pitfalls in learning Tarot is acquiring too many decks when one first begins to study. This often results in the student becoming confused and then, 'giving up'. New students usually alternate between delight and confusion when faced with the large number of Tarots (each expressing its maker's unique personality) available. When asked, 'Which deck is best for me?' I answer, select a deck you feel attuned to: its placement in time – biblical, medieval, renaissance, contemporary, ultramodern, etc;

2 The word Adytum means 'sacred temple within'.

style of artwork – primitive, realist, surrealist, collage, and colours or lack thereof; card names; and symbolism of both the Major and Minor Arcanas. Then learn it thoroughly! Most importantly, be sure there is enough written information accompanying or written about the deck to help you along.

I use the B.O.T.A. deck to teach with. It is a wonderful way to learn the traditional[3] or classical Tarot. Following this tradition is a marvellous way to learn the basics of Tarot study for several reasons. First, because the tradition is aligned with a spiritual hierarchy. Second, these cards were specifically designed to depict the universe and natural laws and principles, plus the results of living by such. Certain vital colours that assist in assimilating the aforementioned laws and principles are used as well. Third, the B.O.T.A., and its close relative, the Waite-Smith/Rider deck, have been widely discussed. Finally, many of the newer decks do not provide detailed written guidelines to instruct you about their particular cards and symbolism. This can be most frustrating for the beginner! To conclude, by learning traditional Tarot first, you will learn the core meanings of each card and then be able to work with other decks despite the differences in symbolism. You will be better equipped to branch out to other Tarots with more ease and confidence than students who dabble with several decks at a time, but do not master one.

I spent my first few years with the Tarot studying the symbolism and philosophy of each card in a highly organised and disciplined fashion. I kept notebooks, coloured in a pre-drawn set of B.O.T.A. cards, exactly like those that appear in this book,[4] and studied at preset times each day. I considered myself a serious student, and applied the same organisation, discipline and desire that had seen me through the rigours of the New York City public school system earlier in my life. As time passed, I began delving into the cards through prayer, dreams, meditation, inspirational quotes, personal statements (affirmations) and divination. My studies have instructed me that each card has a divine essence. I have found that by focusing my concentration and prayers upon that spirit, I have been able to learn about the card's deeper meanings through dreams, meditation and in daily living. These approaches have borne some remarkable

---

3 Traditional refers to embracing the Tarot as a pictorial representation of the ancient Qabalistic Mystery School Tradition.
4 The Tarot cards in this book appear with special permission from the Builders of the Adytum.

revelations for me and my students. I wish to share this knowledge with you throughout this book.

Meditation, or focused concentration, is a way of learning about the unwritten and previously undisclosed aspects of Tarot. By looking at or thinking about a symbol or concept from a card for extended periods, you gain new insight, and a better understanding of what you already know.

Words of inspiration that have come from within and from friends and students, in addition to quotations from my studies of Yoga, the Bible, the Qabalistic Masters and other Wiseones,[5] offer me further perspectives on a symbol or concept. For example, the ancient Sanskrit mantra, So'ham – 'I Am That I Am' – added untold dimensions to the Magician card for me. Plato's, 'There is an eye of the soul which is more precious than ten thousand bodily eyes; by it alone Truth is seen', expanded my comprehension of the Star card.

Personal statements or affirmations bring the concepts I consider relevant to a card into play in my life. They encapsulate and personalise information in simple, easy-to-recall phrases that enable me to integrate a concept or symbol into everyday interactions, to better know and live the Tarot. For instance, I incorporate the Lover's teachings into my decision-making process and personal relationships by affirming, 'My Sword of Discrimination is a useful and most necessary life tool. I have the courage and Self-love to stand naked with my thoughts and feelings.' You can enrich your life and enliven the cards by taking the time and effort to compose and use statements like this. Please be aware that you get only what you put into the Tarot study.

Divinatory questions. Divination for me is not fortune-telling, the foretelling or 'reading' of future events for another. It is a means of bringing the divinity present within each of us and all life situations to the fore. The word divination means, 'to know by inspiration, intuition, or reflection. To bring forth (or down) the divine through augury – the interpretation of signs, omens and symbols'. All we really have before us is the present, which is, of course, the fruit of our past actions and decisions. What those who do predictive work do is, in truth, only based upon the present, and we all know how changeable the present moment may be.

Everyone is psychic to one degree or another: I have experienced

---

5  This is a term I use to denote both the male and female masters of wisdom.

this from earliest childhood. But *the lower psychic world of primal instinct is often confused with the higher spiritual world of intuition.* This point is illustrated on the Tree of Life, a Qabalistic diagram of the interactions that occur between personal and universal consciousness. The Tree of Life is a map illustrating the involution and evolution of consciousness, wherein the subconscious psychic plane of Foundation or *Yesod* (in Hebrew) lies below the self-conscious realm of Beauty or *Tiphareth*, while the superconscious spiritual plane of The Crown, *Kether*, resides as it does in life – above all. I spent years learning how to differentiate between the two planes and aiming to go beyond the lower psychic realms and attune myself to the higher spiritual truths when doing Tarot consultations.

I strongly believe that people who use the Tarot only psychically miss the most important aspect of Tarot. They are attuned to an awareness that is only equal to, or even less developed than, the conscious plane rather than reaching up to superconsciousness. In other words, unless the psychic's subconscious mind is purified to the point where it reflects only what is above, it is subject to error. When seeking guidance, I recommend aspiring to the greater world, something Tarot study can help you learn more about. The Tarot is my pathfinder when I'm lost, confused or disheartened. I have learned that if I turn to the cards with an open heart and mind plus an abiding desire to know how to proceed with what is in accord with the *greatest* or *highest* good, I can always find my way. The Tarot helps one discover which forces, or universal and natural laws and principles, are at work. It then either provides guidelines for harmonising one's thoughts, words and actions with the cosmic order by revealing previously undisclosed options, or helps to confirm the wisdom each of us may already sense to be true.

I've also found that one of the most important goals of Tarot study and spiritual insight, and actually a prerequisite to the final goal of achieving closeness and union with the Most High, is to validate study and insight through practical application. The Tarot's teachings are about transforming and bettering our lives and our world. Because we live in a physical environment and have physical bodies, it makes sense to extend these ideas and awarenesses into daily living. Therefore, instead of just studying the principles of the Strength card one may use these principles in a situation that requires strength. Practical application and integration take ideas, insights and information out of the realms of thought and feeling, and put them into the realm of action. Without this, one will never find out what works and what does not. I have found no better way to learn the Tarot than to make it real, to make it a part of my everyday world by living its teachings. The main purpose of this book is to teach, inspire and invite you to do likewise.

In conclusion, I must confess that I thought about the Tarot's teachings for years before I actually began using them daily. Please consider this: The purpose of spiritual practice is to practise (and practise and practise) making ordinary everyday living better, magical and more enjoyable, with the fringe benefit of cleaning up your past, progressing spiritually and making the world a better place for yourself and others. My message to you is not to hesitate. Make the Tarot more than another intellectual exercise. Take its wisdom beyond the world of your mind and into your everyday interactions now. Don't wait! Get your money's worth from this book. Live the cards now!

With Respect and Love,
AMBER JAYANTI

# *Part One*

## INTRODUCTION TO
## LIVING THE TAROT

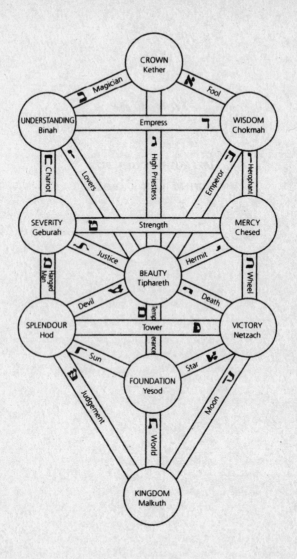

*The twenty-two letters of the Hebrew alphabet and twenty-two cards of the Tarot's Major Arcana assigned to the Qabalistic Tree of Life*

# CHAPTER I

# The Four Steps to Tarot Mastery

At first glance, the Tarot appears to be just a set of pictures. But then, in a way, so is life. Please take a minute or so to consider this similarity. Look around at the 'Tarot' of your life at this moment: where and how your body is situated, positioned and clothed, your surroundings, the presence of other people or creatures, the time of day, even the season of the year. Next, take a few seconds to reflect on your mental and emotional states and consider how these might be expressed in your environment. Now look forward in this book to the Empress and Emperor cards. They, too, are pictures of life: a regal matron sits surrounded by her lush garden; a dignified gentleman is surrounded by his mountainous domain. Take a few moments to 'sense' their mental and emotional states as well. The Tarot's Major Arcana are pictorial representations of the universal and natural laws and principles, what I call the 'Rules and Tools of the Game of Life', plus the results of living by such. The remaining cards – the Minor Arcana, or four suits – illustrate the integration of these guidelines into everyday experience.

According to oral tradition and scattered bits of evidence, the Tarot was conceived by the ancient Wiseones for the purposes of achieving closeness with God/dess and nature; providing posterity with a system that could help meet the challenges of daily living; and establishing inroads to peace and harmony within ourselves and the world at large. The term God/dess used throughout this book means the male and female or positive and negative aspects of the Divine. Qabalists relate to the concept of God as both Father and Mother. The Qabalistic Tree of Life illustrates the existence of this duality and polarity by having male/positive and female/negative limbs: on the Tree of Life, the male limb is topped by Wisdom or *Chokmah* on the right. Understanding or *Binah* tops the left-hand female limb. The neutral trunk, headed by the Crown, *Kether*, rightfully stands above and between the polarities, indicating their origin. Notice how the Tree of Life has 22 paths, each bearing one of the 22 letters of the Hebrew alphabet. Because each Tarot card is linked with a Hebrew letter, the Tarot is a unique way of learning about the Tree of Life and Qabalah they visually represent.

Ordinarily, you are taught to read and interpret the pictures or Tarot of your life by your family, peers, educational and religious institutions, and the media. In early childhood, you are like a sponge, drinking up information indiscriminately as to the workings of the world and your role in it. You are taught not only verbally through words and non-verbally via body language and actions, but also through the emotional undertone of those who instruct you. This process is called the development of a habituated or conditioned perspective.

Experiencing life from this vantage point is sometimes workable and satisfying, while at other times it isn't. Why? In the words of Swami Muktananda, we lack 'right understanding', a term he uses to indicate that everything is divine in origin. This is aligned with the most basic of Qabalistic tenets: God/dess is everywhere, in each person, situation and thing, and at all times. You become unhappy and dissatisfied with life because you lack another context (a spiritual one) to compare it to, something that Tarot work may provide.

You may misread and misinterpret your life experiences because of your habituated perspective – past experiences, training and emotional reactions – and your need to conform to others' desires and expectations in order to be loved and/or successful. This happens because you are not aware that each experience is, in fact, new. Although you are awake physically, you are mentally unaware – unconscious or 'asleep with your eyes open'. The Tarot, as I have come to know and love it, is a potent means through which to encounter life from an awake and aware perspective. You may use the cards to help you perceive what is genuinely called for and view life with 'right understanding'.

Again, the 22 Major Arcana cards represent the universal and natural laws and principles, plus the results of living by these. Because of this, many people learn Tarot to become adept at interpreting, or 'reading' if you'd like, ways to most effectively interact with these forces in daily life. This, to me, is the true meaning of the term 'Tarot Reading'. The Tarot has taught me how to overlay these laws and principles on to the multitude of pictures in my daily life and to interpret what is occurring from the greater, rather than from the lesser, point of view. The Tarot has helped me to see in life situations more of what is there, rather than what I want or have been conditioned to see.

To conclude, because so many of us were habituated in dysfunctional families, a great need to re-habituate or re-parent ourselves has arisen. Many types of work geared to help re-habituate, reclaim and heal the 'Inner Child' have become available to answer this need. The ancient Tarot and Qabalah have offered the tools with which to do this type of transformational work since their inception. When the Qabalist, Jesus of Nazareth, said, 'Become ye as little children,' this is what he meant.

## Learning the Four Steps

Step 1 – *Getting Acquainted with the Rules and Tools of the Game of Life*   This involves cultivating the desire to learn what the cards mean, and then putting in the time and effort to do so. Each chapter of this book begins with a section called 'General Information and Symbolism' to help you along. Caution: please do not feel locked into these interpretations. They are only meant to get you started, to stimulate your mind and intuition.

Mystics say that if you meditate on a symbol long enough, its meaning will become clear to you, even if it has never been explained. This is the process in which any authority on symbolism is engaged. The B.O.T.A. work kindled my own understanding, as I hope this work will kindle yours. But venture out, discover your own meanings for the symbols. There is no right or wrong interpretation of them – a wonderful aspect of the ancient yet living, growing and transforming Tarot.

Step 2 – *Taking the Rules and Tools and Applying them to Everyday Life*   Whether this is accomplished by following the sections of this book called 'Suggestions for Application and Integration', by selecting a card from the deck each morning as a means to approach and better understand the day's events, or by working with your personal numerology, as Mary K. Greer suggests, is of little consequence. This is the point at which your ideas and spiritual insights *must* be applied to the physical world, relationships, work, community, health, etc. This is the juncture where students put the teachings into action. They 'behave as if' they truly believe, and presto, they get results.

This step may be the toughest and most disheartening for many aspirants, since theories must be put to the test. It is the slow and laborious process of replacing obsolete ways of thinking and being – the habituated perspective – with new unhabituated ways of approaching life, quite a challenge in our age of space technology, computers and instant everything.

This is the place in Tarot work where many tend to give up the cards and seek another 'easier' path. Do not be tricked. The nitty-gritty work of integration is an eventuality on every path (and believe me, I've tried to avoid it) no matter what the discipline selected: Tarot, Qabalah, Sufism, Buddhism, Hinduism or Christianity. It was the teachings of Siddha Yoga that directed me back to the Tarot while living and working in the *ashram* in India. It showed me that my spiritual practice (called *sadhana* by the yogis) wasn't just intellectual knowledge and mastery of my guru's teachings, but the actual application of them to *all* aspects of my everyday life.

Those interested in Tarot need to know more about this critical step to inspire and instruct them when they feel stuck, discouraged or impatient, usually because they lack both proper instruction and role models. That is the purpose of this book's sections on Personal and Student Experiences. These segments were taken from tapes of class sessions to show how the students and I do this.

I send students home with this assignment: 'Use in your life what we have discussed and seen here in class. Here are some suggestions on how to apply the cards to what is challenging you in your life at this time.' That's the way I have found to truly learn Tarot. The sections on 'Suggestions for Practical Application and Integration' evolved from my own need to experience each card's teachings in some tangible way. Through these assignments, students return to class knowing the Tarot to be an intimate part of themselves. Please remember, in the process of experimenting with the cards and these techniques, you may discover your own methods of integration. Engage your discoveries. Remember, the purpose of this work is to get you started, to inspire you.

The Third and Fourth Steps are natural outgrowths of the first two.

Step 3 – *Incorporating the Teachings until they Become Second Nature*
At this point, you no longer have to constantly remind yourself to use the Rules and Tools, because they are becoming part of your automatic thinking, feeling and doing. As a result of this change of attitude, your life gradually changes, difficulties become opportunities to do your best, and what was once impossible and debilitating becomes possible and sometimes even fun.

Step 4 – *Completely Mastering the Teachings, thus Achieving Enlightenment* Tarot has the potential to help you reshape your attitudes, which in time will transform your world. Here you continually interact with all aspects of your life – your body, family, friends, career, even the checker in the grocery store – from a fresh perspective.

# CHAPTER 2

# The Four Gateways of Life

Each chapter of this book contains a section called 'Gateway of Life'. This is where the Major Arcana (each of the 22 cards portrayed in this book) are discussed in the light of the four segments, or Gateways, of life: Childhood, Adolescence, Adulthood and Wisdom (old age). This approach is designed to bring the traditional archetypes and their teachings down to earth in order to establish a more personal identification with them, as well as to add to each card's meaning.

This approach or model may be aligned with the Four Steps of Tarot Mastery: Childhood, which is a process of becoming acquainted with the Rules and Tools of the Game of Life – the universal and natural laws and principles; Adolescence, integrating and applying the Rules and Tools to everyday living; Adulthood, an assimilation of the Rules and Tools until they become second nature; and Wisdom, the complete incorporation and mastery of the teachings.

Ordinarily, these terms refer to chronological periods of life. However, in this work the meanings are different. Here, the reference is to an individual of *any age* passing through a particular Gateway due to a life circumstance. For example, the shock of having a serious car accident while driving drunk and angry might catapult an adult back into the childhood stage, to learn more constructive ways of dealing with anger. Or, as another example, a brief encounter with cosmic consciousness, through meditation or a consciousness-expanding technique, may project a stable adult forward to glimpse what the Gateway of Wisdom holds in store. In either case, the event may serve as an incentive to do the work needed to develop one's Self more fully. This system allows for the instances when, although you have an adult body, you may in certain aspects of your personality and maturation process be in Childhood, Adolescence and/or Wisdom as well.

Finally, as you proceed through the various Gateways, you still use the Rules and Tools from earlier points along the way, but in more advanced forms. For instance, in Childhood the Magician might symbolise a generalised excitement about the magic of life. Yet in Adulthood, the Magician might indicate your integrating the fact that you actually 'make magic' in that you help to create the circumstances of your life. In summary, each card within each Gateway also holds the potential for each of the other Gateways. Thus you can be an Adolescent Emperor, an Adult Hierophant, a Child Star, and a Wise High Priestess all at once.

## The Fool's Journey

The *Four Gateways of Life*

Childhood   The Fool to the Chariot (double Gateway)
*includes*: the Fool, the Magician, the High Priestess, the Empress, the Emperor, the Hierophant, the Lovers and the Chariot.

Adolescence   The Chariot to Death (double Gateway)
*includes*: the Chariot, Strength, the Hermit, the Wheel of Fortune, Justice, the Hanged One and Death.

Adulthood:   Death to the Moon (double Gateway)
*includes*: Death, Temperance, the Devil, the Tower, the Star and the Moon.

Wisdom   The Moon to the World
*includes*: the Moon, the Sun, Judgement and the World.

CHAPTER 3

# General Suggestions for Living the Tarot

The Tarot is a powerful tool for growth and transformation. In order to achieve its potentials, it is essential to use the cards in daily living. The purpose of this book is to provide information on how to use the 22 Major Arcana cards beyond the limits of particular spreads. I have found that the most effective way to receive guidance from the Tarot is as follows:

1 Focus on an issue you need guidance about.

2 Formulate a question based upon it; for example, 'Dear Higher Self, what is the best way for me to handle the situation with my stepson for our greatest good?'

3 Ask your Higher Self this question with an open heart and mind, then select one card . . .

4 Without censoring yourself, brainstorm with the card as to what it means with regard to your question.

5 If you don't come up with a single answer at this time, leave the card in a visible place until one becomes evident.

6 You might also meditate on the card daily or 'dream on it' at night until the answer is clear.


## Divinatory Questions for the Cards

For each of the Major Arcana cards, you will find two groups of questions to ask yourself or others when consulting the cards. This question format allows you to affirm or negate what the cards offer, rather than state an absolute conclusion. Phrases such as 'Might you be', 'Are you possibly', 'Have you been', 'Could you possibly be', etc., are useful for this purpose.

## Interpreting Upright and Reversed Cards

The questions are divided into two groups, those for upright cards and those for reversed cards. For many readers, whether a card falls upright or reversed connotes a positive or negative meaning respectively, but for maximum results, these meanings can be expanded to indicate other aspects as well. Unless you are drawing only one card from the deck, a card appears in the context of all the other cards drawn and should be interpreted thusly. We all know that to hear or read something out of context is very limiting, and the same thing applies to upright and reversed Tarot cards. Always take into account a card's position and relationship to the cards around it. Consequently, a reversed card may then be a positive indicator, i.e. Temperance in the future reversed, might suggest the end of an especially trying situation, while an upright card may possibly indicate weakness, i.e. the Devil in the future, upright.

In addition, a sense of the consultation in its entirety, as well as the balance between upright and reversed cards, should be considered in the interpretation.

## Special Guidelines for Reversed Cards

To begin with, it is of the utmost importance to keep in mind that no card is good or bad. This may be likened to a square appearing in an astrological chart or, for that matter, almost any life situation. *It all depends on what the individual does with the situation!*

A reversed card may have a meaning similar to that when it falls upright, but suggests a less conscious or more embryonic state. That is, the concept or behaviour is not fully developed and therefore may be hardly discernible. It is just beneath the surface and awaiting the right time and conditions to appear. It may further indicate that energy is blocked or closed off, either consciously or unconsciously, or that one may be resisting or denying something. Also, there may be a potential present that is not being used or released because it is being unconsciously repressed or consciously suppressed. Therefore, what is under the surface is demanding to be acted out or upon. In this instance, the reversal becomes a turning point and/or opportunity to take action and bring the quality designated by the card into conscious expression.

When a card comes up reversed, it actually becomes physically 'ungrounded', because it is turned upside down. Naturally, this might denote a state of physical, mental, emotional or spiritual instability.

In addition, it might indicate that certain qualities are slow to emerge, are immature or arrested in their development, or are unrealistic or even lacking altogether. However, it may also suggest that the concepts and characteristics represented by the card are being re-evaluated and are therefore temporarily destabilised. In this regard, it may show the beginning of some new cycle or understanding clarity. Remember, everything is constantly changing and, over time, instability tends to bring greater stability.

Finally, the reversed position may indicate that the individual concerned in the consultation (yourself or another) relies on others to do things he or she wants, or more often, needs to do. I call this 'indirect addressing'. For example: A man wants to be an artist, but because he lacks confidence in his ability, he becomes a patron of art. A woman wishes to become a doctor, but fearing the rigours of medical school, she does clerical work in a hospital while looking for a doctor to marry instead. This type of reversal may intimate the need to stretch out and learn something new rather than living through others' achievements.

## Application and Integration of the Cards

At the conclusion of each chapter, there is a list of suggestions for applying and integrating that card in your life. These are designed to offer you a personal and sometimes vivid experience with each card. You may have all the information available on each card in your mind, but to achieve genuine understanding, it must be brought into the arena of daily living.

I recommend doing those exercises first which appeal to you most. Next, I suggest you become the Fool and do an exercise entirely new to you, such as the Rerun, or using the scents and herbs corresponding to each card. Remember, *expect change and it will surely happen*!

At first, you may find your insights and transformations subtle, which is normal. But with desire, dedication, time, patience and persistence you will become increasingly attuned to the workings of the cards and will experience both your life and your understanding of the Tarot growing richer and deeper.

Here are some general directions for using the exercises listed in the 'Suggestions for Application and Integration' section for each card:

1   Colour the enlargement of the Builders of the Adytum card included in this book. I suggest following the *Colouring Instructions* provided at the back of this book. You may, however,

choose to colour it to your own taste. If you are artistically inclined, draw your own version of each card with yourself as the figure(s). This is not a new idea: one of the membership requirements for the world-renowned Order of the Golden Dawn was to create an original Tarot deck. While colouring, notice what you think and feel about the symbols, as well as about the overall mood of the card. This exercise is actually a meditation and one of the best ways I know to become familiar with the symbolism of the cards.

2   Set a card – for example, the Hermit – in a visible place as a reminder to your conscious and subconscious minds to use and absorb its teachings. (Note that the subconscious is always functioning on a subliminal level.) You might use it to remind yourself that the Hermit's teachings are always at your service; to remember to call upon your tools when you get stuck; or to remind yourself that the people in your life may be your teachers. If you keep the cards visible, you'll be more likely to utilise their wisdom than if you keep them in the pack or inside this book.

3   'Dream on' the card you are presently working with. The following steps apply to calling forth the spirit of each Tarot card in your dreams:

   **a**   If you plan to dream on a card, keep it in your thoughts or in view during the day.

   **b**   Don't eat a large meal, drink alcohol or take drugs before retiring (this includes sleep medications).

   **c**   Ritualise the process: pray for guidance, light incense, sleep with a special dream pillow, robe or blanket lightly scented[1] with the aroma of the card you are focusing on.

   **d**   Keep a pen, paper and flashlight next to your bed to jot down key thoughts and images if you are awakened in the middle of the night; or use your pen and paper first thing in the morning after waking. You might also consider sleeping alone to have more dream freedom or to feel more comfortable if awakened by your dreams.

---

1   Because smell is our oldest and strongest sense, each card has been given a corresponding essential oil that will be mentioned further in this section, in each chapter and in the Table of Attributions at the end of this book.

**e** Look at the card you are dreaming on for a few minutes before bedtime and ask your dream source (your Higher Self, your God/dess Self, Jesus, Mother Mary, Krishna or whoever) to put you in touch with the important teachings and information of the card as they relate to you. Write down your request something like this:

> Dear Higher Self – Please reveal to me the teachings and information about this card that are relevant to my life at this time. I will remember my dreams upon awakening.
> Thank you.
> With Love,
>
> (Sign your name)

**f** Experiment with going to sleep holding a natural quartz crystal (referred to as a dream crystal). It will help keep you just a bit conscious, or awake, as you dream and also serve to remind you that you will recall your dream.

**g** Have a sign reading, 'What did I dream?' next to your bed to jar your memory first thing in the morning. It works!

**h** If you cannot recall a dream, stay in bed and try lying in several different sleeping positions. This usually works to rekindle your kinaesthetic dream memory.

**i** Have patience! Be persistent! If the process doesn't work the first night, keep at it. You'll be glad you did!

4 I suggest playing the musical tone of each card (see Table of Attributions) on a musical instrument prior to meditation – a chromatic pitch pipe works best. Hum the note or chant IAO[2] pronounced 'E-Ah-Oh', with the music. Ancient wisdom from both Western and Eastern traditions teaches that the atoms and molecules in everything that exists vibrate at different rates, creating sound and colour. When you intone the specific vibration (musical note) of a card, you are in fact subtly attuning yourself to that card's particular vibratory level. This optional procedure enables you to tune into each card's teachings more completely.

---

2 IAO is the western counterpart to the eastern AUM. The I represents the creative aspect of the Most High; the A represents the preserving aspect of the Most High; while O stands for the transformational and changing aspect of the Most High.

5 Following this process, I advise meditating on the card. Meditation is simply giving your full attention to something for a certain period of time. Experiment with focusing on the card you are exploring, as if it is someone important who has something especially interesting to tell you. This is basic meditation. I also recommend that you imagine sending a long 'grounding cord', or root, from the base of your spine down into the earth as you begin meditating. Take a deep breath or two and as you do so, sense your breath being drawn up through the cord or root from the earth as you inhale, then going back down into the earth as you exhale. This anchors you to the earth so that coming back to your ordinary reality after meditation is immediate. End your meditation by drawing a deep breath up through your grounding cord, holding it for a few seconds, slowly exhaling, next feeling your feet touching the floor and finally opening your eyes. Then, as you go through your day, notice where the card's teachings are apparent in your life. Make note of these occurrences as a way of keeping track of your progress.

6 Go out into the world and pretend you are the archetype in the card. If this is difficult, act as if you were going to a Halloween party characterising the card you are portraying. Imagine how that character would think, feel, behave and, if you dare, dress. Then take it from there. This is a terrific way to integrate the card.

7 The Rerun. After having an experience and realising in retrospect how a card's teachings might have made things different, mentally relive the situation, including your insight. This will help the behaviour become more automatic next time. If possible, actually rerun the situation in real life with this new attitude or behaviour.

8 There is a segment in each chapter that begins, 'Ask yourself any of the following questions.' This will provide you with the opportunity to look at which Gateway of Life you are in or 'growing through' with regard to the cards. Remember that although the card you are studying may fall within a particular Gateway, you have the potential to manifest personally any of the other Gateways. For instance, Justice falls within the Gateway of Adolescence; however, depending upon how you answer the questions presented, you might find yourself in Childhood, Adulthood or Wisdom. Also, you may outline what you need to

do in order to develop yourself further. Note that it isn't necessary to answer all the questions presented. Just address those that are especially meaningful.

9 Use a personal statement or affirmation about the presence of a particular card, hence an attitude, ability, state, or characteristic existing in your personality and/or life. Please note that in order not to set yourself up for disappointment, it is essential to remain open to the fact that in the big picture, *The*, or your, highest good is *always* served.

To affirm something is to acknowledge it as a living reality. You may use the personal statements offered for each card, or create your own (the latter is preferable). The purpose of these statements is to acknowledge and emphasise the existence of various mental, physical and emotional states and attitudes you wish to cultivate. For instance, the statement, 'I believe that God/dess is everywhere, in all people, places and things at all times', states both a belief in this idea and affirms the desire to make this thought reality. The following are some guidelines for creating the most worthwhile statements possible:

**a** For greatest effectiveness, don't flood your mind, but work on only a few statements at once. Tape record and listen to them at bedtime. Repeat them out loud, so you can hear yourself, the first thing in the morning and the last thing at night. Write them out and put them on your bathroom mirror, door or the dashboard of your car to help keep them in mind.

**b** Add power to your statements by having another person say them to you: 'Amber, you believe that . . . ' Or, imagine that someone you respect and love is saying them to you. If that person is unavailable, a photo will work instead. Finally, imagine your best friends talking about you: 'Did you know that Amber believes . . . ?'

**c** Back up your statements with as much feeling as possible. Words without feelings behind them are like a world without sunshine.

**d** Make your statements as real as possible. When my statement is unbelievable to me, it is telling me to examine my reasons for disbelieving it. Putting in the time to make it real helps me clear the air and proceed more successfully.

e   Phrase your statements positively. The use of negatives only causes mental confusion. For example, the negative statement, 'I no longer disbelieve that God/dess is everywhere,' does not work. Instead, say, 'I believe that God/dess is everywhere.'

f   Back up your words with actions. This is critical to making your statements more than just a bunch of words.

10   There are 'Inspirational Words and Quotations' for each card, to serve as further reminders and add other perspectives. You can copy these on index cards and post them on a door, mirror, etc., along with your personal statements.

11   Ask what symbols stand out in each card. This is a sure-fire way to increase your understanding of the symbols. Ask yourself, 'What does this symbol say to me? How might that symbol be useful in daily living?' Next, bring the symbol(s) into your life to integrate the card's teachings. For instance, place a bouquet of red roses as in the Magician's garden on your kitchen table as a reminder to be aware of the desires you are nurturing in the garden of your life.

12   Wear clothing and accessories, or surround yourself, with the card's colour to remind you of the teachings when needed. For instance, wear the Tower's stimulating and activating scarlet when you are moving too slowly. Notice how you are affected. Remember, the atoms and molecules in everything that exists vibrate at different rates, creating sound and colour. Therefore, when you wear or surround yourself with a card's colour, you are, in fact, aligning yourself to that card's specific vibratory level.

13   I advise working with each card's astrological correspondence, its planet or sign. This will add depth to your understanding. Again, it is useful to note what happens to your thoughts and feelings and the outcome of a situation when you experiment with applying these correspondences.

14   You can use the card's Hebrew name to remind you of its teachings and to help in your life process. Remembering that the Magician's Hebrew name, *Beth*, refers to a house has helped me become more aware and respectful of my body as a house of the spirit of God/dess.

15 Use a few drops of the scent associated with each card as an olfactory reminder to integrate its teachings.

16 Have a cup of tea made from, or cook with, the herb listed for each card while you learn about the card. Contemplate the qualities of the herb and the card it represents as you sip or eat.

CAUTION! Please be certain that you are sure about all of a herb's properties before eating or drinking it.

# *Part Two*

## THE GATEWAY OF
## CHILDHOOD

The Fool's journey through life begins with the first of the four Gateways, the Gateway of Childhood. This developmental period includes the first eight cards of the Major Arcana; the Fool through the Chariot. During this time, your survival skills, the Rules and Tools of the Game of Life, are imparted verbally and nonverbally by parents, teachers, and your culture and society at large. Educating you as the Fool-child in the workings of the world prepares you for the behaviours expected of you. To some extent, it also prepares you for what life will bring in return. These guidelines are meant to instill basic values and provide the rudimentary mental, emotional and physical skills needed to ensure your maturation into a happy and well-adjusted adult. These same Rules and Tools develop into instruments for wisdom or self-mastery when applied in more sophisticated ways in later Gateways.

Again, because so many of us grew up in dysfunctional families and were not adequately prepared for adult life, we, as individuals and as a collective, are slowly becoming equipped or re-equipped with the skills we ideally should have received as children; a working knowledge of the universal and natural laws and principles with which to navigate through life successfully. Therefore, when I refer to the 'Rules and Tools of the Game of Life', I am referring to these survival skills rather than to those passed on to us by our dysfunctional families and society. Such tools empower us not only to become functional, but to thrive!

In many ways childhood may be regarded as a time when the individual learns to do what is 'unnatural'. Remember, it is 'natural' to urinate and defecate in our diapers, never brush our teeth and not practice birth control. In truth, in some areas of life, we must teach ourselves to do the unnatural until the unnatural becomes second nature. All self-regulation and discipline may be defined as teaching ourselves to do the unnatural. In conclusion, these traits serve to develop us from childhood into adolescence and through adulthood. It is these same traits that also assist our transformation into enlightened beings.

0   **THE FOOL**   ℵ

# CHAPTER 4

# The Fool

## General Information and Symbolism

The Fool appears to be walking off a cliff into the great beyond, denoting both a trusting attitude and life's infinite possibilities. People engaged in daring or nonconformist behaviour are often labelled 'foolish' by those who don't understand that at some deep level of our being we know precisely what we are doing (including the possible consequences of our actions). Be they walking across hot coals, going into the desert alone with a bare minimum of supplies, or thrusting swords into one's body, as in the Balinese Trance, such acts are indicative of being attuned to the spirit or breath of life, signified by the triple flame worn over the Fool's heart and the Fool's feather. It is interesting to note that such behaviour is recognised in the East as an act of faith and as the power, or *Siddhis*, of the Wiseones. *Siddhi* is the Sanskrit term referring to the 'magical' powers an individual acquires through the practice of Yoga.

The Fool's feather is also recognised as the 'Feather of *Maat*', the Egyptian goddess of Truth. The Fool's feather and leafy victory wreath tell us that the same Divine Spirit that dwells in the Fool lives in all of nature and her creatures. The victory wreath also underscores the truth that, despite how things may appear, spirit is always victorious.

The Dog follows the Fool, attempting to attract his or her[1] attention. This suggests that the ordinary, habituated, or domesticated mind may sometimes try to stop adventurousness and

---

1  Because the Fool is a representation of the Divine Spirit, it contains both male and female characteristics. Because the spirit is neutral, the Fool is also neutral and may be taken for either sex. This is why Qabalists often call the Fool the Heavenly Androgyne.

growth. You must remember that what is right action for one person may be inappropriate for another. Behaviour is destructive ('foolish' in the negative sense) when you abdicate your freedom to choose, inappropriately allow others to make choices for you, choose for another without his permission (young children and the infirm are not included in this one) and/or do not discern what you are honestly capable of before acting. (Although all usually result in some type of self-victimisation or 'foolishness', it is valuable to recall that such results are eventually instructive.)

The Fool wears the Hebrew name for the Most High on its shirt. The letters *YHVH* or *Yod, Heh, Vav, Heh* are known as the *Tetragrammaton*, a four-letter symbol for the ineffable name of God/dess. The *Tetragrammaton* is the Name that the Most High gave to Moses at the burning bush on Mount Sinai when he (Moses) asked who was giving him instructions. It means: I AM THAT I AM, That which was, That which is, and That which shall always be. It communicates that everything originates from a single Source, the Divine Spirit, God/dess, or Qabalists' superconsciousness. The Fool wears the *Tetragrammaton* suggesting that the soul goes on its way with divine blessings and that we always carry the divine essence within us in our heart (another reference to the triple flame).

A white or spiritual sun shines down, showing that the Fool's actions are guided and directed from above. The Fool holds a white rose, showing the clarity of purpose and purity of desire that the incarnating soul brings into the life cycle. Life, like the white rose, is thorny, but pure in essence. The soul, or one's personal piece of the Divine Spirit, is known as the Higher Self by Qabalists and the *Atman* by Hindus and Buddhists. The Fool is a symbol for the soul just prior to its next cycle of manifestation – stepping off the cliff into the physical world below. The Fool brings the wealth of its previous experience and accumulated knowledge, a.k.a. survival skills, for guidance on its present journey – shown by the wand of willing action and the wallet slung across its shoulder. There are two symbols on the wallet, the all-seeing eye of the Egyptian god Horus, and an eagle. The first indicates that the Fool is both dependent upon and watched over by its divine parents. The second, a bird with extraordinary vision, implies the objectivity we have about our previous experiences (in the wallet) just prior to reincarnation and beginning a new cycle.

On the Qabalistic Tree of Life, the Crown, *Kether*, is known as 'The Beginning of the Whirlings', or 'The Source of Life'. The ten circles divided by eight on the Fool's jacket indicate that the Fool personifies not only *Kether*, but the ten kinds of consciousness depicted by the ten *Sephiroth*, or spheres of influence, on the Tree. The other nine spheres flow out from *Kether*, which is the Source. The star and moon reiterate that the Fool is a child of the Divine. The Fool's belt has twelve knots, signifying the twelve signs of the zodiac, through which come the twelve types of personality that also originate from this Source. The belt also symbolises that form temporarily places a limit on the limitlessness of spirit.

The Fool's number, o,[2] shows unlimited potential by its endless egg or womb-like shape. Mathematically, zero is the absence of quantity, quality and mass and therefore, like the Fool, is unlimited. Traditionally, the number represents the entrance of the No-Thing-spirit into the Something-matter. The primacy of zero is emphasised by data showing that the circle is the first intelligible shape in children's drawings cross-culturally.

The Fool's colour is pale yellow, the musical note is E and the herb is ginseng. The Hebrew name for the Fool is *Aleph*, which means 'bull' or 'ox'. The bull is the leader and protector of the herd, in the same way that the Divine Spirit leads and protects us. The ox is a neutered (neutral) bull, a throwback to the Fool's androgynous state. In ancient times, this creature was symbolic of the God/dess: it pulled the plough that tilled the fields which provided food, furnished transportation, did the work of several people at once and supplied food, fuel (dung), clothing and shelter from its flesh. This animal was a major force in sustaining and creating life, and it is easy to understand why certain cultures held (and still hold) the ox (or cow) as sacred, not only deifying it, but refraining from slaughtering it for food.

The Fool is associated with the planet Uranus, regarded by astrologers to be the 'higher octave', the transpersonal, as opposed to the personal, aspect of Mercury, the Roman equivalent of the Greek Hermes, Messenger of the Gods and Goddesses. Mercury refers to interpersonal and socially conditioned communications, whereas Uranus, Greek Father of the Heavens, is linked to inspired or

---

2 The actual value of the Hebrew letter of each Tarot card differs from the number assigned to each card. For example: the Fool is called *Aleph* in Hebrew and signifies the numbers 1 and 1,000, but is numbered o (please see Table of Correspondences). Qabalistic tradition has sequentially numbered the Major Arcana cards o through 22, corresponding to the number of letters in the Hebrew alphabet.

evolutionary thought that seems to descend from higher levels of awareness as well as with the revolutionary and iconoclastic. Uranus may be thought of as life's 'Ah ha's!' It is this planet's idealistic influences that move us to break free from both our own and society's obsolete ways. This is shown by how the Fool's body and attention are directed upwards and outwards, indicating the universal life force drawing humanity on to the path of more highly developed levels of being. Also, Uranus refers to eccentric, unusual and nontraditional behaviour, such as following one's inner or spiritual Self, the God/dess within, which in the ordinary world is relatively uncommon.

A memorable instance of living from the Fool's perspective is seen in the life of the late Indian Saint, Sri Ramakrishna. Ramakrishna was in charge of taking care of the deity of the Holy Mother and outraged the orthodox temple officials when he fed Her sacred food to a hungry cat. The priests did not understand that when Ramakrishna was in such an exalted state, he saw the cat as an aspect of the Divine Mother. He saw the presence of the God/dess everywhere.

Qabalists assign to each path or Tarot card and sphere on the Tree of Life an 'Intelligence'. Because all is one, and we reflect the One, the Intelligences are another way of describing the powers of the Universal Mind, which, through the development of our mental powers or intelligence, may become a force for us to use at will. When we master the teachings of a particular Tarot card it becomes a mental force or tool that helps us to understand how both we and the universe operate. This understanding may then assist us in handling our daily lives and responsibilities more mindfully.

The Fool is called the 'Fiery Intelligence'. The Fiery Intelligence is the spark of life emanating from the Source of all that impregnates all creatures and things, animate and inanimate, with life. When I first viewed Michelangelo's masterpiece, 'Creation', which depicts the Most High igniting Adam with life, I remember saying to myself, 'Aha, there is the Fiery Intelligence!'

## Gateway of Life: Childhood

The soul, or Fool, stands in eternity. If you are a believer in reincarnation, this is the time just prior to birth when you are free from any limiting identification with the body or personality. Buddhist practitioners call this state *shanyata*, the openness of God. Inherent in this objectified state is the ability to take inventory of and understand the various roles or personalities the soul has played (remember the Fool carries its previous experiences in its wallet).

From this vantage point, the soul is able to survey what lies ahead with total clarity. It also has the willingness and desire to do whatever it takes to complete the job. At this point, the Fool-child is about to enter the world, not only from its mother's womb, but from the *Malaprakriti*, a Sanskrit word meaning 'the great womb of all life'. The Fool-child is motivated by some inner knowledge which is often difficult for adults to recall or identify with. Preparing to embrace life, the Fool-child is open, innocent and fearless as well as totally dependent.

Experiencing the Fool at the Four Gateways of Life may result in certain kinds of attitudes and behaviour. CHILDHOOD: A woman impulsively gives up a satisfying business career because friends tell her she should be an actress; ADOLESCENCE: You are learning how to look before you leap and becoming aware of possible consequences before, rather than after, taking action; ADULTHOOD: You are pioneering in a new area, previously unavailable to a person of your sex or race; WISDOM: Rather than saving your partner from a difficult situation, you automatically encourage her or him to do this for themselves, while remaining silent until asked for feedback.

## Divinatory Questions for the Fool

*Upright*: Are new vistas about to open for you? Could you be experiencing more trust in the divine order of things? Are you experiencing the budding awareness that God/dess is everywhere at all times? Is this a time to open to higher insight and inspiration? Might revolutionary (rapid) or evolutionary (slow and more organic) thinking and behaviour be in order? Are you seeking to live life from the greater rather than the lesser perspective? Do you have a sense that you are being guided along your way, that God/dess is behind everything that occurs? Are you feeling more adventurous than usual? Could you use some more adventure in your life? Would you like to be more of a nonconformist? Are you stepping beyond confining thoughts and emotions? Are you daring to do something you have always dreamed of but have hesitated to do because you feared others' reactions? Do you feel as if you are being watched over? Could you be thinking of yourself as a bisexual being? Might you be listening to the sound of a different drummer? Where would a breath of fresh air or spirit be helpful? Are you preparing to live your daily life as a spiritual adventure? Do you consider yourself to be especially honest and open? Do you feel like a novice in some area of your life – family, work, relationships? Have you had a sudden

influx of insight or spiritual energy that has provided you with a
sense of your past lives and how they fit into the present? Might
others consider you foolish or eccentric for your spiritual pursuits?
Could all your experiences be divine lessons and blessings? What is
presently sparking your interest and curiosity?

*Reversed*: Are you overly traditional or conservative in some area of
your life? Do you tend to act heedlessly, impulsively or prematurely?
Has a lack of discernment resulted in pain or destructiveness? Is your
trust based upon fact or fantasy? Might you be feeling timid towards
someone, something or life itself? Have you felt like returning to the
womb? What cliff are you afraid of going over? Where might it be
beneficial for your interest to be sparked? Do you feel that someone
has taken unfair advantage of your openness?

## Personal Experience

Several years into my Tarot studies, which were then predominantly
intellectual, I laid aside my cards during the difficult process of
getting divorced. The disruption and pain of being on my own again
was almost more than I could bear. The fact that I suddenly became
the main parent for my young son on a very small income almost
immobilised me with fear and self-doubt. I spent weeks, perhaps
months, in a state of tremendous anxiety. My skin broke out and I
lost my appetite. I also needed tranquillisers, marijuana, or wine to
fall asleep. One evening, I felt as if I had hit bottom and I began to
pray. Unexpectedly, my forgotten Tarot cards appeared in my
mind's eye. Hesitantly, I located them and after asking for guidance
and direction, drew a card face down from the pack. After slowly
turning it over and finding it was the Fool, I didn't know whether to
laugh or cry. There I was, going off the cliff; but whereas I was
distraught, the Fool appeared serene. What was the difference? After
questioning myself thoroughly, the word 'trust' hit me like a charge
of electricity. I did not feel trusting. Instead, I felt as though my life
were over (and it might as well have been, the way I was caring for
myself). I lacked the trust that what was happening was for my
benefit somewhere down the line.

The Fool's teaching gradually encouraged me to think I could go
on with my life and make the best of things. With this seed
consciously planted, I tacked the Fool card up at the foot of my bed
as a constant reminder of my insight. Although I often felt as if I were
stepping out of bed each morning into the unknown (*off the cliff*), I
started to recognise and actually feel my Higher Self guiding my

actions. Yes, I had made some foolish and immature choices, but those same choices would eventually teach me how to make wiser ones. With this, my depression lifted and I became more confident about getting on with the business of living and caring for my child. What followed was one of the most growth-filled and exciting periods of my life. Since that time, the Fool has served to inspire me whenever I get caught up in fear, distrust or hopelessness.

### Student Experiences

❖ 'Asking myself questions from our homework, as you had suggested, stirred me up,' shared Helen, a mother and teacher who was taking one of my classes. 'For example, the question, "What do I want to revolutionise or evolutionise?" was right on the money. Even the word money is perfect, because that's what it's about for me. I want to revolutionise my attitudes about money. For years I've considered it to be nonspiritual, but now I see that it's the way money is used that makes it what it is.

'I recently got a small inheritance and I've been wondering what to do with it. I've been shopping around, doing some reading about money, and this past week I went to talk with a stockbroker. Well, the broker suggested several different plans for me. And I think I'm almost ready to step off the cliff and be the Fool, not a foolish one, mind you, but one with some information.

'I also feel that my attitudes about money are being *evolutionised* by this decision. There was a time I wouldn't even put a cent into the bank. I kept it under the living room rug. Thinking about investing it is really big stuff for me.'

*I agreed with Helen. 'You're definitely a more mature version of the Fool, stepping above and beyond the world of money you've known that's no longer working for you, into a new world that is more relevant to your current needs. Looks like you're moving into more adult behaviour. I say this because the difference between the grown-up and the immature Fool is that maturity brings the ability to do things to help, not hurt, ourselves and others.'*

❖ New Age computer technology is wonderful, yet it can also strike terror into the heart of a novice. Immediately after taking off her coat one morning, Susan received an e-mail from her boss that she viewed as a direct threat to her job security. 'After reading the message, I felt sick and was just about ready to take my name off my door,' she said. 'And with the message came the realisation that the latest project I was involved in was not thoroughly understood by the message-sender (one of my bosses). What was I to do? In the past I've usually lacked the courage to become involved. But this time was different. As I sat there feeling confused, something clicked. I remembered my homework, to use the teachings of the Fool in my life. Can you believe the timing?

'After thinking about the card's meaning for a few minutes, I asked myself how the Fool would handle it. Why, by stepping off the cliff, of course, while having faith that things will work out for the best in the long run. So I closed my eyes and called on the Fool to help me deal with the situation courageously. Next, I did something I never thought I could do: I rose above my emotions, my fear of being fired, anger at the boss and frustration with myself. I sat down at my computer and sent a clear and concise e-mail back to him.

'A few hours later, another message flashed on to my screen, indicating that the situation had been rectified. I took a few deep breaths (the Fool is the breath of life, you know) and mentally thanked the Fool, my own Higher Self, for helping me to take the risk of explaining myself in a very threatening situation.'

*'You certainly enacted the Fool's spirit of adventure to help you out of that one,' I told Susan. 'You definitely had a direct experience of it when you suddenly remembered your homework. Those jolts that seem to come from out of the blue are the Uranian aspect of the Fool in action. Somehow, the Fool's lightning-quick quality seems to be an excellent symbol for the Computer Age. It is wonderful how, although you initially perceived your situation from the valley below, suggestive of your old reactive patterns, you acted from a higher level of consciousness after recollecting the Fool.'*

❖ 'I was unexpectedly asked to become manager of the beauty salon where I've worked for several years,' said Kit. 'I must admit, the thought of all that responsibility made me nervous. I definitely felt I was in the middle of the Gateway of Childhood.

'With the exception of one new female operator, everyone there is an old friend of mine. Almost as soon as that new woman was hired, tension surfaced between her and the rest of us. When I became manager, things got more and more unpleasant. I'd been thinking I should call a meeting to talk about the general unrest with everyone. But I'd been putting it off because there was the potential for alienating myself from my friends.

'At the beginning of last week, I saw I no longer had a choice. I had to help clear the air. It was getting increasingly uncomfortable for everyone, including the customers. I finally called the meeting, because I put the Fool on my dressing table, and as I prepared for work each day, I'd look at it and see that not dealing with the situation was being childish. I was afraid to "go off the cliff". It was time for me to do with my co-workers what I do with my kids when they fight: be a mediator. But doing this for my kids is one thing; doing it at work seemed very different. Yet, by looking at the Fool, I somehow felt sure I'd do okay, that things in the salon would be fine in the end. I also kept the phrase "possibilities unlimited" running through my head.

'During the meeting I listened carefully to everybody's complaints and found myself in only partial agreement with my friends. I felt scared, but keeping the Fool in mind, I made some suggestions for change. Nobody said so, but I know they all agreed that things had to change. Out of my meeting and suggestions has come a better feeling in the salon, and everyone is still talking to me. I felt as if the Fool were there right over my shoulder backing me up, helping me with my newness as a mediator and with my fear of alienating my friends. I know it will be easier next time, now that I've gone through it once. I think I'm moving into a more adult manner of dealing with this type of situation. I actually feel freer in here (Kit pointed to her solar plexus). I really took the steps to become less of a child and more of an adult and it feels great.'

*I told Kit it was inspirational to see her pride in herself. 'Dealing with conflict is definitely challenging,' I said. 'You used the Fool as an inspiration to bypass your childish avoidance behaviours and it's worked. So often we need to look at the bigger picture, just as you did when you sensed that things would be fine in the end. Welcome to Adulthood. Also, since the phrase, "possibilities unlimited" was so helpful, I wonder what a personal statement such as "open my life to new possibilities", would do for you? Watch out world, here comes Kit!'*

## Suggestions for Application and Integration of the Fool

These exercises will encourage you to bring the Fool into your life to help you cope with and, where appropriate, enjoy the unexpected; increase your sense of spontaneity, trust and adventure; and be more aware of the spirit of life, both within and without. What do you say? You've come this far – isn't it time to head off the cliff and put the Fool's teachings to work for you?

1  Draw or colour your own version of the Fool with yourself as the figure.

2  Set the Fool in a visible place as a reminder to your conscious and subconscious minds to use and absorb its teachings to break loose and try something unconventional; overcome a fear of failure; lighten your heart and mind; sense guidance from above.

3  Dream on the Fool. For in-depth instruction please refer back to number three under the heading of Application and Integration of the Cards, in Part I of this book, General Suggestions for Living the Tarot.

4  Play the note E on a musical instrument. Intone IAO or hum along with the music. Now focus on the card for a few minutes. (Remember to send your 'grounding cord' down into the earth.) While meditating, think about the God/dess's presence in all there is – in all you can see, hear, smell, taste and touch in the world around you. As you sit contemplating this, you might identify with God/dess each image, sound, odour, taste and feeling you receive. Finally, you might ask that the Fool's teachings guide you through some specific situation. Or if you are faced with a worrisome situation, event or problem, such as desiring to feel less apprehensive about some future event or more aware of the oneness of all life, imagine how the Fool would handle it. If it seems feasible, do it. Jot down the times when you became aware of the Fool in your interactions. I was aware of the Fool when? Before/during/after . . .

5  Go out into the world and be the Fool. The Fool is linked with the spirit or breath of life. When I feel fearful or am not being my Self, I think of the Fool while taking some deep breaths. This help to relax and re-attune me to the Fool's energies. I was the Fool and this is what happened . . .

6  The Rerun. After having an experience and realising in retrospect how the Fool's teachings might have made things different – brought greater trust, freedom or confidence in the Self – mentally relive the event, *including* your insight. This will help the behaviour become more automatic next time. If possible, actually rerun the situation in real life with this attitude or behaviour.

7  Ask yourself any of the following questions:

'In what area of life do I need to learn or try something new?'
'What do I desire to change, either quickly through revolution, or gradually through evolution?' 'Where do I wish I were heading?' 'What do I feel fearful about doing or trying?' 'How might my Higher Self be pushing me forward?' 'What do I feel my Higher Self pulling me towards?' 'In what situation(s) might some deep breathing realign and relax me?' 'How would a more carefree and trusting attitude help me?' 'In what area do I lack or fear conventionality?' 'Under what circumstances do I feel or wish to feel guided, protected or inspired?' 'How can I lighten my burdens and my attitude?' 'In what area may I be appearing foolish to others, but true to myself?' 'How am I improving my awareness of God/dess in all?' 'Where is it becoming safe to show my Foolishness, my open and innocent child?'

'What Gateway of Life am I in or growing through in the above?' Indicate: Childhood, Adolescence, Adulthood or Wisdom. Why?

'What do I need to do in order to develop the above further?' I need to . . .

'What step(s) do I want to take towards this and how can the Fool help me?'

8   Use a personal statement about the presence of the Fool in your life at this time, such as: 'I trust that everything has and will happen in my life for my greatest good.' My personal statement is . . .

9   Inspirational quotes and words. Contemplate these in relation to the Fool:

'I am the Source of all, the beginning as well as the end.'

'The power behind every activity of nature is the power of Brahman (God/dess). To realise this truth is to be immortal.'

*Kena Upanishad*

'If a person does not keep pace with his companions, perhaps it is because he hears a different drummer. Let him step to the music which he hears, however measured or far away.'

Henry David Thoreau

10  What symbols stand out in the card? What do they say to you? How might they be useful in daily living? Bring the symbols into

your life in some way so as to integrate the card's teachings. Try wearing a feather like the Fool to bring out your spirit of adventure or a lighter attitude towards daily living. Or, like the white rose, life is thorny but pure in essence. In the midst of thorny situations, I remember that one of the reasons I have chosen to come into this world is to learn how to deal with such.

11 Wear or surround yourself with the colour pale yellow to remind you of the Fool's teachings when needed, such as when you want to feel protected, guided or inspired. Notice how you are affected.

12 The Fool's astrological correspondence is Uranus, ruling transpersonal thought, omnipresent heavenly power, evolutionary, revolutionary and iconoclastic behaviours, the unexpected and unusual. Step out and do something unconventional. Use a transpersonal approach to a strained relationship. Break free from something obsolete. Note what happens: your thoughts and feelings and the outcome.

13 The Fool's Hebrew name is *Aleph*, meaning 'bull' or 'ox'. How might this remind you of the card's meaning or help in your life process? When I feel particularly burdened, I think of the Universal Life Force, the ox, bearing not only my burdens, but those of the entire world, and as a result I feel lighter and not so alone.

14 Try a few drops of the scented oil galbanum, which is associated with the Fool, as another reminder to integrate the card's teachings.

15 Have a cup of the oriental life-giving herb ginseng. Its oriental name translates to mean 'wonder of the world', and it is often called the 'Bringer of Life'. This herb is called an adaptagen, because it possesses so many overall healing properties – tonic, energy booster, and disease preventative – it gravitates towards whatever is weakened and strengths it. Sit quietly as you drink the tea and consider the herb's qualities and the like qualities of the Fool.

1 THE MAGICIAN ⊐

# CHAPTER 5

# The Magician

## General Information and Symbolism

The Magician is traditionally acknowledged as a symbol of the ego – the personality component that is conscious, that most immediately controls behaviour and that is most in touch with external reality. It is assigned the number one – in Roman numerals, one is depicted as I, or self-consciousness. Many spiritual groups teach that the personality, or *Jiva*, as it is known in the Hindu and Buddhist traditions, must be transcended or annihilated in order to reach higher states of awareness. Yet the Magician's physical stance of drawing energy from above down to the earth intimates that it is by developing and directing your ego that you develop your full potential. This shows the essentiality of becoming acquainted with both the weak and strong traits of your personality, plus the importance of employing your strengths to help transform your weaknesses in order to shift the state, or shape, of your life. It is not surprising to learn that the Magician's powers are equated with the shamanic 'Shape Shifter'.

Magic is the art and science of transforming the ordinary individual into the extraordinary individual via the desire to wilfully apply the universal and natural laws and principles to daily living. It is employing the human personality, its gifts and liabilities, as a vehicle through which to transform into one's divine Self and as a vehicle for transforming this planet into Paradise. In this way, each and every one of us is a Magician!

In addition to symbolising eternal life, wisdom, and the constancy of change, the serpent around the Magician's waist swallowing its tail (often called the Ouroboros) portrays the idea of organically shedding, growing beyond or transforming (the Magician is sometimes called the Transformer) the worn out and self-destructive personality traits that compose your immature or negative ego traits. There are two varying yet valid ways of appraising these traits. The first is that these attitudes and behaviours are the barrier that stand in the way of your attaining higher, expanded levels of consciousness. When you encounter life from this perspective, you are closed off to communications from your Higher Self, as well as from other sources of inspiration. The second is that because these immaturities tend to cause you so much discomfort, you will in time do what is necessary to alleviate their effect. Hence, they are ultimately responsible for leading you to enlightenment.

The position of the Magician's body (particularly his arms and hands) instructs us that the heavenly world, the macrocosm, is reflected in the earthly world, the microcosm of humanity or *Adam*.[1] His extended finger of Jupiter, often called the 'Greater Benefic' by astrologers, points down to the earth, suggesting that you benefit from life by paying attention to what it demands and by being present in the here and now. Finally, his physical form is the embodiment of the old Hermetic axiom, 'As above, so below; as below, so above'. 'Hermetic' refers to the work of Hermes Trimegistus, high priest of the Eleusinian Mystery School in ancient Greece (supposedly the third incarnation of the Greek god Hermes and equivalent to the Roman Mercury, Egyptian Thoth, and Hindu Hanuman) and founder of the occult sciences of magic, astrology and alchemy. Your body and personality are the means or channels through which the energies from the Source of Life – the Fool – take shape in the physical world. As the ancient Sanskrit mantra So'HAM beautifully states, 'I AM THAT I AM',[2] the 'THAT' being the energy that animates all of life.

The Magician's robes illustrate this point: the outer robe symbolises the personality which clothes or covers the spirit within. The five red roses above the Magician's head represent your God/dess-given senses, which when directed properly help educate you about the divinity of life here on earth. These are variations of the Fool's white rose of desire and signify how your desires become coloured by your personality. The roses and lilies in the garden are cultivated, connoting the need to direct your attention to cultivating heaven here on earth. The flowers, especially the roses that are both

---

1  In the Qabalah, Adam is used to signify all of humanity. It is a male noun derived from the female root of *adamah*, meaning mother earth. Therefore Adam means child/children of Mother Earth.

2  Notice how the translation of the Hebrew *Tetragrammaton YHVH* and the Sanskrit *SO'HAM* are identical.

above and below the Magician, also remind you that your desires and thoughts are things, and that what you pay attention to, desire and think about (plant in the garden of your life), you tend to manifest. The five roses symbolise the personal desires we wish to fulfil and the five senses we employ to do so. The four lilies stand for a knowledge of the One Reality in the form of the universal laws and truths. Such knowledge may conflict with our personal desires. Yet, it is through the act of cultivating our personal desires that we, in time, gain knowledge of these truths and become aligned with them.

The Magician bears a magic wand and headband. In order to make magic, he must limit his concentration to the task before him. These symbols demonstrate how mental discipline has the potential to transform you and your environment (the garden). Notice that the wand is two headed – it draws energy from both ends – and is held in the Magician's right hand to emphasise that he consciously acts to bring heaven to earth and earth to heaven.

The four implements or mental tools on the Magician's table – Wand, Cup, Sword and Pentacle[3] – are tools of Ritual Magic and are associated with the four elements – Fire, Water, Air and Earth – respectively. These four tools can become practical tools for Practical Magic, the magic of living happy, fully functional and fulfilling lives. Here are the esoteric tools at work in the world.

It is an early spring morning, and as I sit in my kitchen sipping peppermint tea, looking out at my overgrown backyard, I get the idea to plant a garden. The idea being ignited is the Wand. It is also the first plane on the Qabalistic Tree of Life, the Archetypal World of *Atziluth*, known to scientists as the molecular state.

Then I fantasise what I will plant: guavas, gardenias, mangoes, grapes, papayas and watermelons, all on the cool and foggy central California coast. This unrestricted, emotionally oriented imagining is the Cup. On the Tree of Life, it is the second plane, the Creative World of *Briah*, the gaseous state.

Next, I go outside, examine the soil, think about the climate and amount of space I actually have available for planting. The act of mental discernment and of putting limits on my ideas and imaginings in order to actually manifest my garden is the Sword. This is the third Qabalistic plane, known as the Formative World of *Yetzirah*. In scientific terms, *Yetzirah* is associated with the liquid state.

3 These have also been linked to the Spear of Longinus, Holy Grail, Sword Excalibur and Host – the Wand, Cup, Sword and Pentacle respectively.

Finally I get to work and plant, water, weed, cultivate, go out at 2:00 am to de-snail the seedlings and borrow a neighbour's cat to scare off the gophers. Pretty soon I have snow peas for the wok and daffodils for the table. The physical work and resulting products are the Pentacle. The fourth and final plane on the Tree of Life, called *Assiah*, the Manifest World, is the state of solids.

One of the main objectives of Tarot study is the transformation of the rote experiences of ordinary, everyday living into magical events. Another is to come to know your physical body as a home for your God/dess Self. In other words, the goals are to become conscious and appreciative of the presence of the extraordinary in the ordinary aspects of living and being. These perspectives may be cultivated by way of the Magician's teachings.

A horizontal figure eight floats over the Magician's head. It is an ancient Gnostic symbol, representing Christ, the Holy Spirit, eternal life and the interdependency and connectedness between the inner and outer, spiritual and material worlds. All you need do is learn how to direct your attention to its presence. Material existence is proof of spiritual existence. It only takes time and disciplined thinking to become automatically cognisant of this, as shown by the Magician's headband.

The Magician's colour is yellow. His musical tone is E, as is the Fool's (you might wish to take a few seconds to think about why this is so), and the herbal correspondence is the oriental astragalus. The Hebrew name for the Magician is *Beth*, meaning 'house'. Qabalists, among others, refer and relate to the physical body as the House of the Divine. In cross-cultural dream work, the appearance of a house signifies the dreamer. The Magician is the House where the energies of the Fool live (that's why the musical note is the same for both). Each house or body and its residing personality are somewhat different. This is how the many types of lifework or karma are accomplished. When seeing someone with a handicap or disability, we often wonder why they are afflicted. This may be explained by taking a leap of faith and stating that the type of work that person needs to accomplish in life requires them to have that particular body. It is the prerequisite for their job.

The Magician is associated with the planet Mercury. This Roman god is always pictured with wings on his feet, to indicate the speed of thought and the mind's unceasing activity. Mercury facilitated communication between the gods and goddesses, and also brought their messages to mortals. In today's world, as in ancient times, many seek out mediums or channels to guide and advise them, to bring messages down from on high. Remember, however, that the Magician is the channel or message-bearer, *not* the Source itself. Mercury simply represents your intelligence or mental chemistry – your ability to express yourself, reason, perceive relationships, gather facts and adapt to change. Mercury is linked to the Seventh, or Crown (top of the head) *Chakra*, or energy centre, the place where the greater impersonal intelligence enters to become your personal intelligence. On the Tree of Life, the *Sephirah* associated with Mercury is *Hod*, meaning 'Glory' and 'Splendour'. The ten *Sephiroth*, individually termed *Sephirah*, translate from the Hebrew to mean 'precious emanations or gems'. Each of these spheres is like a finely polished gem that reflects the brilliance of its divine Source. Therefore, when our mind is finely attuned, it reflects the brilliance – Glory and Splendour – of the One mind coming through us. Each *Sephirah* on the Tree of Life stands for one segment of the total state of consciousness we call enlightenment.

In the Qabalah, the Magician is known as the Transmitting, Transparent or Clear Intelligence. This refers to the light, life, power and knowledge from above which are conveyed, drawn or channelled through you (your body is the house – *Beth* – of God/dess) and expressed in your own particular way, according to your personality type. When you stay clear and remember who and what you really are, life is magical!

## Gateway of Life: Childhood

The Magician provides the newly born or incarnating Fool (soul) with a physical body and personality in order to do the job it, the soul, has elected to do. In the Gateway of Childhood, the Magician is immersed in discovering his or her gifts, talents, disabilities and shortcomings.

Under the Magician, you begin focusing on and exploring your environment. This is aptly described by Joseph Chilton Pearce in his book *The Magical Child* as, 'The physical interactions with all the possible contents of the living earth, and above all, its principles and laws of interaction.' Those living in the Childhood stage of this card are completely absorbed in the magic of their surroundings and the very wonder of being alive. Psychologists link the Magician with the *animus*, or projective part of your personality, and here you are projecting yourself out into the world. The Chinese term this our *Yang* side.

As a child, you are also occupied with investigating the four tools of life on the table before you – the ability to think, to imagine or fantasise, to discriminate or distinguish one thing from another, and to actually make things. Watching almost any young child, you can see it absorbed in the magic of its surroundings. It is engrossed in discovering (or rediscovering, for someone in later Gateways) the simple wonder of life which most adults cease paying attention to.

Living with the Magician at the Four Gateways of Life, you might encounter certain experiences. CHILDHOOD: You are getting acquainted with the tools of your chosen line of work or profession; ADOLESCENCE: You make efforts to maintain the status quo because you fear change; ADULTHOOD: After receiving the feedback that you could be a better salesperson with better listening skills, you sign up for a series of communication workshops; WISDOM: You are such a clear channel for communications from the Higher Self that you are able to guide others as well as yourself.

## Divinatory Questions for the Magician

*Upright*: Is it becoming increasingly important for you to focus on your work? Is it a good time to take a mental inventory of how you are directing your attention, time and energy? Is it an appropriate time to do some house-cleaning, make some needed changes? How are you experiencing the magic of everyday life? In what ways are you opening up to your higher power? Do you believe that your thoughts are things and you are co-creating the events in your life? Are you becoming or would you like to become more of a channel, a message-bearer? Do you feel clearer than you have in a long time? Where might you be using your tools (directing your will) to make life a magical experience? How are you letting go and allowing your Higher Self to transmit through you? What shapes are you shifting? Might opening up to communication on a difficult subject be essential? Do you know that your personality and body are perfect for both your spiritual and worldly work? Have you underestimated your mental abilities?

*Reversed*: How might disciplining your attention be helpful to your goals at this point? In what ways might you be more in the here and now? Have you been respecting your Self? Has your thinking been muddled? Who or what has brought 'magic' into your life? Might you be so busy 'channelling' information for others that you are not doing likewise for yourself? Has life lost its magic for you? How might you slowly begin making your life more magical? Have you ever considered doing some work on your communication skills? Are your ideas being challenged? Might you presently be thinking or working too hard? Have you been disdainful of your own or another's abilities and disabilities? Could it be important for you to remember where your talents come from ('As above, so below')? How could you show yourself or another greater Self-respect? Might you or someone close to you be alienating others with excessive egotism? Do you feel scattered and restless? Are you feeling especially stressed in some aspect of your life, to the point of thinking that you might break down? How might you be giving your gifts away? Could you be resisting a necessary change?

## Personal Experiences

I want to mention two incidents wherein the Magician has shown me much about the powers of concentration and attention. By way of the roses in the Magician's garden, I've learned that what I pay attention to most consistently – cultivate in the garden of my mind – is most likely to manifest. Now if that isn't magic, I don't know what is! In other words, as within, so without. I spent years dwelling on my lack of a committed partner or love relationship. Yet, it wasn't until I recognised that I was propagating the situation by continuously thinking about it only in terms of 'lack' (I had bought the idea hook, line and sinker), that I finally began to attract potentially satisfying relationships. I recall delighting in the fact that the Aquarian Deck for the New Age renamed the Magician the Changer, substantiating that the act of changing my thoughts helps me to change my reality.

The by-product of a long period of being a single parent, working and going to school simultaneously, was my being absorbed in the past and future while either avoiding or being unconscious of what was taking place right under my nose. Because of this, my life was quite stressful. In an attempt to become centred during an especially demanding time – I was studying for final exams, being mom, working at one job and selling a small business – I convinced myself to colour in another Magician card to remind me that there is enough energy available to do what I need to do (that is, when I allow myself to think so). As I applied the flesh tones to his downward-pointing hand, it seemed to be motioning to me to pay attention to what was going on in my immediate environment, signalling me to focus my attention on one thing at a time. It indicated that I best be in the here and now. Just like the quote from psychologist Fritz Perls scrawled across my first page of study notes on the Magician from several years before reminding me to: 'Be here now!'

From this experience, I recalled that in order to perform the practical magic of living my daily life to its fullest, I must be aware of the present. I then took myself in hand and started spending five to ten minutes a day using all my senses – seeing, hearing, tasting, smelling and touching – to be fully conscious as I did one thing at a time. I began with simple things like washing the breakfast dishes, eating, walking the dog and dressing. I was so delighted at how much more awake and aware I felt afterwards, I began prolonging the exercise and extended it to my studies, work and in relating to my child and friends, as well as using it to help me find the right buyer for my business. In essence, I became the Magician. In addition, I sang and repeated the words of a song my ex-husband, a musician and songwriter, wrote:

> If you're livin' in the past, you're livin' with fear,
> If you're livin' in the future, then you're not here.
> But if you're livin' in the moment, you're livin' with grace,
> And all the pieces just fall into place.
>
> Leni Matlin, *Karma Suite*

## Student Experiences

❖  'While sitting in the front row of a filled-to-capacity auditorium waiting for my turn to speak on the topic of "Death and Dying", I got more and more upset,' began Marilyn, a speaker for the Hospice Foundation. 'As I sat there listening to the other speakers, I worked myself into a mental and emotional frenzy as I compared myself with each one. This one looks more professional than I do. She's a better speaker. He's able to inject humour into this serious subject. I'll only be a let-down after these people.

'The words from our class on the Magician, "Pay attention to what you're cultivating in your garden," magically came to my mind. Right then and there I caught myself and took a rather uncomfortable survey of what I'd been paying attention to. With that, I transformed my non-supportive, undermining and competitively oriented self-talk into supportive statements: "I am who I am. I will definitely do the very best job I'm able to do. I speak from my experiences, which are unique and valuable. These people have their individual gifts of communication, and I have mine. We are all making important contributions here tonight."

'I found myself doing my homework of composing a statement regarding the presence of the Magician in my life right on the spot, and it worked. By redirecting my focus of attention, the tension inside me subsided. When it came to my turn to speak, I was relaxed and able to concentrate on sharing my Self with the audience.'

*I told Marilyn she was absolutely right. 'Your personality is uniquely designed to do what is needed to fulfil the jobs of life before you. And if you are deficient in some ways, you will probably be able to learn whatever is called for – direct your attention, as the Magician does with his pointing finger, to the new traits you'd like to develop.'*

❖ 'I've put the Magician up on my desk at my office as a guidepost during therapy sessions,' offered Carole, a marriage and family counsellor. 'I'm embarrassed to say this, but it helps me listen more attentively to what my clients are saying. My social commitments are so numerous lately, I'm often tired and distracted and sometimes don't concentrate as well as I should during therapy. I guess I haven't been treating my body – house – too well, and it's showing.

'The work we've done with the Magician, especially the homework questions, enabled me to re-establish contact with my clients, so I can direct them in ways I think are most advantageous to their growth. Listening is such an important factor in this process, and the homework question, "In what area can my communication skills – listening, writing and speaking – be improved?" was perfect, just perfect. I'm also trying out a new style – wearing headbands like the Magician does (only mine are made of pretty scarves). It's another reminder for me to use my Goddess-given concentration and intelligence wisely, helping both myself and others transform and change.'

*'Yes, a very important aspect of being a professional message-bearer is being able to tune in and be clear,' I told Carole. 'By doing this you are enacting the Magician as a channel of communication. I respect your willingness to confront yourself and to be so creative about making these changes, transformation and change being two important characteristics of the Magician card.'*

❖ Judith, a communications teacher, came to class with this experience of the Magician: 'I recently revised an Advanced Communications workshop that I haven't given for several years. But the morning I had to walk into the classroom to face the students, I felt nervous and very unsure about the wisdom of my revisions. Well, there was about an hour before class, and as I sat there thinking, I remembered I hadn't done my own homework from this class. Perfect timing! I instantly thought about the Magician's being interpersonal communications. Then, as you suggested in class, I imagined myself as the Magician and actually felt myself bringing the energies from above – my Higher Self – down into my garden, the workshop. I recognised that I wanted to bring as much higher consciousness into it as possible.

'Along with the thought that I wanted to bring as much higher consciousness into my workshop as possible, something very unusual happened. The Magician's pointing finger, which usually makes me feel as if I'm on the spot and responsible, pointed outwards. I interpreted this gesture to mean that this was an advanced class in communication, and I could in fact look to each person present as a source of information. I could draw out what they had to offer, rather than thinking the whole workshop was on my shoulders. I was instantly relieved and was able to progress beyond my initial appraisal of the upcoming day.

'I saw I was letting go of my ego, my immature ego that *always* needs to be in control. Yes, I could be in charge of the class, but I also might be flexible and empower the participants as well. The workshop was a success. It magically, so to speak, became a very enjoyable experience for all involved.'

*'You deserve the Mercury Award for Communications Teacher of the Year,' I said. 'You tuned into and enacted the mediumistic, facilitating and changing facets of the Magician. By letting go of the Magician's immature characteristics of being in charge and having to be the centre of attention all the time, you became the "Changer". And by using (empowering) your students as the resources, you taught them that they are good communicators. Putting your Higher Self in charge of the class was ingenious. I'd say that you've entered either the card's Gateway of Adulthood, or perhaps even Wisdom.'*

### Suggestions for Application and Integration of the Magician

Now it's time for you to wave your magic wand. The following exercises will help you develop mental clarity, improve self-discipline and concentration and your ability to let go and change, bring ideas into form and become more attuned to the magic of life, as well as enable you to experience yourself as a house or vehicle for the God/dess within.

1 Draw or colour your own version of the Magician with yourself as the figure.

2 Set the Magician in a visible place as a reminder to your conscious and subconscious minds to use and absorb its teachings to focus on your goals and objectives at work, be more conscious – awake and aware, be more adaptable to change, pay attention to the shapes you wish to change, etc.

3 Dream on the Magician. Look at the Magician for a few minutes at bedtime and ask that your dreams bring you information and teachings regarding the importance of the Magician in your life at this time.

4 Play the note E on a musical instrument. Intone IAO or hum along with the music. As you do this, focus your awareness on the top of your head, your Crown *Chakra*. You might experience it tingling and warm as you do. Next concentrate on the card for a few minutes. While doing so, you might repeat or contemplate the ancient Sanskrit mantra So'HAM, meaning I AM THAT (the energy of God/dess in human form) I AM. Think about how you are a Magician. Mentally draw the energies from above – your Higher Self – down into your personality and out into your home, work, relationships below. Send energies from your everyday life from below to above by raising your level of awareness – regard all mundane interactions as spiritual work. After a while, you might ask that the Magician's teachings guide you through a particular situation. Or if you are faced with a worrisome situation, event or problem, such as having trouble remembering that God/dess works through your own or another's body and personality; perceiving the inter-connectedness between the spiritual and material worlds; or staying cognisant of what you are cultivating in the garden of your mind, imagine how the Magician might handle it. If it seems feasible, do it. (Did you remember to 'ground yourself'?) Jot down the times when you became aware of the Magician in your interactions. I was aware of the Magician when? Before/during/after . . .

5 Go out into the world and pretend you are the Magician. For example, spend a few minutes a day being fully conscious of what is going on around you. Use all your senses to accomplish this. If your attention wanders, immediately return it to your focus

without chastising yourself. Try this while taking a short walk, eating or bathing. Slowly graduate to more complex interactions. I was the Magician and this is what happened . . .

6 The Rerun. After having an experience and realising afterwards how the Magician's teachings might have made things different – brought clearer communication, helped shed some immature personality traits, brought about a change for the better, etc. – mentally relive the situation, *including* your insight. If possible, actually rerun the situation in real life with this attitude or behaviour.

7 Ask yourself the following questions:

'What goal am I manifesting through my concentrated efforts?' 'How might I better bring the energies of my Higher Self into a particular area of my garden (life)?' 'What communication needs to be made or held back?' 'In what area can my communication skills – listening, writing and speaking – be improved?' 'How can I use my personality attributes to my greatest advantage?' 'Where can I direct my attention to become more aware: family, work, friendships or physical health?' 'In what areas can I be more accepting of the constancy of change?' 'How can I strengthen a weak physical or personality trait?' 'Whose personality would I like to be more at ease with?' 'Where might I be better off being less or more in control?'

'What Gateway of Life am I in or growing through in the above?' Indicate: Childhood, Adolescence, Adulthood or Wisdom. Why?

'What do I need to do in order to develop the above further?' I need to . . .

'What step(s) do I want to take towards this goal and how can the Magician help me?'

8 Use a personal statement regarding the presence of the Magician in your life at this time, such as: 'I'm developing my personality to its fullest.' 'I am an instrument for the will of God/dess.' 'I welcome life's changes.' 'I pay attention to the facets of my life which require care and nurturing.' 'I am who I am and that's okay with me.' My personal statement is . . .

9 Contemplate the following inspirational words and quotes:

'Thoughts are things, thus the very act of thinking something endows them with life.'

'All is flux, nothing stays still.'             Heraclitus

'Knowledge is wakefulness.'            Shiva Sutras

'The human body is the Temple of God. It is the real church, the synagogue, and the mosque made by God.'     Kirpal Singh[4]

'Just as crystal reflects what's near, the mind that's made pure reflects the Self.'            Guru Gita

10 What symbols stand out in the card? What do they say to you? How might they be useful in your daily living? Bring the symbols into your life in some way so as to integrate the card's teachings. The snake wrapped around the Magician's waist reminds me that I'm always growing and changing, also that the only constant is change.

11 Wear or surround yourself with the colour yellow to remind you of the card's teachings when needed, such as desiring to be more accepting of your own or another's personality or physical body. Notice how you are affected.

12 The Magician's astrological correspondence is Mercury, ruling interpersonal communications, mental clarity and trans-formation, among other things. Is some communication pattern asking to be transformed? Try directing your mental energies to it and evaluate what changes are needed. Then formulate a plan to make them. Note what happens: your thoughts and feelings and the outcome.

13 The Magician's Hebrew name, *Beth*, means 'house'. How might this remind you of the card's meaning or help in your life process? Spend some time treating your body like a house for your inner God/dess. Imagine or sense in whatever way you can divine energy flowing down into your house (body) and out into your environment, just as the Magician does.

14 Try a few drops of the scent mastic associated with the Magician as another reminder to integrate the card's teachings.

---

4 Bernard Gunther, Ira Friedlander, and William Hopkins, *Wholly Man*, Macmillian, New York, 1973.

15 Have a cup of tea made from the oriental herb astragalus known as the 'Herb of Outer Strength'. Sit quietly as you drink and consider the herb's properties to build immunity (like ginseng it is adaptagenic), revitalise, balance and energise all of the internal organs, to fortify the 'House of the Most High', and the similar qualities of the Magician.

2 HIGH PRIESTESS

# CHAPTER 6

# The High Priestess

## General Information and Symbolism

The High or 'Supreme' Priestess sits upon her throne at the doorway to the ancient Temple of Solomon. She is the Keeper of the Records, the epitome of memory, and as such is guardian of the 'Great Library' of all knowledge and wisdom. The High Priestess is like a blank tape, receptive, impressionable and operating continuously without the need of conscious consent. In other words, as you read these lines with your conscious mind, your High Priestess, or subconscious mind, is also busy subliminally recording input from your environment. The Priestess's throne is composed of stone, signifying that she is united with the greater world, or higher consciousness, via her accumulated wisdom and understanding, and has thereby earned a right to her position. This is probably the genuine meaning of the term, 'rulership by divine right', used by ancient royalty and political historians.

The twin pillars of the Temple are white and black. The white pillar bears the Hebrew letter, *Yod*, indicating 'yes and positive energy', while the black is inscribed with the Hebrew letter, *Beth*, indicating 'no and negative energy'.[1] The Priestess demonstrates her powers of neutrality by being positioned between these polarities. She personifies neutrality because she is silent, nonjudgemental and nondiscriminating. Accordingly, she is open to influence from both lower instincts and higher intuitions. In the science of physics, the neutron is the part of the atomic nucleus that has no charge; it is neutral like the Priestess. The white and black pillars, on the other hand, may be respectively identified with the positively charged proton and the negatively charged electron. It is by way of the

---

1 Qabalists seat her between the Tree of Life's pillars of Mercy and Serenity on the pillar of Equilibrium.

Priestess's neutrality that you can in time transform your painful and destructive unconscious behaviour patterns into conscious acts.

The High Priestess holds the *Torah*, the parchment scroll on which the body of divine knowledge and law found in the ancient Hebrew scriptures – the first five books of the Old Testament, known as the *Pentateuch* – are inscribed. This scroll may also be associated with the memory of all events on both a personal and universal level since the beginning of time. The collective unconscious, interchangeably termed the universal memory and mass mind, is the common psychic substratum or sea of consciousness shared by all human minds. C. G. Jung says of this: 'In addition to our immediate consciousness, which is of a thoroughly personal nature, there exists a second psychic system of a collective, universal, and impersonal nature which is identical in all individuals. This collective unconscious does not develop individually but is inherited. It consists of pre-existent forms, the archetypes which can only become conscious secondarily and which give definite forms to certain psychic contents.'[2] It is by way of the collective unconscious that we become aware when a friend is troubled on the other side of the world, or know who is on the phone when it rings. What is the difference between the subconscious and the collective unconscious? Simply this: our personal subconscious may be likened to a stream flowing into the ocean of the collective unconscious. On a final note, in Eastern philosophy, her scroll is called the *Akasha*, the archive that superior psychics delve into at will.

The High Priestess or subconscious is numbered 2, and reflects consciousness, the Magician, much as the Roman number II is a reflection of the number I. What you re-enact or react to are the by-products of what you are attentive to and, like a sponge, absorb.

She is crowned by the full, waxing and waning moon, identifying her with the threefold aspect of the Moon Goddess – maiden, mother and crone – and consequently with lunar goddesses throughout the world. The crown also illustrates the High Priestess's astrological association with the moon. The moon rules cycles, changes in mood, instinct, intuition, impressionability, habits, memory, reflection and receptivity. Placement of this luminary in a birth chart also denotes behavioural and emotional

2 C. G. Jung, *The Archetypes and the Collective Unconscious*, Routledge and Kegan Paul, London, 1959, p. 43

tendencies originating from genetic patterning, prenatal and early childhood environments, conditioning and, according to many, past lives as well. On the Tree of Life, the *Sephirah* associated with the moon is Foundation or *Yesod*. This sphere is often referred to as the Automatic Consciousness and contains the vital soul, *Nefesh*, the life-bestowing principle that humanity shares with all of creation. This invisible power automatically enlivens, connects and coordinates everything in the manifest world.

As noted previously, the subconscious is reflective like a mirror. It is not surprising, then, to see water (also reflective) flowing from behind the Temple pillars and down the Priestess's robes, associating her with the stream of consciousness from which all originate. The Qabalists term this stream the *Anima Mundi*, or The Soul of the World. The Priestess's shimmering robes symbolise the Hermetic principle of Vibration, the primal beat of the life force that pulses through creatures great and small.

Behind the Priestess hangs a veil embroidered with palms and pomegranates. It symbolises both the mysteries of life and death which have never been lifted, and her virgin membrane. Because virginity signifies possibilities, these fruits refer to the innate ability to make new or unhabituated choices as well as the essential ingredients with which to do so. The palms signify willpower – the creative-projective energy, while the pomegranates stand for desire – the creative-receptive energy. These forces act in unison to bring forth the seeds of new possibilities. Her potential and virginity are again depicted by the lotus buds atop the Temple pillars. Finally, notice how the pomegranates form a pattern identical to the ten *Sephiroth* on the Tree of Life, regarded as a map of the involution and evolution of consciousness. The Priestess's head is situated directly over it, intimating that within your subconscious mind lies the means to find your path home.

The High Priestess is not only linked to all the lunar goddesses, but is synonymous with the Virgin Mary, Isis and all other virgin goddesses. This can be misleading, as our first association with virginity is that of physical chastity. However, the High Priestess brings with her another, more all-encompassing meaning: here virginity indicates a whole or incorruptible individual, a person so strong in their beliefs and convictions that they might die for them. Relating to the High Priestess as such extends the opportunity to be Priestess-like to everyone, in their own way and time. The equal-armed cross lying over her heart substantiates this potential for wholeness in yet another way. It communicates the uniting of human consciousness possible when subconsciousness – the horizontal female arm – is blended with consciousness – the vertical male arm.

The cross also illustrates the equality and interdependence of male and female energies plus the descent of spirit into matter and ascent of matter into spirit. This occurs in two distinct ways. First, when the cross is perceived as the confluence of fire and water, male and female respectively, which neutralise one another in the form of steam. And second, studying the Tree of Life, you can see the horizontal section of the cross where both the archetypical male – Wisdom, *Chokmah* – and female – Understanding, *Binah* – arise from the vertical neutral section, the Crown, *Kether*, to exist on the same equal plane. From this primal interaction comes not only the rest of the Tree of Life, but the rest of creation as well.

The High Priestess is associated with the colour blue, the musical note $G^\#$, the Sixth *Chakra*, the inner or third eye situated above the nose and between the two outer eyes, and the herb crampbark. She is customarily recognised as the symbol of the original female Eve, the *anima*, oriental *Yin*, the receptive inner side of the human personality, and the subconscious mental activities just below the threshold of the conscious mind. In view of this, she has long been associated with Hecate, goddess of the Underworld. Her Hebrew name, *Gimel*, means 'camel', and like this animal of burden and transportation, the High Priestess bears not only the weight of our experiences, but retains what she is given. The camel is also a ruminating animal that, like the High Priestess, chews over what it has swallowed over and over again. The High Priestess aspect of our personality is responsible for receiving and transporting information to and from our self-conscious and superconscious minds.

Medical science and Tarot agree that all experiences are impressed in our minds and bodies, whether we remember them or not. Dr William Penfield performed neurological experiments wherein patients' long forgotten memories resurfaced when various areas of their brains were surgically stimulated. It is not strange, then, that these memories can surface naturally as well. A particular type of internal or external input – sensory experience, action, emotion, interaction, etc. – can easily restimulate a previously learned or subconscious response. Such responses or imprints are initially transmitted verbally and nonverbally through familial and cultural role models as well as through our surroundings. It is understandable, then, how certain stimuli can induce us to replay or re-enact previous behaviours. It is in this way that the subconscious determines how we experience life in the present and future. In other words, our present actions or reactions may be regarded as planting the seeds of our future.

L. Ron Hubbard, founder of Dianetics and Scientology, named this part of us the 'Reactive Mind': the mind that re-enacts or repeats behaviour based upon previous experiences or impressions of a similar nature, rather than acting in accord with what is presently called for. At times, automatic behaviour is welcomed, such as when breathing, driving a standard-shift car or recalling a foreign language. Yet, at other times, it is worthwhile to stop ourselves and determine the appropriateness of reliving our past actions and attitudes in the present. An example of this would be when choosing a new mate after a divorce.

In the Qabalah, the High Priestess is known as the Uniting Intelligence. To unite is to join pieces, ideas or people together to form a whole or to make peace. The High Priestess is the peacemaker who, by uniting the personality or ego (consciousness) to the Higher Self (superconsciousness) within, brings us inner peace. This Intelligence also bestows the awareness that everyone and everything are united by the collective or universal unconscious.

## Gateway of Life: Childhood

In the previous card (the Magician), the individual in the Childhood stage begins to become conscious of the world. With the High Priestess or indiscriminate mind, you innocently absorb and store information, impressions and reflections from what you have seen, heard and felt within your mind and body and environment, creating a bank of memories. Here, you are trained and conditioned ('programmed') through contact with family, peers, culture, the media, society at large and religious and educational institutions. And according to many schools of thought, past-life imprints, or *samskaras*, a Sanskrit term for present impressions resulting from past lives, are also activated. It is feasible, then, to understand how who you become in later life may be attributed to the High Priestess. Living in the High Priestess stage of Childhood, you are formulating a nonverbal frame of reference for who you are, what the world is about and your place in it.

At this Gateway, you become aware of sub- and suprahuman levels of existence, often in the form of communications with 'special friends', elves, fairies, angels and nature spirits. These awarenesses may also account for your being frightened by things others cannot perceive.

Encountering the High Priestess at the Four Gateways of Life might create certain experiences. Childhood: A student gets A's in all studies that require only memorisation skills, but fails in subjects that require analytical thinking; Adolescence: You experience the budding awareness that many of your attitudes and behaviours have been unconsciously conditioned. Adulthood: the realisation that you are treating your husband like your mother treated your father leads to taking the steps necessary to alter this behaviour; Wisdom: You gain mastery over your autonomic nervous system via biofeedback or meditation in order to keep your blood pressure down.

## Divinatory Questions for the High Priestess

*Upright*: Have you been true to yourself and/or an ideal? What might you be suddenly remembering from an earlier point in your life? Are you feeling more receptive than usual? How have your habits been serving you? Where is neutrality being called for? In what area of your life could you be feeling uninitiated/virginal? Are you becoming more aware of your conditioning or programming? Might you be having otherworldly or psychic dreams or experiences? Have you unconsciously adopted certain behaviours in order to survive in a dysfunctional family or work environment? Could you be feeling more in the flow of life than you have in a long time? What behaviour are your mirroring? Are you becoming increasingly cognisant of what you allow into your subconscious? Might you be recognising hidden motives and feelings in either yourself or another? Whom do you wish to impress? Who is impressing you? What would you like to be the recipient of? Do you desire more time alone for reflection? What foundations are you laying? What message are you transporting, retaining, reflecting?

*Reversed*: Have you been veiling your feelings? Might you be behaving so passively that you are unable to ask for what you need? Where have you been on automatic? What memories, feelings, intuitions might you be blocking? Are you feeling too open? Do you feel excessively private? Who has given you the cold shoulder? Do you feel stuck in a hurtful habit pattern but can't seem to break it? Have you been exceptionally reactive to some person or situation? What foundations have been shaken? Might you be slowly recognising that some of your patterns and coping strategies are outmoded? Are you frightened or confused by precognitive experiences? In what ways has the collective unconscious, universal unconscious or mass mind consciousness been exerting undue influence on you? Are you having difficulty differentiating between what is real and what isn't? How might you be feeling violated? Do you feel disturbed but unable to identify what is disturbing you? Have you been acting without thinking enough first because you are overstressed and tired? Have you remained neutral for too long? What have you suddenly remembered?

## Personal Experience

The following is an account of my first conscious interactions with my subconscious mind. It was a mild autumn afternoon when my five-year-old son ran through the house repeating a long string of swear words. My instant reaction to his behaviour was to think of washing his mouth out with soap. The solution popped up like a reflex, since this was how I was punished by my mother when I swore (I later learned it was done to her by her mother, too). Yet somewhere inside me, I felt that acting on this impulse was wrong. What was more appropriate was simply to ask my child why he was swearing.

After I had sat him down and questioned him, he explained that he was mad because he couldn't find his new fire truck. To which he innocently added, 'I'm saying what you do, mommy.' I nearly fell over, because as little as he was, he was mirroring my behaviour just as I had almost mirrored my own mother's half an hour before. I thought about what had happened for some hours, and the pieces finally fitted together when I recognised it to be the High Priestess in action.

My son had seen how I behaved when angry and frustrated, and duplicated it when he felt that way. In choosing to question him instead of washing his mouth out with soap, I broke at least two generations of subconscious patterning. The realisation that I had taken a different course of action made me recall the veil of potential hanging behind the High Priestess's throne. The palms and pomegranates, the willpower and the seeds of creative possibility are all needed to bring forth meaningful change.

## Student Experience

❖   Laurel was taught that expressing her anger was only for drunks, bad girls and bitches. 'I keep smiling at my boss even though he keeps stepping on me. He takes advantage of me by giving me more work than I can possibly do in eight hours. So I either have to work late or feel terribly pressured most of the day. I'm also not getting paid the salary I deserve. I know that I've contributed to the problem. The High Priestess forced me to look at how I was indoctrinated by my parents and religious school to suppress my feelings and fear getting angry. The homework question, "What state are you seeking to escape from?" hit me right here (she pointed to her gut). My mother told me good girls don't throw fits. Meanwhile, my parents would get drunk when they went out and come home yelling and swearing at each other. The nuns threatened me with going to hell for cursing and having a hot temper. Do you know that the first time I looked at the High Priestess, her robe reminded me of a nun's habit and I didn't want to go near her? I'm glad she turned out to be something else.

'Instead of finding out how to express myself, I've internalised my feelings into stomach ulcers and extra weight. Yet I know it's important, actually essential, for me to express things. A friend suggested I take some classes in assertiveness training to help me do it. It's time to reprogram me myself with what I need, not with what others want me to be. Do you see this lapis lazuli necklace that I'm wearing? It's a reminder to me to get on with this. The blue is the same colour as the Priestess's robes. The necklace belonged to my grandma, and I know she'd want me to be happy.'

*'I'm glad that you're finding the questions and Priestess's colour to be helpful,' I said to Laurel. 'I agree, you could use some additional support in dealing with your situation, and assertiveness training is a good place to begin. You seem aware that the behaviours you've adopted in order to survive are no longer appropriate. You might put the High Priestess where you can see her, and experiment with using a few personal statements to help keep you on the track of throwing off your victim role. You are, in fact, an A.C.A., an Adult Child of Alcoholic parents, therefore doing some reading or group work in this area would also be beneficial.'*

❖ Another student told the class, 'I was trained to expect to be treated in certain prescribed ways around my birthday and holidays. But when I discovered my real feelings about these, I was surprised to find superficial expectations. My training is inappropriate for who I truly am. This past Mother's Day, I saw how I'd been conditioned by my mother, by television, the greeting card industry and floral and restaurant businesses,' said Trish, mother of two teenagers, with a hearty laugh. 'I came to believe I must receive certain gifts and treatment to feel loved and appreciated: cards, flowers, candy, long-distance phone calls and meals I must wait in long uncomfortable lines to eat.

'Studying the Priestess caused me to re-evaluate these attitudes. As I studied my class notes, I decided I honestly didn't care what others did for me on Mother's Day. What I really want is good treatment during the entire year, not just on special occasions. So I told my kids that whatever they did would be completely satisfactory, even if it was nothing. I want them to feel in their hearts what they say and do. My notes on the High Priestess were definitely a catalyst for me. It looks as if I'm being freed from some social conditioning. And, who knows, maybe I'm freeing my kids in the process.'

*I agreed with Trish's evaluation of the situation. 'By wilfully re-evaluating how you were trained and what was projected by the mass mind or collective unconscious, you've begun to take charge of your future,' I said. 'It also seems that you've helped plant some different seeds in your children's future. You're integrating the symbology of the palms and pomegranates into this situation to the best of your ability.'*

❖  'I have a class at school that I don't like, and now it's exceptionally distasteful because we're doing career planning,' said Carol, a sixteen-year-old high-school junior. 'I feel oppressed enough as it is by school, and now I feel like they're trying to control what I'll do when I finally leave. The whole thing makes me so mad; I'm only sixteen and I like to live in the present. But I also know my negative attitude isn't going to get me anything except to bring my grade-point average down.

'I'm willing to admit I'm being very reactive about it, re-enacting similar situations from the past where I've been coerced into doing something, instead of acting as I saw fit. I've decided to begin using the creative visualisation period in that class to pattern the lifestyle I'd like to have in ten years, rather than sitting there crying and frustrated. I can easily visualise my ideal life, and it will be fun. That way I'll be using the more neutral powers of the Priestess to help me make the best of the class. I'll actually be doing something I think is useful, instead of feeling victimised and getting caught up in the Priestess's negative pole (the black pillar).'

*'So, Carol, you've been reacting,' I told her. 'However, your decision to imagine your ideal life is very wise. You'll be using the Priestess's powers of*

*receptivity and memory to create more manageable impressions about being in control than those you've held until now. It seems as though you're well on your way to overcoming your destructive reactive state. Maybe you can see what you're doing as progress into the Gateway of Wisdom in this area of your life.'*

❖   'I have the powerful tendency to put myself in relationships with men who take more than they give,' shared Barbara. 'I'm painfully coming to recognise and explore my long-term pattern of dissatisfying relationships with men. I had a past-life reading and was told it's a deep, deep pattern, originating with my exploitation of women in another lifetime.

'Well, I recoloured the High Priestess twice this past week to reinforce my coming to terms with the problem. The time I spent concentrating and meditating on her was well spent. I was able to explain to the man I've been dating that I'm breaking my pattern of not getting my needs met in my relationships with men. I hope he'll be able to make the adjustment. If he can't, I honestly know I'm better off without the relationship, rather than suffering the way I've been doing. I keep thinking about the Priestess and the idea of her being a virgin, of her being true to her Self. It's about time I do likewise. I know it's going to take a while, but I've suffered too long. She's a great role model for me.'

*Colouring is a wonderful way to contemplate the card's teachings, and it seems as if it helped Barbara to 'see' that she wanted to emulate the High Priestess's virginal attitude. Not only had she been meditating on the card, she adopted its wisdom by standing up for what she believed was right.*

## Suggestions for Application and Integration of the High Priestess

These exercises will give you a clearer understanding of how the magic mirror of the Priestess – your subconscious and the universal unconscious – operates. They will also offer you ways to improve awareness of what you have absorbed and are presently absorbing into your subconscious, and help you become more aware of how to alter your automatic behaviour or habits of mind.

1   Draw or colour your own version of the High Priestess with yourself as the figure.

2 Set the High Priestess in a visible place as a reminder to your conscious and subconscious minds to use and recall her teachings on how we are all interconnected through the collective or universal unconscious; be more in touch with the flow of life; recognise how long our memories are; or be neutral.

3 Dream on the High Priestess.

4 Play the note G# on a musical instrument. Intone IAO or hum along with the music and concentrate on your third or inner eye as you do so (you might experience it feeling warm or tingling just a bit as you do). Now meditate on the card for a few minutes. As you sit there, contemplate the fact that within you is the power to alter your impressions of people, places and things. Think about a situation in which acting would have been more advantageous than reacting. Consider how we are all linked together by the collective or universal unconscious. Request that the High Priestess's teachings guide you in similar events in the future. Or if you're faced with a worrisome situation, event or problem such as wanting to be more receptive, coping effectively with some painful memories or altering an old or initial impression, imagine how the High Priestess would handle it. If it seems feasible, do it. Did you remember to 'ground' yourself? Jot down the times when you became aware of the High Priestess in your interactions. I was aware of the High Priestess when? Before/during/after . . .

5 Go out into the world and pretend you are the High Priestess. I acted like her when dealing with an officer at my bank. I had recently had several unpleasant interactions with bank officers, but was determined to alter the impression. Despite my apprehension, I walked up to the officer's desk with a smile on my face and a desire to transact my business easily, and it did. I was the High Priestess and this is what happened . . .

6 The Rerun. After having an experience and realising in retrospect how the High Priestess's teachings might have made things different – brought less reactive behaviour, increased neutrality, receptivity, etc. – mentally relive the situation *including* your insight. This will help the behaviour become more automatic next time. If possible, actually rerun the situation in real life with this attitude or behaviour.

7    Ask yourself the following questions:

'What survival technique adopted in my formative years is
presently hindering my development?' 'What pattern or habit in
my daily routine would benefit from examination?' 'What do I
instinctively believe about a recurring experience, dream or
memory?' 'Where am I being or becoming supersensitive?' 'How
might I improve my memory skills?' 'Where would a neutral or
dispassionate point of view be helpful?' 'What have I been reacting
to?' 'What state or feeling am I seeking to escape from?' 'How
might I be truer to my Self and what I believe in?' 'How might the
mass mind be influencing how I handle my career, social or family
life?' 'Why have I been blocking out my feelings and instincts?' 'In
what situation might conditioned behaviour be appropriate and
useful?' 'What memory might prove useful to reflect upon?'

'What Gateway of Life am I in or growing through in the above?'
Indicate: Childhood, Adolescence, Adulthood or Wisdom. Why?

'What do I need to do in order to develop the above further?' I
need to . . .

'What step(s) do I want to take towards this goal and how can the
High Priestess help me?'

8    Use a personal statement-affirmation regarding the presence of
the High Priestess in your life at this time, such as: 'I have the
power to recollect whatever I choose to direct my attention to.' 'I
can remain silent, receptive and neutral when needed.' 'I have the
power to act or re-enact.' My personal statement is . . .

9    Inspirational words and quotes:

'The doorway to all-knowing.'

'There is no such thing as "my" consciousness; there is just
consciousness acting as a continuity that is moving across all
forms of evolution, from mineral to man.'        Pir Vilayat Khan[3]

10   What symbols stand out in the card? What do they say to you?
How might they be useful in daily living? Bring the symbol(s)

---

3  Bernard Gunther, Ira Friedlander, and William Hopkins, *Wholly Man*,
Macmillian, New York, 1973.

into your life in some way so as to integrate the card's teachings. The equal-armed cross over the Priestess's heart tells me that the female and male energies are equal and balanced in power. I once hung up a cross to remind me not to be intimidated by all the male energy surrounding me – my husband and two sons.

11 Wear and surround yourself with the High Priestess's colour, blue, to remind you of the card's teachings when needed, such as wanting to be more relaxed, receptive or neutral or to improve your ability to recall information. Notice how you are affected.

12 The High Priestess is astrologically linked with the moon, which rules cycles, mood swings, instinct, reflection, receptivity, past-life inheritances and memory, among other things. Is there some cycle or instinctive response you wish to alter? Some memory you would like to reflect upon, or some idea or person you would like to be more receptive to? Call upon the High Priestess to help this process along. Note what happens: your thoughts and feelings and the outcome.

13 Remember that the High Priestess's name, *Gimel*, means 'camel'. How might this remind you of the card's meaning or help in your life process? When I begin a new course of study, I tack a photo of a camel above my desk to reinforce my potential to store and recall information.

14 Try a few drops of the scent camphor associated with the High Priestess as a reminder to integrate the card's teachings.

15 Have a cup of tea made from the herb crampbark, called the 'Herb of Inner Opening'. Sit quietly as you drink and compare the herb's properties as a muscle relaxant and general calmative to the same qualities of the High Priestess.

3 THE EMPRESS 7

# CHAPTER 7

# The Empress

## General Information and Symbolism

The Empress wears a victory wreath of myrtle, is crowned by twelve six-pointed stars and carries a sovereign's staff. These symbols tell us that she is the immortal Creatrix of the entire material world, and as such is in charge of the forces of nature.

Her flowing robe conceals the belly of the perpetually pregnant Mother of All. Since she is always 'with child', the Qabalists have named her 'the Constant Becoming'. The Empress wears the Greek letter *Delta* (a fertile area of land at the mouth of a river) over her heart underscoring her fruitfulness. She is adorned by a pearl necklace. Pearls begin in a seed-like form, indicating that she holds the seeds for creation within her. Her surroundings are lush compared to those of her pre-decessor, the virginal High Priestess, because she has given birth to life. The ripening wheat-field suggests the ancient agricultural goddesses Ceres and Demeter. Roses and other foliage indicate that the Priestess's seeds of potential have reached fruition. The cypress trees in the background are sacred to Venus as are the myrtle and rose.

The evergreens symbolise the Empress's ever-giving nature. A stream flows through the forest and cascades into a pool, alluding to the stream of consciousness originating behind the High Priestess's temple, now nourishing the Empress's garden. The water shows how feelings fertilise the garden of our lives as well as how the fluidic 'mind stuff' or creative imagination forms the patterns from which physical reality is born.

The Empress's highly visible and comfortably appointed throne is a strong contrast to the stark and barely visible throne of the High Priestess. This shows us that the Empress is a more mature expression of the High Priestess. In other words, the Mother was at some earlier point in time the Virgin. This is further confirmed by the fact that her foot rests upon a crescent moon, the High Priestess's astrological assignation.

The Empress holds a heart-shaped shield. It is a carry-over from her earlier fierce virgin huntress aspect. It shows that she lovingly protects her children. The dove, a Hebrew symbol for peace and a Christian symbol for the Holy Spirit, occupies the shield's centre. This suggests that she is not only motivated by love, but loves unconditionally. It also tells us that peace may be found by tuning into the Self within your heart of hearts to recall who you really are – a child of the Most High.

Her sceptre is shaped like the symbol used for Venus. This glyph was adopted by the Women's Movement as shorthand for the word 'woman' in the late 1960s. The five blooming roses represent the love and desire that motivates us to bring our hopes and dreams to fruition. It is essential to remember that what we yearn for teaches us in time to desire what is for our greatest good.

The Empress's colour is green, her note is F#, that of the Fifth, or Throat *Chakra*, and her herb is the Chinese 'woman's herb', dong quai. She is also related to the physical sense of touch as well as the super-physical sense clairsentience, or 'clear feeling', the power to feel things beyond the range of the natural sense of touch. An example of this would be actually feeling wavelike energies moving towards you through the air from someone sending you either love or 'daggers'.

The Empress's Hebrew name is *Daleth* and means 'door'. As the Qabalistic Great Mother, she is the doorway through which all forms of life must pass in order to become manifest. She is also the portal through which the dead pass to return to formlessness (note how death is often called 'passing-on'). The Empress conducts life into and out of this world.

The Empress is linked to the planet Venus, Roman goddess of love and beauty, sometimes depicted as rising from the sea, or in this case out of the High Priestess, symbol for the sea. Astrologically, Venus is associated with emotion and imagination. Hence your ability to create and maintain balance and harmony within yourself and with your surroundings via your desire for love and love of what is beautiful. Venus is patroness of the arts and music, both of which stem from creative imagination. In your birth chart, Venus indicates your basic emotional tone and nature – feelings, ability to bond, sense of aesthetics, creative self-expression and imagination. Venus is connected with the Throat *Chakra*, the origin of how you express yourself (your voice) in the world. She is also the ruler of love and finances. This is so because the state of your love life, bank account and material well-being are closely related to what you *imagine* yourself with and *feel* deserving of. On the Tree of Life, the *Sephirah* assigned to Venus is *Netzach*, meaning 'Desire, Victory and Attainment'. As noted, the Empress is regarded by Qabalists to be the Creatrix of the world. The Empress is the impersonal force that is behind and stimulates the personal creativity of Venus.

The Empress is linked with all mother deities in both Eastern and Western traditions. She is the giver of unconditional love and solace as well as the guardian of childbirth (her image was next to my bedside when I went into labour). She is also associated with the often misunderstood side of love and creation, limitation, destruction and, as previously noted, death. In the Hindu tradition, the goddess *Kali* represents this type of energy. When the divine spirit assumes a physical form it becomes limited to that form and consequently becomes subject to deterioration and death. Life and death are inseparable. This is further illustrated on the Tree of Life, in which the *Sephirah* assigned to the force of the Great Mother is *Binah*, meaning 'understanding'. *Binah* is ruled by the planet Saturn, symbolic of the restrictions inherent in the world of physical form. Her work is to bestow a bit of the Divine Spirit in the form of a divine soul, or *Neshemah*, to all of her children – creatures great and small.

The Empress is numbered 3, the cementing factor between the numbers one and two and therefore the number of birth and new beginnings. Lao Tsu said of three, 'One engenders two, two engenders three, while three engenders all things.' She is recognised as the combination of the Magician, the *animus* and self-consciousness, and the High Priestess, the *anima* and the subconscious. This union of opposites gives way not only to personal wholeness, but to the beginning of new ideas and forms. Three is also the number of the Holy Trinity, the predominantly male union of the Father, Son and Holy Spirit, which in the Aquarian Age may signify the unity of our divine parents, Father and Mother, with our physical parents, Son and Daughter, to create us, their children. This redefinition includes the excluded Divine Mother and Daughter, who are equal in importance and power to the male deity.

In the Qabalah, the Empress is known as the Luminous Intelligence. Just as the moon is enlivened by the sun, this light and life-emitting Intelligence energises and enlivens what we consistently bestow our creative and emotional energies upon. This is how we manifest or give birth to what we love, passionately desire and nurture.

## Gateway of Life: Childhood

As the child, you are mothered and nurtured. Through this you learn how those around you express affection and caring and create emotional bonds. From this, the child acquires behaviour which evokes love from itself and others. Through experience and observation, you discover what unconditional and conditional love are. This is not a cognitive process. Your self-image and self-esteem are developing. Self-love and love of others are defined. The Empress is linked with the sense of touch and feelings. Here you are touched by and reach out to your environment to learn what feels, looks, sounds, smells and tastes pleasurable. These explorations help establish your basic sense of aesthetics, your emotional tone and sow the seeds of creative self-expression.

Meeting the Empress at the Four Gateways of Life may result in certain attitudes and behaviours. Childhood: Associating extra pounds with being 'motherly', a woman gains an unhealthy amount of weight after giving birth to her first child; Adolescence: You become aware of your tendency to severely chastise and reject others when they make mistakes or do not seem 'perfect'; Adulthood: You are confronting the fact that you have had unhappy love relationships because you tend to love others too much and yourself too little; Wisdom: At this level you might be a master of compassion, such as Mother Teresa or Mahatma Gandhi, or someone like you loving a friend exactly as he is.

## Divinatory Questions for the Empress

*Upright*: Whom or what have you been taking care of or mothering? Where and how are your creative energies being expressed? Are you finding a new voice in the world? What project do you wish to give birth to? Do you wish yourself or another to become pregnant? What are you imagining in regard to your finances? What desire have you recently brought to fruition? Who is deserving of your compassion? Do you feel fertile? What do you desire most? Who or what are you becoming more vulnerable to or is touching you? Is it appropriate to protect yourself or another? Might it be time to develop your female side? To whom are you providing, or who is providing you with, a female role model? What state have you been imagining and feeling most consistently? Might it be stimulating as well as regenerating for you to bring more art and music into your life? Are you learning how to take good care of yourself? Have you

been working towards the regeneration of Mother Earth? Where
have you given or received unconditional love?

*Reversed:* Could your creativity be slowed down, drained or
blocked? What plan, dream or efforts might be aborted? Might it be
necessary to decide whether to continue or terminate a project?
Have you been overly permissive? Is there the resulting need to set
some more appropriate limits? What or whom might you be
behaving overly protective towards? What could you be
'smothering'? Could you be distancing another by being unduly
sensitive? What new bond is slowly forming? Are you slowly healing
a rift with your mother, another woman or with females in general?
Why might you be blocking your feelings? Have you been treating
yourself with less affection and care than you treat others? Whom
might you ask to give you some nurturing? Are you feeling
emotionally or physically deprived or frustrated? Have you been
wasteful or overly indulgent? Could you be refraining from touching
or giving pleasure to yourself or others? Why? Whom have you
possibly withdrawn your understanding or compassion from? When
was the last time you got a good massage? How might you become
more attuned to Mother Earth? What restrictions seem to be
operating in the areas of your work, relationships or creative self-
expression at this time?

**Personal Experience**

In her role as the Great Mother, the Empress has influenced me in
two very important ways. The first was in helping me to open my
heart to heal an extremely painful relationship with my mother. I'll
never forget the night my mom sat among Tarot class members
smiling and cheering me on as I shared my experience of how this
occurred. Afterwards she commented on how the work I did had
inspired her to come to terms with her relationship with her own
mother.

The incident that enabled me to heal the troubled relationship
happened while studying the Tree of Life. I learned that the Creatrix
is associated with the sphere of influence on the Tree called
Understanding (*Binah* in Hebrew). This information immediately
spurred me to pull out the Great Mother or Empress card, and as I
meditated on her, my attention became fixed upon her heart-shaped
shield. I was astounded to realise that her open-heartedness fortifies
and protects her. This simple awareness encouraged me to get on
with the distasteful business of handling the years of hurt, rage and

resentment I held towards my mother. As the door to my heart began opening, I came to agree with the psychological principle that we must love and make peace with our mothers (and fathers) if we are to truly love ourselves. This ideology became symbolised in the Empress card by the dove in the centre of her heart-shaped shield. These insights gave me the understanding (*Binah*) that each troublesome experience I have with my mother is the Divine Mother's way of helping me expand my ability and capacity to love and accept people for who they are and to set limits that are motivated by love.

With this preparation, I dug vigorously into the mental, physical and emotional processes that freed me from the pain and hatred I had been carrying around most of my life. Through the subsequent months of therapeutic work, I learned about the virtues of positive detachment and limit setting. That is, when I do not like what someone says or does, I acknowledge my feelings, and then decide if their words or actions honestly require a response. I detach myself from them with an understanding of, and tolerance for, our differences. In this way, I became able to extend true, unconditional love towards my mother despite her human frailties. Thanks to the Empress, I came to understand, accept and respect her for who she is (and me for who I am). I also became able to let her know when I feel hurt by her actions. Although she is not the perfect person I yearned for her to be, she's perfect in the respect that our relationship taught me about loving unconditionally.

As *Daleth*, the Empress is the doorway through which all enter the world. The second important lesson she taught me has been that innumerable life choices are available. Yet in order to manifest my choices, I must be motivated by loving desire. Without this essential ingredient, I've found myself to be only superficially engaged, merely intellectually committed. Looking at the successful people in my life, I noticed all are motivated by some type of desire: the desire to be loved by a beloved, or the world at large; love for others, such as parents working hard to support their children; love of possessions, money and power; or a love for humanity, nature, Self and God/dess.

Out of this observation have come eight questions I ask myself prior to beginning to manifest (give birth to) something, be it a skill, object or relationship.

**First:** Do I honestly have the ability to do or learn what is required to achieve this? Essentially, this is asking that I appraise my karmic limitations and capabilities – my strengths and weaknesses. For example, if I'm colour blind, I probably won't be a good interior decorator, no matter how much I love design and texture. On the other hand, I had a poor friend who had the aptitude and educational background to be a chiropractor, yet lacked the funds to continue her schooling. Since she desired her goal so intensely, she threw a benefit for herself to raise the money. This woman graduated from chiropractic college last year.

**Second:** Do I desire this 'something' enough to make whatever sacrifices are necessary to acquire it? For example, am I willing to work during the day and go to school at night, foregoing almost all social activities, to earn a teaching certificate?

**Third:** Do I feel deserving of satisfaction? Here I must examine my true motives for wanting what I do. This may mean examining subconscious conditioning, as well as asking myself whether I am looking to perform service or only desire to be recognised and applauded by the community?

**Fourth:** Am I able and willing to devote ongoing love and energy to my goal while also nurturing myself? Can I behave lovingly as a mother nurturing her baby, persevering even when the work involved is especially challenging? This is about caring for the caretaker and taking action despite your own and others' resistance.

**Fifth:** Do I recognise that I am a co-creator and therefore must work with Mother Nature's time schedule as well as my own? I may want to achieve my goal next month, but no matter how great my desire, unless I am in sync with nature, I may have to wait. Put differently, tulips need time and certain conditions to transform from bulbs into flowers.

**Sixth:** Am I getting the supportive feedback necessary to inspire my continued efforts?

**Seventh:** When my part of the work is done, am I willing to 'cut the cord' and offer it to the world without being overly attached to what results?

**Eighth:** Finally, do I realise what ultimately happens is truly for the 'highest good'? I have used these questions again and again to help me get started on my journey towards many a goal.

## Student Experiences

❖ 'Being a single parent for my child's entire life has made me fairly dependent on my relationship with my daughter,' began Gloria. 'But now that she is well into her teens and involved in the process of creating her own life, a life that's getting more and more separate from mine, I must admit I sometimes feel deserted. I know it's time for her to go her own way, yet it's still lonely for me. I know I need to encourage her, but at the same time it hurts when she doesn't want to be with me to share many of the things we've always done together.

'I've been calling on the Empress in meditation to inspire me to be more of the High Mother, to mother and not smother her, to do what is truly loving, to let her go and not make her feel bad or wrong for it. The Empress is helping me to become more objective about my feelings and to start thinking about creating some new experiences for myself, to direct my energies towards me in a positive way. I'm still young, my whole life is ahead of me, and I think I can create a pretty good life for myself.'

*I said to Gloria, 'It's wise to call on the Empress for help with your mothering at this time. You're correct in thinking it's time to be motherly to yourself plus separate yourself from your daughter. Separation begins at birth and is something most mothers spend their years of mothering engaged in. Experiment with using the Empress's powers of creative imagination to think of ways to make yourself feel good. Don't be surprised if you find yourself feeling better and better as a result.'*

❖ Leslie went on holiday with her man friend of several years' standing and discovered that she was afraid of being loved by him. 'Inside, I always think to myself that if I allow him to love me, I'll be lost and end up being hurt. I've had enough hurt in my life already to last me until I die. Just learning that the Empress is a symbol of love helped me to open my heart. I coloured her hair like mine and I'm using her as a symbol of my wise mother within to make me less fearful of being touched (the Empress is associated with the sense of touch), of taking what Bob wants to give, rather than feeling as if I'm on my way to the slaughter. Deep down inside, I know I really want to be loved and intimate.

'So I took a chance. I went to the mountains with him for the weekend and let his sweetness touch me emotionally, and it felt great. I felt energised, rather than drained by my usual resistance. I allowed myself to see how much we care for each other. And I didn't get hurt. Letting myself be loved and vulnerable made me see not only how frightened I am of not being in control, but how I hurt myself with my own controlling and manipulative behaviour.'

*Leslie is overcoming a common, yet often hard-to-deal-with fear. We all want to love and be loved, yet some of us have been so scarred by painful experiences we protect ourselves against the very thing we need. I suppose it's like the Empress card signifying both the protective and overprotective mother parts of yourself. I suggested that Leslie work with some personal statements affirming that what she is doing is good for her and perhaps do some counselling to look more deeply into her feelings. The Empress is a symbol for love and self-love, and cultivating the feeling that we can love ourselves enables us to know that even if we do get hurt – and getting hurt occasionally is part of all normal relationships – we'll be okay. That is, when we have enough love in the bank, enough self-love and self-esteem, we understand what is happening and are more able to seek understanding rather than close down entirely.*

❖  'This year I've given so much to others that I've neglected giving to myself,' Diana began, as her face turned a bright pink. 'I've gained twelve unwanted pounds in the last nine months or so. It's as if I'm pregnant and now I'm ready to give birth. Since we worked with the Empress, I've been honestly thinking about doing my homework and loving myself. I can see that my family really doesn't need me as much as I'd like to think they do. I think I've been using my commitment to taking care of them to avoid handling some issues in my personal life, such as getting in shape physically.

'I actually took a small first step when I went out and bought myself a new green sweater. It's the exact colour of the Empress's dress. I felt it would remind me to treat myself like an Empress. It's strange, but it's been working. I've been imagining new ways to nurture myself and my family besides earning money, cooking and eating, and I'm beginning to feel better. It's as I said earlier: I'm pregnant and ready to give birth to a new me. Look out, world, here I come.'

*'Wearing the Empress's colour is a great reminder,' I told her. 'It's difficult for women to break some of the patterns of nurturing, which are not genuine nurturing, but rote emulation of what we were told a mother is supposed to be and do. In reality, such behaviours may actually create unhealthy dependencies in those around us. Often the most nurturing thing we can do for our family is to take extra good care of ourselves, so that we*

*bring a centred person into the dynamics of the group. I believe that the creation of new role models is part of the important pioneering work our generation of women is being called upon to do.'*

❖ 'Studying the Empress right before Mother's Day was perfect for me,' began Phyllis, a mother and teacher. 'Last year, my children disappointed me. I spent almost the entire week at school preparing my students for Mother's Day, and then my own kids let me down. One of them forgot what day it was, while the other, my stepson, went off to be with his biological mother. So this year, I decided to be nice to myself, to live in the Wisdom stage of life rather than the Adolescent stage. I thought about my wise and loving mother within and gave myself a beautiful day. I even told my husband, "It isn't your place to plan something. The children are old enough. Besides, I'm not your mother." He was shocked.

'Before going to sleep on Saturday night, I propped the Empress up next to my clock so I'd see her first thing in the morning. She'd be there to remind me of my purpose. I got up early on Sunday and went out jogging and came home to find that my older son had made me a wonderful breakfast, complete with flowers from the garden. Afterwards, I decided to work in my garden and listen to the birds singing. I was in complete bliss when I was called to the phone. My stepson had called to wish me a happy Mother's Day. When I hung up, I felt a lot of compassion towards him. I could understand (the Empress means understanding) that he was caught between his two mothers and that his duty is to his biological mother first. I feel that the Empress's teachings have opened my mind and heart to a lot of new ideas.'

*'I felt so peaceful, Phyllis,' I told her, 'listening to you tell your story – you were just like the Empress in your garden. You certainly called forth the Empress's powers of creative imagination for that one. You also gained some important Empress-like compassion for your stepson in the process.'*

**Suggestions for the Application and Integration of the Empress**

The following exercises provide you with the opportunity to make the Empress part of your everyday reality. Her teachings will stimulate your creativity, aid you to express yourself more effectively, alter your negative tendency to 'enable' and enhance your abilities to appropriately nurture yourself and others.

1   Draw or colour your own version of the Empress with yourself as the figure.

2   Set the Empress card in a visible place.

3   Dream on the Empress.

4   Play the note F# on a musical instrument. Intone IAO or hum along with the music. As you do this, focus on your Throat *Chakra*, which is associated with the Empress and this particular note (you might experience it tingling or warm as you do). You might then repeat the following translation of a Sanskrit Prayer to the Divine Mother:

> O divine Mother, fill my heart with light.
> Make darkness distant from me and promote
> illumination within me.
>                                              Gayatri Mantra

Now meditate on the card for a few minutes. As you do so, ask that the Empress's teachings guide you through a particular situation. If you're faced with a worrisome situation, event or problem, such as wanting to get a project started, but not quite knowing how, ask to call forth the Empress's creativity to help stimulate you. If there is a need to get or stop nurture, imagine how the Empress would handle it. If it seems feasible, try it out. Jot down the times when you became aware of the Empress in your interactions. I was aware of the Empress when? Before/during/after . . .

5   Go out into the world and pretend you are the Empress. Treat yourself like royalty. Pamper yourself lovingly. Thank the Divine Mother as you spend the day in nature. Imagine you are the Goddess of Love and Beauty, Art and Music while expressing your creativity. The morning I decided to be the Empress, my teenager left his lunch money on the breakfast table for the

zillionth time. Thinking about the situation from the Empress's point of view, I understood that my reminding him again wouldn't be helpful, as it had not worked so far and was coming from my tendency to overprotect (or enable) him. So I allowed the Empress to rule, and remained silent. He came home from school hungry (not starving to death or weak from lack of food, as my overprotective mother within would have me believe). He hasn't forgotten his lunch money since. I was the Empress and this is what took place . . .

6  The Rerun. After having an experience and realising in retrospect how the Empress's teaching might have brought increased understanding and compassion, or intensified your desire to do or create something, etc., mentally relive the situation, *including* your insight. This will help the behaviour become more automatic next time. If possible, actually rerun the situation in real life with the new attitude or behaviour.

7  Use the Empress's power of creative imagination to re-create a situation. If you find yourself reacting out of habit, stop yourself for a few seconds, take a deep breath and then call upon the Empress's creative powers to imagine how you would like to behave instead. Next, change your behaviour.

8  Ask yourself the following questions:

'Who or what am I overly attached to emotionally?' 'Who could benefit from some compassion?' 'Where might it be compassionate not to be helpful?' 'What is gestating within me?' 'What might I wish to abort?' 'Where am I giving more than I honestly want to?' 'What state are my affections in?' 'What could I do to cease feeling emotionally exhausted?' 'Whom would I like to develop a closer relationship with?' 'What seeds need additional care?' 'How are my finances being affected by my imagination?' 'What feelings need to be expressed?' 'Who or what am I mothering, smothering or enabling?' 'When was the last time I asked someone to take care of or nurture me?' 'How might dealing with my feelings help release and stimulate my creative energies?' 'In what ways have I become more fertile?' 'What ideas, projects, etc., are requiring my creative energies?'

'What Gateway of Life am I in or growing through in the above?' Indicate: Childhood, Adolescence, Adulthood or Wisdom. Why?

'What do I need to do in order to develop the above further?' I need to . . .

'What step(s) do I want to take towards this goal and how can the Empress help?'

9   Use a personal statement regarding the presence of the Empress in your life at this time, such as: 'I give as much to myself as I give to others.' 'I take pleasure from life's beauties.' 'I give and receive love and nurturing.' 'I am getting better and better at co-creating my goals.' My personal statement is . . .

10  Inspirational words and quotes:

'Desire is half of life; indifference is half of death.'
                                    Kahlil Gibran, *Sand and Foam*

'As we desire, so do we will, as we will, so do we act, as we act, so do we attain.'

'There are two tragedies in life. One is not to get your heart's desire. The other is to get it.'
                        GEORGE BERNARD SHAW, *Man and Superman*

11  What symbols stand out in the card? What do they say to you? How might they be useful in daily living? Bring the symbols into your life in some way so as to integrate the card's teachings. Her crown reminds me to treat myself like a queen. At one point, when my self-esteem was especially low, I braided my hair in a crown to remind me to love and respect myself.

12  Wear and surround yourself with the Empress's colour, green, as a reminder of the card's teachings when needed, such as desiring to be more creative, commitment to nurturing your goals, or loving. Take a walk in the woods or a botanical garden and think of the Empress and notice how you're affected.

13  The Empress corresponds astrologically to the planet Venus, ruling emotions, love, creative imagination, the arts, music, money matters and your voice in the world. Is there some area of your life listed above which would benefit from a jolt of love and creativity? Use the Empress as a visual reminder to carry this out. Note what happens (what was born): your thoughts, feelings and the outcome.

14 The Empress's name, *Daleth*, means 'door'. How can this remind
   you of the card's meaning or help in your life process? While
   writing this book, I've been imagining myself as a door through
   which the ideas for this book are coming and going. Hence, in my
   small way I'm being the Creatrix.

15 Try a few drops of the scent myrtle associated with the Empress
   as a further reminder to integrate the card's teachings.

16 Have a cup of tea made from the oriental herb dong quai (if
   appropriate, because this is a 'woman's' herb). Sit quietly as you
   drink and consider the herb's properties of increasing fertility in
   women, nourishing and purifying the blood, improving bodily
   warmth and circulation and consider the like qualities of the
   Empress. This herb should not be used during pregnancy or with
   excessive menstrual flow.

**4 THE EMPEROR 7**

# CHAPTER 8

# The Emperor

## General Information and Symbolism

The ram's head and horns on the Emperor's shoulder armour, crown and throne associate him with the cardinal (initiating and of foremost importance) Fire sign Aries. Aries rules the head, especially the eyes and frontal lobes of the brain linked with reasoning and analysis, or multi-dimensional thinking. It is these frontal lobes that distinguish humans from the rest of the earth's creatures, making us the most evolved and responsible intelligence on earth and consequently, its ruler. The Emperor wears a crown with twelve triangles (reminiscent of the Empress's twelve-star crown), signifying his dominion over the ordering of the world, as well as the fact that his mind is always open to new ideas. Although he is dressed like a warrior, he bears no arms. This states that he bears goodwill and is intent upon finding non-violent resolutions to conflict.

The Emperor stands for all the father deities in both Eastern and Western traditions; Jupiter, *Adonai*, *Agni* and Zeus among others. He is the male Creator, as the Empress is the female Creatrix, and as such bears as his sceptre an Egyptian *ankh*, or 'Cross of Life', in his right hand to indicate his powers as the male giver of life. The ancient Egyptians believed that human survival depended upon having an *ankh* because it was endowed with the power to connect them to the life force. The Emperor sits upon a stone cube, signifying the material world. It also shows that his reign is founded upon divine law and wisdom. The fact that he, the Creator, is seated upon it indicates the principle that God presides over, protects and is seated within everything on the face of the earth. The Emperor's hair and beard are white, providing additional evidence that he is the Qabalist's wise 'Ancient of Days'. This point is further reiterated by his head appearing in profile – his left eye looks out at the world around him, while his right eye looks to the infinite and universal truth (another symbolic reference to his rulership by divine right). Owing to his universal perspective, the Emperor loves, as does the Empress, unconditionally.

The Emperor holds a globe topped by an equal-armed cross in his left hand representing his ability to carry out the divine plan (the cross indicates the descent of spirit into matter), watch over the world and be an objective observer. Objective observation, or the ability to look carefully and without emotional bias, is the Emperor's ally in much the same way as the Empress's heart (her ability to feel) is hers. The Emperor protects himself with armour. When scrutinising an individual, 'body language' – the information we give out nonverbally about our thoughts and feelings via our physical posture, facial expressions, gestures or armouring – may prove insightful. Armouring, the act of maintaining body stances that are protective and keep others at a distance, such as keeping your arms folded across your chest, or looking away when being spoken to, may be understood as a way of holding fast to certain mental attitudes, or helping someone separate from their too-soft inner nature and make more accurate observations. This suggests that the Emperor may be someone who is either so entrenched in his attitudes and behaviour that he arms himself against external influences, or is protective, because he is tender-hearted. There are times when you have to do something that others will not like you for, such as firing a habitually tardy employee. In instances like this, the armour becomes a way to healthfully distance yourself from another's unpleasant reactions and dissatisfaction. Being truly loving often means that we must behave in ways that do not reinforce self-destructive patterns in others. This aspect of the Emperor's personality may be characterised by the term 'Benevolent Despot'.

In contrast to the fertility of the Empress's garden, the Emperor sits in stark surroundings, indicating that a prerequisite for attaining mental clarity (getting a handle on reality) is divesting oneself of excessive emotion. On the other hand, the water and fertile earth at the mountain's base remind you that reliance upon intellect alone, without emotions such as love to temper it, is usually problematic. In other words, the true ruler must have a heart as well as a mind. Please note that, according to tradition, each card contains the attributes of the cards preceding it, indicating here that the Empress's emotions exist within the Emperor. In response to this it is sometimes said that the Emperor gazes in the direction of his love, the Empress.

Although the Emperor is usually linked to the rational or thinking part of your mind, identified with left-brain linear perception versus right-brain holistic perception, working effectively with the Emperor activates whole-brain perception.

The Emperor is associated with the colour red, the musical note C and the herb ginger. His Hebrew name is *Heh*, meaning 'window'. We appraise what is going on in the world around us by looking through our eyes, or windows. Being the best of military strategists, the weaponless Emperor courageously appraises what he sees according to the Greater Reality, or Higher Self within. The Emperor knows life will be less warlike if he is willing to look at events honestly. A true warrior is brave enough to see what is there, rather than what he or she wants or has been conditioned to see. It is in this way that the Emperor can help free you from the need to impose your false perceptions, which ultimately bring hurt and disappointment, on yourself and others. This aspect of the Emperor's personality is partially what Carlos Castaneda's character Don Juan meant when he spoke of 'learning to see'. Finally, when a window is said to open in our mind, it is regarded as an opportunity to see something new or differently than before. The Emperor has this window open at all times.

As the first cardinal (initiating and of foremost importance) sign of the zodiac, Aries ushers in springtime and the beginning of the yearly life cycle. From this comes the desire to manifest plus the will to act and lead. The enthusiastic Arian personality says: I am, will, can, do, order, motivate initiate, define, activate and energise. These assertive and aggressive qualities challenge the Arian personality to balance his mental energies with his feelings, as the rigid belief that 'there is only one way – mine' often results in hurtful inflexibility, arrogance and the alienation of others. The evolved Arian extends compassion and awareness towards those he seeks to lead.

The word 'Emperor' means 'He who sets in order', as the word 'Empress' means 'She who sets in order'. Being mates, they empower and complement each other. They are interdependent co-creators, each respectful of the other's role and abilities. The Empress produces the egg and the desire to receive, the Emperor produces the sperm which enlivens the egg and the will to give. Please keep in mind that since they symbolise archetypes, only some of their functions are applicable to human relationships, wherein roles are not meant to be so rigidly defined.

*Living the Tarot*

Mastery of the Emperor's teachings is essential for happiness and well-being. This is communicated by his being numbered 4, indicating rulership of the material world, implying the order, balance, stability and discipline necessary to govern. I remember once telling a teacher of mine that 'All I want is to be free.' He smiled, and with a mischievous glint in his eye, replied, 'Freedom is the choice of your disciplines.' It took me years to believe that discipline could bring me freedom. Yet once I began applying order and logic to what I did, the principle became increasingly believable and easier to enact.

The Emperor is linked to both your sense of sight and the superphysical sense clairvoyance, or 'clear seeing'. The Emperor is a visionary who has the ability to see things out of the natural range of human senses (remember that one of the Emperor's eyes looks to the infinite). The ability and willingness to 'see' your options in life are well worth cultivating. Using the cube the Emperor sits upon is one sure way to get started. This is what I mean: Suppose I am faced with a need to live alone, but because my income is small it seems as though I must share a home. In addition to being a symbol of the material world, the cube is identified with multidimensional thinking and reasoning. So in order to problem-solve more effectively, I draw a cube (please see the illustration which follows) like the one the Emperor is seated on. Next, I think out and imagine (the Empress gets into the act, too) as many possible solutions to my problem as the cube has edges and faces. Then I carefully examine each one with the willingness to see what is there, rather than what I want to see. Through this process, I have become better equipped to make decisions.

The Emperor is regarded by the Qabalists as the Creator, the Divine Father who is responsible for his children's protection and well-being. The *Sephirah* on the Tree of Life associated with this force is *Chokmah*, meaning Wisdom. As the father of his people, he is the lawmaker who pays close attention to what is best for them, although they may at times misunderstand and misinterpret his actions as harsh and unreasonable. Until we are all self-regulating, laws and rules are essential: the Hebrews' Ten Commandments; Buddha's *Daca Paramitas*, or Ten Truths; *The Twelve-Steps*; the American Constitution and *Bill of Rights*; to name a few, are the touchstones for millions.

## Using the Emperor's Cube to Solve a Problem

(Reference page 104.)
Sample problem: I need to live alone, but my income is small.

**Step one** **Step two**

**Step three**

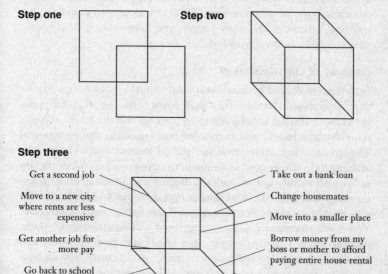

Get a second job
Move to a new city where rents are less expensive
Get another job for more pay
Go back to school for another degree to make more money

Take out a bank loan
Change housemates
Move into a smaller place
Borrow money from my boss or mother to afford paying entire house rental
Get new housemate who agrees to the rules in writing

Forget the whole thing until next year

My solution: the cube helped me see my options. As it turned out, the real issue was not my need to live alone, but to have a housemate who fulfilled his or her agreements. I decided to ask my housemate to leave because she refused to live up to the house rules we had verbally agreed upon. The next person to share my home agreed to sign a written contract to abide by the rules.

In the Qabalah, the Emperor is known as the Constituting Intelligence. This Intelligence inspires and activates you to organise and compose the fundamental rules, laws and processes necessary for effective and efficient daily living. These principles and disciplines make up your moral and ethical codes of behaviour, and function to help run society, as well as your personal life. Please note that it is important to review and, if necessary, revise your personal constitution as you mature. The word 'constitution' may also refer to a person's prevailing state of health, suggesting that if one's constitution – the aforementioned rules, laws, etc. – is strong, one will lead a healthy life. Very simply, the Constituting Intelligence keeps stability in the motion of daily living.

## Gateway of Life: Childhood

At this juncture, you as the child are shown order, reason, boundaries and discipline; through this you learn how to regulate your behaviour at home, school, places of worship and the world at large. As with the mother, you encounter unconditional and conditional love. In this stage, your moral and ethical senses begin to form; self-image and self-esteem continue to grow. The focus is on self-assertion, discipline, and the beginnings of clear and logical thinking. Encountering the Emperor at the Four Gateways of Life, you may be aware of certain attitudes and behaviour. CHILDHOOD: You learn elementary time management and organisational skills; ADOLESCENCE: You discover the difference between aggressively and assertively pursuing your independence; ADULTHOOD: You initiate action to overcome your long-time maths anxiety in order to get a Master's Degree; WISDOM: A corporate executive runs her business with an eye towards employee well-being rather than excessive production, knowing that this attitude will naturally yield higher output.

## Divinatory Questions for the Emperor

*Upright:* Is it time to reorder your life? What part is discipline playing in your life at this time? Have you considered that armour is a necessary tool? Might it be time to develop your male side? Are you working through the relationship with your father or some male authority figure at this time? Whom are you providing with a male role model? Has a window of opportunity opened? What are you in the process of initiating and planning? Where might logic and careful attention to details pay off? Is there a benevolent male in your life at this time? Where have you transformed your aggressive behaviours into assertive ones? Where and why are you becoming increasingly reasonable? What have you possibly 'seen' for the first time? Are you feeling creative? Are you having an encounter with some rules or system? Where are you being called upon to use your organisational abilities? Where might it be necessary to take a 'hard line' approach to setting boundaries? Whom are you lovingly disciplining and setting standards of behaviour for? How has 'tough love' been paying off? What new vision has come to you?

*Reversed:* Where would it be helpful to take your own or another's feelings into consideration before making further plans? Have you been too linear in your thinking or seeing only what you wish to see? Could you be experiencing chaos due to a lack of discipline and order in your life? Might you be at odds with or fearful of your father, men in general or of a male-oriented system? Is this rift slowly healing? What oppressive situation is on the wane? Where could it be beneficial to share or delegate power and responsibilities rather than always being the person in command? Could you be domineering, overly controlling or aggressive in some facet of your life? Has someone misinterpreted your behaviour as harsh and inflexible? What did you previously avoid seeing that is now causing you to question your reasoning? Is it possible that your attitudes and behaviour have been too rigid? How might your vision be clouded? Whom might you be empowering beyond what is appropriate and reasonable? Has your behaviour become less aggressive and more assertive? What personal rule or discipline might it be worthwhile to review and perhaps revise? Is it likely that a more thorough investigation of your options would be beneficial? Has your mind been working overtime? What rules have you broken? What are you rightfully armouring yourself against? Might you be tired of wearing armour or of being so invulnerable?

## Personal Experience

When I first began working with the Emperor card, I encountered so much personal discomfort and difficulty, I often could not continue studying. Compared to the warmth and lushness of the Empress, I perceived the Emperor to be cold, sterile and even forbidding. I finally discovered my main problem with him was his association with the Father principle, because my relationship with my own father had been so tumultuous. When, after considerable time, I finally became able to interact with the Emperor without trepidation, I realised I needed the prerequisites of understanding and open-heartedness gained by working with the Empress, the Mother principle, to work with the Father principle.

My father was a strict disciplinarian who so wanted me to live the life he envisioned for me that he imposed very rigid behavioural standards on me, thinking these would help me fulfil his picture of who I 'should' be. Unfortunately, I didn't agree with his strategy and vehemently refused to do as I was ordered. My defiance served only to frustrate and infuriate the poor man, resulting in his beating and punishing me severely. This, in turn, only heightened my resistance. What a no-win situation for us both!

By way of my studies and meditation on the Empress and Emperor cards, I learned that the Emperor is the Empress's mate, the wise, all-loving, Divine Father, who, because of His wisdom, knows it is only a matter of time until I 'see' what I must attend to in order to lead a fulfilling life.

In contrast to my own father's over-attachment, I found the Emperor to be the epitome of loving detachment. Due to his universal viewpoint, the Emperor loves unconditionally and is not attached to my reactions and responses. He knows that I will live and learn, whereas my father's mundane and limited point of view created tremendous pain, guilt and conflict.

In light of the severity with which I was raised, I vowed I would not discipline my children and became a very permissive parent. But on the hot summer day my three-year-old insisted on repeatedly undressing in the supermarket, my attitude definitely began to shift. Despite his loud and embarrassing protests – he loved being free of the encumbrances of clothing – I told him it was not okay to be naked in the market and helped him back into his clothing. Being a strong-willed child who usually got his way, he persevered. As he began his next round of undressing, I reminded him of the carousel ride I had promised him after shopping and threatened to cancel it if he didn't stop taking his clothes off. Since I had often gone back on my threats, he continued unzipping and untying as if he didn't hear me. Suddenly I saw that I had to discipline him for his own good and mine, and quickly headed for the checkstand. With him screaming in the back seat of the car and me feeling somewhat like a mean mother, we headed directly home.

While manoeuvring through traffic, the words, 'for his own good and mine', echoed through my mind, and for the first time I could see the similarity between my father and the Emperor. Yes, my father did overdo disciplining me, but an essential part of loving is creating order, setting limits and boundaries, a basic teaching of the Emperor card. In my efforts to heal my painful childhood, I had gone to the other extreme and created an often impossible situation with my own child. Over the years, this vivid encounter has enabled me to bear my children's anger when I take on the role of 'Benevolent Despot' and lovingly impose certain standards of behaviour upon them.

## Student Experiences

❖  Mike, a businessman, husband and father, began, 'I grew up in a disorganised and dysfunctional family and became a very in-charge person to compensate for it. I know it's an expression of my fear of losing control and living in the chaos of my childhood, but it has also become synonymous with loving others and it's hard to shake. Sometimes I've alienated others by being overly capable and needing to be commander-in-chief and protector of everyone and everything. I've been trying out the Emperor's teachings to feel my power inside, to know how strong and competent I am, and not have to prove it to anyone or run things when I have no business doing so. I keep meditating on the card to help me and using the affirmation, "I am quietly powerful".

'I'll tell you something else: I've been wearing the red underwear my wife gave me for Valentine's Day (red is the Emperor's colour) as a reminder to turn my energy inside. Like my underwear, I know I'm wearing it and have possession of it, but the world doesn't. With all this, I'm beginning to give others more of a chance to express themselves, to be more powerful, without feeling I'm any less of a person for it. I see I can share some of the control with others, especially my wife. And I know that my next step will be to ease my dictatorial attitude towards my kids. I actually think I can learn something from others. What a surprise!

'I find I get along better, especially at home. My wife and I argue less – or should I say I'm disciplining myself to shut up. I think she appreciates my efforts. We've talked about this power struggle for years now. We even spent time with a counsellor. Now, thanks to the Emperor and my red underwear, I'm finally ready to do something about it.'

*I shared with Mike that it's often difficult to let go of control, especially for someone with a dysfunctional family background. 'Yet once you do, you begin to find that you have a new and more effective kind of control instead, as your affirmation so aptly states. It's just wonderful that you thought of using your wife's gift of love – her Valentine present to you – to remind you to be more loving towards her and yourself. It's amazing to notice that when we empower others, rather than always having to be the powerful one (because it's brought us so much: security, attention, admiration, etc., but has also*

*alienated us from others), we can be loved for it. You might say you've been
living the less mature side of the Emperor's astrological sign of Aries.'*

❖    Sixteen-year-old Carol has a school-sponsored radio talkshow
and came to class relating her most recent programme on parent-
child relationships. 'I kept thinking about what I learned here in class
about the Emperor while preparing my part of the discussion. I
thought about how the Emperor is the loving parent who lays down
the rules and regulations that are good for his children. When I got
on the air, I talked about the importance of discipline from a kid's
point of view.

'At first, some of the other panel members were reactive towards
what I said. They felt as if they could be completely in charge of
themselves. But as we kept talking, they came to agree that it's
important to have rules from the child's viewpoint because it shows
your parents care about what happens to you. We agreed that
discipline and rules are basically meant to protect us and teach us
how to be responsible adults, not hurt us. The problem comes when
we think we're being dictated to.'

*'Yes, Carol, the Emperor addresses the use of rules and discipline, which can
relate to both the positive and negative facets of the card. To restate what I
said in class earlier, the Emperor is the benign Divine Father who truly
does what's best for his children. It's only when he operates through the
imperfect human personality that problems with inflexibility, more
specifically a lack of vision, arise.'*

❖    'I lived with a lot of misunderstanding about orderliness until we
worked with the Emperor,' offered Karen, a chef at a gourmet
restaurant. 'I have a lot of fixed signs in my birth chart and usually
see the effects in my life being too orderly: my home, work,
relationships, even what I choose to do with my free time. I've often
been down on myself for my lack of spontaneity. It was a revelation
for me to see these qualities in a positive light, to appreciate them
and myself, to see how they've aided my success, my ability to be
proficient in what I do at the restaurant.

'Also, the Emperor's teachings have helped me see how much I
want to make more time for fun. This means letting go of a little of
my overly structured and scheduled free time. I honestly think I'm
going to enjoy doing whatever it is I decide to do during that time,
even if it's taking a nice long nap.'

*'Order and discipline are important at the right time and in the right place and amount,' I said. 'It is good that you are appreciating your ability to use these essential tools. Your decision to allow some of your free time to remain unstructured is a good way to counterbalance the effects of too much of a good thing. You might find that at first you're uncomfortable with the free time. But I think you'll find yourself enjoying it more as you keep experiencing it. If you are anything like me, it will probably serve to freshen your perspective on the routine stuff you do.'*

❖ 'I usually limit myself severely when approaching problems,' shared Ellen. 'I ordinarily don't allow myself to see more than just a couple of black-and-white possibilities. But having the Emperor's cube to play with has been extremely stimulating for me. It's allowed me to be relaxed rather than uptight with a problem, to be creative and almost feel like I'm playing with it, rather than wrestling with it and feeling crazed in the process.

'I must decide about beginning a Master's programme in the autumn, and used the cube to help "see" (as the Emperor sees) that I can begin small. For me, it's not a question of going or not going to school, but how it can be combined with my family and work schedules. I let myself get silly with some of the possibilities, like hiring a French chef to do the cooking. It made me see that we could go out to eat; my older children or husband can cook or easily bring dinners home. Even skipping a meal or having breakfast food for dinner occasionally won't hurt any of us. I feel like a kid with a wonderful new toy.'

*'You really went to town with the Emperor's multidimensional potential,' I told Ellen. 'I'm glad it helped lighten things up. Although the Emperor is linked to linear perception, working with the cube activates your whole brain, both the analytical and creative sides, for true clarity.'*

❖ Edyth, a secretary at the local university, told the class the following story about how the Emperor is affecting her work situation: 'The woman who has been running my office is retiring and the place is undergoing a major reorganisation because of this. We waited until she retired to modernise. And, in anticipation, last year my boss sent me to computer school. Now I've been called upon to use everything I learned and more.

'I'm the person who's in charge of creating the new systems. *Me*, one of the most disorganised people I know! The homework question, "What have you been called upon to organise?" would have made me laugh if my head didn't ache so much. I feel as if I am "Emperorising" the office. And it takes a great deal of mental work and discipline to stick with it. I've been meditating on the Emperor every morning before going to work, asking to see the office through his eyes and for the inspiration to bring order to the disorder, both in my mind and at work. I feel myself drawing on his energy and it's definitely helping me develop the more thinking and reasoning parts of myself, something I should have learned as a child, but somehow, probably because I'm a female who was raised without a father and with a mother who was very emotional, didn't.

'Do you know that the other evening was the first time I can ever remember making a meal and not having to practically scrub down the entire kitchen afterward? This stuff's dangerous! I'm doing the job I've been dreading and feeling more and more confident about it and myself as things are progressing. I think I'm finally growing up in this side of my personality. I think I'm being jet-propelled from Childhood into Adulthood, thanks to the Emperor.'

*'Your morning meditations are certainly paying off,' I told her. 'Be careful you don't overdo it. Getting a headache is a possible sign of "too much Emperor" because of his astrological rulership of the head and frontal lobes of the brain. It may also just be a sign that you're stretching less used or new parts of yourself.'*

## Suggestions for Application and Integration of the Emperor

This is an opportunity for you to be the Emperor. These exercises are designed to 'set your world in order' and open your eyes to 'see' what is going on within your mind and in your environment with greater clarity, as well as improve organisational abilities, rational thinking processes, boundary setting, inspire self-discipline, assertiveness, multidimensional thinking and creative problem-solving skills.

1   Draw or colour your own version of the Emperor with yourself as the figure.

2   Set the Emperor in a visible place as a reminder to your conscious and subconscious minds to apply and integrate his teachings.

3   Dream on the Emperor.

4 Play the note middle C on a musical instrument. Intone IAO or hum along with the music. Now focus on the card for a few minutes. While meditating, ask that the Emperor's teachings guide you through a particular situation. Or if you are faced with a worrisome situation, event or problem, such as resisting your need to become more organised; wanting to be more rational and less emotional; or needing to take a 'tough love' approach to a relationship, yet fearing a loss of love from that person; imagine how the Emperor would tackle it. If it seems feasible, do it. Jot down the times when you became aware of the Emperor in your interactions. I was aware of the Emperor when? Before/during/after . . .

5 Go out into the world and pretend you are the Emperor. I've behaved like the Emperor as I've been writing this book to help me break down the work into small manageable tasks rather than feeling overwhelmed by the enormity of my project. I was the Emperor and this is what took place . . .

6 Use the cube mentioned in this chapter to problem-solve, brainstorm and become aware of your options.

7 The Rerun. After having an experience and realising in retrospect how the Emperor's teachings might have made things different – brought clarity of thought, improved your ability to see things more realistically, helped you be a more effective leader, assisted you in being less dominant or more reasonable, etc., mentally relive the situation, *including* your insight. This will help the behaviour become more automatic next time. If possible, actually rerun the situation in real life with the new attitude or behaviour.

8 Ask yourself the following questions:

'In what area of my personal or professional life could my vision benefit from expansion?' 'What would I like to see more clearly?' 'What do I want to avoid seeing?' 'What plan or project needs to be thought out more thoroughly?' 'Am I being as reasonable as necessary?' 'Who has been unreasonable towards me, and how do I feel about this?' 'What vision am I sharing with others?' 'Whom have I authorised to act on my behalf and why?' 'Why or how have I abdicated my power?' 'What area of my life could use more or less discipline?' 'What have I been called upon to head or organise?' 'How might I hold my ground or boundaries more successfully?' 'In what ways might being less controlling and more flexible be of benefit to both myself or others?' 'What rules and regulations am I learning to trust and follow?' 'What area of my life needs ordering or reordering?'

'What Gateway of Life am I in or growing through in the above?' Indicate: Childhood, Adolescence, Adulthood or Wisdom. Why?

'What do I need to do in order to develop the above further?' I need to . . .

'What step(s) do I want to take towards this goal and how can the Emperor help me?'

9    Use a personal statement regarding the presence of the Emperor in your life at this time, such as: 'I'm willing to see the truth behind what I want to see.' 'My ability to lead, initiate and organise is valuable to myself and others.' 'My head is in balance with my heart.' 'My visions are becoming realities.' My personal statement is . . .

10 Inspirational words and quotes:

'Freedom is the choice of one's disciplines.'

'The Weaponless Warrior.'

'Father of All.'

'Call no man your father upon the earth: for the One is your Father, which is in heaven.'                        MATTHEW 23:9

11 What symbols stand out in the card? What do they say to you? How might they be useful in daily living? Bring the symbols into your life in some way so as to integrate the card's teachings. I identify the Emperor with the Weaponless Warrior. This identification tells me that I can meet life armed with reason, goodwill, self-discipline and breadth of vision.

12 Wear or surround yourself with the colour red to remind yourself of the Emperor's teachings when needed, such as desiring to see as completely and clearly as possible, or wanting to bring more order and self-discipline into your life and surroundings. Notice how you are affected.

13 The Emperor's astrological correspondence is Aries, governing traits such as self-assertion, leadership, motivation, analysis and the sense of sight. Survey your life and 'see' where the Emperor might help motivate you so that you might assert yourself or lead others more effectively. Notice what happens: your thoughts and feelings and the outcome.

14 Remember that the Emperor's Hebrew name, *Heh*, means 'window'. How can this remind you of the card's meaning or help in your life process? Knowing that I can see through both my outer and inner eyes (windows) often encourages me to look for the truth behind what I see with my outer eyes to avoid unnecessary suffering.

15 Try a few drops of the scent pine associated with the Emperor as a reminder to integrate the card's teachings.

16 Have a cup of tea made with or cook using the herb ginger. Sit quietly as you drink or eat and consider the herb's properties to increase circulation, calm the stomach and intestines, reduce swelling and inflammation when applied externally and consider the like qualities of the Emperor.

5 | HIEROPHANT | ‎ו

# CHAPTER 9

# The Hierophant

## General Information and Symbolism

The word Hierophant is derived from Greek word *hierophantes*, meaning 'one who shows or brings to light'. The Hierophant, regarded as the revealer of Sacred Things Within by Qabalists, is both a term and a position that originated in the ancient Greek and Essene Mystery Schools. Dressed in the garments of the autocratic medieval church and commonly thought of as the Spiritual Father or Pope (note that he wears the customary 'Shoes of the Fisherman'[1]), a Hierophant may be of either sex. In traditional or *exoteric* religion, the High Priest acts as the intermediary between those seeking guidance and the Divine. This arrangement works well for those lacking the belief or know-how to accomplish this directly, and also functions for those who are not ready to take personal responsibility for their fate. However, there are many seekers who have contacted their internal Source by creating a personal synthesis from the various religious and philosophical systems, practices, doctrines and rituals so readily accessible in today's world. It is essential to bear in mind that *both* ways fill important roles and serve important functions. Traditional practices not only give followers models from which to understand their personal evolution and place in the scheme of things but, in time, may become stepping-stones to the inner more non-traditional ways of getting in touch with divinity.

The Hierophant represents the Spiritual Parent. It is interesting to note that in many of the Eastern spiritual traditions, the Wiseones are often referred to as 'Baba' or 'Ma', father and mother

---

1 When Christ conferred the name Peter, meaning 'rock' in Aramaic, upon Simon the fisherman, He said: 'Thou art Peter, and upon this rock, I will build my church.' Because Simon Peter was a fisherman and is regarded as having been the first bishop or pope of Rome, his successors are said to wear 'the shoes of the fisherman'.

respectively. The state of wisdom and dispassion are symbolised by the Hierophant's traditionally grey stone throne, background and four black and white circles at his feet. Grey is the colour of wisdom while black and white suggest balance as together they make grey. These circles also suggest the recognition of God/dess in all levels of life – animate and inanimate. The Hierophant wears a crown and bears a four-levelled sceptre in his left hand, illustrating his automatic attunement with the four aspects of creation, or Four Qabalistic Worlds. The Hierophant is associated with hearing in both the ordinary physical sense and the superphysical sense of clairaudience, or 'clear hearing'. In the genuine state of clairaudience, you hear what is outside the normal range of human hearing; the voice, or knowledge, of your inner teacher or Higher Self. This is alluded to by the Hierophant's earflaps which cover and uncover his ears. This suggests that in order to tune into truth or your Inner Self, you must be able both to block out the distractions from the outer world, *and* listen to the wisdom of others. A pair of crossed keys (customarily gilt with the silver of subconsciousness and the gold of superconsciousness) adorn the ledge of the Hierophant's throne, demonstrating that the keys to revelation lie in the ability to discern between our unrefined instincts and intuitions, the sub- and superconscious minds respectively, plus have them work together.

The Hierophant and two monks wear yokes around their shoulders. A yoke is intended to conjoin and train creatures to work together. The Hierophant's yoke illustrates his conscious and serviceful union with God/dess; those of the monks show the forces of desire, symbolised by the roses, and knowledge of the One Reality, depicted by lilies, within the human personality working in concert.

The Hierophant stands for the power of intuition. Intuition is the power of attaining direct knowledge or cognition without rational thought and interference. The word 'in' relates to things of an internal nature, while 'tuition' means the act of teaching. Hence, intuition may be explained as the act of inner teaching. From this explanation, we can better understand this facet of the Hierophant or Inner Teacher.

To tap into intuition is another thing. First, there must be a willingness to put aside preconceived ideas and desires in order that higher truth may have a place to enter. This openness is depicted in the card by the monk's physical gestures. Both kneel before the Higher Self indicating surrender and supplication. The monk wearing the lilies of purity sends out a prayer for help, while the monk wearing the roses of desire shows the openness necessary to receive such. The monks also have Franciscan haircuts, a reminder that the followers of St Francis were nonconformists in the eyes of the traditional Church. Appearing in this card, they suggest the unorthodoxy of seeking truth through your Self.

Next, sincerity is vital. After laying aside what you think you know and want, a sincere request that the truth be revealed – no matter what it is – *must* be expressed. When the truth does reveal itself, it feels so completely right and natural, you immediately recognise your answer. In fact, it is sometimes so clear and simple, you may almost doubt its validity. Be mindful that answers may not come in the form of an actual 'Inner Voice', but may take the form of a deep feeling of certainty, or be the reiteration of a fundamental law or principle of life such as, 'You must work with nature, not against her.' Please know that your answers may not present themselves while you are sitting and waiting for them, but in God/dess's own time. The key is to keep asking with a heart and mind open for revelation, while remembering to remain alert for answers. The Hierophant's hand gesture, 'Be still and listen', emphasise this point. His gesture is also one of blessing, reminding us that it is usually a blessing to be still and to listen before acting.

Finally, to paraphrase Paul Foster Case, answers usually indicate what area requires attention or development in order to attain and learn what it is you truly desire. For example, you might be moving too fast, thus you might hear or suddenly become aware it is important to 'Slow down and look around you.'

In a time when 'channelling' has become popular, we had best be cognisant that listening to just *any* voice may be dangerous. In other words, as you develop spiritually you become increasingly open, open not only to the higher spiritual plane, but to the lower astral plane, too. Because the astral plane is populated by disincarnate entities, many of whom are little more evolved than we are, we *must* use discernment regarding the information we receive. We are wise to keep in mind that the true Inner Teacher or Hierophant will never predict the future, issue judgements, flatter, or promise how successful you will be if you adhere to his or her advice. Above all, genuine revelations *always* communicate what is best for your spiritual growth.

Both the Hierophant's right hand and his shoes bear the sign of the cross. These symbolise his commitment and ability to bring the

*Living the Tarot*

teachings of heaven down to earth, and raise the consciousness of those on earth up to heaven. The fingers of this hand point above and below reiterating this.

The Hierophant's musical note is C#, the colour is red-orange and the herb is sage. The Hierophant's Hebrew name, *Vav*, is used both as the conjunction 'and' and as the nouns, 'hook, nail, or link'. The revealer of Sacred Things Within functions to connect you to the teachings of truth as well as to your own divinity. With this in mind, you might contemplate the dictionary definition of religion: 'A bond or link between man and God'. As stated previously, exoteric religion teaches that this cannot occur without an intermediary, whereas esoteric teachings hold that although helpers, teachers or gurus are important at certain times in your development, they are ultimately unnecessary. In other words, you may contact the Source of life, the God/dess within, directly. Whichever path is selected is best determined by your personal needs and degree of evolution.

Five is the number of the Hierophant and humanity. Number 5 is regarded as the number of mediation, because it falls in the middle of the sequence of the single-digit numbers one to nine. This intimates that humans are the mediators, intermediaries, or links between the realms of God and nature.

The Hierophant is related to the astrological sign Taurus, signified by a pair of bull horns on the top of his throne. This fixed (stable, nonvolatile) Earth sign governs the ears, lower jaw, mouth, thyroid and larynx. The Taurean personality says: I own, have, endure, persevere and listen. Because the bull is a ruminant animal, the evolved Taurean is capable of states of deep meditation and contemplation. Natives are usually practical and stand firm in their beliefs and convictions. They must aim not to be bound too tightly to possessions, people and ideas. Since the card is associated with the larynx or 'voice-box' in addition to inner teaching and the sense of hearing, the Hierophant is known as the 'Fool's Voice'. Hence the tendency towards over-possessiveness may be overcome by listening carefully to the voice of your conscience.

The moon, symbol of instinct, intuition and memory, is exalted in Taurus. Therefore, the lunar crescent worn at the Hierophant's throat suggests that 'The Voice' reveals not only what is hidden in our past and instinctive side, but provides intuitive guidance for our future as well.

The ancient Hebrew, Christian, Hindu and Buddhist teachings state that we not only have the ability to contact divinity within, but are capable of becoming that saint, Buddha, Christ, or God/dess. This is another reference to the ancient Sanskrit mantra mentioned in the chapter on the Magician: So'HAM – I AM THAT I AM. This is further affirmed by the Bible's statement that humans are created in the Most High's image. Bearing in mind that we take after both our natural and divine parents, we can see the necessity of loving and respecting ourselves, since God/dess lives within us. In his priestly aspect, the Hierophant may stand for your personal initiation into this type of belief system.

In the Qabalah, the Hierophant is known as the Triumphant or Eternal Intelligence. This Intelligence teaches that you may triumph in life by tuning into and heeding proven internal and external sources of inspiration – that which attunes you to the eternal or universal truths. Call upon this ever-available Intelligence to bring the light of greater awareness into the darkness of ignorance and confusion. The Hierophant is a lesson in Self-empowerment.

## Gateway of Life: Childhood

The Hierophant brings forth the Fool-child's awareness of conscience, the small quiet voice of truth within you which offers wise counsel. At this immature stage, however, you usually do not listen to what you hear. It may also be programmed by others' needs and desires. In any event, the voice is again sought in later stages of development when its value is known and appreciated. Here, too, you tend to give your parents, mates or other significant persons God/dess-like status, something which usually takes several life stages to outgrow.

Living through the Hierophant in the Four Gateways of Life may give way to certain behaviour and attitudes. CHILDHOOD: You dislike eating meat, yet continue doing so unquestioningly because your family doctor tells you that you must have animal protein to remain healthy; ADOLESCENCE: Knowing that it's wrong to steal, you do so anyhow, for the thrill of getting a new sweater free; ADULTHOOD: A successful businessman finds he has material security, but lacks inner security and begins investigating various spiritual practices to balance himself; WISDOM: Encountering difficulties with your mate, you automatically bypass your first instinct of fleeing the relationship to instead learn the truth about what is occurring and how to handle it through a deep and fearless intuitional quest.

## Divinatory Questions for the Hierophant

*Upright:* Are you exploring the differences between religion and spirituality? Could you be ready to break with a worn-out tradition or custom? How has a long established tradition served to support you? Are you becoming increasingly practical? In what ways might you empower your Self in a challenging situation? Are you exploring a new religion, tradition, ritual, spiritual teacher or belief system? Have you been learning how to listen more carefully? Would it be wise to discern if the information you are receiving originates from your unrefined instincts or intuition? Are you seeking to understand how you gave up your power and became co-dependent? Are you being motivated by a particular religious, social or political cause? Are good listening habits paying off? Are you becoming more attuned to your own inner wisdom? Is it possible that you've been questioning the musts, shoulds and ought to's in your life? How have you contacted your own inner teacher? Might you be saying, 'No', to another, but, 'Yes', to your Self? In what situation could it be beneficial to stop, look and listen before proceeding?

*Reversed:* What religious, political or traditional belief might be oppressing you? Whom or what have you deified? Might you be identified with a group or another individual's goal to the exclusion of your own needs and desires? What is preventing you from seeking out your inner teacher? Are you subscribing to a certain behaviour you no longer believe in for the sake of others? What might you be unduly possessive about? Is it possible that remaining quiet is currently working against you? Are you paying too much attention to what others are telling you? Have you given someone too much authority or power? Could you benefit from being more practical? Would you be better off listening more carefully before acting? Is it inappropriate to respect a certain authority figure at this time? Has a certain religious or political figure proved unworthy of your support and trust?

## Personal Experience

Owing to the evolution of consciousness, modern technology and worldwide communications which aid in disseminating formerly inaccessible teachings, an increasing number of people are now eliminating a middle person between the Divine and themselves. These individuals hold the common belief that all knowledge and wisdom lie within us and that the true role of spiritual teachings and teachers is to put us in touch with this Source.

The first time I experienced this personally was after studying the Hierophant card and wishing intensely to meet such a being in the flesh. I marked the start of my extended search by attending many lectures and workshops, reading numerous spiritual books and staying alert to all the new teachers passing through the area. In the midst of this, at my best friend's suggestion, I gladly agreed to attend a Yoga retreat with a well-known and respected Indian meditation master. Not only did the retreat grant my wish to see the personification of the Hierophant, but I got to encounter my own inner Hierophant as well.

The teacher was exceptionally inspired and the weekend-long retreat seemed to fly by. It was delightful to be in his presence, as he was to me the embodiment of the Hierophant and of spirituality. Then on the last morning of the weekend, he lectured heatedly on the topic of celibacy, insisting that his followers observe it as a means of focusing completely on their inner selves. Most group members nodded and murmured affirmatively as he spoke. I myself was almost convinced, except for the meditative experience I had following his powerful talk.

As I sat repeating the *mantra* the guru had given me, I found myself unable to totally clear my mind of his lecture. Then, as an accidental (it seemed) result of repeatedly asking myself, 'Is celibacy appropriate for my highest good at this time?' I tuned in to my own inner teacher. I realised by way of an overwhelming sense of rightness in my heart that celibacy is indeed a valuable tool. I could see its appropriateness in my life at some point in the future, yet was certain that now was not the proper time for me to practise it.

Excited by my revelation (the Hierophant is called the Revealer of Sacred Things Within), I shared it with some friends during lunch, but I was surprised and somewhat shaken by their response to me. This was a combination of irritation at my not wanting to follow the holy man to the letter, plus the subtle message that I was being egotistical by thinking I was beyond his teachings. It was unnerving to differ with the Master and my friends. Yet I didn't give in to the pressure. I followed my own inner teacher – my intuition – which proved to be the correct action for me.

Out of this situation came the understanding of the part that teachers play in my life. One: Teachers or gurus (translated from the Sanskrit, the word guru means 'dispeller of darkness') provide tools that help put me in touch with my own Higher Self. Two: Teachers are human beings who are just farther along than I in some vital areas. Most still have karmic knots (life work) to untie. Three: these individuals impart what has worked for them, which does not necessarily mean that it's going to work for me. Four: I must take their teachings and filter them through my own Self, as I inadvertently did at the Yoga retreat. As one perceptive student put it, 'You must separate the dogma from the catma.' Five: Genuine spiritual teachers teach that they are only a symbol of my own Higher Self, not that Self. The teacher is present primarily to remind me to turn inward to the Source inside me, or outward to what will do likewise. Six: Persons such as these live what they teach and see their students as equal to them. Seven: I've found that I should avoid any teacher who seeks to create unhealthily dependent or co-dependent, rather than independent or interdependent, relationships with students.

## Student Experiences

❖  'I have a good friend who keeps wanting to move out of the city,' said Shari, a student. 'Life is too much hustle and bustle for him, and every once in a while he dreams of going off for a few months to live in the quiet of the mountains. This week he came to me and asked if he could leave. He didn't say, "Should I leave?" but actually asked my permission. It was a strange experience for me.

'My first internal reaction was to say, "No, you can't do that. I'll miss you." Later on, as the Hierophant caught my eye – she looks out at me from my bookshelf – I became aware that he should do what his own inner voice told him to do. He should listen to his Self! I also decided that I don't want to be responsible for what he does. So I told him I couldn't tell him what to do, but that he must listen to his own heart about the situation and then reach his own decision. He was surprised by my answer, but understood what I was telling him. I felt completely relieved and happy after I had talked with him. It turned out to be a great lesson for me, in listening to my Self.'

*I explained to Shari and the class, 'The Hierophant is that certain knowledge within that alerts you to what is really going on. The Hierophant reminded you that rescuing your friend by telling him what to do was improper. The card is a lesson in self-empowerment, and you did just that. By passing up your initial response to his request and listening to your intuition, you not only empowered your friend to choose his own course of action and learn from his Self, you also reinforced your own powers. What a great learning experience for both of you.'*

❖ Plagued by severe allergies, Kate is under the care of an expensive allergist. 'Because of my allergy problems, I have to follow a very strict regimen of health care. I think I should be feeling better by now, but I'm still ill a lot of the time. The doctor charges much more than I can honestly afford right now. I'll admit that I really put him in charge of me, and I'm afraid of pursuing other alternatives. That question in the homework about putting others in charge of my life really made me stop and think.

'So the other morning, when I awoke feeling miserable, I did something different, something very non-traditional, very Hierophant-like and self-empowering. I kept thinking about an old and practical remedy of aspirin, Vitamin C and calcium, but at first kept pushing it out of my mind because of the doctor's instructions. Then I said to myself, "There must be some reason why it keeps coming back into my thoughts. Let me check it out." So I meditated and tuned in to my inner Hierophant and felt a strong sense that that remedy was okay, despite the fact that my doctor would deem it a "no-no". So I took it and felt better remarkably fast (this sounds just like a television commercial).'

*The Hierophant often refers to breaking with external authority figures. And as Kate found, doing so clears the channel through which you can tune into and respect your own inner authority. It also seems that Kate's experience is telling her to acknowledge her ability to be practical, a trait linked to the sign of Taurus and the Hierophant.*

❖ 'While recovering from cancer several years ago, I learned how to find my invisible inner healer,' began Joan. 'I found her observations and suggestions to be invaluable during my convalescence, but when I was well, I put her aside. Lately, I've been dealing with a residual disability from the operation, but I honestly didn't think of turning to my healer again until we began working with the Hierophant. Last week – right after class, as a matter of fact – I focused inward and she pointed me in the right direction. It was amazing, genuinely amazing. I surrendered to her just like the monks in the card. I guess I did my homework and put the symbols to use. I got a lot out of the encounter. But I believe the most important information is that it's time I got a prescription from my doctor for some physical therapy to improve my mobility and alleviate the pain I have in my shoulder. Hooray for my inner healer and the Hierophant who showed me my way back to her!'

*Joan had definitely put the symbols to work for herself. She used the Hierophant's staff, a symbol of the power to employ the Magician's tools – inspiration, imagination, discrimination and manifestation – to help take charge of her pain. The card inspired Joan to recall her own inner healer. Her imagination then brought the healer into being. After that, Joan's discrimination enabled her to select the appropriate means from those suggested, and finally she was moved to manifest change by arranging for some physical therapy.*

❖ 'I'm a Taurus, and like the aspects of that sign, I love things,' shared Nora. 'So here I am, a buyer for a small speciality store. This past week, the manufacturers came to town and I had to use the voice of the Fool, my conscience, to deal with them.

'There they were, all these salespeople trying to sell me goods I knew weren't right for my store. The products were very appealing; I loved most of them, but so many weren't for my customers. I felt like a child being tempted by goodies I couldn't have.

'I got taken out for great lunches (you know how Taureans love good food) and was offered excellent purchasing terms. But I was able to say, "No", even though I'd had a few glasses of wine, because I remembered to listen to my inner voice. I just kept checking in with my Hierophant and was able to stay fairly well centred throughout the showings, meetings and lunches. I thought about the homework questions, "Where is your conscience guiding you?" and, "What pressures are making you feel oppressed?" In the past, I would have been pressured into buying at least a few useless things and then taking a loss on them later, just to take the pressure off myself. But this time I didn't buy a single thing I didn't think the store could sell. I feel as if I behaved in an adult rather than a childlike fashion, and I'm proud of what I accomplished.'

*Like a well-developed Taurean, Nora was able to stay in possession of her Self, rather than accumulate a lot of unnecessary merchandise. The Hierophant is sometimes called the 'link' because its astrological sign, Taurus, rules the neck, the link between the head and body. It sounds as if listening to her conscience, the Hierophant, helped Nora link the two kneeling monks – her resolve (head) and desires (body) – together to help her move forward into the Gateway of Adulthood.*

**Suggestions for Application and Integration of the Hierophant**

The Hierophant may teach you how to 'be still and listen'. The following is designed to offer ways of getting more attuned to your inner teacher or intuition, ways of becoming a good listener and a better authority on what is best for you, plus how to reclaim power that has been lost in unhealthy co-dependency.

1   Draw or colour your own version of the Hierophant with yourself as the figure.

2   Set the Hierophant in a visible place as a reminder to your conscious and subconscious minds to use and recall his or her teachings to tune in and listen; to be the final authority on what is correct for you and not be intimidated by either religious or 'New Age' dogma.

3   Dream on the Hierophant.

4   Play the note $C^\#$. Intone IAO or hum along with the music, then focus on the card and contemplate spending a few minutes a day listening carefully to what is going on around you, be it another person talking, the sounds within your environment, nature, or your own conscience. Activating this particular aspect of the Hierophant can prove to be an excellent tool for daily life. Or meditate on a question or problem in the way described earlier in this chapter. While meditating or contemplating, ask that the Hierophant's teachings guide you through a particular situation. Or if you're faced with a worrisome situation, event or problem, such as gathering with your family, whose religious or political beliefs are no longer viable for you; desiring to empower yourself, but lacking the know-how; or saying, 'No', to another and, 'Yes', to your Self; imagine how the Hierophant would tackle it. If it seems workable, do it. Jot down the times when you became aware of the Hierophant in your interactions. I was aware of the Hierophant when? Before/during/after . . .

5   Go out into the world and pretend you are the Hierophant. I behaved like the Hierophant as I sat in my dentist's chair, prepped for surgery and 'knowing' that I needed to be put to sleep for the procedure instead of going ahead and 'gutting it out' in a waking state. I was able to be still and listen to the voice of truth within me, although it somewhat inconvenienced the

dentist (since I left and went to an oral surgeon). I did what was in my best interest, and he was also glad in the long run. I was the Hierophant and this is what took place . . .

6 The Rerun. After having an experience and realising in retrospect how the Hierophant's teachings might have made things different – facilitated unification, truth, made you a better listener, or encouraged you to ask for help and surrender to a higher good, etc. – mentally relive the situation, *including* your insight. This will help the behaviour become more automatic next time. If possible, actually rerun the situation in real life with your new attitude or behaviour.

7 Ask yourself the following questions:

'How might I be a better teacher?' 'What internal issues are calling to be listened to?' 'Where is my conscience guiding me?' 'Whom might I turn to for information and assistance?' 'What is the difference between instinctive and intuitive guidance?' 'What group, belief system or organisation am I placing before my own well-being?' 'What person, group or ideal am I united with in a common cause?' 'What am I discovering by centring myself within?' 'Where might it be valuable to become a better listener?' 'Whom would I like to listen to me?' 'What intuitive guidance do I wish to receive?' 'Why am I avoiding becoming centred and/or listening?' 'What truth am I avoiding surrendering to?' 'What outside influence(s) must I shut out in order to tune in to my Self?' 'What dogma may be running my life?'

'What Gateway of Life am I in or growing through in the above?' Indicate: Childhood, Adolescence, Adulthood or Wisdom. Why?

'What do I need to do in order to develop the above further?' I need to . . .

'What step(s) do I want to take towards this goal and how can the Hierophant help me?'

8 Use a personal statement regarding the presence of the Hierophant in your life at this time, such as: 'I am inspired by learning from the teachers in my life.' 'I'm in charge of my thoughts and actions.' 'I'm connected to my inner teacher.' 'Because I listen to others, others listen to me.' My personal statement is . . .

9   Inspirational words and quotes:

'Let your conscience be your guide.'       Jiminy Cricket

'To thine own self be true.'       Shakespeare, *Hamlet*

'Kneel to your own Self. Honour and worship your own Being. Meditate on your own Self. God dwells within you as you.'
       Swami Muktananda Paramahamsa

'Intuition is soul guidance, appearing naturally in man during those instants when his mind is calm . . . truth cannot be created, but only perceived.'       Paramahansa Yogananda[2]

10  What symbols stand out in the card? What do they say to you? How might they be useful in daily living? Bring the symbol(s) into your life in some way so as to integrate the card's teachings. The Hierophant's hand gesture reminds me to slow down, look and listen to both myself and other sources of inspiration before doing things I might later regret.

11  Wear and surround yourself with the Hierophant's colour, red-orange, to remind yourself of the card's teachings when needed, such as productively uniting yourself with others, being more tuned in or cultivating the habit of being still. Notice how you are affected.

12  The Hierophant's astrological correspondence is Taurus, governing traits such as practicality, prosperity, possessiveness, endurance and intuition. Get in touch with your inner Hierophant to learn where your intuition can inspire you in these or other areas. Note what happens: your thoughts and feelings and the outcome.

13  Remember that the Hierophant's Hebrew name, *Vav*, means 'hook', 'nail' or some type of linkage. How can this remind you of the card's meaning or help in your life process? I'm united with others on this earth who want world peace and believe in the importance of non-violent resolution of conflicts.

14  Try a few drops of the scent vanilla associated with the Hierophant as a reminder to integrate the card's teachings.

2  Paramahansa Yogananda, *Autobiography of a Yogi*, Self-Realisation Fellowship, Los Angeles, 1946, 1981, p. 177.

15 The etymology of the word sage is 'to save'. Have a cup of sage
   tea or cook with or burn the herb sage. Sit quietly as you drink,
   eat or inhale the fragrance and consider the herb's properties as
   an aromatic, tonic and as a balm for irritated tissues, and consider
   the similar qualities of the Hierophant. Try burning sage or
   sagebrush as an incense. It has been used for many generations in
   native American ceremonies as a purifier.

6 THE LOVERS

# CHAPTER 10

# The Lovers

## General Information and Symbolism

The Archangel Raphael, Angel of Laying-on-of-Hands, of the eastern quadrant of heaven and the element of Air, presides over the Lovers card. The name Raphael means both 'Healer of God' and 'God is our healer', suggested by the Angel's hands raised in benediction, as the radiant sun, symbolic of *Kether*, the Crown or Source on the Tree of Life, beams down blessings from above and through him. Because love is about devotion, Raphael's presence states that your Higher Self is completely devoted to healing you (making you whole) and loving you unconditionally. Two Lovers and an angel are depicted, but what you may also see is your whole Self.

The naked Lovers are Adam and Eve in Paradise. Adam, symbol of self-consciousness, looks to Eve, symbol of subconsciousness, intimating that looking to the subconscious for your responses, before it is completely aligned with superconsciousness, brings difficulty. We must remember, however, that difficulties bring wisdom, understanding and maturity in their wake. Adam's attention to Eve instead of the Angel also illustrates how, in order to reach higher consciousness, the Angel, you must deal with your subconscious or dark side. For example, you cannot transcend the fact that you were sexually abused as a child until you consciously face it again as an adult (this is why psychotherapy is often regarded as going through 'the dark night of the soul'). Eve's attention to the Angel depicts the concept that when your subconscious is able to turn to your superconscious or Higher Self for its responses, the obsolete habit patterns that prevent you from having a better life change, ushering in great self-transformation and liberation. Remember, your subconscious is the ever-receptive passageway to the Higher Self that in time will consistently reflect what is above, rather than what is below. The nude man and woman further signify that true love empowers you to have the courage to stand naked with your thoughts and feelings respectively, to be yourself without shame. In reality, the dynamics between the Angel, Adam and Eve depict how habit patterns are established, reinforced and change.

Because most versions of the Lovers card make reference to 'The Fall', the Bible story of Adam and Eve in the Garden of Eden, it is essential to contemplate its symbolism. God warned Adam and Eve that eating from the Tree of Knowledge of Good and Evil, the apple tree behind Eve, would bring them death. But the wise old serpent, coiled around this same tree, claimed, 'Ye shall not surely die: For God doth know that in the day ye eat thereof, then your eyes shall be opened, and ye shall be as gods, knowing good and evil.' Being innocent, desirous, curious, and perhaps bored, they ate and became aware.

Eating the apple was a death, as God forewarned – the death of their lack of awareness, yet only a symbolic death, as the serpent promised. In the end, it proved the catalyst for Eve and Adam's transformation to a conscious state of mind. The apple was actually the key to the door of Paradise that brought about the 'The Rise' of humanity rather than 'The Fall'. This act acquainted us with the process of attaining God/dess or wholeness by way of intelligent self-gratification. Adam and Eve had to eat the fruit (experience their desires and feelings); otherwise they would have been obsessed with their craving until they yielded. These first people needed to experience their desire in order to find out who they were and what they truly wanted. Travelling the spiritual path is much like eating the apple; once you taste it, you cannot go back. Raphael hovers over the clouds, symbolising how confusion and lack of clarity ultimately lead to order, clarity and expanded awareness.

It is often impossible to take another's word in place of your own experience. Banishment from Paradise brought Adam and Eve pain, but that same pain guided them to know truth and develop into mature adults. This leads me to believe that the 'curse' of childbearing bestowed upon Eve was symbolic of the pain and joy that occurs when giving birth to one's own Self. Consequently, what is pictured in the Lovers is an image of and formula for finding and embracing our whole Self.

The mountain in the background indicates the recognition of your potential to reach the highest – to be the best and most you can be. The tree with twelve flame-like leaves behind Adam (self-consciousness) represents the twelve essential types of human consciousness, as Adam is a symbol for all human personalities. Since studying Tarot and the Qabalah, I've come to regard trees as symbols of the human body. Thus, the serpent coiled around the Tree of Knowledge in this card may symbolise the arousal of personal and spiritual knowledge – the ability to tell right from wrong or make distinctions – that occurred in Eden and occurs when you learn from your experiences. The serpent was responsible for this, although not acknowledged for it by exoteric religion. In numerous esoteric circles, the word 'serpent' is synonymous with the Redeemer or Messiah. This symbol reiterates that what occurred in the Garden of Eden was the awakening and the rise of consciousness. Adam and Eve were oblivious to the fact that they lived in Paradise. It was through their expulsion that they became cognisant of what they had left behind and became motivated to seek their *conscious* return to it.

The Lovers is associated with the musical note D, the colour orange, and the herb parsley. The Hebrew name for the Lovers card is *Zain*, meaning 'sword'. The sword has long been used in mythology to symbolise both knowledge and power (Excalibur) as well as the agony and ecstasy of romantic love (Sir Lancelot). A sword has two edges, illustrating life's many possibilities, sides and consequences. By figuring out how and when to use the Sword, you gain the knowledge of the kind of life you wish to cut out for yourself. Unless you use the Sword from the Magician's table to choose (in some Tarots the Lovers are aptly named the Choice) which seeds to plant when and where, the garden of your life will never grow to fruition, but will remain forever in the realms of thought and imagination (the Wand and Cup, respectively). The Sword is the tool responsible for the transformation of ideas and imaginings into plans, actions and, subsequently, finished products.

I was once given a beautiful Balinese batik for a birthday present, but could not decide what to make with it. Impulsively, I hung it on the wall near my bedroom window, and the sun shone in on it and faded it. I kept it on the wall for a long time afterwards to remind me of the importance of making more thoughtful decisions. Discrimination or discernment is the power to make fine distinctions between things in order to reach viable decisions. When you are unable to pick up this essential tool, decisions seem to get made for you that are often less desirable than those you might have chosen for yourself.

By picking up the Sword of Discrimination, you define your

needs, set limits, choose what you want to keep and nurture, and eliminate whatever is not viable. If you feel uncomfortable with the concept of the Sword, you might consider its cousins, the pocket knife, scalpel and scissors as alternatives. The Sword enables you to move forward, instead of being trapped in fearful indecision. Despite this, the Western world tends to regard it as an instrument of destruction and conquest. On the other hand, in Eastern religions, the deities of transformation wield the Sword to serve truth. Proper use of this essential and powerful tool helps you to take greater charge of yourself and your environment, a definite step on the road back to Eden.

The Lovers is associated with the mutable (It combines the qualities of cardinal energies with fixed energies – adaptable and changeable energy that can either move or remain still.) Air sign Gemini. Coincidentally, in East Indian astrology, the sign of Gemini is called *Maithuna*, meaning Lovers. Gemini governs the arms, hands, shoulders, lungs, bronchi and nerves. The Gemini personality says: I invent, adapt, change, think, communicate, am restless, quick-witted and curious. Generally, natives are highly articulate and socially oriented individuals who possess adaptive yet sometimes restless minds, tend to adjust well to their immediate surroundings, possess artistic and literary abilities, and are attracted to most types of communication – writing, theatre, public speaking. Being both mentally oriented and changeable, they often experience boredom and may lack the stability, interest and will to follow through on what they initiate. As a dual sign, the Twins (the Lovers) are capable of perceiving both (or all) sides of an issue, indicating their potential to be extraordinary mediators and decision-makers. The immature Gemini, however, may lack grounding and tends to get blown about by the winds of change. This causes not only problems in making decisions, but a nonstop flood of mental activity as well. Or, as a Gemini student humorously shared about himself, 'I sometimes get diarrhoea of the mind.'

The Lovers card is numbered 6, the number of the sixth *Sephirah* on the Tree of Life, seat of the human heart called *Tiphareth*, Beauty, Love and Harmony. Genuine love creates a beautiful and harmonious state between and within lovers. Therefore, the number six stands for twin action, reciprocation, union, the act of mutual exchange or interchange. This suggests what the Lovers card depicts, that the interrelationship between your Selves is reciprocal and indivisible. Your subconscious reflects to your self-conscious what it pays attention to, while self-conscious attention dictates what we absorb. Although we may divide human awareness into three parts, Adam (self-consciousness), Eve (subconsciousness) and the Angel (superconsciousness), every interaction is actually the One consciousness (superconsciousness) at work. It also addresses the fact that having a harmonious relationship with various parts of yourself elicits both love of self and others. The Angel's presence shows that all actions are rendered possible by interdependent interaction with the One, your superconscious Self.

Qabalists correspond the Lovers to the sense of smell, considered to be our most primitive sense. As human animals, we usually respond instantly to this acute sense. Studies show that we are either attracted or repelled by how others smell. It is not surprising to learn that one of the first signs of falling out of love is no longer being attracted to how a partner smells.

When I first began meditating, I burned a particular incense. Now just the slightest whiff of it, or even something similar, puts me into a meditative mood. Aromatherapy uses a wide variety of scents to alter stressful and traumatic impressions and experiences. It has been proven to lower blood pressure, slow heart rate and overcome fears and phobias, as well as induce higher states of consciousness. Psychological and scientific researchers agree that scents and naturally secreted pheromones[1] have the ability to bring about the whole range of emotional reactions. This substantiates what we have learned from the High Priestess, that our innate associations bear a wide range of experiences. So when making decisions, it is best to sniff out the truth with care.

The Lovers portrays the many paths of love through the triad of Angel, man and woman. Beyond the traditional identification of Adam with masculinity and Eve with femininity, he is the *animus* or inner man within each woman, and she is the *anima* or inner woman within each man. It is of interest to note that in Eastern religions, this psychic duality is paralleled by cosmic duality, as gods and goddesses are often depicted as *Ardhanarisvara*, half-male and half-female.

Ordinarily, you fall in love with someone who embodies your ideals. Jungians say this is projecting your own inner man or woman

---

1 A pheromone is a chemical substance produced by an animal and serves especially as a stimulus to other individuals of the same species for one or more behavioural responses.

on to another. In this type of union, disillusionment often occurs when you find the objects of your affections to be who they are, themselves, not who you want them to be, yourself. Others find fulfilment in loving someone of the same sex, their mirror image, and a handful fall in love with themselves first and then go on to love others from a place of wholeness and self-satisfaction. Finally, this same dynamic interchange shows how excessively dependent or co-dependent relationships eventually lead to independence and interdependence. Whatever route is taken, in time, integrating the principles of the Lovers card brings interdependence, independence and true love to all.

In the Qabalah, the Lovers are known as the Disposing Intelligence. This Intelligence guides you in the process of sorting through ideas, feelings and information in order to arrive at the best decisions possible. You must often take some thing or situation apart in order to learn about, repair or reorder it more satisfactorily. This Intelligence enables you to get to the heart of an issue or situation by disposing of what is extraneous, so that you may take wise and loving action. Or, as a student wisely quipped, 'The Disposing Intelligence takes out the garbage.'

## Gateway of Life: Childhood

With the Lovers card within the Gateway of Childhood, you begin figuring out how to make distinctions. An important part of being, like the child, is that you often have to learn for yourself, as did your predecessors, Adam and Eve. Consequences are necessary, as mental, emotional and spiritual maturity evolve from them. Problems occur in all stages of development; it is just that our methods of problem-solving improve over time. Eventually, you comprehend that there are no mistakes, just life lessons to be learned. Because the Lovers are in the Gateway of Childhood, desire for personal gratification comes before all else. Yet from this extremely egocentric state, the basics of good judgment become apparent in time. In other words, you discern that whom or what you have a passion for may not always bring you happiness and satisfaction. Again, it is through trial and error that you learn to how to discern.

Finally, as the child nears the end of this Gateway and brinks on adolescence, she or he feels the stirrings of sexuality. Although children are not sexually mature, they still may feel sexual. This is especially true in today's world because of the tremendous amount of sexual stimulation being projected by the media.

Meeting with the Lovers card at the Four Gateways of Life may give way to certain attitudes and behaviour. CHILDHOOD: A doctor takes your sudden inability to sleep at face value, prescribing sleeping medication without asking you whether you are experiencing any undue worry and anxiety; ADOLESCENCE: You have a contraceptive available, but decide not to use it because it is 'inconvenient', and you get a sexually transmitted disease; ADULTHOOD: A woman becomes aware that her decision to become a dentist like her father stems from an unconscious effort to satisfy her demanding parent, not her own desire to be in the profession; WISDOM: Aware that you have a choice of whom to be intimate with, you automatically decline involvement with an unsuitable mate instead of conforming to your old co-dependent pattern of rejecting yourself in order to please another.

### Divinatory Questions for the Lovers

*Upright:* Is your life being energised and revitalised by a new love? Might you be finding out the value in loving your Self? Might a love relationship, despite its discomforts, be bringing you closer to knowing and being yourself? Where is honesty essential? Is your ability to stand naked with your feelings and thoughts bearing unexpected fruit? Have you gained new respect for or understanding of the opposite sex? Are you experiencing a sexual awakening? Are your confronting certain co-dependent tendencies? Are you learning the value of what you lost? How has a love relationship been serving to crush your immaturities? What 'forbidden fruit' might you desire to taste? Where might your mediation skills be called for? Have you recognised that the Garden of Eden is a state of mind? Are you sorting through some new information or old difficulties successfully? Have you become aware that problems bring forth clarity? What might be tempting your curiosity at this time? Is it time to distinguish between what you want and don't want from your relationship or career?

*Reversed:* What state or feeling might you be trying to recapture? What or whom might you now miss that you formerly took for granted? How might the sword help get you out of limbo? Is it inappropriate to hide your feelings from someone you love? What apple have you decided not to eat? Have you alienated another or yourself by lacking discrimination or being overly discriminating? Whom or what have you been obsessed with? Have you insisted that someone you love be who you want them to be, rather than who they are? Is it possible that you fear intimacy? Are you slowly becoming more independent or interdependent rather than dependent or co-dependent? Is a new experience causing you growing pains? Have you suffered disruption, separation or loss of trust and intimacy in an important relationship? Are you confused and immobilised by seeing too many sides to a situation?

## Personal Experience

For me, the Lovers card holds the special significance of learning, like Adam and Eve, how to make choices via the process of trial and error. Until a few years ago, I wasn't aware that I always make the best decisions possible, so when things didn't work out as planned, I'd adolescently lament, 'If only I would have done, if I could have done, I should have done . . . such and such would or would not have happened.' (I call this singing the 'If I Woulda, Coulda, Shoulda Blues'.)

But the Lovers card has shown me that my decisions reflect my level of maturity and that from the broader point of view, there are no mistakes, just opportunities to learn. I am slowly accepting and integrating the idea that pain, disappointment and dissatisfaction have the potential to teach me to make better choices next time around. The Archangel Raphael, Angel of Healing, presides over the card, letting me know that all is okay in the greater scheme of things.

My main forum for becoming a better decision-maker has been in the area of love relationships. Owing to the early childhood survival pattern of caretaking others, I was consistently attracted to partners who needed nurturing, but who didn't nurture me in return. From this I derived the short-term satisfaction of being 'Big Mama', powerful bestower of love and healing. But in the long run, these relationships gave way to much pain and frustration, as each man rejected me once he no longer needed what I had to give. I was continually being left in a depressed and depleted state until the Lovers card showed me, through its potent symbolism, that I was so involved in loving others (Adam the personality looks to Eve), I neglected to love my Self (Eve looks to the Angel).

By the time I met my present husband, my trials and errors with various partners had helped me to become more discriminating. I was outgrowing my need to be in control and suffer. I also discovered the shocking truth that two people love each other only when they are very capable of living without each other, but *choose* to live together. The Lovers card played a very significant role because it inspired me to do as Eve does, to look to my Higher Self in order to know when to turn outward and love others and when to give love to myself. It was difficult facing and undoing years of self-defeating habits, but I kept the image of the Lovers in mind almost constantly, as a reminder to love and heal myself. It also helped to remind myself that the work I was doing was preparing me for a real love relationship.

The Hebrew name for the Lovers card is *Zain*, 'sword', and in order to alter my patterns I needed to learn how to use it. Initially, it was exceedingly uncomfortable for me to pick up the Sword of Discrimination, because of my associations with its functions as an implement of war and pain. After considerable thought and meditation on my problem, I changed the symbol into scissors and became able to relate to it more easily. Then, when faced with making a choice about a possible new relationship, I'd ask myself how I could use my tool from the Magician's table to cut out from the fabric of my life what was best for me. It was difficult saying no to men who needed caretaking; they were so sweet and sad; I was lonely and mothering was so validating for me (short-term). But because I was so intent upon my desire of learning to love and befriend my Self, I was eventually freed from my fear of being abandoned, alone and loveless.

During this long and uncomfortable readjustment period, my scissors helped me formulate several guidelines for decision-making in relation to men. I don't give more than I can give freely, that is, without wanting love or certain treatment in return. When I desire something in return for my love, such as help with a task, I ask for it directly beforehand, instead of waiting anxiously for another to read my mind and grant my wishes. Rather than giving or overextending myself to someone solely because I desire love and attention, I do something loving for myself – take a delicious bath, meditate, read an inspirational book, go for a swim, listen to my favourite music, take a long walk in nature, or have a massage. Instead of abandoning myself, as I learned to do as a child, I support and comfort myself.

I am presently carrying over what I learned in the area of male-female love relationships into relations with children, parents, siblings and friends. I'm learning to be more open with my concerns and needs, to stand naked with them as the Lovers are naked in the card. I am now creating independent and interdependent situations rather than draining dependencies. I do my best when I remember to follow Eve's example and look to my Higher Self before acting, and when I'm honest in my communications. Even if I lose another's love or friendship in the process, I gain my own love and self-respect.

**Student Experiences**

❖    Elaina, an avid Tarot student and astrologer, returned to class to share this encounter with her born-again Christian friend: 'I have a dear friend who's convinced I'm going to hell unless I take Jesus as my saviour. Out of love and concern for my salvation, she invited me to attend her Bible study class yesterday morning. My first reaction was, "Oh Lord, what am I getting myself into?" But there was the Lovers card sitting right in the middle of my study desk, so I opted to examine the situation more carefully because I want to make decisions from my centre. So I meditated on the card and the situation and reached the place where I wanted to go to the class because it could provide me with a chance to better understand my friend and her beliefs. I decided I would go, with the attitude of seeing the events through the eyes of the Angel Raphael, as our homework suggests.

'Well, I was nearly bowled over. There were almost one hundred women present in the sanctuary, studying a passage from the Book of John. It was absolutely fascinating to hear how the teacher interpreted it to fit the group's beliefs. As I sat there in a meditative state – being the Angel as best I could – it dawned on me that the Bible can be like the Tarot. You can read the universal truths from it, or you can read it to suit your more personal needs. I could understand how the teacher's mundane interpretation gave purpose and meaning to those women's lives. I was also able to see again how my path with the Tarot and astrology is perfect for me.

'After class, my friend and I sat and talked for a while. She cried when I told her I wasn't interested in joining her group. But she seemed pleased when I told her I could appreciate its healing powers with her.'

*I felt that Elaina had certainly had a valuable insight. When we are willing and able to rise above our personality – take our cues on life's events from the Angel's perspective – we may distinguish that, like the flaming tree of personality types behind Adam, contrasting points of view are essential to the gestalt of life. We are all God/dess's children finding our way back to the Garden of Eden. And we do so in accordance with who we are. It is our personal distinctions that in fact determine which path back to Eden we follow, whether born-again Christianity, Buddhism, astrology or Tarot study, among others. It helps to keep the Angel's perspective and remember that all paths have the potential to bring healing and wholeness.*

❖  Sunny was very quiet throughout the sharing period that class always begins with, and then in a small voice she said, 'This is uncomfortable, but the Lovers are showing me that I need to be truthful and tell you all that I'm not ready to share my encounters with the cards. I'm not ready to take the risks involved. I have some parts of me that are afraid the group might not like what I have to say, or who I am. I'm an expert in my profession, and it's hard for me not to be number one in everything I do. That's a problem of mine. It's hard not to have a handle on everything, and I'm willing to own up to it.' Then she laughed. 'After hearing myself tell you all this, I guess I'm ready to share my experiences with the cards with you.' Sunny's sharing was followed by applause from the entire group.

*'Well, Sunny,' I said, 'we all certainly appreciate your honesty. You realise, of course, that you have just lived the card's teachings? By being open with your thoughts and feelings, you imitated our naked Lovers, who have nothing to hide.'*

❖  'I've recently been spending a great deal of time with a very depressed and negative friend,' began Lin. 'And I find that in order to take better care of myself, I have to use the Sword of Discrimination from the Lovers card, the Hebrew letter *Zain*. I must continually make choices as to when to be comforting to her and when not to be. Sometimes it's difficult not to get hooked into being negative along with her. It think it's contagious! I've been consciously using the Sword to choose between being assertive, passive or aggressive with her.

'I see the man in the card as my aggressive side (Yes, I know men can be assertive, but in my life I've known them to be mostly aggressive); the Angel as my assertive side; while the woman in the card is the passive, subservient side of my personality. I wasn't brought up to say, "No", to another's needs. But it's time for me to define myself with the Sword, especially with people who drain my energies. I'm getting closer to this by picking up the fearful thing. It's up to me to choose between old conditioning and Self love, doing what is being communicated in the Lovers card.'

*'I love the way you associate the man, woman and Angel with the aggressive, passive and assertive aspects of your personality,' I told her. 'It seems that you are actively engaged in using the card's symbols and teachings. I agree that using the Sword isn't comfortable at first, yet the more positive experiences you gain by using it – feeling energised rather*

*than depleted and drained, for example – the more you will welcome picking it up. People like your friend often lack the positive experience of having someone draw the line with them, setting limits. I have actually seen the Sword work to facilitate healthy independence after the person gets through the initial feelings of hurt, anger, rejection, etc. By using your Sword, you are giving a gift of love, not only to yourself, but to your friend as well.'*

❖   Jan, a university librarian, brought this realisation to class: 'Over the last few months I've been seriously analysing my feelings about sex and love. This started when I took a class on Human Sexuality. And now, after learning about the Lovers, I'm reaching a decision about myself. It's strange, but I've been so involved in learning and studying, so involved in the mental process, that I've been celibate. Yet I don't feel denied. I feel enriched.

'I think the Lovers are learning to look to higher consciousness in the place of the Angel, which reinforces my ideas about sex being something that is above culture and society. I believe that not only is everyone sexual, but we have the possibility of being so in a variety of ways. Nobody is born to be a certain way, but like the Lovers we have the choice of how to express our sexuality.

'I've been meditating on the card, using it to look into my heart and Higher Self to determine who I really am in this area. I'm not looking at my ego or to the world outside. I'm going deep within. I feel as if I'm finally getting free of having my love life influenced or defined by others. I'm defining and choosing who I am for myself. And this card is definitely helping to reinforce and confirm it.'

*I agreed with Jan that the card shows the many different types of love and sex relationships we may pursue. It's sometimes helpful to be able to step out of what we are accustomed to, or told we 'should' be, etc., in order to gain perspective on what is genuinely best for us. We may very well wind up back where we started, but at least our decision will be the product of our conscious choice.*

❖   'The study we did last week with the Lovers made me come to terms with my fear of being open and honest – naked like the Lovers – in my communications,' shared Valerie, a student. 'I'm actually terrified to let people know who I am and what I think and believe. Over this past week, I've been scrutinising my reasons for being like this, and I'm making a concerted effort to be less guarded. I'm wearing a little bit of orange (the colour of the Lovers) to remind me to do this, to open my heart to myself. I also see that one of the best ways to expand and get in touch with your Higher Self is by having open and honest relationships. I think that is what being truly loving means.

'And after taking a good look at myself, I think I'm not as bad as I've made myself out to be. I think I'm slowly opening up to a real love relationship, one with my own Self. Loving me first will surely help me to love somebody else. I want to feel okay about who I am and not be ashamed, not have to cover myself in excuses and fear, but to stand naked in the light. I'm writing this affirmation at bedtime and have gone so far as to play a tape of it in my car when I drive over to school in the city: "I love myself unconditionally!" '

*I think the Lovers card illustrates the fears we all have about being intimate and consequently vulnerable. I also believe relationships are magic mirrors through which we can see ourselves. And as our responses become increasingly grounded in our Higher Self, the more accepting and loving we become towards ourselves and others. The upshot of this behaviour is that relationships can't help but become less threatening and more supportive.*

❖   Beth, a marriage and family counsellor, offered her insights from a meditation period on the Lovers card: 'The other evening while I sat meditating on the Lovers card at bedtime, asking that its meaning be shown to me in my dreams, the Bible story of Eve and the apple took on a whole new meaning. I suddenly recalled my first experience with the consciousness-expanding drug LSD a long time ago. I remember how it brought me the awareness that I already lived in the Garden of Eden, but was so conditioned to perceiving my life as a constant struggle, I didn't see it that way. After this awareness, I refocused on the card and saw how I'm still like Eve and Adam before eating the apple. Here I am with this great life. I'm young, healthy and have more than enough money. I'm standing in Eden, but not having earned my way consciously, I lack appreciation for my circumstances. I'm using the personal statement, "Eden is a state of mind", to redirect my thoughts when I forget where I truly am and get caught up in my conditioning.'

*I told Beth she was using her affirmation to remind herself to look to the Archangel, or her higher mind, for her responses to life. 'I understand how you can equate what occurred in the Garden of Eden with your LSD experience. Drugs like LSD can be great "apples" or awakeners when taken with great care. However, it's always up to us to integrate our perceptions into our everyday patterns, something which takes a lot of intention and time. I might suggest taking the Angel's eternal and loving perspective on the integration process as well. It took time to formulate your present patterns and it will take time to alter them. Be patient, persistent and above all, loving towards yourself.'*

## Suggestions for Application and Integration of the Lovers

The following will help you to know the teachings of the Lovers card more intimately. This is a chance to become better acquainted with your male and female sides, improve your ability to discern, make decisions wisely and work with problems more effectively. You might also learn to look to your Higher Self when interacting with others, communicate more freely, increase your intimacy and interdependence with others and examine the many paths of love.

1   Draw or colour your own version of the Lovers with yourself as the figures. Designate them in any of the following ways: Angel-Higher Self; Man-consciousness or *animus*; Woman-sub-consciousness or *anima*. Or if you are a woman: Eve is your outer self, your body and personality; Adam is your inner self, your subconscious; Raphael, your Higher Self. If you are a man reverse the aforementioned. Think about how the three interact.

2   Set the Lovers in a visible place as a reminder to your conscious and subconscious minds to integrate and absorb its teachings such as being more willing to examine situations carefully before acting, being unashamed of your feelings and looking to your Higher Self for responses to life situations.

3   Dream on the Lovers.

4   Play the note D on a musical instrument. Intone IAO or hum along with the music. Focus on the card for several minutes. Contemplate how the dynamics between the Angel, Adam and Eve actually depict how your habit patterns are established, reinforced or changed. Experiment with perceiving the events in your life through the eyes of the side of your personality which you desire to become more unified with or aware of – female/feeling, male/reasoning or Higher Self. Next, consider how some problem is helping you to grow; imagine how your Sword of Discrimination might be useful. While meditating, ask that the

Lovers' teachings guide you through a particular situation, event or problem, such as having to take a difficult course of action, choose between two or more possibilities or overcoming your tendency to be more loving to others than towards yourself. Imagine how the Archangel Raphael, Angel of Healing, would handle it. If it seems workable, do it. Jot down the times when you recognise the card's presence in your interactions. I was aware of the Lovers when? Before/during/after . . .

5   Go out into the world and use your Sword of Discrimination for analysis, differentiation and discernment in a situation which requires you to cut something apart for examination, define yourself, take action, make a choice, cut off, eliminate or terminate something, or set limits of some type. 'I used the Sword and this is what took place . . . '

6   The Rerun. After having an experience and realising in retrospect how the Lovers' teachings might have made things clearer or more loving, provided definition, unity or healing, or enabled you to turn to your Higher Self for aid, mentally relive the situation, *including* your insight. If possible, actually rerun the situation in real life with your new attitude or behaviour.

7   Ask yourself the following questions:

'What am I afraid to lose by taking action?' 'How is loving another a distraction from, or an attraction to, loving my Self?' 'Must I mate with myself first before I am actually ready to have a mate?' 'How am I embracing and expanding my male and female sides?' 'What incompatabilities am I making an effort to overcome?' 'Is the relationship I am in supportive of who I truly am?' 'What issues need to be decided or acted upon?' 'What communication might be uncomfortable yet healing at this time?' 'How am I getting to be more intimate with myself and others?'

'What Gateway of Life am I in or growing through in the above?' Indicate: Childhood, Adolescence, Adulthood or Wisdom. Why? 'What do I need to do in order to develop the above further?' I need to . . .

'What step(s) do I want to take towards this goal and how can the Lovers card guide me?'

8 Use a personal statement regarding the presence of the Lovers in your life at this time, such as: 'I am getting better and better at making decisions.' 'My Sword of Discrimination is a useful and most necessary life tool.' 'I have the courage and self-love to stand naked with my thoughts and feelings.' 'I love myself without condition.' My personal statement is . . .

9 Inspirational words and quotes:

'Unity through honesty.'

'The sword is the tool of a sharp mind.'

'Communication heals!'

'Our first and last love is – self-love.'        Bovere

'Love in its essence is spiritual fire.'        Swedenborg

'If man realises that east and west are the two halves of our human consciousness, comparable to the two poles of a magnet which condition and correspond to each other and cannot be separated, he will become a complete human being.'

Lama Anagarika Govinda[2]

10 What symbols stand out in the card? What do they say to you? How might they be useful in daily living? See or bring the symbols into your life in some way so as to integrate the card's teachings. The Archangel Raphael blessing the Lovers reminds me that God/dess, my Higher Self, is blessing me with the experiences that help me become a better and more whole person.

11 Wear and surround yourself with the Lovers' colour, orange, to remind you of the card's teachings when needed, such as opening your heart to yourself, being more honest and affirming your ability to make viable decisions, or recalling that difficulties bear wisdom, understanding and maturity in their wake. Notice how you are affected.

12 The Lovers' astrological correspondence is Gemini, governing traits such as adaptability, interpersonal and artistic communications, social activities and the ability to mediate. Step

---

2 Bernard Gunther, Ira Friedlander, and William Hopkins, *Wholly Man*, Macmillian, New York, 1973.

out and communicate in an area in which you would ordinarily hesitate to do so: give a talk, write a poem, or engage in a social or political gathering or protest. If appropriate, act as a mediator within your family, socially or at work. Note what happens: your thoughts and feelings and the outcome.

13 Remember that the Lovers' name, *Zain*, means 'sword'. How might this remind you of the card's meaning or help in your life process? When I first approached the Sword, I mentally substituted for it my scissors because this was more comfortable for me as a tool of practical, everyday magic. Each time I pick up my scissors, I think about my relationship to the Lovers card: defining myself, setting limits or eliminating something useless or excessive.

14 Try a few drops of the scent wormwood associated with the Lovers as a reminder to integrate the card's teachings.

15 Have a cup of tea made with or cook using the herb parsley. Sit quietly as you drink or eat and consider the herb's properties as a diuretic, aphrodisiac, laxative and expectorant (it cleanses and purifies as does the sword) and consider the like qualities of the Lovers.

**7 THE CHARIOT**

# CHAPTER 11

# The Chariot

## General Information and Symbolism

The Chariot bears the Charioteer beyond the city's walls or known world. The Charioteer, who may be of either sex, wears an apron and belt like those used in the rites of esoteric groups such as the Masons. Decorated with astrological symbols and talismans of ritual magic, these garments illustrate that novice initiates have help and protection available on their journey through the degrees[1] of life. These symbols suggest that life is the experience of turning ritual magic into practical magic by using the tools of the art in the rituals of daily living; in other words, the application and integration of the teachings of truth. The symbols also serve as reminders of the Charioteer's basic training and initiation – the previous seven Tarot cards.

Contrasting Sphinxes pull the Chariot, stating that the rider's adventures will be a varied combination of black and white, positive and negative forces, aimed at teaching the rider how to master his or her everyday circumstances and less evolved (or animal) self. This is beautifully alluded to in the *Bhagavad-Gita*: 'The Self is the rider in the Chariot of the body, of which the senses are the horses and the mind the reins.' You might now notice that the driver's left hand appears to hold the reins with which to direct the Sphinxes mentally. Because the Sphinxes are portrayed with human heads on animal bodies, they symbolise the evolution of consciousness. In other words, you are distinguished from the animal kingdom by your forebrain or intellect. In this card, the Sphinxes represent how your mind identifies and classifies the polar experiences of joy and suffering – joy, the white Sphinx, and suffering, the black Sphinx. Your primary aim is to use your mental tools, the previous seven

---

1 Degrees: the series of steps or stages defined by esoteric organisations which brings the initiate to mastery and wisdom.

cards, to have loving dominion over your senses, emotions and desires, rather than allow them to dominate you. The Charioteer wear a laurel victory wreath bearing the message that victory (Victory is a name older decks give this card) comes from self-control and emotional stability. At this level of development, initiates (although novices), know better than to allow their obsolete instincts and feelings to victimise them. They emphatically believe that they may not be in control of what is happening in others and in the world, but they are in control of *their* responses to such.

Two crescent moons wearing expressions of joy and sorrow rest (or weigh, depending on your attitude) on the Charioteer's shoulders. Traditionally, these are called *Urim* and *Thummim*,[2] objects worn inside the breastplate of the High Priests in ancient Israel. Worn within, these served as private reminders that the priest was to consciously draw down and be receptive to the will of the Most High. Because the Charioteer is positioned in the middle, these symbols emphasise the initiate's role as a mediator between the positive and negative polarities. Eastern thought terms this the development of your 'witness consciousness'. The Charioteer holds a staff in his right hand – the dominant, conscious or wilful side of the body – continuing the theme of dominion. The staff is composed of a lunar crescent and figure eight. This states that when the subconscious works in conjunction with the conscious personality, 'above' is brought to 'below', 'below' is brought to 'above', and Self-empowerment is spontaneous. The Chariot itself is made from the cube that appears in prior cards, suggesting that mastery over the material world occurs when the rider's actions are founded in the eternal truths. The cube also states that the will of God/dess underlies all and therefore predominates over all.

The number four stands for order, discipline and the material world; four pillars rise out of the Chariot to support a star-studded canopy. It is through the process of ordering and disciplining your daily life that you ascend to higher consciousness. Conversely, God/dess descends to earth, becoming apparent through the human personality (the Charioteer) and the four elements of nature – Fire, Water, Air and Earth. The canopy, symbol of holy matrimony, further implies that the driver is protected by and married to heaven. Consequently, when feeling driven by life circumstances all he or she

2  Urim and Thummim are mentioned in Exodus 28:30 and Leviticus 8:8

need do is turn upwards for guidance and recall that it is the Higher Self who truly drives them.

The winged emblem on the front of the vehicle bears the Hindu *lingam-yoni* signifying the union of heaven and earth, the male and female forces respectively. This shows that being a divine vehicle becomes feasible when you acknowledge that all earthly interactions originate from and are influenced by the Source of life, the winged solar disk, an Egyptian symbol of the Logos or Divine Word.

The Charioteer wears a crown composed of three five-pointed stars. The five-pointed star, or pentagram, symbolises evolving human intelligence and tells us that the Charioteer has developed a basic working relationship with all three levels of being: subconsciousness, self-consciousness and superconsciousness. The crown and wreath also suggest that the driver knows that you do nothing by yourself; genuine victory is to acknowledge humbly that all human activities are empowered by the interconnectedness of heaven and earth.

Along this same line, there is a certain mystical Hebrew teaching known as the 'Work of the Chariot'. Evolving out of interpretations of Chapter One of the Book of Ezekiel, this 'work' has not been taught publicly for many centuries. Recently, there has been speculation that this work may be speaking of extraterrestrials coming to this planet. But after considerable thought, it's my guess that this writing actually symbolises the realisation that God/dess descends to earth in the chariot of the body (human form). I believe the work to be an ancient harbinger of the present Messianic or New Age, during which humans will not only realise that they are vehicles (chariots) for God/dess's work on earth, but through loving intention will be victorious over their lower selves. In other words, the Higher Self drives the Chariot, not the Charioteer (the personality), or Chariot (symbol for the physical body and instinctual self).

In addition to wearing the Emperor's armour, the Charioteer wears a four-sided emblem embossed with the T-cross of Saturn. This refers to the initiate's heartfelt dedication to work within the limitations of the material world and his/her personality to master the restrictions these present. The T-cross also underscores the fact that victory requires self-discipline. Water flows in the background as a reminder that the universal forces continue to flow into the individual personality.

The Chariot's colour is orange-yellow, its musical note is E, and its herbal correspondence is dandelion. The Hebrew name for the

Chariot is *Cheth*, meaning 'fence'. Each of our bodies is like a fence, since it encompasses, protects and defines the inner Self within. Also, when we become protective of our personality, our 'de-fences' are said to be up. The walled city in the background shows that the Charioteer is stepping out of a protected environment into the world at large. In many schools of thought, it is said that, in order to know your Self, you must venture out and leave what is familiar behind.

Qabalists assign the function of speech to this card. In defining and protecting yourself with words, it's essential to note that they are shaped by and mirror your encounters with life. Therefore, two people might say the word 'family', yet be referring to two entirely different concepts. Speaking your mind and heart tells others about your personal frames of reference and level of awareness. It may be helpful to recall that when others speak to you – complain or exclaim about life or you personally, they are really telling you about how *they* have come to see the world – their previous experiences and associations. In truth, we are all at different levels of personality development, although we ostensibly share the same human form. If you disagree or are irritated with another's statements, think of the old native American adage, 'Judge not a man till you have walked in his moccasins for two moons.'

The Chariot is associated with the cardinal (initiating and of foremost importance) Water sign, Cancer. Because this sign is governed by the moon, it is also known as the Moonchild (the driver wears lunar crescents on his or her shoulders). The reflective quality of both the lunar nature and water reminds us that the Charioteer or human being is, in truth, a reflection of the Divine Self. Cancer governs the chest cavity, breasts, stomach, diaphragm, oesophagus and mucous membranes. The Cancerian personality says: I feel, receive, imitate, change, nurture, protect, pinch, domesticate and take comfort in repetition. Moonchildren tend to be sensitive, tenacious, value country, home and family, and have excellent memories and imaginations. Depending on their level of maturity, they may employ their memory and imagination to cling to old hurts, dwell in the past or dream endlessly as a means of denying or avoiding (sidestepping, like their significator, the Crab) conflict or present demands. They may also step beyond their sheltered world (their crab shell) to greet life from the greater perspective, calling upon their innate sensitivity to tune in to new possibilities instead of hiding in their shell, home or behind their fence to fantasise and avoid hurt, change and confrontation. An important lesson that evolved Moonchildren learn is to feel at home within their bodies and personality. Experiencing your body as a comfortable place to be may decrease excessive dependence upon external circumstances and increase dependence upon the Self within.

The Chariot card is numbered 7, denoting victory, conquest, initiation and accomplishment. Genesis states that on the seventh day, God rested. It is good to stop after we have worked to appreciate our efforts. The seventh *Sephirah* on the Tree of Life is *Netzach* or Victory. The state of Victory is knowing that we are the vehicles through which the One Self does its work. All is the Self. The card depicts the state of centredness that occurs when you become aware of this concept and begin to lovingly take charge of your behaviour. The Chariot is the culmination and incorporation of the teachings from the previous cards, and an initiation into worldly life, connecting it further to the number seven. This state brings the following with it: first and foremost, the Fool provides the knowledge that all is God/dess, and that life is an ongoing adventure initiated and guided by this Force. With the next six phases of training come the Rules and Tools of the Game of life.

The Magician familiarises you with your particular personality and informs you that you are the house for the Self. He communicates that by paying attention to your interactions and acknowledging where your abilities and shortcomings originate ('As above, so below'), ordinary life becomes magical and challenging.

The High Priestess stirs your memory to recall that your subconscious powers hold the potential to refine your gifts, overcome your immaturities, and bring you higher consciousness.

The Empress offers you the loving and compassionate assurance that you have entered the right door – parents, environment, circumstances, etc.

The Emperor guides you to see and think clearly, so that you may order your life in such a way as to find your place in society.

The Hierophant teaches that if in the midst of confusion you will momentarily put aside your concerns, peace and wisdom are close by.

The Lovers introduce you to the Sword of Discrimination and the concept of comparative analysis, through which you learn to make better and more mature choices. The Lovers also depict your Guardian Angel ready to help you celebrate and heal your differences with yourself and others in order to become a well-integrated individual.

The Charioteer is the embodiment of all this, showing you poised and ready to use these tools in pursuit of your destiny. Here, too, you are equipped with the knowledge that the Self always triumphs in the eternal time frame.

In the Qabalah, the Chariot is called the Intelligence of the House of Influence. The word influence means 'in-flowing'. Know that you are influenced or guided by your Self. When you allow this Self to influence, or flow, into you, you can exert a positive influence upon the world. This Intelligence directly prompts how you think, feel and express yourself. It may be likened to a loving mentor guiding a promising co-worker. It is the way in which the Higher Self manifests itself through every human personality.

## Gateway of Life: Childhood to Adolescence

The Chariot is a double Gateway, marking the Fool-child's passage from the realm of Childhood into Adolescence, and as such denotes the completion of your elementary education. After you become familiar with the Rules and Tools of the Game of Life (also known as survival skills), you naturally become motivated to explore the world on a larger scale and prove that you can care for and protect – *Cheth*, 'the fence' – yourself. Here your inner life is about to become a sound basis for your outer life. Like any hero or heroine, you must leave home to seek your fortune. Climbing into your Chariot equipped with armour and magical talismans, you go forward into life, where you will strengthen and further develop through trial and error the teachings gathered from the cards up to this point. Because you evolve organically, patience is the key to fulfilment and victory.

Living the Chariot at the many Gateways of life may result in certain types of behaviour and attitudes. CHILDHOOD: Because you were so impatient to get into the wilderness, you get caught in an early snowstorm without enough warm clothing; ADOLESCENCE: A 'typical' American has difficulty being hospitable towards a foreign family who move into the neighbourhood because their customs and clothing are 'different'; ADULTHOOD: Recognising that she has been holding on to certain trivial hurts and jealousies towards her sister since childhood, a woman decides to forgive and forget; WISDOM: You employ your tools to master a family crisis in which everyone is very distraught.

## Divinatory Questions for the Chariot

*Upright:* Are you being influenced to head in a new direction? What initiation or rite-of-passage are you experiencing? Have you overcome being pulled in several directions at once? Might it be appropriate for you or another to withdraw into your shell? How has self-discipline been rewarding you? What type of behaviour or activity could you be outgrowing? Have you completed a cycle of learning and are you now applying new skills to everyday living? Have you been feeling more emotionally stable? What aspect of your life are you getting under control? What circumstances have you triumphed over? Are you feeling more connected to your spiritual body? Where is your Self helping you gain better self-control? Are you keeping up with the responsibilities being placed upon you in a calm and centred way? What tools and information do you have at your disposal? What might you be learning from a conflict in your home? Where are you experiencing success? How are you feeling protected? Are you keeping certain thoughts and feelings in check? Where would it be of benefit to appreciate your progress? In what situation might it be beneficial to hold your tongue?

*Reversed:* What passions are tearing you apart? Who or what has been running your life? What are you feeling impatient about? Should you be careful not to indulge in your weaknesses? What circumstances are presently driving you? What are you hesitating to leave behind you in order to grow? Where are you avoiding confrontation? In what situation(s) have you been either indirect or overly emotional with others? What reward are you getting from clinging to old hurts and anger? Why are you feeling defensive? Could you possibly benefit from being less or more sensitive? Why might you be clinging to some attitude or behaviour that serves no useful purpose? Are you resisting or fearing a promotion, or success? In what area of your life do you feel defeated? Have you been dreaming rather than acting? Is it possible that you are hiding out from your own Self? What tools or information have you rejected or avoided putting to use? In what situation might humility be useful? What journey are you completing? What initiation are you denying yourself? Are you feeling uncomfortable with being led, rather than leading? Are you focusing on your weaknesses? Might it be helpful to cease hating yourself and others for shortcomings and weaknesses?

## Personal Experience

It has been all too easy for me to become disappointed and frustrated with my own and others' shortcomings and weaknesses, which I also call immaturities. Yet these personality traits have taught me about the workings of the Chariot card. As the parent of two teenagers see-sawing between immaturity and maturity, Childhood and young Adulthood, I lived through innumerable situations in which these characteristics were displayed. A prime example of this is the number of years my husband and I spent countless hours discussing with our boys the importance of doing their chores. Despite our incessant pleas and in-depth talks on the importance of personal responsibility, the chores slipped their young minds time and again. Bernard and I even resorted to punishments such as reduced allowances, then no allowances and the withholding of privileges. These efforts yielded only temporary changes, plus tons of frustration for all.

After several years of this drama, the boys unexpectedly started fulfilling their obligations more efficiently. While asking myself what had finally clicked into place, the answer appeared in the form of the Chariot card. I had been thinking almost constantly about the Tarot in relation to the Four Gateways of Life when I understood that my sons were passing through the Gateway of Childhood into that of young Adulthood symbolised by the card. Because of this transition, their mental and emotional wiring was becoming more complete, and they were behaving more maturely. I excitedly contemplated the Chariot card for further insights.

First I thought about the card's association with Cancer, the zodiacal sign most connected to the home (and subsequently the development of the human body and personality, home of the Higher Self). I also pondered its cyclic ruler, the moon. Next, I meditated on the Chariot card itself and recalled how the human body is a vehicle (like the Chariot) that matures much as the cart's wheels turn, rolling along steadily, but on the driver's time schedule. Finally, I came to the realisation that all personalities develop within their Higher Self's time frame. This insight helped me recognise that I may communicate how I would like others to behave, but unless they are mentally, emotionally and physically mature enough to act on their own, there is nothing more I can do. This thought inadvertently shed some important light on the negative attitudes I held towards my own developmental process as well.

There are times when I frustrate, disappoint and anger myself when I don't function according to capacity: I react instead of act, am lazy, lack compassion, or don't listen to my Higher Self. Gaining the understanding that I am in many ways just like my teenagers – mature on the outside while certain facets of my personality are immature within – was priceless. It allowed me my humanity, giving me the leeway to love and accept my Self despite myself. I know that by way of time, loving patience and persistence, my personality and capabilities are maturing just like my children's are. Wow, did I feel victorious!

## Student Experiences

❖ David told us about his bad habit of waking in the middle of the night and stuffing himself with whatever he can find in the refrigerator. 'After going over my class notes on the Chariot on Saturday morning, I put the quote from the *Bhagavad-Gita* on the nightstand next to my bed and on the refrigerator door: "The Self is the rider in the Chariot of the body, of which the senses are the horses and the mind the reins." Since then I've been working at putting it all together. When I wake up famished at 2:00 am or so, I immediately turn on the light next to my bed and see the quote staring at me. I have it memorised! Then I ask myself, what do I really want to happen next? Who's in control, my Self or my mouth? I use my tools to be loving towards myself. I pick up the Sword and discriminate between actual hunger and the habit of eating. In that way, I stop myself from being pulled in directions I really don't want to go . . . towards the fridge. If the bedside quote doesn't work, and I make it to the kitchen, I run into the quote again on the fridge door. I'm training myself to have a glass of milk or cold water at that point and then march back to bed.

'I must admit that some nights it's hot cocoa, but at least I'm not cleaning out the pantry. My Self, with a capital S, is in charge of my body, not the other way around. It's hard, but it's working. I know I'm succeeding and being victorious like the Charioteer. I've gone so far as to record the quote on my tape deck and play it before I fall asleep.'

*'By calling on your greater Self and the Sword from the Lovers card to empower you to be more in charge of and at home in your body, you're undoubtedly "living" the card, David,' I assured him. 'You might also have or imagine another saying the quote to you. Perhaps there is someone like a grandmother or parent who has encouraged you to eat more than you need*

*to as a means of assuring your nourishment or pacifying you when you felt upset? It would also be valuable to check out what you are feeling and thinking when you feel driven to eat. Remember, the problem is usually not what you're eating, but what's eating you. You've enacted two of the main themes of the Chariot: who's in charge, and the role of physical and emotional comfort.'*

❖ 'People are certainly at different places in their lives and personal development,' began Kim, a single parent and elementary school teacher. 'When I first met my man friend, it was summertime. I was on holiday from school, and my daughter was visiting her father up north. My life was free and easy with no cares or responsibilities. This man has no responsibilities other than himself and it was great being with him. But I honestly wasn't thinking rationally about the relationship. I was living in the "now", not the "later", like I usually do. It was wonderful just being spontaneous. I really hadn't had so much fun in years. But now that life is back to normal, I'm miserable because his lifestyle doesn't mesh with mine.

'I've been thinking about asking him to be more definite about his plans to be with me. It's hard for me to just drop everything to be with him. I've also been considering making it a point to be clearer about my own needs and plans, letting him know when I have free time and can be with him. My commitments to my daughter and school usually prevent me from doing a lot of outside activities, and that's ordinarily okay. But I had a taste of something new and I liked it. I suppose the question, "What journey are you beginning?" from the homework applies to my situation. Only for me it's, "What journey are you ending?" because I'm worried that, because of the way I am, he'll want to find someone who is like I was last summer. We are clearly in different places in our lives. We were adolescents then, but now I'm back to my adult role.

'I feel I may need to let go of the relationship unless we can make some immediate compromises. It just isn't working out the way it is. Neither of us is getting what we want. I feel as if I'm living the Chariot in Reverse. I'm fighting the situation and allowing it to run me. It's painful and depressing, but I know it's time to resolve things in some way and make the Chariot go forward again. I guess I've been doing my homework, but it sure isn't fun.'

*'It sounds as if you feel bogged down with your roles in life, Kim, as so many of us often do. The Chariot card addresses your need to play the roles that*

*are correct for who you truly are – what the Eastern traditions call your*
*dharma, or life role. The personality has many different facets, only some of*
*which can shine at once. It's normal for you to want to step out of the*
*ordinary, to let loose and experiment. What you did last summer was as*
*right for the person you were then as what you're presently doing is correct*
*for you now. Maybe this is showing you that you need a bit more flexibility*
*in your life? Perhaps it's time for you to use the Charioteer as a model and*
*step beyond the walls of your home and classroom to develop some of your*
*interests or personality traits that have been on the shelf. Remember, your*
*Higher Self has a miraculous knack of steering you towards what's*
*appropriate.'*

❖  'My good friend's husband is dying, and one of his last requests
has been for her to buy a funeral dress and then wear it so he can see
how lovely she'll look at his funeral,' began Jean. 'It's an almost
impossible task for her, so she's been putting off going shopping for
weeks now, and spends her time compulsively talking about how he
wants her to buy the dress with everyone who comes to visit. I've
been going over there almost daily and it never fails that, at some
time during my conversation with her, she mentions that she hasn't
been able to find the right dress yet. It's weird, because I'm positive
she hasn't gone to even one store.

'At first I made a few suggestions as to where she might shop, even
offering to accompany her or sit with her husband while she went.
She responded by ignoring my offer and repeating like a zombie how
she isn't able to find the right dress. It's all so very unreal. Several
times I've been tempted to tell her she's acting crazily, but held back
because she's under such tremendous stress.

'Then the other evening she called and invited me to lunch the
next day. It was unusual for her to leave her husband unattended, but
I didn't ask any questions and agreed to meet her.

'After finishing our lunch and letting her pick up the bill – she
insisted – I finally got the picture. She was born into an Asian culture
that believes it isn't correct or polite to ask people to do things for
you unless you're either a man or an elder. I checked my watch and
saw that I had over an hour before my next appointment, so I took
the cue and asked her if she'd like to go shopping for a dress. With
the appropriate protocol taken care of, she instantly agreed.

'We soon found the perfect dress, and while she was in the
dressing room trying it on for the last time, my mind wandered over
the things I needed to do. It was then that I remembered my Tarot

homework, to use the Chariot's teachings in my life. I soon realised, well, here it is, the Chariot come alive. I had to respect my friend's way of doing things and let her be herself. Being able to accept her for her Self was for me the Chariot in action. It was a lesson I can apply to some other relationships I've been trying too hard to change. I tend to want people to be me, rather than themselves.'

*'Looks like you've learned one of the card's most important teachings,' I said. 'Basically, you accepted the fact that the Self takes many different forms. The Chariot is sometimes called "Victory", and you've had a victory in facilitating a complex situation.'*

## Suggestions for the Application and Integration of the Chariot

You now have the opportunity to become more comfortable in your Chariot and from this place of Self-confidence head forward into life. The Chariot provides opportunities for the following: to be more centred and Self-reliant, to exert greater self-control via application of the Tarot's teachings, to be more accepting of your level of development and to be successful in the roles you play in life.

1  Colour or draw your own version of the Chariot with yourself as the driver.

2  Set the Chariot in a visible place as a reminder to your conscious and subconscious minds to use and pay attention to its teachings to feel more Self-assured, confident that you will succeed, more patient and in command of your senses and emotions.

3  Dream on the Chariot.

4  Play the note D$^\#$. Intone IAO or hum along with the music. Focus on the card and imagine yourself in the driver's seat. You are now driving the Chariot: sense the wand in your right hand, the reins in your left, the two Sphinxes, the starry heavens above and the world before you. Sense or imagine in whatever way you can the power and influence from above flowing into you. Now ask that the Chariot's teachings guide you through a particular situation, such as feeling as if you are being pulled apart by what is going on in the world and others' opinions, allowing yourself to be led by your Higher Self rather than lead, or becoming more accepting of your level of personal development. Or, if you are faced with a worrisome situation, event or problem, imagine how the Charioteer would tackle it. If it seems appropriate, do it. Jot

down the times when you became aware of the Chariot in your interactions. I was aware of the Chariot when? Before/during/after . . .

5   Go out into the world and pretend you are the Charioteer. I was the Charioteer when I gave my first public talk on the Tarot. I knew I had the tools at my disposal and could draw on them, through my personality, just as I do when I teach regular Tarot classes. Before speaking, I focused my attention on the card, imagining myself as the Charioteer. While giving my talk, I kept the image and feeling in my mind to remind me that the power was flowing down from my Higher Self through my body to help me accomplish this. I was the Charioteer and this is what took place . . .

6   The Rerun. After having an experience and realising in retrospect how the Chariot's teachings might have made things different – you might have used skills and tools more accurately, not spoken unnecessarily, been in greater command of your thoughts and feelings, accepted and celebrated a small success although you were aiming for a larger accomplishment, felt you were doing the best you could at the moment, etc. – mentally relive the situation, *including* your insight. This will help the behaviour become more automatic next time. If possible, actually rerun the situation in real life with your new attitude or behaviour.

7   Ask yourself the following questions:

'In what situation is it best for me to be accepting and non-judgmental of my level of maturity?' 'Where might my life be moving along too fast?' 'What skills and abilities am I about to develop further?' 'When do I experience my Higher Self operating through me' 'What victory have I achieved?' 'What am I being initiated into?' 'What aspect of my personality requires additional self-control?' 'With whom or what have I lost patience?' 'Why am I feeling defensive?' 'What journey am I beginning?' 'What issues or commitments am I sidestepping?' 'What personality traits would I like to be more in charge or accepting of?' 'How have I been more in control of myself and consequently less anxious about the state of the world and others?' 'Am I behaving like the driver or the driven?'

'What Gateway of Life am I in or developing through in the

above?' Indicate: Childhood, Adolescence, Adulthood or Wisdom. Why?

'What do I need to do in order to develop the above further?' I need to . . .

'What step(s) do I want to take towards this goal and how can the Charioteer guide me?'

8   Use a personal statement regarding the presence of the Charioteer in your life at this time, such as: 'I meet life's adventures equipped with the Universal Teachings.' 'I'm doing the best that I can.' 'The Self works through my personality.' 'Joy and suffering stem from the same Source.' My personal statement is . . .

9   Inspirational words and quotes:

'To conquer oneself is a greater victory than to conquer a thousand in battle.'

'God is the job of life at hand, the One who does the job, and the means for completing it.'

'Now there are varieties of gifts, but the same spirit.'

                                                I CORINTHIANS

'You may not be in control of what others say and do or what goes on in the world at large, but you are in control of your responses to such.'

10   What symbols stand out in the card? What do they say to you? How can you bring the symbols into your life so as to integrate the card's teachings? I have a pair of crescent moon earrings and wear them as a reminder that I interpret, and am responsible for, my moods, thoughts and feelings.

11   Wear or surround yourself with orange-yellow, the colour of the Chariot, to remind you of the card's teachings, such as when heading in a new direction, recognising the potential of becoming enmeshed unproductively in your own or another's feelings, or remembering that you are in charge of your senses. Notice how you are affected.

12   The Chariot's astrological correspondence is Cancer, the Moonchild, governing traits such as memory, creativity, the

ability to 'hang in there', avoidance or denial of unpleasant situations, receptivity, changeability and sensitivity. If you are avoiding an unpleasant situation (hiding in your shell or side-stepping like the crab) remember that things are always changing and that others are entitled to their point of view. Doing this, you will feel less threatened and become more receptive and willing to do what life is asking of you. The sooner you accept the situation, the sooner it will change and you will feel better. Note what happens: your thoughts and feelings and the outcome.

13 Remember the Chariot's Hebrew name, *Cheth*, means 'fence'. How can this remind you of the card's meaning or help in your life process? When entering into a situation in which I feel excessively vulnerable, I mentally surround myself with a fence of protection.

14 Try a few drops of the scent sandalwood associated with the Chariot to remind you of the card's teachings.

15 Have a cup of tea made from the herb dandelion. Sit quietly as you drink and consider the herb's properties as a diuretic, tonic to the stomach, detoxifier and blood purifier, and consider the similar qualities of the Chariot. Or try some dandelion root coffee instead, following the same procedure.

# *Part Three*

## THE GATEWAY OF
## ADOLESCENCE

The next cards bring the Fool-child through Adolescence to Adulthood. The Fool-adolescent vacillates between the worlds of Childhood and Adulthood. On the one hand, you may insist on complete independence, while on the other hand, resist and resent having to care for yourself and your surroundings. At this stage of development, you may have a mature body but lack the mental and emotional maturity to go along with it. Because adolescence is a time of individuation and rebellion, questioning and testing of parental and other types of authority usually ensues. Remember, this is natural and *must* be done before adulthood may be fully claimed.

Development from Adolescence to Adulthood involves the slow and sometimes painstaking process of learning to apply the Rules and Tools provided during Childhood to everyday encounters. In essence, the adolescent needs to practise and succeed at daily living in order to become an adult. At this juncture, experience slowly becomes the great teacher.

In Adolescence, practice starts out as a sometimes faltering and inconsistent repetition and application of what you have learned in Childhood to slowly mature you into Adulthood. The Adolescent (remember that, in this model, Adolescence is a state of mental and emotional development, as opposed to solely physical age or bio-logical development) becomes increasingly mindful and confident of thoughts, words and actions. The transition occurring between Adolescence and Adulthood may be simply described as learning to think before you speak and look before you leap. In the Gateway of Adulthood, on the other hand, practice slowly evolves into the idea of spiritual practice, the conscious and *continuous* application and integration of the same Rules and Tools of the Game of Life until they are perfected in the Gateway of Wisdom.

Adolescence to Adulthood may be defined as the stage during which you are slowly gaining more consistent control over your instinctive drive and emotional impulses, and as a result, become increasingly aware and responsible. Early efforts are mainly aimed at satisfying the ego's demands. Because of this, whatever it regards as good is accepted, and whatever it regards as bad is rejected and unconsciously repressed, or consciously suppressed and put on hold. At this time of life, you are generally unable to realise that many rejected factors accumulate in the subconscious mind and must be dealt with in the Gateway of Adulthood. Confronting significant repressions and/or suppressions in one's life is an unavoidable prerequisite for entry into the Gateway of Wisdom.

On a final note, many individuals may get stuck within the Gateway of Adolescence because they have not previously learned the skills required to cope with what the world now offers. Here you may get caught in the trap of endlessly blaming others for your inadequacies, failures and damaged personality. However, part of our developmental process involves accessing the strength to re-parent and/or re-educate ourselves in order to get on with living our lives in the present.

8  STRENGTH  ל

# CHAPTER 12

# *Strength*

## General Information and Symbolism

What appears in this card is in sharp contrast to earlier versions of the Strength card known as *La Force*. Although the words *La Force* may refer to the life force within everyone, the older cards depict a warrior brandishing a club and illustrate the outdated philosophy of dominion by force. Most contemporary versions of Strength, however, show a serene Woman standing on an open plain, calming the King of Beasts. This states that love is the superior means to rulership. Taming a wild animal (or your own wild side) requires much awareness, suggested by the fact that the scene occurs in full daylight.

The Woman is an extension of all the previous female archetypes. Because she embodies the receptivity and subconscious force of the High Priestess and Eve in the Garden of Eden as well as the desire, nurturance, unconditional love, and creative imagination of the Empress, she conveys two important facts. The first is that someone in her position of strength is motivated by purified desire or love and the Divine Intelligence rather than fear. This is communicated by the serene expression on her face and by her white robe. Second, through her willingness to engage with life, she becomes able creatively to control, direct and articulate (the Lion's mouth is open) *La Force*. She wears a crown of flowers, signifying that her powers are blossoming owing to loving rulership over both herself (her instincts, emotions and biological drives) and her interactions with the Lion (practice makes perfect).

An infinity sign floats over her head as it does in the Magician card, showing her connection with the infinite. This symbol is used to indicate a state of balance and inter-connectedness: heaven/earth, mind/body, human/animal, intuition/instinct, etc. In addition to the aforementioned, it suggests that the Woman's personal will is focused on the desire for right action, the importance of balancing teachings or philosophies, and study with application and action.

The Woman realises her powers by *applying* her knowledge of the Rules and Tools of the Game of Life to the challenges of daily living. Life has undoubtedly become her guru, and so she seeks its infinite laws to guide her finite actions. Turning the infinity sign upright, it becomes the number 8, the number of Strength, affirming the courage, discipline and loving care necessary to accomplish these feats. It is interesting to note that the eighth *Sephirah* on the Qabalistic Tree of Life is called *Hod*, Splendour or Glory, which may be interpreted to mean how splendid we feel when allowing the glory of God/dess to shine and operate through us. The bodily function of digestion is assigned to the card. Digestion converts food into energy, whereas Strength converts knowledge into actions. The serpentine figure eight feeds upon itself, showing that the application or digestion of the universal and natural laws and principles result in both personal and spiritual development. Simply, we are learning to take our experiences, digest them, keep what is nutritious and eliminate the rest.

The Woman and the Lion are entwined by a chain of red roses. This suggests how, whether we know it or not, we are chained to our desires. Desires are the part of being human that keep us alive and evolving spiritually. Spiritual development requires that we face all of our feelings and desires. Of course, this does not mean we must act all out. It suggests that, as our consciousness evolves, we become more able to desire what is for our highest good. This concept may be summed up by a quote from II Corinthians 12:9, 'My strength is made perfect in weakness.'

Furthermore, the chain connecting the Woman, or the creative and loving application of will, with the Lion, the kingdom of nature and personal desire, forms yet another figure eight. Since red roses also refer to love and desire, this interconnection shows how, by linking desire to will and creativity that is motivated by love, you may tame not only your own wild side (passions and desires), but the forces of nature as well. It is important to note that, in either case, love and the ultimate desire for union with God/dess is the stimulus. Therefore, the Lion symbolises what we are wise to fear and consequently respect; our personal desires, emotions and biological drives; the realm of nature; and life as the guru all in one. The Woman opens the Lion's mouth, suggesting the necessity of courageously expressing and yet lovingly controlling your passions. She directs the Lion, not the other way around, as is more often the case. Both his position, beneath her, and red colouring show his passionate nature being dominated by her love. As the brave King of Beasts, he stands for the will and stout-heartedness it takes to engage with and transmute the grosser forms of human awareness within, referred to in Qabalistic teachings as the animal nature. Proof of this willingness is seen by the mountain in the background shown smaller than it was in the Lovers card – the journey has come a bit closer to its end.

The final reference to the number eight is my association of it with The Middle Way or Eightfold Noble Path of the Buddha. Until the advent of Buddhism, most Eastern schools of spirituality taught their students to check their senses and subdue their passions by austere practices and repressive actions, rather than through the use of intelligence or sense and sensitivity (depicted in the Strength card). The Buddha's enlightenment was precluded by years of such severe ascetic practices that his body became debilitated. Then, one morning after bathing in the river, he was so weakened he could not get back to shore and nearly drowned. Fortunately, a passing woman pulled him out of the water and gave him some badly needed food. Following this incident, he realised that asceticism brought about illness and enfeeblement instead of leading him to the goal he sought. As a result, he gave up all ascetic practices and began a period of reflection and self-examination, trusting that his own intelligence would enable him to find the higher consciousness he sought. In time, he achieved his enlightenment and from it came the components of the Eightfold Path: Right View, Right Thought, Right Speech, Right Behaviour, Right Livelihood, Right Effort, Right Mindfulness and Right Concentration. For countless generations, these eight paths have taught millions the importance of applying creativity and intelligence on the path to enlightenment.

The colour of the Strength card is yellow, its herb is cayenne and its musical note is E. The Hebrew name for Strength is *Teth*, meaning 'serpent'. Both the Hebrew letter and the figure eight over the Woman's head resemble a serpent devouring its tail. In Western exoteric religion, the snake is equated with Satan. Yet, in both Eastern and Western esoteric circles, it is recognised to mean not only the Redeemer and transformation, but the awakening of the spiritual nature or life force (*La Force*) within. This energy is known as *Ki* or *Chi* by the Japanese and Chinese respectively, *Kundalini* by Hindus and Buddhists, *n/um* by the people of the Kalahari Desert in south-western Africa, *Shekinah* – the Glory of the Most High on Earth – by the Qabalists, the Holy Spirit by Christian mystics and the Force by New Agers. In addition, the Quakers quake with it, the

Shakers shake with it and the Pentacostals voice it, indicating its power. When the spiritual energy is aroused, you consciously commence your journey back to Paradise, to your own God/dess Self. Rising from its resting place at the base of the spine, it slowly inches its way through the body's spiritual centres (*Chakras*) until it reaches the brain. This process is accompanied by increased personal and transpersonal power and awareness. Now, exactly how does this transformation occur?

In the Eastern traditions, the process originates from the 'Guru's Grace', or initiation rites, wherein there is an actual transfer of energy from teacher to pupil via touch, as well as through ancient rituals, practices, tests and trials that purify the student.

In Western metaphysics, the Guru of Life stirs the Holy Spirit into action. The same end is achieved by way of the individual's wilful, loving and sometimes painful interactions with the guru of daily living, depicted in the Strength card as the Lion. It is right understanding coupled with the right use of the Rules and Tools of the Game of Life in the right time and place that bring about transformation and liberation. As one student wisely stated, 'It is doing today what feels good tomorrow.' Please note that this does not mean a human teacher cannot play a part in your growth here in the West. It merely suggests that the Western culture and lifestyle often give way to a different type of process.

Strength is associated with the astrological sign Leo. A fixed (stable, non-volatile) Fire sign, Leo rules the heart and spinal cord. The Leonine personality says: I love, forgive, risk, control, play, perform, master and empathise. I'm protective, intense, in charge, generous, warm, emotional, lazy, powerful, creative, proud, courageous (lion-hearted) and helpful. Many a Leo's life lessons are aimed at discovering how to use their power wisely and how to open their hearts to themselves and others in well-balanced proportions; learning to differentiate between times when opening their heart is a truly loving and generous act, and when it is an overextension, a call for excessive validation or power play. In other words, distinguishing between the Self-centred versus the self-centred perspective. Evolving Leos might want to cultivate their ability to check their pride, the desire to be the centre of attention and the need for recognition, since these traits may interfere with their counter-need for self-acknowledgement, self-love and self-discipline.

In the Qabalah, the Strength card is known as the Intelligence of the Secret of All Spiritual Activities. Qabalists tell us there are no secrets because nothing is kept hidden from those who desire to 'know'. This Intelligence is the courageous application of what you know – your spiritual tools and knowledge – to what life presents you with. Putting these concepts to work in everyday living is the secret of both worldly success and inner tranquillity. Finally, this Intelligence relates the great secret that all behaviour and activities are spiritual in nature and origin.

### Gateway of Life: Adolescence

The Charioteer has prepared you for the next phase of maturation: the testing and further development of your tools, skills and perceptions by way of ongoing interactions with the sometimes fierce yet ultimately loving guru of daily living. At first, meetings with the world at large may be like encountering a wild beast (yes, it can be a jungle out there!). When conditions are adverse or fail to work out as planned, a person in the adolescent stage may decide that the world is the enemy, and react with anger, fear, depression, vengefulness and inflexibility. Essential to the journey of life, however, is meeting its Lions. As an adolescent, your task is learning to tame them, to experience the Lions of life as the challenges and opportunities they are. This type of approach encourages and allows such interactions to strengthen and mature you into adulthood. Essentially, the Strength card addresses the necessity for self-confrontation; growth comes from wilfully and lovingly taking yourself in hand.

As mentioned earlier, the Strength card had been previously named *La Force*. Such a method bullies and dominates, but does not tame (a hint at dealing with adolescent behaviour). At this stage of development, you start learning that you can tame a Lion only by approaching it with sense and sensitivity.

Experiencing the Strength card at the Four Gateways of Life may give way to certain situations. CHILDHOOD: Without thinking, you instinctively dive into a swimming pool to rescue a drowning friend, although you can barely swim; ADOLESCENCE: In the midst of a more experienced group of applicants, an enthusiastic novice applies for a managerial position in a large corporation and gets hired because of his eagerness and bravado; ADULTHOOD: Realising that a co-worker is aiming to intimidate you, you confront her and handle the situation with the Rules and Tools rather than running from it; WISDOM: Having mastery over her alcoholism, a woman now helps others with this problem.

**Divinatory Questions for Strength**

*Upright:* What are you subduing with love/reason, sense/sensitivity? What challenges are being presented that you are meeting bravely? Where do you need to hold your ground and be strong, yet loving? Where might fear be healthy? What pleasures are you learning to live happily without? In what way are you being called upon to turn the knowledge – teachings and philosophies – into actions? Where is love motivating a change in your own or another's behaviour? What situation might you cease forcing? Have you learned that it sometimes takes a strong person to show weaknesses? Do you need to make yourself or another purr? What should you be feeling proud of? What person or idea have you been warming up to? What new-found strengths are blossoming? Whom or what have you forgiven? What are you doing in moderation rather than to excess? What thoughts, desires or passions have you been expressing constructively?

*Reversed:* Where have you been forceful or been forcing 'The Force'? Who or what has forced you? How have you bullied yourself or another by not applying sense and sensitivity? What personal weaknesses are troubling you or another? Are your passions running you more than usual? What substance, emotion, etc., are you excessively dependent upon? What undesirable personality trait have you finally accepted having? What are you keeping the lid on that you know in your heart needs to be expressed? Where would a more moderate attitude be useful? What compulsive or addictive behaviour is overwhelming you? Why has your heart been closed – unsympathetic or unforgiving? Is it possible that your strength can be a weakness? Is your need for recognition excessive? In what situation has fear proved detrimental? What need is your pride stopping you from attending to? Whom have you tried to manipulate through unsolicited help and generosity?

**Personal Experience**

Aleister Crowley renamed the Strength card Lust, saying of it, 'Be strong, O man! Lust, enjoy all things of sense and rapture: fear not that any God shall deny thee for this.'[1] Insightful advice, yet Crowley lived his credo to a self-destructive end. Appreciating the wisdom of his words, but not his actions, I adapted this statement to mean that

---

1 The Master Therion, Aleister Crowley, *The Book of Thoth*, Samuel Wieser, York Beach, ME: 1974, p. 92.

it's okay for me to enjoy my pleasures because I am a physical being and my senses are both God/dess given and a means through which to experience the divine. Yet it also reminds me that I need to be in command of my sensual satisfactions instead of them being in command of me. Subsequently, the Lion in Strength represents not only my sensual pleasures, but the wide range of challenges presented by daily living: adverse or stressful circumstances, overwhelming emotional reactions, an un-controllable passion, addictive behaviour or habits, etc. The incident that follows illustrates one of my many encounters with the Lion.

I love chocolate, but became fearful of my passion, since eating too much results in allergic reactions, a sugar hangover and terrible constipation. Over the course of time, my desire became an exceedingly powerful Lion, because after even the merest nibble, I could not prevent myself from going on a binge. I intermittently fought off my craving, but found that it only roared louder and sometimes pounced on me when my guard was down.

This occurred most memorably when I was attending a Christmas party where, after a couple of relaxing glasses of wine punch, I pigged out on chocolate divinity fudge (and I mean *pigged out*). As I lay in bed the next morning, overwhelmed by a sugar hangover, I reflected on how I had managed to succumb. I remembered walking into the party and, as the smell of chocolate wafted across the room, resolving not to eat so much as a morsel. I carefully sat out of sniffing distance and enjoyed some delicious *sangria* instead. Despite this, the chocolate won out once the wine had relaxed my guard.

Feeling weary and sick to my stomach, I turned to the Tarot for guidance. As I sorted through the cards while sipping warm lemon water, the Strength card hit home. I carefully contemplated it for the next few hours and finally came to acknowledge that my desire for chocolate, like the Lion, is a part of me and that I probably would always have this, or some other, passion to deal with. I saw how the Woman's gentle yet firm relationship with the Lion could help me tame my chocolate Lion. The key to the situation was in copying her behaviour.

I continue to eat chocolate, but in a new way. I grant myself permission to have small bits of it, whereas in the past it had been a definite no-no. Once it's in my mouth, I savour it, rather than quickly stuffing down several pieces in rapid succession because 'I'm not allowed to have it'. By behaving like the Woman in the Strength card, I have courageously taken charge of my Lion and no longer fear my appetite. It's worked so well that I'm slowly taking this strategy into other areas, such as taming my fiery lioness temper. I have learned that by allowing my Lions to exist, and accepting them as part of myself, I can lovingly restrict them so as not to injure myself or others.

When confronting other Lions or challenges, the Strength card has also shown me how to recognise my options. I may act in several ways: I may become immobilised; I may delay acting until another, more suitable time (sometimes this is avoidance behaviour for me, while at other times it is what is needed); I may feel so anxious, fearful and insecure that I flee; I may also take out my verbal weapons and engage in a no-win, all-out contest of wills; or if necessary, I can go off and roar (vent) for a while to let off steam and then, at the right time, approach the Lion with sense and sensitivity – love, reason, compassion and a willingness to understand. Through this analysis, I taught myself that when I must come to grips with a potentially difficult person or situation, I can imagine them (or it) as the Lion, take a few deep breaths and think about being the Woman in Strength. This results in my recalling my options and becoming able to take charge of the challenge at hand more effectively. The Lion has often symbolised my ex-husband, with whom I need to have a functional relationship because of our son, yet fear interacting with because of our stormy past history. Through Strength, I have learned to behave in a friendly but businesslike manner. Imitating the Woman in the Strength card has helped me calm many frightening and potentially disturbing Lions, as well as strengthen my own character and self-reliance.

## Student Experiences

❖   Don came to class with these thoughts and feelings: 'I've always been such a "good boy", doing what I "should" and what others have expected of me. Well, I see from the Strength card that it's time to be a little wild. I feel it's an important part of being human. I feel as if I've suppressed my passion for life, that I've been very repressed, especially emotionally. Yes, I'm opening my Lion's mouth and expressing in words and acts things I've held in check for so long – too long. I feel I'm becoming a more balanced person, and that makes me happy. I've put the Strength card up on my clothes-closet door (you should see what I've been wearing to work) to remind me of this understanding and how important it is to have a little fun each day.

'As a kid I loved playing jokes on people, but I had to stop when I mistakenly did it inappropriately a couple of times – when I acted like a kid. So I've decided to let my joker side out. I'm using this affirmation along with it: "Laugh and let the Lion roar!" '

*I reminded Don that astrologers relate the aspect of our personality that wants to perform, play a part, be an actor or actress, to the sign of Leo. 'Judging from what you disclosed about yourself, it certainly seems as if it's time for you to be in the limelight a bit. I would say that you are venturing out of the unhealthy "good little boy" into the healthy "playful adolescent" stage of life, a necessary requirement for the Gateways that follow.'*

❖  A few weeks after working with the Strength card, Carin returned to class with this hair-raising story: 'I was roughly awakened in the middle of the night last weekend by a man kneeling next to my bed holding a large hunting knife. He had entered the house through an open window. Waving the blade at me, he told me in no uncertain terms that he was going to rape me, and if I screamed or protested in any way, he'd slit my throat. I was terrified, but couldn't allow my emotions to get the better of me the way they usually do. So I held back my own inner Lion, my emotions, and began talking to him. It was incredibly difficult, but I took a chance and saw him as the Lion in the Strength card who needed taming. I'm not even sure where the idea came from, probably from me holding back my own Lion, my fear and panic. It was a miracle. We talked for a couple of hours about his loneliness. I appealed to him with reason and compassion and convinced him not to hurt me, but to leave instead. I am a Leo and tend to have an overly emotional personality. This situation taught me more about positively controlling my often overwhelming feelings than any other in my life thus far. It showed me who I can be, my potential. I feel that studying the Strength card definitely prepared me for this incident.'

*What a dangerous situation! Carin is one lucky woman. Taming a wild animal or person of this type who is more beast than human is extremely touchy. And as I said before, it requires much good sense and sensitivity. 'You were blessed that he didn't turn on you,' I told her. 'Situations like this have the potential of rendering us impotent. You, however, took a chance and enacted yet another Leonine trait, the ability to improvise. You took your power and made instant decisions, and because you didn't succumb to either your own Lion or the intruder's, you exhibited admirable self-control and courage. You were extremely fortunate to be able to accomplish what you did.'*

❖ 'The Strength card has shown me about civilisation's next step in dealing with social and political conflicts,' offered peace-activist Lois, after her experiences at the protest against the opening of the Diablo Canyon Nuclear Power Plant. 'Non-violent protest was first evident in Thoreau's civil disobedience, developed by Gandhi's passive resistance movement in India in the 1940s, then in the "sit-ins" in the southern US during the early '60s, gaining increased support with the anti-war movement of the late '60s and '70s, and now gaining worldwide attention, support and recognition with the anti-nuclear campaigns today. I believe more and more people are becoming fearless enough to face the Lions of conflict without violence, but with true Strength – love and reason. This hopeful insight came to me while sitting with many others outside the gates of the power plant in San Luis Obispo.'

*'What an inspirational thought,' I said to Lois. 'You're correct in that the dictionary defines strength as the power of resisting force. Thus, genuine strength is not dominance by force, but the ability to be attuned to the Universal Life Force and work with it towards a higher purpose. The oriental martial arts work on this principle. For practitioners, it's a matter of availing themselves of the life force, the Chi or Ki, that we have been talking about in relation to the Strength card. The martial-arts student practises working with that force, rather than against it. Like the woman in the Strength card, you are turning your philosophy into actions!'*

❖ 'I did Yoga exercises for many years, but when I began working full time again, I stopped,' began Joanne, a busy accountant. 'After talking about the *Kundalini* energy in relation to the Strength card, I started thinking about how I've been neglecting my body, how I've been sitting slumped over my desk and how closed down my Heart Centre is because of it. So I'm relying on the Strength card to remind me to stay more erect and open. I've even begun doing a few Yoga postures before going to work in the morning. The first few days were a painful reminder of how off track I've been. Right now, I still feel a little stiff and sore, but I'm disciplining myself to keep at it. I want to keep going along with the spiralling *Kundalini* energy.'

*The class and I then discussed how Yoga has a way of opening the mind and body to the life force. There are seven basic types of Yoga, each of which awakens the* Kundalini *or Holy Spirit. However, the* Kundalini *doesn't actually require special practices to become awakened; it wakes of its own accord at the right time. Yet, once it's been roused, whether through Yoga practice or life experience, you become able to sense when you are in or out of tune with it. Practices such as Yoga are wonderful ways to keep the fire burning. But I must caution you. Many people are in such a hurry to have 'Kundalini experiences' that they hurt themselves by doing what they are not prepared for just to get that special 'jolt'. They force The Force, something which often causes damage in the long run.*

❖ 'There's been so much transition going on in my life for weeks now, I feel like I'm being pulled in many directions all at once,' shared Mary, a working woman, mate and parent. 'Some moments, I almost feel panicky that I can't possibly keep up with all that's happening around me: work, my three kids growing up and behaving crazily, my friendships, my mate, the housework and keeping my body in shape. Just listing all of it makes me nervous. Now my mother is thinking of moving into town to be closer to me and the children – as if I don't have enough to cope with already!

'But working with the Strength card is helping me see that I have to be in control of the Lion. And I want that! I have the power to upset myself and calm myself down. I ask myself, "Who's in charge here?" With that, I take command. I become the Woman taming the Lion, which in this case is my own stressed-out life, instead of being dragged around by him. I feel that the process is very much like petting my cat when he's out of sorts. I get him to let go and relax and pretty soon he's purring.'

*I told Mary, 'It sounds like your question, "Who's in charge here?" is working as both a command and an affirmation to take charge of yourself. For the most part, we've been trained to be hard on ourselves, to demand that we do more and more. It isn't easy to treat ourselves gently without feeling somewhat self-indulgent. As I've mentioned before, a certain amount of Self-indulgence is both necessary and healthy. Again, the key is moderation, one of the central concepts expressed in the Strength card.'*

❖ In the midst of ceasing her heavy smoking habit, Ruth is using the Strength card to inspire her efforts. 'I've been calling on Strength a lot while quitting cigarettes. Unlike you with your chocolate, I can't seem to moderate myself. It's all or nothing for me. Right now, I feel like a nonsmoker in a smoker's body. My hunger for nicotine is intense. And with a lot of personal pressures in my life lately, I've wanted to smoke almost constantly. Yet I know I really and truly don't want to give in, that is, my Higher Self doesn't. I carry the Strength card in my handbag, and when I want to pull out a cigarette, I look at the card instead. And when that isn't convenient, I think about it. I know I have the resources to be the Woman in the card. I also believe I need to be very kind to myself in other ways while I'm undertaking this task. I'm quickly growing from Childhood to Adulthood in being able to use my willpower to master this habit. The part in our homework questions about the steps to take to achieve my goal has made me become creative. I know I need to get as much help as I can to accomplish this.

'So I had a great message the other evening. I'm reading about other people who've quit and I think I'll buy some smoker's chewing gum in the morning. My doctor prescribed it and now I think I can use its help. I'm also wearing all this yellow to keep me on track. I used to associate yellow with being a coward, but I now know it as the colour of the will. Have you ever seen socks like these? (She pointed to her yellow and black bumblebee striped socks.) And the figure eight has become a symbol of balancing infinite strength with finite strength, which is what I'm doing. I find myself doodling eights when I feel nervous, or want to smoke. Somehow, it helps.'

*I congratulated Ruth. 'What a job you're doing! It takes creativity, love and backbone to stand up and do what you need to do for yourself, referring to Leo's characteristics, as Leo rules both the heart and spine. I suggest you might also muster your strength to join a nonsmokers' support group as another way of getting additional strength during this challenging time. This would be another way to integrate the card's teaching of being strong enough to admit your weaknesses.'*

## Suggestions for Application and Integration of Strength

Now is the time to become stronger. The exercises below will enable you to experience life as your guru more fully. They will also help you become more attuned to your inner strength, build pride in your accomplishments, be more generous with yourself and others and more playful, become strong enough to admit your weaknesses as well as lovingly and sensibly interact with the immature or unevolved parts of yourself and others.

1  Draw or colour your own version of the Strength card with yourself as the Woman and/or the Lion if you are working on therapeutically articulating or enacting suppressed or repressed aspects of your personality or feelings. You might also want to

assign the Lion to an aspect of your personality you are expressing or mastering, such as anger, a love, or substance addiction.

2   Set the card in a visible place as a reminder to your conscious and subconscious minds to use and absorb its teachings to use love and reason, be courageous when facing a challenging situation or individual, refrain from overextending yourself, balance knowledge with actions and express your Lion (a strong emotion) constructively.

3   Dream on Strength.

4   Play the note E on a musical instrument. Intone IAO or hum along with the music, concentrating as fully as possible on the image of Strength as you do. Now meditate on the card for a few minutes. While meditating, ask that Strength's teachings guide you through a particular situation, such as needing the confidence or self-reliance to confront certain uncomfortable circumstances, to decide whether it is for your highest good to let go and roar, or to lovingly, creatively and sensibly harness a compulsive behaviour. Or if you are faced with a worrisome situation, event or problem, imagine how either the Woman or the Lion would handle it. If it seems workable, do it. I was aware of Strength when? Before/during/after . . .

5   Go out into the world and be the Woman in Strength, and where appropriate gentle or tame some beast. Or let your Lion's mouth open to judiciously express something that withholding has proved detrimental to your growth and development. I enacted Strength and this is what happened . . .

6   The Rerun. After having an experience and realising in retrospect how Strength's teachings might have inspired you to create new options, be empathetic, be more or less prideful, or better able to resist a harmful force. etc., mentally relive the situation, *including* your insight. This will help the behaviour become more automatic the next time. If possible, actually rerun the situation in real life with your new attitude or behaviour.

7   Next time you feel the need to release frustration, anger or tension, do so. Try this: Go to the mirror and spend a few seconds looking at yourself while growling and roaring like a lion. Notice how you feel afterwards.

Please note: When expressing feelings that have previously

been held in check – through conscious suppression or un-conscious repression – it is essential that your expression be used as a positive force for change, not one that is aimed at hurting or destroying others.

8 Ask yourself the following questions:

'Where do I need to turn my philosophy into actions?' 'What are my options in dealing with a particularly challenging situation/person?' 'In what area of my life could being more playful be of value to myself and others?' 'Where am I struggling to remain in control?' 'Where have I gained loving control? In what situation(s) might I benefit from giving up control?' 'What aspect of my personality needs to be expressed or tamed?' 'What habit do I desire to master?' 'What part of my personality is being strengthened through a challenge by the guru of daily living?' 'Where is pride a help?' 'Where is pride detrimental?' 'How has my spiritual energy been awakening?' 'Where is courage or generosity required?' 'Would someone call the Society for the Prevention of Cruelty to Animals on me for mistreating my inner lion?' 'In what situation would it be best for me to remain out of/in the limelight?' 'What lion has become less imposing?'

'What Gateway of Life am I in or developing through in the above?' Indicate: Childhood, Adolescence, Adulthood or Wisdom. Why?

'What do I need to do in order to develop the above further?' I need to . . .

'What step(s) do I want to take towards this goal and how can the Strength card guide me?'

9 Use a personal statement regarding the presence of Strength in your life at this time: 'My actions speak as loudly as my words.' 'Daily life is my teacher.' 'I take pleasure in being in charge of my pleasures.' 'I courageously face the challenges of life.' My personal statement is . . .

10 Inspirational words and quotes:

'May the Force be with you.'                    Ben Kenobi, *Star Wars*

'Enjoyment is essential to happiness; decadence is not.'

'Passion and compassion are tempered by reason.'

'Do today what will feel good tomorrow.'

'My strength is made perfect in weakness.'

II CORINTHIANS 12:9

11 What symbols stand out in the card? What do they say to you? How might they be useful in daily living? Bring the symbol(s) into your life in some way so as to integrate the card's teachings. The chain of red roses reminds me that whenever my inner lion tries to take over my life inappropriately, I can restrain him or her by lovingly tugging on the chain.

12 Wear and surround yourself with Strength's colour, yellow, to remind you to integrate the card's teachings when needed, such as in getting your courage up, wanting to be more playful, feeling more freedom to express yourself, or as a reminder to use your tools in a potentially adverse situation. Notice how you are affected.

13 Strength's astrological correspondence is Leo, governing traits such as generosity, pride, playfulness, creativity, leadership, courage, self-control and empathy. Select a trait from those listed that is weak and use the Strength card to remind you to play at fortifying it. Note what happens: your thoughts and feelings and the outcome.

14 Remember that Strength's Hebrew name, *Teth*, means 'snake'. How can this remind you of the card's meaning or help in your life process? For instance, knowing that the guru of daily living stirs the serpent of spirituality and transformation to life within me gives me the strength to engage my circumstances with more hope, understanding and awareness.

15 Try a few drops of frankincense associated with Strength as a reminder to integrate the card's teachings.

16 Have a cup of tea sprinkled with, or cook with, the herb cayenne pepper. Sit quietly as you eat or drink and feel your body warming with its energies. Cayenne aids digestion, relieves internal inflammations and fevers, increases circulation (when someone has 'cold feet', he is said to be weak or cowardly rather than strong), tones the heart and blood vessels. When cayenne is added to other herbs, it increases their potency. Consider the herb's strong flavour, yet soothing abilities, and the like qualities of the Strength card.

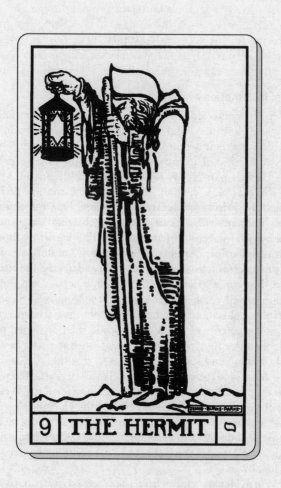

9 THE HERMIT

# The Hermit

## General Information and Symbolism

The Hermit[1] stands alone on a mountaintop, shining his lantern so that those below may find their way to where he lovingly and patiently awaits their ascent. Because the lantern is held in his right or conscious hand, it intimates that it is kindled by his deliberate efforts. He has plotted his own way up the mountain. Qabalists regard the Hermit's light to be a symbolic extension of his own inner light or Wisdom, *Chokmah*, the second *Sephirah* on the Tree of Life. The lantern is illuminated by a blazing six-pointed star formed by two interconnected triangles. This shows that God/dess reaches down to us, the descending triangle, as does the Hermit, while we reach up to our Higher Self and truth, the ascending triangle. The star also suggests the blending of the male and female principles of self-consciousness and subconsciousness respectively. In metaphysical symbolism, the upward pointing triangle indicates the mental elements of fire and air, while the downward pointing triangle signifies the emotional elements of water and earth. This symbol of union and synthesis informs us that thinking and feeling must be combined to achieve wisdom. It also suggests that when the Hermit is embodied in human form, that individual is a Wiseone or master of worldly life. When you relate to the Hermit as a particular spiritual teacher, it is essential to recognise that he was at some earlier point aided to the mountain-top by the teachings of truth, the Rules and Tools of the Game of Life, or another helper standing where he now is.

The Word 'Hermit' comes from the Greek, *eremites*, meaning 'one of the desert', and is possibly derived from the contemplative journeys Moses and Jesus took into the desert. It seems that most

---

1 Although the Hermit is depicted as male, a hermit may be of either sex.

serious seekers must periodically journey to solitary places to aid their quest for wisdom, insight and inspiration. In all cultures and religious groups throughout time, there have been Wiseones who have chosen to withdraw from the outer world into the solitude of the inner one. Note: Genuine Wiseones or Hermits have graduated from the school of life and may now assist others, by shining their light of wisdom, in doing likewise. They are not dropouts. Nor are they fleeing from life's responsibilities. Having completed their worldly business, such persons have earned their retirement. This is stated by the Hermit's being clothed in a grey robe, the colour of wisdom, and being numbered 9, the final single digit in our numbering system, indicating achievement, realisation, perfection and accomplishment. If you look at the Hermit carefully, you can see how his body actually takes on the configuration of the number nine. This completion is also noted by the fact that he holds his staff in his left or subconscious hand, substantiating his assimilation process further. In addition, this is exemplified on the Tree of Life, where the ninth *Sephirah*, Foundation or *Yesod*, deals with the assimilation of knowledge into one's automatic consciousness. To conclude, the number nine reminds us that our experiences may serve as a support to both ourselves and others.

The Hermit is associated with the colour yellow-green, the herb liquorice and the musical note F. The Hermit's Hebrew name, *Yod*, means 'an open, creative or helping hand'. This brings to mind ideas of giving, receiving and reciprocal action (remember, when you are receptive, you give another the opportunity to show affection and thoughtfulness). Notice how the Hermit's cap is shaped like the letter to remind us that he directs his mental attention to the highest. Our hands and bodies serve our mind and heart, but, in time, our hands, mind and heart learn to consciously serve the spirit. Therefore, everything we do in life can be looked upon as service to the Higher Self. Recalling this in the midst of daily living definitely makes its sameness more palatable. Buddhists refer to this attitude as 'The One Taste'; yogis relate it as *Guru Seva*, service to the highest teacher; and Western mysticism identifies this concept as the dedication of one's actions and the fruits thereof to God/dess, Higher Self and the good of humanity.

*Yod* is the letter in the Hebrew alphabet from which all others are derived, and as such, states that all life originates from the same basic Source or substance. Because the Hermit is wise, objective and patient, he views life from the mountain-top, the eternal rather than temporal viewpoint. In regard to ordinary human behaviour, this pertains to the fact that at the right time we will all turn to and seek the light in order to make our ascent to higher consciousness. He is confident that, although our personalities, lifestyles and particular journeys through life vary, we are all eventually headed for the same place, up to the mountain-top to Self-realisation and union with God/dess, the Source of life.

The Hermit's elevated position also symbolises that we have the opportunity to look to the light and attune ourselves to the greater meaning in problematic situations. Adopting this attitude, we perform not only service to our Self, but the added service of setting living examples – being Light Sharers, for others to follow. Furthermore, such an attitude serves to increase the critical mass necessary for group transformation. However, this type of behaviour can make you a Hermit or engender isolation, because you will no longer be a part of the larger group, which is bogged down by excessive emotion and negativism. Although the Hermit stands alone, he is not lonely. The evolved Hermit has withdrawn from the world figuratively, not literally. He participates in the world, but is not subjugated by it. The Hermit is more singular because he has withdrawn from the ordinary attitudes and beliefs shared by the mass mind in the valley below. He is not lonely because he receives the satisfaction of living discerningly and joins the company of others who are doing likewise.

The Hermit is associated with the mutable (combines the qualities of cardinal energies with fixed energies; adaptable and changeable energy that can either move or stand still.) Earth sign, Virgo. Virgo governs the small intestine and pancreas, which break down, assimilate and separate waste products from nutrients in order to nourish the body. This process illustrates the analytical, dissecting and utilitarian aspects of the Virgo nature. The Virgo personality says: I utilise, serve, harvest, dissect, worry and sympathise. I'm selective, modest, serious, industrious, health-conscious, humane and adept at details. With these traits arises the tendency to be overly analytical, preoccupied with trivia, and the inclination to be perfectionistic and set unattainable standards for both self and others. In Virgos' industrious dedication to serve, there is sometimes the danger of becoming so enmeshed in a cause or ideal that they fail to enjoy their accomplishments, as well as life in general. One of their lessons is to acknowledge the greater order of life – the perfect order of the universe – to free themselves from worry, excessive sympathy and over-attachment to the fruits of their labours. The developed Virgo tends towards utilitarianism, the philosophical doctrine that considers that all moral, social or political action should be directed towards achieving the greatest good for the greatest number of people.

As I mentioned previously, a teacher may come in many different packages. With the Hierophant, I discussed the truth coming through a highly evolved person or guide such as the Hermit, in addition to your own inner teacher or intuition. I did not mention, however, the teachings of truth in other forms, which I have also come to identify with the Hermit card. Since many people think of the Hermit solely in terms of a highly evolved individual who shines the light of wisdom, this often causes the card to be indistinguishable from the Hierophant. Unlike the Eastern spiritual traditions wherein one customarily has a single guru for his/her entire life, the Western lifestyle offers teachers in myriad forms. The Western aspirant may have many different teachers along the path. Consequently, I identify the Hermit with the teachings of truth, the Rules and Tools from the previous cards, as well as other resources or sources of inspiration we may reach out to, or which reach out to us (offer a helping hand) when we are in need.

These teachings or helpers can be embodied in any and all of the following spiritual, mental or physical disciplines: meditation; the various Yogas; Tai Chi; karate; jogging or swimming; Bible study and inspirational reading material and tapes; the Tarot cards; I Ching and the Runes; and many others. I have found the teachings presented in experiences such as Gestalt, Reichean or Jungian therapy; Twelve-Step and other types of recovery programmes; dreams; the use of a consciousness-expanding drug under expert supervision; fasting, a change of diet or cleansing colonic; Holy Communion; automatic writing; out-of-body experiences; communication with the dead or other types of psychic awareness; and traumatic or near-death situations, accidents or illnesses. Of course, guidance and inspiration may also come by way of someone in the helping professions, such as a physician, therapist, clairvoyant, astrologer, etc. Finally, teachings might also become evident through a mentor, friend or loved one who has mastered what you are presently struggling with and who can share his insights. It's important to remember that we are *all* vehicles for the teachings and serve both knowingly and unknowingly as aid and inspiration for one another (we shine our light for others to see by).

The message is simple: the Hermit is a beacon of light in the darkness, and if on the road of daily living you run out of gas, get lost, become despondent, or your chariot's tyres go flat, you may seek out the Hermit in whatever form needed to help you regroup, fix what needs fixing and get back on your path again. Qabalists assign the function of Coition[2] – union with your inner or Higher Self, by getting in touch with the Greater Reality – to the Hermit. Seeking the light of support, guidance and inspiration from the Hermit's lantern via the various resources available – disciplines, rituals, practices, tools, groups and teachers – helps you navigate through life and up to the mountain-top whereupon you will at some time stand side by side with the Hermit. In view of this concept, the Tarot for the Aquarian Age has aptly named the Hermit card the Seeker.

In the Qabalah, the Hermit is known as the Intelligence of Will. The power or will to get in touch with your Higher Self or higher truth is at your service if you are determined to access it – will it. Through deliberate and diligent control over your thoughts and actions you may will to reach out (or in) towards this Source.

## Gateway of Life: Adolescence

While travelling the road from Adolescence to Adulthood, you often require guidance and direction, as mishaps are a natural and intrinsic part of the journey and are opportunities for additional maturation. The Hermit offers these in the form of a Wiseone or consciousness-expanding tool or teachings (the Rules and Tools of the Game of Life), any or all of which may be either consciously sought after or magically stumbled upon. In other words, ancient wisdom states that a teacher and teachings appear when the student is ready for them. Their purpose is to remind troubled or unconscious travellers that they need help, as well as to turn to their resources to learn what must be done in order to find their way to a more fulfilling life. Yet in early adolescence, you are often unable or reticent to acknowledge your inadequacies, and when confronted tend to react with denial, and shy, angry, fearful or 'smart' attitudes and behaviours. Also characteristic of this stage of growth is the

2 The Hebrew letter, *Yod*, is often associated with the male sex organ. Therefore, its projective nature may initiate a state of divine union and ecstasy through a non-physical or spiritual type of insemination as well as via physical contact, i.e. Tantric practices. Perhaps this is the true meaning of immaculate conception.

emergence of and fight for independence, usually manifesting as the desire to be 'left alone'.

Experiencing the Hermit at the Four Gateways of Life, you may display certain attitudes. CHILDHOOD: You may be 30 years old, intelligent and able-bodied, yet remain dependent on others for financial assistance because you do not want to 'work your way up' the corporate ladder; ADOLESCENCE: You intermittently enjoy and fearfully avoid being independent; ADULTHOOD: Finding herself at an impasse in her career, a woman turns to a mentor, trade magazine, career counsellor, Tarot cards and particular meditations for counsel and guidance; WISDOM: You 'know' when it is appropriate to serve others by not helping them.

## Divinatory Questions for the Hermit

*Upright:* How has your Self been guiding you? What help or services are you offering or receiving? What level of attainment are you reaching for? In what area of your life have you ceased denying that you need help? Might it be necessary for you to be alone in order to seek out a new direction? How might you go into your community and shine your light – share your knowledge and wisdom? What benefits would a period of retreat give you? How are you reaching out for the support you need? What group or ideology are you helping along, or is shining the light for you? What tools are at your disposal? What would you like others to be receptive to? How are your experiences upholding your present position? What discipline could be keeping you on track? Who or what is 'there' for you? How has time alone been serving you or another near and dear to you? How might your ability to deal with details be of service to others? Have you released yourself from the mass mind, in the valley below, to join those on the mountain-top?

*Reversed:* Why have you felt unable to be alone with yourself? Could you be isolating yourself? What facts or data have you failed to gather? Why won't you give others the opportunity to support you? Have you been reluctant to share your skills and abilities with others? Whom or what might you need to stop guiding? Are you on the verge of reaching out to others for help, friendship, companionship or love? In what situation might support actually be non-supportive? Have you been forcing guidance upon another without being asked? Why are you afraid to ask for help when you need it? What aspects of your life-relationships, finances, career, health are worrying you? What problem(s) are you hiding by withdrawing? What input have you been lacking? Are you feeling bad because your offer of support/assistance has been rejected? Could you be losing perspective in evaluating a particular situation or relationship alone? Who might you be serving in order to validate yourself, rather than because of a genuine need on the part of that person? Why might the attainment of a higher level of awareness or position in life make you fearful?

## Personal Experience

Through my years of spiritual and metaphysical study and questing, I have gained the insight that a teacher and teachings may come in many different packages. The teachings are any tool, person, or experience which acts as a 'Cosmic Alarm Clock' to awaken you to right understanding and right action; to help you better understand your circumstances and how to effectively cope with them. The following is an account of a life-threatening situation that was not only a purveyor of the teachings of truth, but deepened my understanding of the Hermit card more than any other experience.

I was a bit over four years old and felt as if my parents did not love or understand me. Believing that I somehow did not belong with them, and as a way of escaping my pain and discomfort, I spent hours in psychic reverie fantasising about the family I *really* belonged to.

Then, one hot, sticky, New York City summer morning, my family and I drove the many miles to the seashore. My father carried me out into the beautiful ocean (I love the water) to play in the cooling waves, and after a happy time of bobbing over them hand in hand, we headed back to shore. Suddenly, an unusually large wave came up behind us, hit my father, and accidentally catapulted me from his arms into the pounding surf. While swirling around under the water (I can still see it as I write these lines), my life flashed before me as if it were a movie. In addition, my mind became strangely adult. In a few short moments I was 'told' I was here (in my family) to learn from my parents, and that my parents had the job of learning from me as well. Also, I realised that we are different from one another, but this is where our learning is to come from. I was 'shown' my connections to them from past lives and could see clearly why we were now all together. Finally, I was 'informed' that it was not my time to die, that I had 'work' to do, and found myself instantaneously swept up on to the beach.

It was impossible to share my experience, because I returned to my four year-old mentality and lacked the words and reference points to express what had happened. Yet it has lived inside me as a constant reminder of the existence of a Greater Reality since that summer day so many years ago. As an adult, my spiritual and metaphysical studies, especially those on reincarnation and the Hermit card, have helped me fit the puzzle pieces into place. I have finally been able to integrate and understand that what happened was a vehicle for the teachings of truth that somehow got me through my difficult childhood – a small ray of hope from the Hermit's lantern. The Hermit card serves as my enduring reminder to look for the wisdom in everyday experiences and people.

## Student Experience

❖  'I acted like the Hermit in my office this past week,' began Lin. 'One of the secretaries I work with has been having an awful time of it for months now. She's finally getting up enough nerve to break up with her abusive husband. He drinks too much and then hits her. You should see her coming in to work with long sleeves to cover her bruises and looking so terribly sad. I could recognise what she's going through because I went through it myself a few years ago. You know the old saying, "It takes one to know one." I asked her out to lunch and she let it all out, tears included. She's taken it for this long because she's scared of being alone and believes her husband has so much potential when he isn't drinking.

'I told her how for years I did the very same thing, and after seriously contemplating suicide, I decided I needed to get out. I also told her about remembering my mom standing for the same treatment from my dad. I think my mom died young because she was so miserable and couldn't find any way out, since my parents didn't believe in counselling or divorce. I made up my mind to break the pattern, and with a lot of hard work and support, I did. I could see that this woman really got something from talking with me. Like the Hermit, I was able to shine some light for her to take a good long look. I could do it because I've been where she is now. I could also let her know that when you have more of yourself, you can be alone, but you don't necessarily have to be lonely. I'm enjoying my life although I don't at present have a mate, and I believe she can do the same.'

*'Being alone without being lonely is an important facet of the Hermit card. All too often we have a hard time learning that being alone can be a joy and, in some instances, a welcome relief. Perhaps this stems from childhood, when many of us were sent to our room to be alone as a form of punishment.*

*It is a blessing that Lin reached out to her co-worker and that this woman allowed herself to be reached. Lin not only acted as the Hermit, but put the symbol of the six-pointed star to work as well.'*

❖ 'Something happened to me just this morning that reminded me of the work we're doing with the Hermit,' remarked Ilene, a hard-working single woman. 'I do a routine of Yoga and meditation for about two hours every day before breakfast, which for me is in the late morning because I work at night. Today, my housemate's lady friend came by with her three small children for a visit. He knew what I was doing in my room and tried to keep the kids fairly quiet, but I heard them running around anyway. After I had finished, I sat down and chatted with the visitor over tea, and I felt an incredible wave of resentment coming from her. She finally got around to telling me, "I can't imagine having all that time in my life to do what you do in there." At first, her words stunned me and I felt as if she were saying I was selfish. I got defensive and reacted and explained how hard I work and how the Yoga and meditation are essential to my survival.

'Then the Hermit suddenly came to mind. I'm sure it was because I was trying to tell her how the Yoga helps me to function better, how it's my tool. The Hermit reminded me that she has her path in life, just as I have mine. I felt him reminding me to step back and look at how I'm living and feel okay about the choices I've selected and the service I'm able to do as a result. Both selectivity and service are Virgo traits. Later, I decided to use the affirmation, "I serve myself in order to serve others", to support and reinforce my lifestyle.'

*'By dropping your defensive attitude, Ilene, you were able to see the service you perform by leading your life as you do,' I told her. 'It takes quite a lot of will (the Hermit's staff) and self-discipline to work hard, as you do, and stay centred. It's good to recognise that you are performing Self-service, rather than being only "self-serving." '*

❖ Dee came to class with this incident about her teenage daughter and the Hermit card: 'My daughter hasn't been honouring her agreements with me and has been forgetting to do her chores around the house. Yet she wants to be treated like an adult. She wants to drive, stay out late with boys, smoke, drink and the like. We've been in a terrible power struggle for months now, and I'm honestly exhausted by it. When we worked on the Hermit and talked about how he could be someone in the helping professions, I got to thinking. I meditated on the situation and it became clear that we needed to get some professional help, pronto! With only the two of us living together, things aren't always clear. Then, after going over the homework questions, "What tool, teacher or teaching might be of help in your work or relationships at this time?" I became even more certain that another person could bring some light into this dark and draining situation. I talked with my daughter about it. I told her I was having a problem living with her and that I wanted it to change. I told her I wanted to visit a therapist with her. Owning up to the problems and not blaming them on her really helped, because she agreed immediately.

'It was a great session. We both got support for our needs. The therapist shed some light on our difficulties and how we might compromise on some issues, while on other issues there could be no compromise, like her obeying her curfew and not drinking and driving. Our relationship is already better for it, and we went only a few days ago. Thanks to the Hermit, I was able to take some action instead of continuing to complain and suffer. I feel like I (and the Hermit) did a great service for us both.'

*'You certainly did. Often we have to experience a whole lot of pain before we reach out and get help,' I told Dee. 'This is the Hermit card in its immature, weakened, or, if you like, reversed form. In other words, it's fine for us to help others, but needing help is different. Sometimes our analysis of a situation is off – we think we should be able to handle everything all by ourselves. That kind of thinking usually stems from our familial and cultural conditioning. Many people had role models who could not show their humanness, and subsequently suppressed or denied having problems. Your experience serves as an excellent example for all of us to follow.'*

## Suggestions for Application and Integration of the Hermit

Now is the time to let your own light shine as well as to turn to the light available to you. The following are resources through which you may become more comfortable with your path through life and feel less isolated, become more open to seeking and offering help when needed, be of greater service to your community and self, worry less and become increasingly aware of and utilise the tools and disciplines at your disposal or start to cultivate new ones.

1    Colour or draw your own version of the Hermit with yourself as the figure.

2   Set the Hermit in a visible place as a reminder to your conscious
    and subconscious minds to use and recall his teachings to offer
    others your services, to be more open in your need for help and
    to feel less isolated in your spiritual quest.

3   Dream on the Hermit.

4   Play the note F on a musical instrument. Intone IAO or hum
    along with the music while you focus your attention as
    completely as possible on the image of the Hermit. Now
    meditate on the card for a few minutes. As you do, imagine the
    light from the Hermit's lantern shining down upon you. Next,
    recall the many tools you have at your disposal. Ask yourself if
    you are using them to the best of your ability. Or if there is a
    new tool you wish to gain access to, consider the service it would
    perform. Finally, contemplate a situation in which you might
    presently use a tool you already have, or apply a new skill or
    discipline. If you are faced with a worrisome situation, event or
    problem, such as deciding which skills or tools will best handle a
    difficult boss, mate, parent; or the need to reconcile yourself to
    the fact that another's path is different from yours; imagine how
    the Hermit would handle it. If it seems feasible, do it. Jot down
    the times when you became aware of the Hermit in your
    interactions. I was aware of the Hermit when? Before/during/
    after . . .

5   Go out into the world and pretend you are the Hermit. For
    example, go somewhere alone, and although you would like to be
    with others or one special person, have the best time possible
    being with yourself. I enacted the Hermit and this is what
    happened . . .

6   The Rerun. After having an experience and realising in
    retrospect how the Hermit's teachings might have made things
    different – enabled you to reach in or out for needed help, be less
    worried, not press help on another unsolicited, be of greater
    service to yourself or others, be more selective, etc. – mentally
    relive the situation, *including* your insight. This will help the
    behaviour become more automatic next time. If possible, actually
    rerun the situation in real life with your new attitude or
    behaviour.

7   Ask yourself the following questions:

'What tool, teacher or teaching might be of aid in my personal or professional lives at this time?' 'In what situation(s) might taking some time off help me gain a different perspective?' 'Where have I aligned myself with higher consciousness above, rather than with the mass mind below?' 'What can be derived from living alone at this time?' 'How am I reaching for the ever available light when I feel engulfed in darkness?' 'How could I derive greater understanding from a problematic situation?' 'How am I seeking needed inspiration?' 'How may I best serve my family, community or country?' 'What skills/abilities am I negating or underestimating?' 'How can I best serve my Higher Self?' 'How am I letting my light shine?' 'Who am I punishing by withdrawing?' 'Why am I feeling lonely?' 'Why do I worry and how could I worry less?' 'In what situation would it be more helpful to temporarily withhold help than to give it?'

'What Gateway of Life am I in or growing through in the above?' Indicate: Childhood, Adolescence, Adulthood or Wisdom. Why?

'What do I need to do in order to develop the above further?' I need to . . .

'What step(s) do I want to take towards this and how can the Hermit serve me?'

8  Use a personal statement regarding the presence of the Hermit in your life at this time, such as: 'I am happy and comfortable being alone with my Self.' 'I share my light with others, as others share their light with me.' 'My Higher Self always stands ready, willing and able to guide me.' My personal statement is . . .

9  Inspirational words and quotes:

'The Lighthouse.'

'The Most High reaches down to us, when we reach up to our Higher Self and Truth.'

'The Light-Sharer.'

'Keeper of the Flame.'

'This little light of mine, I'm gonna let it shine.'
African-American Traditional

'Light is the task when many share the toil.'     Homer, *Iliad*

10 What symbols stand out in the card? What do they say to you? How might they be useful in daily living? Bring the symbol(s) into your life in some way so as to integrate the card's teachings. I refer to an old lantern over our fireplace to remind me to use the tool of meditation to bring me closer to 'the light' and to help return me to my centre when I get off my path.

11 Wear and surround yourself with the Hermit's colour, yellow-green (lime or pale chartreuse), to remind you of the card's teachings when needed, such as telling you to do a physical discipline, read inspirational material, worry less and pray more, feel less alone in life, or pay more attention to important details when undertaking a project. Notice how you are affected.

12 The Hermit's astrological correspondence is Virgo, governing traits such as selectivity, analysis, service, industriousness, the importance of good health, utilitarianism, and facility with details. Is there some area of your life in which the development of these qualities would be of service to you and/or others? If so, use the Hermit to remind you to develop them. This aspect of the Hermit reminds me that cultivating good health helps me to perform better service. Note what happens: your thoughts and feelings and the outcome.

13 Remember that the Hermit's name, *Yod*, means 'an open, creative or helping hand'. How can this remind you of the card's meaning or help in your life process? For instance, the open hand reminds me to reach in to my Higher Self with increasing frequency.

14 Try a few drops of the scent pettigrain associated with the Hermit as a reminder to integrate the card's teaching.

15 Have a cup of tea made with or eat some liquorice. Sit quietly as you drink or eat and consider the herb's properties to reduce the unpleasant taste of tonics and detoxifying herbal formulas without interfering with the beneficial aspects as a thirst-quencher, mild laxative, expectorant, stress reliever, replenisher of the adrenal glands and the like qualities of the Hermit card.

10 WHEEL ᵒˢ FORTUNE ♄

# CHAPTER 14

## The Wheel of Fortune

### General Information and Symbolism

Surrounded by other-worldly creatures, the Wheel of Fortune hangs suspended in space. Journeying through life, you often question whether your adventures and misadventures are pure happenstance or due to destiny's hand. The answer to this lies within the Wheel's symbols. The Roman letters around its circumference spell out the word 'ROTA', meaning 'wheel', and stand for the idea of cycles and evolution; 'TORA', the body of divine knowledge and law found in the ancient Hebrew scriptures, the first five books of the Old Testament; 'ORAT', an oracle, speaker or messenger through which hidden knowledge and divine purposes are revealed; 'TAO', the Way, path or teachings of truth which lead to enlightenment; 'TAR', an abbreviation for Thoth, the Egyptian messenger of the gods and goddesses and advisor to King Osiris; 'ATOR', a shortened version of the Egyptian goddess of nature, Hathor; and, of course, 'TAROT'. Therefore, the Tarot is an oracle, speaker, advisor or messenger from the gods and goddesses or Godhead that communicates a body of divine knowledge and natural law, which leads the way to higher consciousness and ultimately enlightenment. The Hebrew letters, *Yod, Heh, Vav, Heh,* spell the Hebrew name for the Most High, suggesting that the force that grasps, propels and guides the Wheel and us through fortune and misfortune alike originates from the Greater Universe. This name, usually referred to as the *Tetragrammaton*, is the primary formula for the universal creative process.[1] The Wheel of Fortune symbolises the

---

1 Qabalists believe that prior to creation God/dess existed in an undifferentiated state of infinite potential. The foundation of existence, or the four elements – fire, water, air and earth – were the first result of the God/dess's utterance, often called 'The Word'. Consequently, Qabalists assign the Most High's Hebrew name, the Tetragrammaton, IHVH, *Yod, Heh, Vav, Heh,* to the elements – fire, water, air and earth respectively.

laws of cycles: as surely as we have peak experiences – reach the Wheel's top – we will head towards its bottom, only to aspire upwards again from this point. We are continuously in motion, both as separate beings and as part of the ever-moving and changing universe. Adulthood follows Adolescence as certainly as summer follows spring.

The alchemical glyphs surrounding the Wheel's centre, Mercury ¡, Sulphur ꝗ, Salt O and Water ô, hint at the goal of esoteric alchemy. Daily experiences have the potential to transform ordinary people (ordinary elements) into enlightened beings, or the legendary alchemist's gold. These symbols, known in the East as the *gunas*, show how life works. Form is initiated by the *Rajasic* or sulphury fire energy; is preserved in form by the *Tamasic* salty earth element; is modified into a different form by the *Sattvic* mercurial air element; and finally dissolves in the element of water.

The hub and radiating spokes illustrate that what the Wheel's motion brings to pass originates in the Macrocosm, or *Ain Soph Aur*, a Qabalistic term meaning 'the Source of all animate and inanimate life'. If you look at the Wheel itself carefully, you can see that it is composed of four circles, symbolising the Four Qabalistic Worlds. In the Bible, the Wheel of Fortune card is almost perfectly described in Ezekiel 1:15–16, 'Now, as I beheld the living creatures, behold one wheel upon the earth by the living creatures, with his four faces . . . and their appearance and their work was as it were a wheel in the middle of a wheel.' This speaks to the essential meaning of the Wheel of Fortune; the continually changing and evolving nature of every living thing; the Hermetic principles of Rhythm and Cause and Effect. The eight spokes refer back to the horizontal figure eights floating above the Magician and Strength, stating, 'As above, so below; as below, so above'. This is reiterated on the Tree of Life where the physical world is signified by the tenth *Sephirah*, Kingdom or *Malkuth*, which is recognised to be a reflection of the divine *Kether*.

The Snake warns, 'Hang on, life can be a rollercoaster ride!' It also serves as a reminder that each cycle has the potential to enable us to shed our old skins. The jackal-headed figure of Anubis, the soul's guide through the underworld, whose eye is shaped like the letter *Yod*, gazes up towards this letter on the Wheel, hinting that the hand of God is present and available even in our darkest hours. Substantiating this are the four Archangels, mentioned in the Bible's book of Revelation, arising from the clouds in the card's background. The Archangels serve as cornerstones, illustrating the indisputable and fundamental truth that everything the Wheel brings us originates in heaven. According to the Greater Reality, all are opportunities for growth and development clouded by immature thinking, over-emotional reactions, a lack of understanding and excessive attachment. The Sphinx sits upon, yet above, the Wheel, witnessing its movement. Having mastered control over its animal body, or habitual responses (symbolised by its human head), the Sphinx interacts with the Wheel, but does not interfere with its movement. The Sphinx's position illustrates the concept of living *in* the world, but not being *of* the world, an idea that is further communicated by the card's number, 10, a combination of one, the Magician (the personality), and zero, the Fool (the One consciousness). This mythical being bears the Sword of Discriminating Detachment, indicating that he or she knows when to hold fast and become involved and when to 'let go and let God'.

The four beings who surround the Wheel of Fortune represent not only the four Archangels of the four corners of the universe and four fixed signs of the zodiac, Aquarius (the Man), Leo (the Lion), Taurus (the Bull) and Scorpio (the Eagle), but four of Christ's apostles as well. Rachel, a student of Tarot and Art History, reminded me that they symbolise Matthew, Mark, Luke and John, who were changed into these creatures by the heavily repressive atmosphere of the early Christian Era. The Man is Matthew, referring to Christ's humanity; Mark, the Lion, symbolises Christ's kingliness and dignity; Luke, the Bull, a sacrificial animal, indicates Christ's teachings and the sacrifices He made in their name; and John is the Eagle that soars through the heavens, signifying Christ's divinity.

The colour of the Wheel of Fortune is violet, its musical note is A# and its herb is slippery elm. The Hebrew name for the Wheel of Fortune is *Kaph*, meaning 'a grasping hand'. To grasp something is to know, understand or comprehend it. *Kaph* intimates your ability and willingness to comprehend the role you play, consciously or unconsciously, in co-creating your circumstances. I use the term co-creator because of the fact that we are all bound to work *along with* the divine plan, and therefore are co-creators, not the Creator/Creatrix. As co-creator, you may participate in your fate by putting forth your best efforts, while bearing in mind that you will be able to make the most of what the Wheel of Life, Cause and Effect, or Karma Wheel (other names for the Wheel of Fortune), bestows upon you in God/dess and nature's time. To conclude, we must consider the fact that there are times when things simply 'happen' (you have probably seen the bumper sticker, 'Life Happens'). The point here is not so much to think about how you got caught in a flash flood or tornado, but what you can do about it. Situations like these are chances to graduate to a higher level on the spiralling wheel of life.

Jupiter, the Roman Heavenly Father, supreme patron of the Roman state and husband to Juno, Mother Earth, is associated with the Wheel of Fortune. 'Jupiter' means 'the Heavenly-Father-Who Rains', and as such was deemed a fertility god who ruled over thunder, lightning and rain. On the Tree of Life, the sphere assigned to the planet Jupiter, Lord of Greater Fortune, is Mercy, or *Chesed*. This corresponds remarkably well to the east Indian astrological system, wherein this planet is called the Guru who is recognised throughout the East as the incarnation of divine mercy. Experience and investigation, plus your grasp of the Rules and Tools of the Game of Life, help you recognise that the conditions of your life may serve as merciful gurus or teachers. Although they are sometimes uncomfortable and disconcerting, you have the opportunity to seek out the guru or teaching to your benefit in all your encounters (astrologers often refer to Jupiter as the Greater Benefic). Approaching life from this perspective results in your stepping above and beyond your over-attachment to having things a certain way, allowing you to experience conditions from a more objective vantage point and to understand that although you may not get what you *want*, you do get what you *need*.

Jupiter is also linked with the solar plexus centre (Third *Chakra*), ordinarily assigned to the expression of your personal power in the world. In metaphysics, however, the solar plexus is termed the abdominal brain and is associated with your instinctive memories and gut feelings versus more cognitive channels of information. Because this centre is below the heart, action taken from the solar plexus tends to be motivated more by the desire for personal advancement, than by the desire to advance all concerned.

It is essential to acknowledge that the Wheel's turns do not always make sense or appear fair. Austrian psychotherapist, Viktor Frankl, spent several harrowing years in Nazi prison camps, where he developed his famed *Logotherapy*. Frankl's writings relate how differently people coped with imprisonment. Some became embittered, animalistic and morally depraved, while others searched for the higher meaning in what had befallen them. This latter group aspired to the *Logos*, a term referring to the cosmic purpose, will or Word of the Most High, in their circumstances. These individuals rose above their personal suffering and used the situation as an opportunity to aid and comfort others. From this, Frankl concludes: 'Man has the potential to behave like a swine or a saint. Which one is actualised depends on decisions, not on conditions.'[2] There are endless ways of relating to everyday life, and it is essential to bear in mind that whatever the fruits, you sow the seeds. Frankl re-emphasises the truth that we may not have control over circumstances, but we do have control over how we deal with them.

The Wheel of Fortune is customarily associated with the ideas of success and failure. It is helpful to note that these evaluations are defined and influenced by many forces: society, your particular cultural or peer group, religious beliefs, even geographical locale. This point became ironically obvious to me through the following experience: I was appreciated and well-compensated for teaching Natural Foods Cooking in an alternative high school in northern California in the early 1970s; yet, when I offered the identical course in the suburbs of Pennsylvania a year later, it failed to draw a single participant.

In the Qabalah, the Wheel of Fortune is known as the Conciliating or Rewarding Intelligence, inspiring you to overcome your distrust of life and nature and to realise that all events, circumstances, persons and things are ultimately harmonious. In return for adopting this attitude of compatibility, you become seasoned by your experiences, and daily life becomes more rewarding. A reward is something given in return for something done. This Intelligence rewards you with an understanding of the concept of karma and the potential effects and affects of your actions.

## Gateway of Life: Adolescence

While travelling the road to Adulthood, the Fool-adolescent learns about fortune and misfortune, success and failure. Simply stated: All actions result in some consequences. Despite your efforts to maintain the status quo, karma (consequences) are intrinsic and unavoidable aspects of being human. You simply cannot stop the Wheel of Cause and Effect from turning. At this point, as an adolescent, you are learning how to navigate through the maze of life (the Royal Maze is the name the Aquarian Deck for the New Age has given the Wheel of Fortune).

Eastern thought defines karma as the force generated by your

2 Viktor E. Frankl, *Man's Search for Meaning*, Washington Square Press, New York City, 1963, p. 213.

actions which perpetuates or terminates the process of reincarnation and certain behaviour patterns. Your actions have certain moral, ethical and spiritual consequences that determine present conditions, future destiny and what your next incarnation will be. Those in an adolescent stage may react to so-called 'bad karma' or misfortune like a victim of chance, denying the part they have played in what has come to pass, and/or avoiding the occasion to use or develop their skills. With maturity, they come to understand that they co-create their circumstances (consciously or unconsciously), and that everything is cyclical. This is perfectly summed up in the popular adage, 'What goes around, comes around.'

Experiencing the Wheel of Fortune at the Four Gateways of Life may cause certain attitudes and behaviour. CHILDHOOD: You are so set on having things done a particular way, you throw a tantrum or sulk at the slightest opposition or deviation; ADOLESCENCE: A woman believes she's been fired from her job because of her skin colour, rather than seeing that her own sloppy work, tardiness and forgetfulness is the cause; ADULTHOOD: As a result of becoming more attuned to the natural cycles of her life, a business consultant plans her work schedule according to when she is most mentally alert and energetic; WISDOM: During a heated argument with his brother, a man watches himself and the situation from the perspective of the Sphinx and is subsequently able to resolve things amicably.

## Divinatory Questions for the Wheel of Fortune

*Upright*: What have you got a grip on? Where are you gaining new comprehension? What seeds are you consciously sowing? How has a more detached attitude been helpful or hurtful? How have you profited from your difficulties and misfortunes? With whom have you shared your good fortune? What opportunities have you taken advantage of? Where might you do your best and then surrender? How have you grown by dealing with some unfortunate circumstances? In what situation have you become more able to go with the flow of life? What event or interaction are you being rewarded by? What good might heeding a gut feeling be to your personal or professional life at this time? How have you recalled God/dess's presence during a down cycle?

*Reversed*: What opportunity, project or relationship has failed to work out as planned? Although things haven't worked out as planned, what gains have occurred through it? Where have you been generous to a fault? What experience have you had difficulty understanding? Could you be slowly adapting to the new flow of things? How might impatience with your own or others' natural rhythms be causing you problems? How have you felt victimised or dragged around by the Wheel of Fortune? In what area of your personal or professional life might your judgment be clouded with feelings of over attachment? Where has it been beneficial to avoid your gut feelings? Are you becoming able to equate wealth with good friends and learning experiences, not just money? Where have your needs or ideas proved to be out of sync with others?

## Personal Experience

The week my seventy-six-year-old mother moved to California from New York, I had scheduled a large holiday dinner. Little did I know that my oldest son would have a car accident, and I would need to have a tooth extracted as well – all this compounded with my regular work schedule! As I began to be drawn into an emotional cyclone, I sought out my friend, the Tarot, for some first aid. After meditating and requesting guidance, I turned over the Wheel of Fortune from the downward facing pile of Major Arcana cards and had a good laugh. The Wheel fitted my situation to a T, and I immediately began associating with it.

First, I was reminded to see the situation like the Sphinx sitting above the Wheel as an observer of events wherever possible, while also doing my best to make myself and others comfortable. This clearly meant recruiting help from others. My holiday dinner instantaneously became a potluck; I asked a friend to take me to and from the dentist, making sure my husband and sons would do my usual household chores after the surgery; and rescheduled several business appointments.

Next, the Wheel reminded me of the law of cyclicity. I recalled how apparent this became when, at a friend's suggestion, I had had my biorhythms charted. I remembered studying the ups and downs of my physical, mental and emotional cycles and thinking about being a moody teenager, half listening to my father's counsel. He would say, 'When things get so bad they can't get any worse, they have to get better.' And he was right! With this thought in mind, I decided to use his statement as my affirmation to support me through the challenging and emotionally charged situations at hand: coping with my mom's nervous and insecure state, the insurance companies, injuries, fulfilling my work obligations, organising the dinner turned potluck and my anxiety about having my tooth pulled. *What an opportunity!*

It's impossible not to be touched by circumstances such as these while going through life. The point is not to emote endlessly about them, but lovingly and efficiently to do whatever you can to ease things along. I took a break to wash some lunch dishes and accidentally caught sight of the Alcoholics Anonymous Serenity Prayer hung on my kitchen wall:

> God grant me the serenity to accept the things
> I cannot change,
> The courage to change the things I can,
> And the wisdom to know the difference.

This prayer embodies what the Sphinx's sword has come to symbolise for me: discriminating detachment.

The Hebrew letter, *Kaph*, associated with the Wheel, means the 'grasping hand' (I cannot emphasise enough the value of referring to each card's Hebrew letter). Looking at my own hand as it grasped, I could see that it actually forms a spiral. *Kaph* helped me recall that life cycles and their symbol, the Wheel of Fortune, are spiral in nature. That is, I may *think* I repeat the same experiences over and over again, but they are really on another loop of the spiral, since I have the option to apply what I have learned from my previous experiences to guide me along. Essentially, I have certain karmas to work out and with during my lifetime, only some of which will disappear completely. The remainder will slowly dissipate if I treat each recurrence as an opportunity to grow wiser. Hence, anxiety, fear, family events, accidents, teenage behaviour, physical ailments, etc., are often an unavoidable part of life. What is avoidable is my repetition of old worn-out (reactive) attitudes and behaviour in relation to them.

Finally, I reflected on the meditative work I have done with the Wheel, which has taught me that all problems are solvable, requiring only desire, time and the willingness and patience to locate the proper tools and information to do so. With this, I have learned that my own immaturity, over-emotionality, lack of information and understanding are the primary obstacles to success and the Wheel's upward movement. I am sure that whatever I am faced with has been earned and bestowed by my Higher Self. At this point, I made a list of how my problems benefit me, and this is what I found out:

My problems help me to develop compassion and generosity towards myself and others; enhance my ability to handle immaturity, weakness and physical limitations; remember that there is more to life than excessive material concerns and satisfactions (destitution may also be an inability to feel and love); embrace whatever life serves up as a challenge and teacher to be met and learned from; surrender to the truth that it is sometimes impossible to know the 'whys' of things, that the complete story is inaccessible. The very fact that a situation exists indicates that I must surrender and handle it. In such circumstances, I recall the wise words of one of my teachers, who said, 'You eat what you've cooked,' and I get on with the job on hand.

As you can see, I lived through the week I described, and from it and the Wheel of Fortune gained a more conscious model with which to approach other such times in my life.

## Student Experiences

❖ 'I had to go to court again last week and was petrified with fear and anxiety,' began Christine, mother of three sons and stepmother to two daughters. 'It's a dirty custody battle between my husband and his ex-wife, and our attorney thinks it's important for me to appear at this next court date. I've been through it three other times already and found it to be frustrating beyond belief. Listening to my husband and his ex saying these terrible things about each other made me absolutely sick to my stomach. But the work we've done with the Wheel of Fortune helped me to see the situation differently this time. I recognised that I had the choice to go on another emotional rollercoaster ride – the Snake – or behave more like the Sphinx to witness and watch, rather than becoming drained and anxious. All last week before going to court, I used the Wheel of Fortune for meditation and practised being the Sphinx. I used these affirmations: "I'm doing everything appropriate to be of help", and "I surrender to the will of the Higher Self".

'Before going to court on Tuesday morning, I repeated the whole procedure and reminded myself that when things got rough, I could do something to make myself feel a little better. Later on in the courtroom, when I felt myself getting frustrated, I took a deep breath or two, closed my eyes and repeated my affirmations. I couldn't believe it, but I felt normal afterwards. Even the feelings between my husband and me weren't as tense as they've been in the past. I believe my dispassionate, Sphinx-like attitude somehow rubbed off on to him.'

*I feel that sometimes the best thing we can do is to assume a detached attitude. However, as I said to Christine, it's a skill to know when and when not to do so. In order to make the right choice, we can use the Sphinx's sword, the concept of critical analysis explained in the Lovers card, to help us discern what is right action and then proceed to enact it.*

❖ 'I finished grad school last spring, much to the relief of myself and my family,' began Paula. 'My boys are three and six years old and it had been a real strain on them. At first, I really enjoyed being at home, gardening, cleaning out the closets and cooking real dinners. But before long, I started thinking, "You're not working. You slaved for your degree and now you may as well not have it for all the good it's doing you."

'What you said in class about the Wheel of Fortune's connection to life cycles somehow made me realise that now is my time to be home with my kids. I'm lucky enough to be able to afford it. I have friends who'd trade places with me in a second. Soon the kids will be big enough for me to comfortably pursue my career. I asked myself, "Why did you have them? To put them in childcare centres so you can work with other people's families?" So I've let go and I honestly feel okay about my life now. I know I'll be glad later on. Come to think of it, I'm already glad.'

*Paula was able to let go, which can really allow the Wheel to move. By being cognisant of where we are, when we are there, we can become more aware of our options and opportunities. For example, Paula is taking this class, and there are other things she now has the chance to pursue, since she isn't working full time. The Wheel of Fortune is called the Rewarding Intelligence. I recall how difficult it was at one point for me to give myself fully to being a parent. It wasn't easy for me to see things in perspective, but somehow I knew I had to surrender myself to it fully – and the rewards have been indescribably great.*

❖ Bill, a new attorney, shared his experience: 'In spite of my efforts to have a client acquitted, he was convicted of a crime I know he didn't commit. Finally, I had to give up. I've come to realise through the Wheel of Fortune's teachings that I can't always understand why things work out as they do, that reasons aren't always apparent. This is nearly impossible for someone who relies on his mind and rational thinking as much as I do. I wouldn't even be in this class if I weren't here with my wife. It's easy for me to be excited and celebrate when things go as I plan. But then it's just as easy for me to complain and be in a bad mood when they don't.

As it turns out, the judge is taking my advice and sentencing my client to a rehabilitation programme that will help him with his alcohol problem. I suppose it did all work out for the best: no jail time and he's getting help. But I sure did go down fighting. I think I'll try to remember this one to guide me through my next go-round, like the little guy winking at me from the side of the Wheel (Anubis). I'll admit I'm very childish when I don't get my way. I'm hell to live and work with. I certainly wouldn't want to be around somebody like me, and that's something I plan on changing.'

*I told Bill that it's hard for most of us when we don't get our way – when things go contrary to how we believe they 'should, must, ought to' be. It's definitely a step towards more adult behaviour for Bill to admit his shortcomings and accept that things did work out well for his client despite the initial struggle. With the Magician card we learned that the only constant is change. With the Wheel of Fortune, we have to come to terms with life's fluctuations in yet another way. Remember that the Wheel is a spiral – there's always another opportunity to put what you've learned to use. I suggested that Bill use a personal statement or two to reinforce his plan to be more open.*

❖ Elisa, a graphics designer, was home from work sick for nearly a week and returned to class with this experience: 'Being home sick all last week made me realise how much I love being at home. At first, I got very upset because I've used up all my sick leave for the year, but soon decided that being upset wasn't going to help me get better. After giving my situation some thought, I got a better grip on it. I needed to accept my position on the Wheel, at the bottom, in order to head back up. I needed to learn how to go with the flow. That's pretty good self-talk for me. Then I began doing everything possible to heal myself. I believe that accepting my situation helped me start the upward spiral.

'Out of all this has come the realisation that I want to have a more flexible work schedule. I want to be able to spend more time with my daughter. She'll be a teenager soon and then off to her own life. I'm going to put some things into motion to make this happen within the next year, a full cycle from now. I think the Wheel of Fortune will help me watch my progress intelligently. As our homework suggests, I'll use the card's Hebrew name, *Kaph*, to remind me of what I want to grasp on to.'

*'Elisa, it looks as if you got a great deal from your illness,'* I told her. *'After you surrendered to the fact that you were sick and stopped being upset about not having any more sick leave, you were able to maximise your time and even plant some important new seeds. Having goals for ourselves is an essential part of enabling us to ride out the inevitable down cycles and doldrums of life.'*

❖ 'This is the busiest time I can ever remember,' began Karin, a mother, student, worker and mate. 'Just this morning, I happened to catch a short piece in the newspaper while standing up gulping my juice in the kitchen. It said that June is the most stressful month of the year, both good and bad stresses. I know exactly what they mean. For me, it's my son's high school graduation, my sister's wedding, the end of the fiscal year at work, getting ready for our annual family holiday and doing papers and final exams for the two classes I'm taking.

'I made up my mind that instead of feeling crazed by it all – and I almost was – I'm going to face the whole situation and do my best. This means being sure to schedule some time for myself, for exercise and/or a nap every day. I bought some gorgeous African violets the exact colour of the Wheel of Fortune's violet and put them next to the card and my telephone. They remind me of my promise to myself each time someone calls and asks me for something. They're reminding me I have the power to decide whether to take on another commitment or not. It's that Sphinx's ability to witness and then make choices we talked about in class. These are also reminders that this is simply the cycle I'm going through right now, and a lull is sure to follow it.'

*Learning to work effectively with the current cycle is providing a great model for Karin. While listening to her speak, I recalled a retired friend commenting, after I told her how busy I was, that she could remember herself at my age doing the same thing and how she wished for some of that busyness now! She recommended I keep the never-ending flux and reflux of life in mind. These are the teachings of the Wheel of Fortune that Karin now appears to be profiting from.*

## Suggestions for Application and Integration of the Wheel of Fortune

The following are opportunities for you to take the teachings of the Wheel of Fortune into your life. You may use them to get a better grip on a particular issue or situation, develop your 'witness consciousness', become more adept with the Sword of Discriminating Detachment and more able to comprehend life's endless fluctuations. Or they may help you get unstuck, derive increased benefit from all your experiences, ride the rollercoaster of life more easily, become more attuned to and comfortable with your own cycles and co-creative abilities.

1   Draw or colour your own version of the Wheel of Fortune with yourself as the Sphinx.

2   Set the card in a visible place as a reminder to your conscious and subconscious minds to use and absorb its teachings to go with or become more attuned to the natural cycles of things, become more sensitive to your own or another's cycles, see the potential benefit in all that befalls you, and recall that the Higher Self guides the Wheel through its turns.

3   Dream on the Wheel of Fortune.

4   Play the note A# on a musical instrument. Intone IAO or hum along with the music and concentrate on your solar plexus or Third *Chakra* as you do so (you might experience it feeling warm or tingling as you do). Now meditate on the card for a few minutes and, as you do so, consider a situation in which you would like to be a witness – more Sphinx-like. Mentally place yourself in the position of the Sphinx outside the Wheel and contemplate your situation from this perspective. Think of ways in which you might become less attached, involved or controlling. Then imagine a thin cord going from your solar plexus to this situation. If you would like to take another step in detaching yourself, sever the cord. After doing so mentally, apply some healing herb or medicine to both yourself and the situation. Now request that the Wheel's teachings guide you through these circumstances.

Or if you are faced with a worrisome situation, event or problem, such as needing to be more understanding, open and flexible, or to derive gain from the cycles happening within or around you, imagine how the Sphinx would handle it. If it seems feasible, do it. Finally, note as many benefits and rewards as you can imagine resulting from engaging with and handling a difficult cycle, person, situation or problem. Does this inspire you to get started? Jot down the times you became aware of the Wheel of Fortune in your interactions. I was aware of the Wheel of Fortune when? Before/during/after . . .

5 Go out into the world and pretend you are the Sphinx or 'witness'. I enacted the Sphinx and this is what took place . . .

6 The Rerun. After having an experience and realising in retrospect how the Wheel's teaching might have given you the opportunity to help yourself and/or others through a particularly difficult cycle, recognise that you may not get what you want, but you will surely get what you need, or offered a bit of objectivity. Mentally relive the situation, *including* your insight. If possible, actually rerun the situation in real life with your new attitude or behaviour.

7 Ask yourself the following questions:

'What rollercoaster ride would I like to end?' 'Where might it be beneficial to become more of a "witness", or practise discriminating detachment?' 'What gut feeling(s) need to be handled?' 'What cycle would I like to begin or end?' 'Where have I done my best and now must surrender to my Higher Self?' 'What points am I at in my various cycles – mental, emotional, physical and spiritual?' 'What challenging predicament have I unconsciously co-created?' 'What new concept have I grasped?' 'What tragedy is making me mature and/or encouraging me to use or develop my skills?' 'Which cycle can I help to spiral upward?' 'What situation is making me feel wealthy or poor?' 'What unfortunate circumstances have I unexpectedly benefited from?' 'What fortunate circumstances have become unexpectedly difficult?' 'In what area are my ideas ahead of my time?' 'Where might my needs be out of sync with others?' 'Am I gaining new understanding as to how a present situation was set in motion?'

'What Gateway of Life am I in or growing through in the previous questions?' Indicate: Childhood, Adolescence, Adulthood or Wisdom. Why?

'What do I need to do in order to develop the above further?' I need to . . .

'What step(s) do I want to take towards this and how can the Wheel of Fortune guide me?'

8  Use a personal statement regarding the presence of the Wheel of Fortune in your life at this time, such as: 'My witness consciousness grows stronger and stronger.' 'Wherever I am in my life cycles is workable.' 'I'm open and flexible during periods of transition.' My personal statement is . . .

9  Inspirational words and quotes:

'Witness consciousness.'

'A wise man is out of the reach of fortune.'
Sir Thomas Browne, *Religio Medici*, 1643

'Not my will, but thine, be done.'                LUKE 22:42

10  What symbols stand out in the card? What do they say to you? How might they be useful in daily living? Bring the symbol(s) into your life in some way so as to integrate the card's teachings.

11  Wear and surround yourself with the Wheel of Fortune's colour, violet, to remind you of the card's teachings when needed, such as wanting to feel more flexible within, detached from, or understanding of the cycle you are now in. Notice how you are affected.

12  The Wheel's astrological correspondence is Jupiter, ruling generosity, circulation of energy, self-improvement, trust in the beneficence of the universe, among other things. Examine the cycles you are now involved in – work, relationships and health. Notice where these Jovian qualities might benefit yourself or others.

13  Remember that the Wheel of Fortune's Hebrew name, *Kaph*, means 'a grasping hand'. How can this remind you of the card's meaning or help you in your life process? For instance, I grasp the importance of doing the best I can when I do Tarot consultations for others. Therefore, before working, I relinquish my personal hold by placing the question(s), client and myself in the hands of God/dess, with the trust that God/dess will do the rest.

14  Try a few drops of the scent balsam associated with the Wheel of Fortune as a reminder to integrate the card's teachings.

15 Have a cup of tea made from the herb slippery elm. Sit quietly as you drink, and consider the herb's properties as a nutrient for children and convalescents, an anti-inflammatory especially good for calming the intestinal and urinary tracts, treating burns, wounds, ulcers and boils. Consider how slippery elm may help you to digest and soothe what the Wheel of Fortune brings you.

11     **JUSTICE**     ל

# CHAPTER 15

# *Justice*

## General Information and Symbolism

A sighted Justice bears a raised sword in her right hand and scales in her left, suggesting that the discerning (the sword) individual balance (the scale) and transcend their mental and emotional prejudices, mind and emotion (pans), in order to achieve the wisest application of law, or Justice. Maturity brings the ability to weigh, measure and critically analyse circumstances and their potential consequences before acting. Accompanying this concept is the faith that whatever results follow such considerations are relative to what an individual needs to learn and grow from. Now, I think I hear you saying, 'What about poverty, racism, sexism, wars, accidents, natural disasters that wipe out hundreds, sometimes thousands, and other such things?' The uplifted sword shows the necessity of doing your best to act to eliminate these things when and wherever possible (it's hard to stop an earthquake, but you can be prepared for it, or perceive catastrophic events and restrictions as opportunities for people to be their best selves, to grow and perfect skills). The sword's handle is shaped like a 'T', shorthand for the planet of limitation, Saturn, and underscores this fact. While intervening, it is essential to recall the understanding gleaned from the Wheel of Fortune. You can't always understand the 'whys' of everything and must trust the harmony and equanimity of the universe. Pain, in time, impels you to locate the appropriate tools and intervention strategies to meet the challenges at hand. Having compassion for inequality, misery, affliction, brutality and deprivation, as well as personal experience with such things, encourages you to look truthfully at people and circumstances. Justice instructs us on the moral imperative of performing acts of love, mercy and kindness, what the Qabalists call *mitzvah*, whenever possible. To conclude, Justice bears the Sword of Righteousness. When justice is not served (and only God/dess may judge this), there always is karmic feedback from on High. True justice is sometimes severe and difficult to administer owing to social, political and cultural bias, but, in time, less severe than taking unjust action. Julia Ward Howe's *Battle Hymn of the Republic* sums it up quite simply: 'He hath loos'd the faithful lightning of His terrible swift sword, His truth is marching on.' It is interesting to note that *Geburah*, the fifth *Sephirah* on the Tree of Life, is called both Justice and Severity.

Justice extends her foot, showing that she is ready to act. The figure of Justice may be likened to the Celtic Goddess of the Land, who acts to lawfully protect its inhabitants. This assures us that whatever group or individual does not respect the law, or enacts laws for a country that are not aimed for its greatest good, become responsible for the demise of its people and environment. Consequently, they subject themselves to the wrathful side of this goddess. The fall of the Soviet Union and the demise of the South African government demonstrate this principle at work. It is not surprising that Work and Action are the Qabalistic functions assigned to the Justice card.

Justice's crown refers to *Kether*, the Crown or Source of life on the Tree of Life. This implies that the justice acted out in our everyday world, is related to the divine Justice represented by this card, symbolised by the square in the centre of the crown, and the small circle within the square. In the greater scheme of things all eventually fits together.

Justice's red robe of courage and desire is draped with a green capelet of creativity. It indicates desire under the dominion of wisely directed creativity. Furthermore, red and green are complementary colours and combine to make grey, the colour of wisdom. This combination suggests how, by desiring to dress and address our daily experiences with courage and creativity, we become wise.

The colour of the Justice card is green, its musical note is F# (as is that of the Empress card, Venus) and its herb is plantain. The Hebrew name for the Justice card is *Lamed*, and as a noun means 'ox-goad', the implement used to keep an ox on its path. *Lamed* may also be used as a verb, signifying 'to educate'. The fruits of your actions may serve to keep you on the spiritual path, since straying often brings some type of pain that motivates, educates and ultimately goads you back on the track to living more responsibly and harmoniously with the teachings of Universal Truth. This is called 'living the *dharma*', or according to the teachings of the Buddha.

Justice is linked to the cardinal (initiating and of foremost importance) Air sign, Libra. Libra governs the kidneys, adrenal glands and lower back area. The Libra personality says: I balance, equilibrate, adjust, agree, idealise and harmonise. Ruled by the planet Venus, Libras desire fairness and harmony, especially in the area of relationships. Or as a Libra friend once joked, 'Balance and harmony at any cost.' This attitude tends to ignore the fact that imbalances, which may be perceived as the down cycles of the Wheel of Life, are necessary in achieving a more stable balance. As in most instances, conflict and disequilibrium facilitate deeper under-standing, with time. Evolved Librans observe that Justice is faithfully served – all is ultimately for the greater good, even if the initial outcome does not meet with their personal desires or ideals. This is communicated by Justice's sightedness, showing that she can 'see through' illusion. This type of personality aligns its sense of Justice with the higher truths rather than with what the mass mind presents. Simply, these people trust that the laws of the universe work for, not against, them.

If you look at Dickens's character Ebenezer Scrooge, you can perceive the principles of Justice at work. Scrooge chose to enact the same behaviour time and again, but was plagued by many sub-conscious fears, as evidenced by his dreams and visions. (Scrooge was unfortunately being dragged around by the Wheel of Fortune.) Yet this same misfortune – pain, suffering, and dissatisfaction – caused him to do some intense soul-searching and led him to the opportunity to adjust his future by adjusting or modifying his behaviour (in his Thoth deck, Aleister Crowley renamed the Justice card Adjustment). Like Scrooge, by accepting responsibility for the state of our lives, we take the first steps in adjusting our karmic patterns.

In Qabalah, Justice is recognised as the Saturnian, or disciplining and lovingly restrictive, aspect of the Empress. This is illustrated by the fact that the figure wears a 'T' over her heart. This symbol underscores that Justice feels all of her feelings, but knows she does not necessarily need to *act* upon them all. This principle is essential both to the administration of Justice and to our spiritual growth. It also states that whenever our actions are followed by pain or discomfort, these are usually prodding us to make better choices in the future. The exception to this would be when we are first modifying an old behaviour, wherein discomfort is due to the absence of what is familiar and is often a natural response to a period of readjustment.

Note that part of the readjustment process is sometimes an over-reaction to and over-compensation for past guilts and errors – indiscriminately weighting Justice's scales in the opposite direction.

For instance, if you have been miserly and then become unsuitably generous, you may set in motion another set of unfortunate circumstances or learning experiences. For this reason, it is best to be centred, the fulcrum of Justice's scales, before making a decision. A friend who, after inheriting a large sum of money, felt it was 'politically correct' to give his less fortunate friends generous cheques, was unprepared when a few later turned against him, calling him a 'Capitalist Pig' when he refused to continue sharing. Justice's Sword of Discrimination and balancing pans offer the consolation that in time you will learn to act *after* weighing the pros and cons of situations carefully. By doing this, you derive value from your experiences and learn what is truly being called for, what is in accord with the basic and unalterable laws of the universe, as symbolised by Justice's stone throne. This is further suggested by the card being numbered 11, a double Magician, symbolising the power of the personality over its environment through will, desire and intelligent action. It is interesting to see how the throne's columns actually form the number 11. This arrangement refers to the Tree of Life and the fact that the middle path, leading to the one temple of higher truth, stands hidden between and behind life's dualities. This is again emphasised by the space in-between the drawn curtains and the three points on the top of Justice's crown.

In the Qabalah, Justice is known as the Faithful Intelligence. This Intelligence addresses the essentiality of remaining faithful to the teachings of truth or keeping to your spiritual belief. It is a constant undeviating allegiance to the laws of God/dess and nature in all life situations. The modification of behaviour gives way to the mitigation of karma, which in turn alters the quality of your life and in time brings enlightenment. The light streaming through the parted curtains behind Justice reiterates both that the light is always behind us, and when you take an active part in co-creating your life situation and karma, the workings of the universe become less mysterious.

## Divinatory Questions for Justice

*Upright:* What are you carefully weighing and measuring? Where are you having to use your Sword to do what is just? What value are you deriving from your experience? How has an uncomfortable, yet right action, worked in your favour? How has your ability to analyse a situation carefully brought balance to your personal and professional life? Where is the Sword of Righteousness evident? In what situation is your ability to finally feel pain a blessing? How has your desire to do good manifested? Could you be more aware of the power of your input in your daily interactions? What behaviour are you modifying? How has Justice been on your side? How are you mitigating your karma? What change are you adjusting to? How is your faith helping you through a difficult time? Where has pain or being wounded acted as your teacher? Would it be advisable to get centred before making an important decision?

*Reversed:* Where has an injustice been upsetting? How might this be testing your faith? Are you forgetting to balance your words with your actions? How could being in too much of a hurry be bringing upset and disharmony? Might you be having difficulty adjusting to someone or something? How might you benefit from modifying a particular habitual way of thinking and behaving? In what area of your life are you avoiding responsibility? In what situation is your inability to feel pain or deny its existence proving detrimental? Could you be reaping the results of not having examined the pros and cons of a situation carefully? Where might you be overcompensating for a past injustice or lack of understanding? In what area of your personal or professional life are you experiencing a period of adjustment or readjustment? Is it possible that you or another are using your 'need' for peace and harmony to avoid clearing up some festering conflict? How could more faith help at this time? In what situation have you inappropriately allowed your emotions to lead you? How have the scales been unfavourably weighted? What important action have you put off taking?

### Gateway of Life: Adolescence

While experiencing enough unpleasant reactions from the Wheel of Fortune, in advanced adolescence you start acknowledging that you are contributing to the state of your life. With Justice, you begin assuming responsibility for your choices and actions – for yourself. The maturing adolescent starts shedding the role of victim and heads towards becoming a conscious co-creator working along with the Universal Life Force. This is accomplished by adjusting or modifying behaviours according to what is just (that is, what one thinks is correct at one's particular level of development). At this juncture, you realise that the Wheel, or new cycles, is set spinning by how you choose to relate to your circumstances, not by your mother, father, teacher, lover or environment. This does not imply that these are not an important influence; they definitely are. It means that how you presently interact with your past is up to you. At this point in our journey, we comprehend that it is our response to these circumstances – people, places and things – which helps determine consequences or karma, so-called fortunes and misfortunes.

Certain actions and attitudes may be observed within the realm of the Justice card. CHILDHOOD: You feel that everybody and everything is against you, that everything is unfair and you must suffer. There's no justice; ADOLESCENCE: Instead of taking the time to adjust her treatment of a difficult student, a teacher chooses to remains locked into the idea that the child is a problem and cannot possibly be otherwise; ADULTHOOD: Facing the fact that she has been lazy and not been working up to last year's sales figures, a woman takes steps to get into gear rather than continuing to work towards dismissal; WISDOM: Presented with the choice of becoming embittered and victimised for life by a car accident in which he loses his leg, a dancer assumes responsibility for the fact that he drove too fast on an icy road. With this attitude, he gets on with his rehabilitation and starts imagining himself as a choreographer.

## Personal Experiences

The creation of karma, also known as movement of the Wheel of Fortune, is a basic, unalterable, unavoidable law of the physical and spiritual worlds. Through this law, I have learned about the potency of my input into what comes to pass from my interactions (conscious and unconscious) with daily circumstances. Since Justice is associated with the process of education, it has taught me much about my freedom of choice. That is, making conscious choices as to what seeds I wish to plant in the garden of my life. I have learned that this type of participation, or Right Action, as it is termed by Buddhists, tends to yield sweeter and easier to digest fruits than those of wild or unconscious chance. When actively operating as a conscious co-creator (working with the Creator/Creatrix), I opt for actions and behaviour which adjust or mitigate my karma, and as a result my life is happier and more acceptable.

I often get a sense of future events (based, of course, upon present and past conditions) and vividly recall a particularly upsetting instance that happened within weeks of moving from the San Francisco Bay Area to Santa Cruz, a small town on the central Californian coast. I envisioned myself and my small child barely being able to survive economically. I had chosen to leave friends, students and security behind to raise my son in a less urban environment and live in the same town with the man I loved. But as the universe would have it, just prior to our moving, a brutal murder with which the Tarot and black magic were associated was committed in our new home-town. Needless to say, work for a Tarot teacher and consultant became almost non-existent, and the interest I did manage to generate was quite unsavoury. Yet, instead of being immobilised by what I sensed, which until that point was how I tended to deal with my precognitions, the teachings of the Justice card (which I was blessed to be studying at the time) inspired me to use my freedom of choice and do everything within my power to co-create a better, less painful, alternative.

I prayed, meditated, weighed and measured the facts, information and my feelings. In time, these efforts yielded the idea of baking home-made bread and delivering it door-to-door to support us. It took a lot of very hard work, but by taking action to counteract the possible long-term effects of the murder, I successfully helped mitigate my karma.

Through this encounter, I recognised how conscious choice and actions can enable me to take some genuine shortcuts through life. When I feel impotent or pained about the state of my life (in actuality, the state of my mind and emotions), I recall my role in co-creating what is, and from this my potential to recreate a more acceptable alternative surfaces. It also works to remind myself that I am sometimes like the adolescent (the stage in which the Justice card falls) who is mature on the outside, but not fully developed within. Directing my thoughts to the Faithful Intelligence connected with the Justice card renews my faith in the perfect balance of the universe. This focus serves to reinforce and strengthen my faith that as I am educated by the guru of my life – my experiences – in time, my choices and actions will become more adult and aligned with the teachings of truth.

## Student Experiences

❖ 'I'm embarrassed to say I tolerate my husband's terrible habit of yelling and screaming at me because my self-esteem is low,' began Vicki, meekly. 'Well, it's getting to be more and more upsetting for my son (his stepson), who becomes hostile towards my husband after such tirades. I know he's defending me, something I see I need to do for myself. I feel I've been stuck, because I've let my husband do this ever since we got married, over three years now.

'After we discussed Justice and how it can help change our karma,

I did my homework and took a gigantic step forward in a way I didn't do even after taking a course in assertiveness training. I sat down with my husband and told him to *stop*! I told him I didn't want him to yell and scream at me anymore, that I would understand if he spoke to me in a normal voice just as well, in fact, a whole lot better. He nearly fell off his chair. I also let him know that if he does it anymore, I'll get up and leave the room or wherever we are immediately. It's true it's not going to be easy to undo the damage I now realise I co-created, but at least I feel like we're on the way. It's amazing that I didn't do this for myself, but only after seeing the harm it was doing to my son. It's making me work on changing my karma – actually the karma of our entire family. I think that this is the end of my being a little girl and victim, and the start of being more responsible and womanly. I keep rehearsing (doing the Rerun from the homework) how I'll handle things the next time he yells. I see myself gently, but firmly, telling him that I can hear him if he speaks to me, that he doesn't have to yell, and then leaving until he cools down. I must keep reasserting my request and back up my words with action. I think he'll eventually get the message.'

*'You've used Justice's symbols well,' I said to Vicki. 'You've weighed and measured the situation carefully and have now taken up your Sword. Whether we like it or not we – our Higher Self – are always asking for Justice to be served. As you've learned, not doing what is just creates even more karmic knots. Yes, it will take time. It took time to establish your other pattern of being a victim, but now you are definitely headed in a better direction. You are also enacting the Qabalistic function of the card – Action.'*

❖   Sara, an even-tempered accountant, shared her experience with the Justice card: 'I always strive for peace and harmony, and I'll be the first to admit that strong negative emotions and upheaval terrify me. But coincidental (are there really any coincidences?) with studying the Justice card, my oldest daughter is having a difficult time in her new marriage. It seems she doesn't know how to express her negative feelings. Talk about karma!

'It hasn't been easy, but I've been communicating my wrongdoing to her. I've been telling her about how scared of conflict I've been, yet now I'm learning that conflict and disagreements are necessary for bringing important feelings out into the open and deepening relationships. You can't solve a problem unless you admit you have it. I'll tell you, she's furious with me and rightfully so. And although it's awful to bear, I allow her to express her emotions. I hope we can learn about this together. I keep meditating on the Justice card for the faith and inspiration to persevere. I honestly believe that it's going to rebalance our family. But it's going to take time, hard work and perhaps some good counselling. I'm using the statement, "All circumstances of my life are just", to alleviate my guilty feelings and remind me of this as I learn.'

*As Sara pointed out, often the first step in changing our behaviour is to own up to what we've done – to admit to ourselves and others that it would be better to have behaved differently. It's often hard to take responsibility for our actions because we not only 'look bad', but must also become educated in new ways. One of the meanings of* Lamed, *Justice's Hebrew name, is 'education', the second step in the process. During the re-education process, it's important to keep a patient and loving attitude towards ourselves, because it helps us learn faster. Using our energies to hate ourselves for what we've done only drains, distracts and slows things down.*

❖ 'Work has been absolutely mad. New people to train, deadlines to meet, overtime and meetings. I've been totally swamped,' began Ira, a Silicon Valley executive. 'Learning about the Justice card (I couldn't even make it to class and had to get it on tape from you), I got that my life is out of whack. All I'm doing is working, eating, going to the bathroom and sleeping. Making it to class is almost a miracle for me. I'm realising that I've created this and now it's time for me to create something else, like relaxing and having fun; otherwise, I'm going to be one burned-out non-functional executive. I'm in this state of physical, mental and emotional bankruptcy. Sure, I get pleasure from some of it, but it's gotten to be much too much. I'm not even sure how things got this way, but they have, and that's what I've got to deal with. I can find reasons later, when I'm able to think more clearly.

'With this long weekend coming up, I'm going to give myself some quality relaxation time. I'm going camping with my best buddy before jumping back into it all on Tuesday. I'm going to head out into nature's greenery. Green is the colour of the Justice card, and I need all of it I can get to become rebalanced. The green of nature is so soothing to me. That's it. I'm getting back in balance. Green salads, green trees, my green tent and me.'

*It's a wise person who recognises that he feels out of sorts and then takes some constructive action to elevate himself, as Ira did. It is sad how instead, so*

*many depend upon substances such as food, drugs and alcohol to stop feeling
and keep on going. In the process of readjusting our behaviour, we
ordinarily must confront situations which are similar to those we are
altering. Here it's essential to be aware that even though we are in the
process of changing a pattern, there always seems to be an intermittent
transition or readjustment period. However, during this time of not having
completely transmuted our pattern, we may observe ourselves getting wise
to our actions sooner and sooner. This tells us we can, at some point, look
forward to being aware even before we act.*

❖  Sam, a secretary and mom to three children under twelve, came
to class with this experience: 'My kids have been unbelievably ornery
lately. I ask them to do things, leave notes everywhere, and come
home from work to find my requests and communications ignored. I
ask them what's going on and they say, "Sorry Mom, I forgot." But I
think I've found out why this is happening, thanks to Justice.

'While meditating a few nights ago at bedtime, it occurred to me
to use the dream process you've suggested so many times in class. I
honestly hadn't had much of a connection with the Justice card, but
since I hadn't done my homework, the thought of dreaming
appealed to me and I decided to give it a try. I asked that my dreams
show me the teachings from the card relevant to my family life at this
time.

'And you'll never guess what I dreamed: I dreamed about taking
my kids to a big amusement park. The dream was so intense, it woke
me up. Lying there thinking about its significance, I remembered
that I had promised to take my kids to the big amusement park near
here for months now. But since my partner and I are usually so tired
from the work week, we don't want to budge on weekends. Also, my
money's been short. But you know what I decided to do? I decided to
take all three of them with a friend each to the amusement park at the
beginning of June. I think I have to balance my words with some
actions. I need to keep my promises so they'll learn to keep theirs. If
I improve my credibility, I bet things around the house will change
for the better.'

*'What a helpful insight, Sam. It's disconcerting enough to see our
immature behaviour mirrored by our children, yet even more challenging
to admit that we're the ones who teach them how to behave irresponsibly.
Fortunately, we always have the chance to adjust our behaviour; then it's
only a matter of time before our children stop acting up and follow suit.'*

❖ 'My fifteen year-old daughter's been spending hours on the phone since she and her boyfriend got together,' began Flora, a longtime single parent. 'Each time I ask her about her studies, she tells me, "Don't worry so much, Mom. I've got it covered." I remind her how important her grades are, because our income is low and she definitely needs a scholarship to go to college. Well, I found out this week how much she has it covered. Her grades arrived. What a disaster! She went down in every single class, including PE. And not just from As to Bs, but to Cs and one D. So I made a rule – the Saturnian mother principle you spoke about – she must finish her homework before getting on the phone and limited her talking to one hour a night.

'Well, wouldn't you know it! On Sunday, a friend came over for a visit, and as we were walking out the door to catch a movie, I saw her pick up the phone. For some reason, I didn't remind her of her limit and left. When we came back over two hours later, she was still talking. I felt like wrapping the cord around her neck. God, she was pitiful, whining and begging to stay on the line for just another five minutes. She was just asking for the Sword of Justice to come down and terminate her behaviour. After she was forced to hang up, she went off to her room to sulk and didn't even come out for dinner. Of course, I felt guilty, but the next morning she was the most pleasant she's been for a month. I couldn't believe it. I finally realised she was just testing out the laws of the household and asking for Justice to be served. It's a way of knowing she's loved.

'She apologised and we talked over breakfast. She asked me how I felt about her staying on the phone longer on weekends, if she's done her homework. I told me I'd think about it. And after weighing it in my mind, like Justice's scales, I felt it was fair to allow her this. I think the question, "What discord in your life is bringing harmony in its wake?" accurately described my situation.'

*The question really did describe Flora's situation. It can be so uncomfortable to deal with conflict. That is probably why she went to the movies without enforcing her rule. Yet, because personalities are so varied, discord is inherent in the human condition. Justice is called the Faithful Intelligence and may inspire us to believe that keeping on track, or maintaining our spiritual perspective, and trusting that we are honestly doing the best we can will lessen the discomfort of dealing with these kinds of situations.*

*Remember, Justice wears the green cape of creativity over the red dress of courage and loving desire. We are slowly developing the creativity, desire and courage to work in ways that are in accordance with universal and natural laws and principles. I would say you are getting taught about the Great Mother who makes rules, regulations and disciplines for the good of her child!*

## Suggestions for Application and Integration of Justice

The following will give you a clearer understanding of the workings of the Justice card, in addition to some actions you can take in order to incorporate its teachings into your life. These exercises suggest ways in which you might become more aware of your potential to be a co-creator in your life process, educate yourself about how to mitigate your karma, be more understanding of life's harmonies and disharmonies, heal a wound, take increasing responsibility for your actions, and remain faithful to the teachings of truth.

1   Draw or colour your own version of Justice with yourself as the figure.

2   Set Justice in a visible place as a reminder to your conscious and subconscious minds to use and integrate her teachings, to have more faith in the path you are following, to remember that you help co-create the events in your life, and to be more willing to take a modified course of action.

3   Dream on Justice.

4   Play the note F# on a musical instrument. Intone IAO or hum along with the music. Now meditate on the card for a few minutes and, as you sit there, contemplate your freedom of choice. Zero in on a situation in which you can make different choices and imagine what each might be, as well as their possible outcomes. What would be the most responsible action to take? Now ask that Justice's teachings guide you through that particular situation. Or if you are faced with a worrisome situation, event or problem, such as being uncomfortable with what you must now learn in order to grow, the harmony of disharmony, or bearing the liability for not weighing the pros and cons carefully before acting, imagine how Justice would handle it. If it seems feasible, do it. Jot down the times when you became aware of Justice in your interactions. I was aware of Justice when? Before/during/after . . .

5   Go out into the world and pretend you are Justice. I enacted Justice when I felt like fleeing from a good friend's anger towards me. But recalling the card's teachings, I remained to hear her grievance. Doing this made some needed changes to our relationship and in time deepened our friendship. I enacted the teachings of Justice and this is what happened . . .

6   Examine a difficult life situation and acknowledge the part you have played in its co-creation. Now actively adjust your behaviour (and karma) accordingly. Remember, have patience with yourself as it usually takes time to modify old deep-seated behaviours. Appreciate each step you take!

7.  The Rerun. After having an experience and realising in retrospect how Justice's teachings might have brought equilibrium and understanding to discord, encouraged you to bear fair witness, stopped you from acting purely from your emotions, or adjusted your attitude towards some injustice, mentally relive the situation, *including* your insight. This will help the behaviour become more automatic next time. If possible, actually rerun the situation in real life with this new attitude or behaviour.

8   Ask yourself the following questions:

'What discord in my life may be bringing harmony in its wake?' 'What injustice am I struggling with?' 'In what situation might I benefit from feeling all of my feelings, but not necessarily need to act upon them?' 'What social or political situation is disturbing me?' 'Where do I desire to become more balanced and centred?' 'What state (karma) would I like to mitigate?' 'How might pain, or a deep wound inflicted in childhood, be God/dess's way of helping me to grow spiritually?' 'Do I erroneously believe that the only way I change and mature is through painful experiences and have I become attached to being in pain?' 'Where is a period of adjustment called for?' 'Where might enacting some extreme behaviour for a short period of time serve to balance me out healthfully?' 'Do I understand that pain does not indicate punishment or spiritual failure, but a sign that I am out of sync with universal and natural laws and principles?' 'How might I be going overboard in seeking to make up for a past immaturity or error in judgment?' 'Although it is not the easiest route to take, where and how am I directing my energies towards bringing the greatest possible reward by doing what is best?' 'What behaviour am I modifying?' 'What justice can I now perceive within an injustice?' 'In what situation(s) have I borne fair witness?'

'What Gateway of Life am I in or growing through in the above?' Indicate: Childhood, Adolescence, Adulthood or Wisdom. Why?

'What do I need to do in order to develop the above further?' I need to . . .

'What step(s) do I want to take towards this goal and how can Justice guide me?'

9  Use a personal statement regarding the presence of Justice in your life at this time, such as: 'I make tomorrow today.' 'I am centred and balanced in the midst of imbalance.' 'I have the ability and capacity to mitigate my karma.' 'My daily life is constantly educating me in the workings of the greater universe.' My personal statement is . . .

10  Inspirational words and quotes:

'As surely as day follows night, harmony follows disharmony.'

'Justice is not merely compliance with written laws.'          Cicero

'God's mill grinds slow, but sure.'                    George Herbert

'Faith is the force of Life.'                                      Tolstoy

11  What symbols stand out in the card? What do they say to you? How might they be useful in daily living? Bring the symbol(s) into your life in some way so as to integrate the card's teachings. Each time I see my bathroom scale, it reminds me of the importance of eating a balanced diet and not worrying about gaining weight. As result of eating in this way, I have maintained the same weight for many years.

12  Wear and surround yourself with Justice's colour, green, to remind you of the card's teachings when needed, such as desiring to feel more able to adapt and adjust when necessary, be centred and balanced in the midst of disequilibrium, or wanting to weigh and measure information carefully. Notice how you are affected.

13  Justice's astrological correspondence is Libra, governing traits such as agreement, balance and harmony. Is there some situation

in which you would like to feel more agreeable and balanced, confident about lovingly eliminating what is unnecessary, or less subject to over-compensating for past guilt and human error? Is there some extreme behaviour you would like to balance out or need to experience in order to achieve equilibrium? Remind yourself to do this via the Justice card. Notice what happens: your thoughts and feelings and the outcome.

14 Remember that Justice's Hebrew name, *Lamed*, means both 'ox-goad' and 'to educate'. How can this remind you of the card's meaning or help in your life process? The ox-goad reminds me to keep on my spiritual path, to live as responsibly as I possibly can, in accordance with the teachings of truth. It also underscores the fact that when other means fail, the goad's pain pushes me from a lower level of consciousness to higher one; reminds me how blessed it is to be able to feel; and impels me to cease denying a difficulty and pay attention to handling it.

15 Try a few drops of the scent peppermint associated with Justice as a reminder to integrate the card's teachings.

16 Have a cup of tea made from the herb plantain. Sit quietly as you drink and consider the herb's properties to draw pain when applied as a poultice to bee stings, as a soother of headaches, revitaliser and promoter of fertility and consider the similar qualities of the Justice card.

12    **HANGED MAN**

# CHAPTER 16

# The Hanged Man

## General Information and Symbolism

Out of all the Tarot cards, the Hanged One (although 'man' refers to humanity, I prefer to call this card the Hanged One, because this being may be of either sex) has shown me the most faces; and as each has presented itself, I have renamed the card accordingly: the Hanged, Surrendered, Reversed, Hung-up or Suspended One. Tradition associates the Hanged One with the idea of sacrifice and even crucifixion, which led me to entitle the card the Surrendered One. Sacrifice is the act of forfeiting or surrendering something of value for something considered to have a greater value: a lucrative but excessively demanding career given up for peace of mind and more time with loved ones; rich foods for a healthier body; one's life for an ideal of God/dess. The hands of the figure are unseen, symbolising that something has been 'handed over' or surrendered. Furthermore, this individual has temporarily given up personal control in order to receive impersonal guidance.

The Hanged One is suspended upside down from a treelike gallows. If you superimpose the Hanged One over a diagram of the Tree of Life (you might want to look at the Tree of Life at the beginning of this book), the being's head is positioned right over the ninth and tenth *Sephirah* called Foundation, *Yesod*, the subconscious mind, and Kingdom, *Malkuth*, the physical world, while his/her feet reach to the Crown or Source, *Kether*. This tells us that as a natural consequence of imbibing the spiritual laws and truths, or Rules and Tools of the Game of Life, the Hanged One contemplates their application to daily living. The figure's jacket is divided into two parts, bearing two crescent moons and four buttons on the lower portion, and six buttons on the upper. Because the Hanged One is reversed, the bottom of the jacket points upwards to the top of the Tree of Life, suggesting the spiritualisation of the subconscious mind via the principle of reversal. This is the process of transferring and incorporating the teachings of the greater world or macrocosm (the upper *Sephiroth*) into the microcosm (the lower *Sephiroth*) and everyday living. The lunar crescents recall the High Priestess in which the qualities of receptivity and neutrality are highlighted. These are now used to represent the Hanged One's inner state. Finally, this position tells us that the Hanged One's roots are in heaven, although he or she is attending to life on earth, the ultimate in attitude adjustment.

The card's number, 12, adds up to three, *Daleth*, the door, the number of the Empress. The haloed figure is suspended in a doorway (the trees or gallows form an arch), suggesting that suspension gives way to passage through an important door. We all arrive at doors, gateways or crossroads (The Crossroads is an obscure title for the Hanged One) from which it is advantageous to suspend, or hang-up, our worldly activities for a bit and turn inward for regeneration, inspiration (the halo) and contemplation, appraising life from the position of a witness, that of the Sphinx sitting above the Wheel of Fortune. This concept is depicted by the inverted position of the Suspended One's body, and implies not only suspension of activities and judgment, but viewing life from an out of the ordinary, centred or spiritual position. Suspension, or the attitude of 'Let go and Let God', is another reference to the fact that the Hanged One's hands or personal efforts are out of the picture.

To conclude, the reversal of physical posture represents the mental and spiritual turnabout that come through the disciplined use of meditation, study and other types of centring techniques. In this sense, the Hanged One is often compared to the supreme Norse god, Odin, who suspended himself from the World Tree as a means of seeking wisdom. Finally, it may help to recall the physical principle that when anything is hung in this way, it will swing like a pendulum, until it is perfectly centred.

Since the Hanged One is often linked to the ideas of crossroads and crucifixion, I'd like to take a few lines to consider these concepts. Medieval practitioners of magic considered the crossroads the optimal place to practice their art since it was the power spot where all four directions came together. It was also where the ancient pagan 'God of the Hanged' – Christ's symbolic ancestor – was ritualistically suspended on a crucifix or gallows. When examining Christ's crucifixion, we can trace its origin to an important crossroads, that of His choosing to go the way of heaven and the Self, versus going the way of the world. Along this same line, the figure hangs by a rope umbilicus in the upside-down birthing position, signifying this type of re-birth or emergence.

Accountability to your Higher Self is a sure sign of increased maturity, and what becomes evident through it is what the card illustrates: in reality, your only true and lasting attachment is to the Source of life above. This connection is what, in truth, sustains you. The Hanged One's hair is white, symbolising the clarity acquired from seeing the world from this perspective.

The figure is tied by one leg, yet seems content with this limitation, suggesting comfort within the bonds and constraints of daily life. It is through your evolving attitudes towards these ties that you grow. For instance, by deciding to own a puppy you are bound to certain feeding, walking and training schedules. You may also have difficulty locating a place to live that accepts pets. Yet, at the same time, you gain the pleasure of watching your pet grow up with your children, and you have it as a companion and guardian. In the East, this attitude towards your everyday work, relationships and responsibilities is the practice of *Karma Yoga*, by which you learn that daily life not only restricts you and creates and mitigates karma, but in time serves to connect you with the Divine (another reference to the Hanged One's halo). Simply, you have the options to be hung up, or drowned by the physical world, or liberated through it.

The legs of the white-haired Hanged One form the number four, as do the white-bearded Emperor's, linking the two. Since four is the number of order, stability and the material world, and the Emperor is associated with the sense of sight, this symbol indicates that by reversing normal perspective, the Hanged One sees the ordering of the world in a new way. The white hair further states that when the Hanged One consistently reorders his or her life so that it is based upon universal truth and the ancient wisdom liberation is achieved. The Hanged One, like the Christ, is a role model for us to follow, as he or she wilfully and lovingly submits to doing the work of his or her divine parents here on earth, despite the fact that it will entail sacrifice.

The Hanged One is associated with the musical note G#, the colour blue and the herbs Irish moss[1] or kelp (the sea-grown variety of Irish moss). The Hebrew name for the Hanged One is *Mem*, meaning 'water'. Water can nourish, purify, suspend, protect, destroy, reflect and baptise. In the practice of alchemy, water is

---

[1] It is interesting to note that Irish moss hangs down from trees as does the Hanged One.

known as the Universal Solvent, the liquid capable of dissolving all substances. In several old tarots, the Hanged One is depicted as the Drowned Phoenician sailor, or Drowning Man, emphasising this correspondence. As a mirror, water suggests the process of Self-reflection via meditation, which suspends the small mind while activating the Greater one. Self-reflection aligns us with our true ties while dissolving (or drowning) our false ones, as indicated by the halo around the figure's head. The last letter of the Hebrew alphabet (look at the World card), *Tav*, referring to the greater world or macrocosm, resembles the Hanged One's gallows, accenting this truth.

This card is associated with the planet Neptune, Roman god of the seas and oceans, who was supposedly guilty of encroachment (eventually water eats away all land) upon the earth goddess's domain. Astrologers refer to Neptune as the higher octave of Venus, the transpersonal versus personal aspects of the principles of love, affection, desire, creativity and motherhood, such as self-sacrifice and renunciation, because of its power to attend to the greatest good. Neptune is linked with dissolution, purification, illusion, martyrdom, compassion, intuition, self-examination and the subconscious acceptance of the knowledge of the Rules and Tools of the Game of Life. Neptune may inspire you to intuitively and compassionately clear your mind of hurtful self-indulgences, addictive and compulsive behaviour, and delusions. You need to renounce what is injurious in order to alter your perspective on life, so that you can expand your vistas and your capacity to grow. Inherent in these processes, however, is the danger of overindulging in self-examination and purification as a means (often unconscious) of escaping reality, holding fast to illusion, and as a defense against pain and letting go of what may be destructive and hurtful, yet familiar.

The Hanged or Suspended One offers the option of viewing life from an altered or transcendental state. The need to actually base ordinary interactions upon this reality in time becomes more apparent. At this juncture, self-esteem begins springing from right understanding, not only from the right clothes, home, car, friends and bank account, but from the more important truth that you are nourished, protected and provided for by a combination of your individual efforts and ties to the Source of life. Humbled by this, the potential for permanently reversing your perceptions of the world at large emerges. The evolving individual begins surrendering to the idea that proceeding in obsolete old ways violates what is for the greater good. Finally, individuals who seek their own path are often thought to be weird. However, in archaic German, the word *weid*, a synonym for the word weird, means 'to find one's way'.

When you arrive at the place where you can carefully examine and appropriately dissolve your judgments about what and who you 'must, should and ought to' be and do, you are transformed. Becoming more accountable to and reliant upon your Higher Self, you are less likely to be swayed by what others – known in metaphysics as the Race Mind Consciousness – suggest and dictate. Here you may extricate yourself from the fierce competition for prestige and position by developing the trust that you are provided for. Please don't misunderstand, this is not a message to renounce work and the world, but to perceive it from a different, reversed point of view. And as an added benefit of taking this crossroads, you begin relating to external influences, such as the messages of doom and gloom continually broadcast by the media, in another light, seeing them less like overwhelming threats and more like issues to be approached from a centred and intelligent position.

Following Justice, the Hanged One reminds the life traveller or Charioteer that the world is not merely a place to struggle, but can be enjoyed and celebrated as the path back to Eden. This awareness is often accompanied by some type of rebirth or spiritual experience. Although rebirth is customarily referred to as the Second Coming of Jesus Christ, it may be known in other forms: the spontaneous awakening of the Christ Consciousness – Christ's way of embracing life – within the ordinary person; the stirring of the *Kundalini* (another reference to the rope tying the Hanged One to the gallows) energy owing to an altered state of perception through meditation and contemplation, or an especially enlivening encounter with the guru of daily living; formal initiation rites; or baptism.

The number 12 confirms this, suggesting the assertion of personal will and concentrated effort; one, the Magician, to reverse detrimental subconscious patterns; two, the High Priestess, to both bring forth a new or reborn individual and usher us through a new door of perception; and three, the Empress (the sum of one and two).

In the Qabalah, the Hanged One is known as the Stable Intelligence. In times of insecurity, trauma or self-doubt, this Intelligence may remind you of the availability of permanence and stability by calling upon your knowledge and application of the Rules and Tools of the Game of Life – the teachings of truth. These constant, dependable, eternal teachings fortify your resistance by opening your mind and heart. Doing this offsets unnecessary disruption and maintains or restores equilibrium.

## Gateway of Life: Adolescence

At this juncture, individuals in the adolescent stage experience additional effects from the act of taking responsibility for themselves (initiated in the Justice card), and as a result their world view continues to shift. Experiencing themselves less as victims, they frequently consider bypassing or sacrificing obsolete behaviour patterns and impulsive short-term gratifications, which usually give way to long-term difficulties, for more mature choices. Not only do their perspectives of the world change, but they start accepting the limits of their daily duties and obligations with increasing grace. Such adolescents are safely on their way to Adulthood, since they are beginning to care more about how actions appear to themselves (their Higher Self) than how they appear to others.

The Hanged One may present itself in certain ways at the various Gateways of Life. CHILDHOOD: Despite the fact that a man has asthma, he refuses to give up smoking because 'Smoking didn't kill my father and he had asthma'; ADOLESCENCE: Although her friends are always trying the latest new illegal drug, a woman begins to think about her own drug experiments differently after she gets deathly sick; ADULTHOOD: Rather than denying her Self, a new mother acknowledges her need for regeneration by leaving her baby with another new mom, while taking an hour of exercise four times a week; WISDOM: A teacher of spiritual material is faced with the difficult question of whether to allow an unstable, hypersensitive student to continue working in a haphazard fashion, or communicate that she would be more successful if she gets better organised. After meditating on the situation, the teacher realises that allowing her to continue working as she does is a disservice to both the student and the teachings, so the teacher has no choice but to share her concerns with the student.

## Divinatory Questions for the Hanged One

*Upright:* How might your perspective be changing? What is sustaining and stabilising you through your present difficulties? Where might surrender to your Higher Self be of benefit to yourself and others? How are you being purified or initiated into more expansive ways of approaching life? How might you be extricating yourself from the negative influences of the Race Mind? What issue(s) have you reversed your position on? How have you freed yourself from being a martyr? In what situation have you been hanging by a thread? What supports your need to 'hang in there'? How have you been able to gain stability? What are you in the process of dissolving? What vision is being revised? Could a short-term sacrifice bring you some important long-term gains? What insight or inspiration have you received? How might you be seeking your own path?

*Reversed:* What are you drowning in? Would it be beneficial to work on attaining inner stability because both the world and others around you are unstable? In what area of your life are you behaving like a martyr? Are you in the midst of dissolving a deeply ingrained, yet obsolete, habit pattern? What circumstances are encouraging you to 'Let go and Let God/dess'? Why might the idea of sacrifice be abhorrent to you? Why won't you surrender to what you know to be best for you? Has some old hang-up returned to haunt you? How might your perspective be enhanced or restored? What could you be resisting your need to cleanse and purify? What initiation do you fear? In what areas might the Race Mind Consciousness be dictating your behaviour? How does surrender mean winning rather than losing? Why do you continue to meddle in things that are clearly out of your jurisdiction and control?

## Personal Experience

It was a couple of months before the winter Holy Days, and while reviewing my finances, I found that I was definitely going to be short for my projected expenses. I love the work I do, yet cannot depend upon it for a set income. On the other hand, I must leave my schedule as open and flexible as possible to accommodate clients and students. What to do? I sat down with the Major Arcana and asked to be shown how best to approach the situation for my greatest good. Turning over the Hanged One, the card's Hebrew name, *Mem*, meaning 'water' and its properties of dissolution, suspension and reflection, came to mind. These led me to hold off making an immediate decision in order to slowly contemplate the circumstances in one of the ways I often do, while swimming.

After several days of swimming on my question and glancing at the Hanged One sitting on my desk, I concluded that it was best to put some of my work on hold temporarily, due to my strong desire to be generous during the Holy Days. I felt genuinely relieved and comfortable thinking about the next step, applying for a holiday sales job at one of the many local department stores. What followed my decision still amazes me: within twenty-four hours of zeroing in on where I would submit applications, a phone call gave me the opportunity to work with a lovely couple who wanted to study Tarot privately according to their schedule. As it turned out, this would provide more than the money I had imagined needing. After setting a starting date, it dawned on me that surrendering to what I thought and felt to be of greater value in my situation was emulating the card, not as the Hanged or Undecided or Hung-up One which the card is sometimes associated with, but like someone who surrenders to doing what is best.

The other face of the card I wish to share is how I use the Hanged or Reversed One to help me alter my perspectives. Whenever I make a public presentation, I get jittery. No matter how well I am prepared, these feelings manage to creep up on me. Yet, instead of allowing myself to be overwhelmed, I focus on the card, which I then relate to as the Reversed One, and I reverse my attitude.

I start by doing a few *Hatha Yoga* postures because the Reversed One's body reminds me of its many inverted positions. Yogic philosophy teaches that performing these postures reverses the flow of your physical and mental energies, and hence enhances your perspective. Next, I reflect on the memory of the last time I gave an excellent presentation and both pictured and sensed the sequence of events as if they were happening now, right before me. This experience (or re-experience) leaves me feeling calm and confident, and as a result my presentation goes smoothly. In other words, by changing my perspective – by looking at the situation as the Reversed One does, from its opposite polarity, success and confidence, not failure and fear – I reverse not only how I feel, but the outcome as well.

## Student Experiences

❖ 'Going over the Suspended One's associations with water and purification and then meditating on the card, I realised I've been putting off purifying my body for way too long,' began Ro, a busy adult graduate student. 'I've been eating too many rich, sugary snack foods since I started working on my thesis. I know it's not out of hunger, either, but to break up the boring routine I'm in. I also recognised that I've somehow stopped fasting one day a month, something I've done for a few years now. It just slipped away from me. So last week I went to a spa with a friend and took steam and sauna baths. I'm in the middle of a healing crisis, my skin is broken out, and I'm craving salt and sugar – definitely signs of withdrawal for me. This is all only confirming what I already know, what the Suspended One showed me: suspend the junk food. Purification is long overdue!

'Do you know what else I realised? Here I am, almost a middle-aged woman, eating like I did when I was a teenager. I think that becoming a student again somehow triggered my subconscious into allowing me to behave as I did when I was last a student. Well, it's clearly time to move into more adult habits.'

*'Great realisations, Ro,' I told her. 'As I've said before, we have an unconscious way of wanting to return to states that seem comfortable or familiar even if they prove to be genuinely uncomfortable and destructive. And it looks as though you've caught yourself in the act. You've done your homework well and will soon recognise that you're not only cleansing your body, but your mind, too. You've definitely tapped into one of the functions of the Suspended One, purification of the habit mind.'*

❖  'I felt "out of it" this week because I had to work a lot of overtime,' said Ken, a production manager in a local electronics firm. 'I hadn't given my homework with the Hanged One so much as a single thought. Then, while standing in a very long line at the post office the other afternoon, the card "appeared" in my life. That line was so long it almost went out the back door, and it seemed as if everyone in it was complaining.

'At first I felt that way, too. Here I was on my way home from my first day without overtime out of the past ten and I had to wait in line just to return a shirt. But after a few minutes of feeling increasingly uncomfortable, I recalled that I could handle the situation another way. I could do as the Hanged One does, and be contrary to the world, contrary to the consciousness surrounding me. I didn't have to partake of others' negativity, what you call the Race Mind. I could reverse my attitude. So I smiled to myself and took some paper from my organiser and outlined a letter to a friend that I've been putting off because I've been so busy. Before I knew it, it was my turn at the counter. I left the post office with a feeling of accomplishment. Not only did I get the letter started, but I did my Tarot homework, too. I'd reversed my attitude and turned a waste of time into a productive one.'

'Ken, that's a wonderful example of living the Hanged One,' I said. 'The pull of the Race Mind is usually so all-pervasive it's difficult to be able to differentiate it from your own mind. When you do, it's not always easy to extricate yourself from its grasp. This is one of the Hanged One's main teachings and you did a great job with it.'

❖  'My husband's college roommate came to California last week on business and then spent the weekend with us,' shared Beth. 'It was the first time my husband had seen him in over a dozen years, and I hadn't met him before. He turned out to be nice, but too serious (very much an Easterner), and his politics were anything but liberal. After I heard his views on abortion, I found myself gradually retreating. When he finally asked me about my interests, I had fun watching him squirm when I told him about my study of the occult and Wicca.

'Sunday mornings are my time for doing Tarot homework. I usually begin by rewriting my notes to be sure I understand the teachings thoroughly. Well, lo and behold, I latched on to the Intelligence of the Hanged One, the Stable Intelligence, the eternal truths that offer stability in times of insecurity. There it was. I immediately saw that I was feeling threatened and invalidated by our visitor. I also guessed that he was probably feeling likewise. So I sat in my meditation chair with the Hanged One and asked how to stabilise myself. It soon became apparent that I had to open my heart to who he really is – his Higher Self – and hang up my self-righteous attitudes of he's wrong and I'm right. We're both right for who we are.

'Later I found him in the kitchen busily preparing coffee and some sweet rolls he had bought in town. I greeted him with a warm, "Good morning," and didn't get upset when he judged the quality of the baked goods as "not too bad". Instead, I joked with him and said, "We're farther from Paris than you Easteners, you know." He smiled and almost laughed. We definitely became more at ease with each other throughout the day, thanks to the Stable Intelligence.'

'Beth, you've demonstrated how the Hanged One can teach us not to get "hung-up" on being right,' I told her. 'In reality, each of us sees the world from our own "correct" perspective. We can best achieve stability amid ego conflicts as you did, by tapping into the eternal truths. You lived the Hanged One's teachings by remembering what your real ties are, and it was your visitor's personality that helped you achieve this.'

❖ 'This card has become very special to me because I'm using it to help curb some reactive attitudes,' stated Tina, a woman who lives in a large household and works at a busy restaurant. 'When I first looked at the card, something about it seemed familiar. I laughed to find that the entrance-way my house is shaped like the symbol of the Hanged One's gallows. So each time I walk through it, I stop and do a little ritual. I pause under the arch and consciously recall that in each world I enter through it – the worlds of home and work – I wish to be as aware as I can, to see as much as I can through the eyes of the Hanged One. I'm overcoming patterns of being reactive to what goes on in both places: specifically, of giving more than I can afford to give and do. I've resisted taking charge of my life because I want others to like me. I know that way of behaving is childish. Now I've begun to feel less overextended and put upon, because I say, "No more," and I feel less defensive when I do. I know my responses to people are helping them respond differently to me. There, I said it: responses, not reactions.

'I'm behaving more like myself, instead of like my mother and grandmother, who took care of everyone except themselves. They were behaving like martyrs, a negative side of the Hanged One and sacrifice. I've been wearing a lot of blue, the Hanged One's colour, to reinforce my new role.'

*'Yes, Tina, it looks as if you have been working with the Sacrificing One, still another name for the Hanged One,' I explained. 'This particular facet of the card addresses the courage and willpower it takes not to fit in with a group that's important to us, yet whose behaviour hurts us; to sever such ties and act differently than prescribed by important people in our lives. But you're doing it, and you seem to be making the transition from Childhood to early Adulthood in the process.'*

❖ Barb recently began a freelance secretarial service and came to class wanting to discuss the effect the Hanged One was having on her. 'I've been terribly concerned about work and money for the last few weeks. It's interesting, but I feel as if I've somehow been led into working for myself. I know that I need to learn more about trusting my Higher Self, and believe that my Self set this one up for me. If I didn't feel so bad, I'd feel terrific!

'Well, I've been a very bad example of trust: waking up at night filled with anxiety, not acknowledging how much I'm doing to make my business work and thinking about failure almost constantly. The

Hanged One teaches a lesson I really need to incorporate into my life. I'm cared for by the universe. I'm tied to the Tree of Life. My Higher Self loves me. I know that I'm doing everything possible to make my business work, and new businesses take time to get going. But, on a gut level, all my negatives have been coming to the surface. I've actually been drowning in them.

'This week I took myself in hand and used a simple affirmation like you've been suggesting, a statement affirming the presence of the card's teachings in my life. So simple, yet so hard to do in my anxious state. This is the one I came up with: "Both my Self and myself provide for me."

'I also went to see my counsellor and took a look at where my overwhelming fears are coming from. I remembered being young and my dad's business going bankrupt and hearing my mom putting him down for years about it. Since I've identified more with him than her, I think that's where my fears and insecurity are coming from. I'm using my affirmation and have brought the card to my office. I've been crying a lot, too, cleansing myself with tears. Oh, no, the card's association with water just hit me! It's not easy, but I know I'm going to have to face these issues sometime, so why not now? And why not have my business be successful in the bargain?'

*'Ah, you have lived the Surrendered One, Barb,' I assured her. 'An essential part of this card is surrendering to what must be done, even though it might be uncomfortable to set things right. Yet you've come to the point in your development where it isn't so much a question of taking the harder road, the road of sacrifice, but of surrendering to what is for the highest good. It is very adult to consciously surrender to some short-term discomfort for the long-term satisfaction of doing what is best. Looks like you're moving right into the Gateway of Adulthood!'*

## Suggestions for Application and Integration of the the Hanged One

The following are means through which you may come to know the Hanged One's teachings more personally. These exercises will provide you with the means to 'Let go and let God'; be more stable and reverse, suspend or surrender a point of view; not give up more than is genuinely necessary, or overextend yourself.

1   Colour or draw your own version of the Hanged One with yourself as the figure.

2 Set the card in a visible place as a reminder to your conscious and subconscious minds to use and absorb its teachings not to sacrifice what you honestly cannot, to reverse an obsolete perspective or attitude, to surrender to new vision, or to gain stability by turning to your belief system.

3 Dream on the Hanged One.

4 Play the note G$^\#$ on a musical instrument. Intone IAO or hum along with the music. Now meditate on the card for a few minutes. While doing so, contemplate an especially challenging or anxiety-provoking task from its 180-degree opposite or reversed position. Or mentally recreate a similar situation in which you were successful. If you lack one to recall, create your ideal. Try this several times before actually doing the task. Request that the Reversed One's teachings guide you through this situation. Be aware of how you feel and perform afterwards. Notice how the card helps to create stability. If you are faced with a worrisome situation, event or problem, such as an inability to quit recreational drugs, realise you are hanging on to some false support or system, or feel excessively emotional or unstable, imagine how the Hanged, Surrendered or Suspended One would handle it. If it seems feasible, do it. Jot down the times when you became aware of the Hanged One in your interactions. I was aware of the Hanged One when? Before/during/after . . .

5 Select an appropriate aspect of the card – the Surrendered, Hanged, Reversed, Sacrificed One – and enact it in the world. I enacted the — One and this is what happened . . .

6 The Rerun. After having an experience and realising in retrospect how the Hanged One's teaching might have resulted in the suspension of certain behaviour, increased stability, encouraged surrender to a higher good, or prevented you from drowning in your emotions, mentally relive the situation, *including* your insight. If possible, actually rerun the situation in real life with this new attitude or behaviour.

7 Ask yourself the following questions:

'Where would I like to feel more secure and stable?' 'What attitude, behaviour, condition or person would I like to reverse my experience of, or know from a new and different perspective?' 'What thoughts or actions would I benefit from suspending?'

'What am I excessively hung-up on achieving?' 'Where might I be sacrificing more than I can afford to?' 'What do I hope to gain from the sacrifices I'm making?' 'What have I been avoiding through extended periods of meditation, fantasy, or over-indulgence in food, sex, drugs and/or alcohol?' 'In what area of my life is contact with my Higher Self starting to provide me with new-found stability?' 'How might I better relinquish my tendency to over-control myself, others and situations and, "Let go and let God?"' 'What is it best to suspend acting upon right now?' 'What can I do to cease feeling as if I'm drowning?'

'What Gateway of Life am I in or growing through in the previous questions?' Indicate: Childhood, Adolescence, Adulthood or Wisdom. Why?

'What do I need to do in order to develop the above further?' I need to . . .

'What step(s) do I want to take towards this goal and how can the Hanged One guide me?'

8   Use a personal statement regarding the presence of the Hanged, Suspended, Reversed or Surrendered One in your life at this time: 'I surrender the little me to the big me.' 'I gladly sacrifice my addiction to cigarettes for better health.' 'I am willing to suspend my small perspective of life in favour of a greater one.' 'When appropriate I go contrary to the ways of the world.' My personal statement is . . .

9   Inspirational words and quotes:

'How different the world appears through the eyes of your true Self.'

'God will supply every need of yours.'          PHILIPPIANS 4:19

10  What symbols stand out in the card? What do they say to you? How might they be useful in daily living? Bring the symbol(s) into your life in some way so as to integrate the card's teachings. The position of the Reversed One's body reminds me of the importance of doing *Hatha Yoga* postures daily to reverse and balance the flow of energy in my body.

11  Wear and surround yourself with the Hanged One's colour, blue, to remind you of the card's teachings when needed, such as

wanting to be more active in purifying your body, becoming more reflective or perceiving a person or situation from a more centred point of view. Notice how you are affected.

12  The Hanged One's astrological correspondence is the planet Neptune, which governs traits such as an excessive fantasy life and the creation of illusions, hurtful self-indulgences, martyr-like behaviour, plus the desire to cleanse away or dissolve these traits. Also, loving self-sacrifice, renunciation and the sub-conscious acceptance of the universal and natural laws and principles. Is there some situation in which you might lovingly use the aforementioned in order to dissolve, renounce or give up any of the aforementioned traits? Use the teachings of the Surrendered, Suspended or Sacrificed One to remind yourself of this. Notice what happens: your thoughts and feelings and the outcome.

13  Remember that the Hanged One's name, *Mem*, means 'water'. How can this remind you of the card's meaning or help in your life process? Because water is a mirror, it reminds me that every time I look into the mirror and find fault with what I see, I may also reflect on the truth I have been given the perfect physical body to do the spiritual work of this lifetime.

14  Try a few drops of the scent myrrh associated with the Hanged One as a reminder to integrate the card's teachings.

15  Have a cup of tea made from or cook with the herb Irish moss or kelp. Sit quietly as you drink or eat and consider this mineral-rich herb's properties as a demulcent (soother of abraded mucous membranes) and nutrient and consider the similar qualities of the Hanged One.

# Death

## General Information and Symbolism

The Grim Reaper, age-old symbol of death, clears the fields of life, so that what is dead will not impede the new growth that is sprouting up. Death's scythe is shaped like the glyph for the planet Saturn, indicating that all born into the physical world are limited to mortal form and, therefore, will in time die. In the right season, the Harvester arrives to extract each ripened soul from its body.

The man and woman represent the spheres of Wisdom, *Chokmah*, and Understanding, *Binah*, on the Tree of Life respectively. Death is not only a physical transformation, but the change from a subjective to an objective state of mind. After our soul exits the physical body and world, we become wise and understand what life truly was, is, and will be, about. In life we are constantly challenged to expand our awareness and become enlightened, while in death we are enlightened. A white rosebush appears in the card's corner. The Fool, or incarnating soul, carried this rose to signify the impersonal clarity of purpose, objectivity and purity of desire that the incarnating soul sets out to bring into the life cycle. Upon physical birth and the advent of self-conscious awareness (the Magician), the rose becomes coloured (red) by personal desire and subjectivity. Returned to white in Death, the flower intimates how the death experience re-clarifies and purifies our consciousness so that our perceptions are again impersonal and unified into the single desire for truth.

The crowned man and youthful woman also emphasise that Death is the great equaliser, since neither power, prestige nor youth can prevent it from doing its work. This reminds me of the strange story of a wealthy businessman who, near the end of his life, attempted to fend off death by drinking human milk in a fruitless attempt to restore his youth.

Terms such as 'passing-on', 'crossing-over' and 'life's last great journey' are often used to refer to Death. A foot rests on the earth to show that the soul has moved onwards. The foot alludes to the Qabalistic function of Motion assigned to this card. It is the un-stoppable forward motion of life that bears all to Death. Because the astrological sign of Pisces rules the feet, the foot also suggests the passing or death of the present age of Pisces (the last 2,000 years). In contrast to the Piscean Age, wherein power has been garnered through limiting knowledge, fear, control of others and greed, the Aquarian Age will be a time when power will come through knowledge, open-mindedness, trust, self-control and humanitarianism.

One hand lies upon the ground illustrating that Death puts the work of life to rest. Two others reach heavenwards to seek life's greater meaning. Such comes via the higher wisdom and under-standing that accompany the Death process. Again, many believe Death to be a state of temporary enlightenment for as long as one is out of the physical world, whereas life is the work one elects to do to evolve into permanent enlightenment. This may explain why so many people who have had very difficult birth experiences often say, 'I know I didn't want to be here.'

The skeleton is yet another symbol of Death's equality. Death subjects all to the same universal and natural laws and principles and eventually reduces all to the same basic skeleton or component parts. The skeleton symbolises the act of taking out the old to bring in the new. This is about the demise of antiquated and dysfunctional dogma, laws, rules, regulations, and practices that attempt to prevent people from thinking for themselves or questioning the omnipotence of organised religion, science and certain political leaders and systems. Lastly, in certain occult and shamanic schools, the skeleton represents the one eternal self. Trainees work to perceive this Self through mind-expanding substances, trance, meditation, or even going so far as to remove the living flesh from their bodies while in such altered states.

Now, if you think the skeleton looks strange, you are right! Looking carefully, you can see that the skeleton is reversed at both the centres for reproduction and creative self-expression. Because sex and personal self-expression are no longer needed in death, these energies are turned inward to help the soul regenerate and assimilate its life experience.

When asking students, 'Does the sun rise or set?' they reply, 'Both'. It is true that when the sun rises here, it sets elsewhere and vice versa. This implies that when the sun of an individual's life sets on the physical plane, it rises on the spiritual plane. The sun, symbol of the One Self or Source, is the cause of all dualities. Death, however, puts an end to the illusion of separateness. From the perspective of the Higher Self, Death is neither positive nor negative; it just *is*. The wise know that in the end, all is One. The exquisite words of Kahlil Gibran further illustrate this concept and its symbolism: 'For what is to die but to stand naked in the wind and melt into the sun?'[1] The sun also underscores the fact that death is always preceded by some type of transformation, regeneration or rebirth. Therefore, in time, you become able to welcome death as the end of painful, unproductive or self-destructive conditions, such as a compulsive habit, a diseased and hopeless relationship, writer's block, or a comatose and severely brain-damaged child. Here, you may fear the unknown, as well as the pain and adjustment these changes bring. This transition may be likened to the image of the Fool about to step off the cliff. His trusting expression encourages us to have faith and believe that the life force always knows best and does what is ultimately right.

The stream of life first seen in the High Priestess appears here to tell you that death is part of the natural flow of life. In death, its waters travel like the transitioning soul, moving from the narrow stream of personal consciousness back into the wider ocean of impersonal consciousness beneath the sun, or Source.

The colour of the Death card is blue-green, its musical note is G and its herb is elder. *Nun* is the Hebrew name for the Death card, meaning 'fish' when used as a noun, and 'to grow' or 'productivity' as a verb. Death often seems cold-blooded like the fish, yet the Greek word for fish means 'womb'. These words may also bring to mind Jesus' miracle of feeding the multitudes from a few loaves and fishes, in addition to His name, 'The Fisher of Men'. Death comes from the greater reality to fish us from the sea of life when we have completed our earthly work.

Death is linked to the fixed (stable, non-volatile) Water sign of Scorpio and governs the organs of reproduction and elimination. The fact that orgasm is often called the 'Little Death' creates a link between death and new life. The connection between death, rebirth and transformation is undeniable. One of life's greatest miracles is a species' ability to reproduce itself. Inherent in this process is sometimes the death of the parent. The plant dies to yield the seed;

1 Kahlil Gibran, *The Prophet*, Alfred A. Knopf, New York, 1964, p. 81.

fish often die after spawning. This is communicated by a seed appearing in the Death card's upper left-hand corner. The Scorpio personality says: I'm vital, powerful, resourceful, energetic, secretive, argumentative, vengeful (stinging like the scorpion), desirous, forceful, creative, a transformer and survivor (like the Phoenix rising from the ashes, also a symbol of Scorpio), and perceptive (like the eagle, yet another significator of the sign). Evolved Scorpios get what they desire by seeking their Higher Self through what they desire. These individuals apply their creativity, vitality and resourcefulness to transform adversity, rather than by forcefully manipulating or deviously eliminating it.

Arriving at the Death card, the following help from the previous cards is available: Strength shows how to handle lovingly inner and outer conflicts and adversity; the Hermit makes you aware of the multitude of tools and resources available when assistance is needed on the road to maturity; the Wheel of Fortune communicates the unavoidable laws of cause and effect; Justice relates that you may choose to adjust your actions and mitigate your karma by weighing, measuring and then choosing your responses to life carefully; the Hanged One indicates the possibility of reversing your beliefs about the world and what it expects from you. This card offers you the encouragement to pursue your inner promptings, resulting in a conscious spiritual awakening or rebirth.

Death is the last state you encounter and must master in life, yet it is difficult to prepare for, because you usually do not know what to expect. Many believe that knowledge of death comes only from experience. Hence, initiatory procedures involving mock death take place in many cultures. Death is more real to humans, because we are the only species that seems to know of its inevitability. Out of this have naturally evolved a number of belief systems regarding what death bestows. In the Western world, the prospect of death is usually grim, embodied by the symbolism of the Grim Reaper. Family, friends, possessions and body are left behind as we go to spend eternity with God in heaven or with the Devil in hell. Those with minor sins are allowed to repent in purgatory. The ancient Egyptians coped with death by subscribing to an afterlife much like the physical one just completed, sending their dead off to the next world equipped with life's necessities and comforts, often including living servants and animals.

Eastern philosophies teach reincarnation, or 'dropping the body' when its work or karma has been fulfilled, and 'taking a body' when there is need to resume another phase of worldly activity. This system is based upon the concept that death is an often welcomed and temporary break from the labours of life. Here you are instructed that both the physical body and its possessions are merely loaned to you to facilitate your life's work. Death is celebrated as freedom from your karmic indebtedness and body simultaneously. This attitude is summed up by a quote from the renowned Indian master, Meher Baba: 'Instead of looking upon death as the opposite of life, one inevitably comes to look upon death as the handmaiden of life.'[2]

The contemporary works of Elisabeth Kübler-Ross, *On Death and Dying*, and Raymond Moody, *Life after Life*, and the public testimonials of such personalities as Shirley MacLaine, are giving increased credibility to the existence of reincarnation. The practices of past-life and hypnotic regression strongly indicate that consciousness withdraws from the body when the latter becomes too old, diseased or injured. The spirit then dwells in another realm, assimilating its earthly interactions, until the Higher Self deems it time to re-enter the physical world to continue growing closer to perfecting the God/dess Self. It is speculated that the more evolved the soul, the faster it returns to the physical world and body. In other words, when a soul finally comprehends what it must do in order to merge with the Most High, it cannot help but become highly motivated to complete its allotted work and achieve this oneness.

Many who doubt the validity of reincarnation claim past-life memories to be ancestral experiences originating from our gene pool, encoded along with genes for eye colour, handedness and a predisposition for playing the violin. Others claim that such come from the many lives that are occurring simultaneously with this one, but in other dimensions. Whatever the perspective taken, the results serve to inspire many to accept their life circumstances, do the best job possible with them and be the finest person they can be. The Death card indicates that these new perspectives are helping many to face one of life's greatest challenges, death, with increasing ease and dignity. This is emphasised by the card's number, 13, a combination of the will and concentration of number one, the Magician, with the creativity, desire and imagination of number three, the Empress, to

2  Meher Baba, *Listen Humanity*, Harper & Row, New York, 1967, p. 96.

produce a more realistic vision of Death – seeing it as part of the order of life – and number four, the Emperor (the sum of one and three). Finally, the number thirteen has long been considered 'unlucky'. This is primarily because Jesus was said to have been crucified on Friday the 13th. But Jesus did rise from the dead on Easter Sunday, reminding us that inherent in death is resurrection.

Along this line of thinking is the belief that we not only choose our time and manner of death, consciously or unconsciously, but the death experience itself reflects our belief system. For example, highly developed Yogis often perceive their death in meditation before it actually happens. Also, it has been learned from persons who have died and then been revived, that if they believed in hell and that their actions warranted going there, they did. Or, if you are convinced death is the end of everything, it will be. Finally, in regard to the matter of examining how one dies, accidentally, through long- or short-term illness, or suicide, we must also consider euthanasia.

Individuals are now considering their 'right to choose' merciful tools to put an end to extreme and terminal physical suffering. Here they must be exceedingly careful that they are not wilfully inflicting harm upon others by their decision, or seeking such an alternative as a means of avoiding necessary, yet painful, growth.

In the Qabalah, the Death card is known as the Imaginative Intelligence. Imagination is the link between the world of mind and the world of matter. Contemplate this Intelligence as your own, or the One Great Creative Imagination, that reproduces, or ceases to reproduce, a thought over and over again, resulting in the life or death of the imagined form.

### Gateway of Life: Adolescence to Adulthood

The Death card, like the Chariot, is a double door marking the passage from Adolescence to Adulthood. Knowing the pain certain behaviour brings, individuals in the final throes of Adolescence either suppress, sublimate or relinquish this behaviour instead of continuing to suffer. Recognising and accepting that the immature aspects of your personality are holding you back from the privileges of Adulthood, you allow some immature needs and desires to die, keep some in close check and sublimate others in order to move onward. The maturation process may be inadvertently accelerated owing to the emerging adult accidentally brushing with death – your own physical mortality or that of another. Feeling the preciousness of life, you are motivated to do what is necessary to partake of it more fully. In addition, you begin to cultivate the ability to view death as the changing and transforming aspect of life, paying attention to and even welcoming the mini-deaths that continually surround you. The ability to accept death as part of life is a sure sign of maturity.

Like the Chariot, Death is the sum total of the previous cards. From the Magician to the Chariot, you are like a child being educated in the skills required for encountering daily living. Between the Chariot and Death, you as an adolescent grow to maturity by way of your encounters with the guru of everyday living. You seek personal fulfilment and the world at large responds, causing certain behaviour to be enhanced, modified, or die either a natural or unnatural death. At this point on your journey through life, you are learning about suppression, the conscious exclusion of painful desires or thoughts from awareness, and sublimation, the conscious modification, elevation and transformation of your inappropriate instinctive impulses into more suitable behaviour. The former process is illustrated in the Death card by the skeleton's twisted spine (at the reproductive or procreative centre and at the throat, the centre for creative self-expression). These twists imply that there always are options available when deciding how to express your creative energies, passions and desires, *if* you wish and will yourself to imagine them.

Encountering the Death card at life's Gateways may lead to certain attitudes and behaviour. CHILDHOOD: After a man's longtime companion dies in his sleep, the man becomes fearful of going to sleep and not awakening; ADOLESCENCE: Although she desires to continue having spontaneous love affairs, a woman attempts to restrain herself when she recalls that a good friend is dying from AIDS; ADULTHOOD: When a gardening fanatic is fined for using more water than his fair share during a drought, he is able to acknowledge his wrongdoing, and although it means that some of his plants will die, he alters his behaviour for the good of the community; WISDOM: Accepting that her body is dying and that she will soon pass on, a woman prepares to meet the next stage of her life, death, by completing her personal business matters, including the signing of a legal document stating that she does not want her life prolonged by artificial measures.

## Divinatory Questions for Death

*Upright:* What are you allowing or helping to pass away? What part of your life has died – gone forever – youth, childbearing, parenting, an ability for a certain line of work? Where may your desire for something new be functioning as a motivation to let something old and worn out die? What have you tried to eliminate? What has died in order to be reborn in a new form? How might your perceptions about death be changing? What desire have you sublimated instead of suppressing or repressing? Where might a period of mourning be appropriate? What attitude is in the process of being transformed? What relationship is no longer viable? Are you preparing for a complete transformation in the area of your career or living situation? What are you letting pass on naturally? What experience have you suppressed in order to survive? How has greater wisdom and understanding come through loss? What thought forms are you reproducing or allowing to die?

*Reversed*: What project, relationship, etc., have you been fighting to keep alive? What new thing or situation is about to emerge? Might your present feelings about death be related to childhood feelings of abandonment and isolation? What death and rebirth have you been struggling with? What are you afraid to surrender to or give up on? In what ways or areas could your desires and imagination be working against you? How might you have abused your power? How has your body, project, or relationship become regenerated? Is it possible that your prolonged state of mourning is an avoidance of getting on with the business of living? What ideas would it be wise to let go of? Where has death proved to be a blessing? How might death be bringing a oneness of mind or purpose with it? How might death be an initiation and transformation into something greater? What would you have been better off sublimating rather than suppressing? What have you miraculously survived?

## Personal Experience

My initial reactions to the Death card stemmed from my early childhood during which images of skeletons, monsters, ghosts and cadavers rose from the dead on Halloween night to haunt, scare and punish. I was also taken to several graphic murder movies while quite young, owing to the unavailability of a sitter, which caused me to further associate fear and violence with death. Yet, as in most modern American families in which relatives are sent to hospitals, 'homes' and sanatoriums to die, I was sheltered from the everyday realities of death. In my formative years, familial discussions and dialogue about the interconnection between living and dying were non-existent. Looking back, I believe I would have been much better off to have been protected from the images of death promulgated by the retail and entertainment industries, and instead to have had more open communication within my family regarding this fact of life.

It was with tremendous relief and excitement that I discovered the other perspectives on death through the teachings of the Tarot and Yoga, getting acquainted with it in terms of the transition and transformation from one state to another, a natural phenomenon that happens to all of creation. These studies also helped me gain additional understanding of the near-death experience I had as a child.

Viewing my first cadaver in an anatomy class, I was immediately struck by its lifelessness. I knew intellectually that the body is the vehicle for the soul, but I had not actually experienced it. Standing in that first anatomy lab, I understood what metaphysicians and yogis say about the body being the house or temple of the spirit. The body lying on the lab table was obviously vacant; its inhabitant, the spirit, was definitely elsewhere. In fact, the first thought I had while looking at the remains was that it was like a piece of meat sitting in a butcher shop showcase.

During recent years, I have been close by when both a family member and a friend have died and watched with almost embarrassing fascination how the death process, when allowed to proceed naturally (without machines or heroics), is the polar opposite of birth. As death nears, lung capacity decreases; unlike a newborn's first deep inhalation, a dying person's last breath is a complete exhalation of the life force. The breath of life associated with the Fool, the spirit, seems pulled from the body at the moment of death, the moment of surrendering or 'giving up' the body, as reincarnationists term it. These experiences further transformed my theoretical understanding of the interrelationship between life and death communicated throughout the Tarot into something more personal. Undoubtedly, the same force which manifests life also manifests death.

Two primary teachings depicted by the Death card are that God/ dess gathers all back to itself and Death has precedence over all of creation at any time. Yet, why is it difficult, especially for those from Western cultures, to accept its authority? After considering this carefully, I recognised it to be the prevailing idea of death's finality. When death is apparent, I notice that most people tend to re-evaluate their lives, and when feelings of incompletion and dissatisfaction arise, resistance and fear are heightened. Some leave the world under dire protest; others, however, take advantage of whatever time remains to complete whatever they can and make peace with the rest.

I plainly recall my father hoarsely calling from his hospital bed, 'But I'm not ready yet, this isn't fair,' then slipping into a coma. His words chilled me to the bone, until I came to recognise his death to be a lesson in living life. I realised that I must not only live my life to its fullest, but must also be ready to die at any time. I discovered that the more I know and believe in the spirit or non-physical world, the less upset I am by thoughts of death. These insights, plus the meditations I did on the Death card, gave birth to my way of preparing for death, that of going to sleep each night at peace with myself and the world, repeating the personal statements I associate with the Death card: 'Life is my preparation for death, and death my preparation for life. I completely forgive and am completely forgiven.'

### Student Experiences

❖ 'Speaking of death, what a week I've had,' began Theresa with a deep sigh. 'I got the flu so badly I felt as if I was going to die. I never, ever get sick, but I've been working hard and taking care of the rest of my family who've been sick, too, so "it" got me. I was absolutely miserable; I ached all over; my stomach was cramping and the very thought of food made me retch. Out of the corner of my eye, I could see the Death card lurking on my dresser. It was eerie; I kept thinking to myself, Did I bring this one on to learn more about the Death card? To do a better job on my Tarot homework? Hey, there's a limit!

'Yet, as I lay there half dead, I could imagine how somebody who is very sick, whose body is failing, would want to die. I could see that death can be a great relief from suffering. After the weekend, I took a turn for the better and actually felt reborn, kind of how I used to feel as a kid after being in bed for a week and then going out to play. Everything looks new and shiny, somehow. Yes, it's definitely like some type of birth.'

*Illness and death may well bring transformations and openings in awareness such as the one Theresa told us about. It is often said that the secrets of death cannot be known in life, yet I think we've just heard one of its most important secrets. We can gain a direct perception of what it's like to welcome death as a relief and a release from suffering.*

❖ 'The aging and dying processes are very real, and up until recently, I've denied their existence,' shared Elliot, a potter, retired attorney and father of three sons. 'I was diagnosed as having leukaemia last summer and now there's a definite weakness in my body. I've refused to pay attention to its presence, but each time I overextend myself physically, I pay, pay, pay. I'm seeing the Death card as the slow demise of my body, which is natural. I think I'm more willing now to surrender to my limits and therefore hopefully look forward to suffering less. The nature of the physical world is change and transformation, death and rebirth. Without death, nothing new could find a place in the world.

'I know my spirit is immortal and that's what really counts. I think I need to take care of my body as best as I can, to respect and love it, but also accept its obvious transientness. I've been using an Indian chant I know as an affirmation:

> I am not my body. My body is not me.
> I am not my body. My body is not me.
> Immortal soul am I. Immortal soul am I.
> Immortal soul am I. Immortal soul am I.

'I'm also learning that my old attitudes about death are dying and that I'm becoming wiser and wiser as they go. The hardest part of this whole thing is leaving my children behind. I've been open and I talk with them, yet it's still very painful.'

*It's true that the work of life naturally wears the body out. I remember reading the autobiographies of several great Indian saints and vividly recall how, when a Wiseone of an especially elevated nature lay dying of cancer, his devotees begged him to cure himself as he had cured others. His response to their pleas was to tell them two things, both of which are integral to understanding the Death card: one, God or some higher power must take us all from the world at some point; and two, always keep in mind that the soul, not the body, is immortal.*

*On the other hand, it's undeniable that no matter what we believe happens after our body dies, and how much explaining we do, our physical presence is no longer around, and people can't help but miss and mourn this part of us. However, Elliot, like the Indian sage, couldn't be facing death in a more conscious or courageous fashion.*

❖ 'My job requires me to fly several times a year, and I absolutely dread it,' admitted Dee, a corporate saleswoman. 'It's embarrassing, but it's the truth. I'd been thinking about the Death card and hadn't been able to connect with it very well, and then my boss got sick and couldn't attend an important meeting. So I was asked to represent us instead, and had to take an unexpected flight on Wednesday morning. We hit some awful weather over the Rockies. I'll tell you, it was just like being in a popcorn popper. My fears kept mounting until something very strange happened to me, and I think to everyone else on the plane. We became very, very quiet. I think it was a sort of silent resignation. Maybe it was just in my mind, but I sensed that we were all – me, the other passengers, the crew and the plane – being held in God's hands, and I somehow knew everything would be okay, even if we crashed. It sounds crazy, but it was a genuine transcendental experience. I guess that's my integration of the Death card, knowing that death is all right.'

*I think Dee saw clearly that death is a part of life and, although we can try to forestall it by taking good care of our bodies and being aware of our actions, there's always the unexpected, such as natural catastrophes and accidents. Often, when we are forced to face our fears, we no longer fear them. When most people come face to face with death, the ego has a way of taking a back seat to the Higher Self. And as a result, the fear we feel has a way of being transformed into surrender, as it did with Dee (and most likely the others) on her plane trip.*

❖ 'I failed to pass the nursing exam for advanced emergency room procedures,' said Nan sadly. 'I studied and studied for it, but I guess not hard enough. It means that I won't get the raise I've been counting on, and I'll have to continue having my work supervised, then study for the exam again in a couple of months. Ugh! When I got the notice of failure in the mail, I felt like crawling off into a hole and disappearing. At first, I denied my feelings and tried to keep my spirits up for a day or so. I joked with my co-workers about wanting to stay at the poverty level. But it didn't work; I finally gave in. I started doing my homework and mourning my loss, rather than avoiding it. I've allowed myself to feel it, be angry at the people who wrote the test, feel sorry for myself, indulge in not cleaning the house, eat sweets and even wear black (she pointed to her clothing). It's been a good process for me to go through. I think it will help me to move on with getting ready for the next exam without feeling bitter.'

*I believe we must mourn losses so we can more fully celebrate and appreciate our gains. Elisabeth Kübler-Ross states that there are five stages involved in dealing with death: Denial, Anger, Bargaining, Depression and Acceptance. I have added Mourning to this list. Nan's responses are right on target. It's sometimes difficult in a world that moves as fast as ours, and places so much emphasis on pleasure and being happy, to give ourselves the space to fully deal with death in whatever form it may come in.*

❖  'You mentioned that death can be the passing on of old patterns and habits. And I have patterns of remaining close to people even if they treat me badly,' said Elaina, a long-time student of religion and spirituality. 'My spiritual side says, "They aren't developed and don't really mean to hurt you." But lately I've been coming to grips with the fact that my acceptance reinforces their behaviour, actually sanctions it. I've come to see that it would be better for all concerned if I'd communicate how hurt I feel, instead of making excuses for people. But it's scary, as I might lose friends. I've even opted to wear all my turquoise jewellery, like the colour of the card, to keep me focused on my purpose.

'Anyhow, the other day, my best friend, who is having a lot of marital problems, lashed out at me unexpectedly. Here was my chance to put my new philosophy to work. I told her I was hurt and felt that she was letting her frustrations out on me. She didn't like hearing what I had to say, and our conversation became strained during the remainder of our time together. I had a lot of doubt and guilt afterwards, but knew deep down I was doing the right thing.

'When somebody kicks me and I come back for more, it's not good for anybody. I need to be more protective of myself. And guess what? She called me the next morning to apologise and it felt great, so good I cried. This was the death of an old, immature pattern and the rebirth of a more adult one.'

*'I agree, Elaina, you're clearly moving into a new Gateway of Life. At some point, we become able to appreciate and even welcome death as deliverance, and that it is a helpful part of our maturation process, without which we would stay stuck in the rut of our immaturities forever. It is just wonderful how you killed off your pattern of giving your friend permission to abuse you just by being honest about your feelings. It seems that you have really deepened your friendship as well.'*

❖   'I've been thinking about how I can use the Death card in my life,' said Mara, a secretary and single parent, 'and part of that has been to review (or Rerun) my childhood experiences with death, which, like yours, weren't conducive to accepting it as a natural phenomenon. One of the main things I've been doing is trying to raise my daughter with a more open attitude. You know, not avoiding the subject and even getting kids' books from the library about it. Also, my mother's health has been declining and I can envision a time not too far off when my daughter will experience death more personally. On Friday night, as we unlocked our front door, we heard this chirping sound right under our feet, and my daughter said, "Look, Mommy, a baby bird." We have these big trees next to our apartment complex and somehow a baby had dropped out of its nest. So we picked it up and brought it in. I remembered that if a baby bird is kept warm and not handled or fed, there's a chance that the mother will pick it up again.

'We fixed a cosy nest in a shoe box and put it on a warm shelf in my daughter's room. It was hard for her not to touch it, and she kept wanting to feed it parts of her dinner. But she finally understood that we were trying not to put our scent on it so the mother might take it back when we put it out in the morning.

'It was so sad when she woke me up early on Saturday to tell me, "The birdie isn't moving, Mommy." The poor thing had died during the night. Well, here was another opportunity for me to handle death. As we buried the bird in the planter box, I told her how the bird, like all of us, comes from Mother Nature and is made of her elements – Fire, Water, Air and Earth. And that putting the bird into the earth is like giving it back to Mother Nature. I've been wanting to plant some flowers for a while now; this was the perfect chance to do it while at the same time showing my daughter something about life and death. We went to the nursery and picked out a miniature pink rosebush and planted it over the bird. I told her that each time we see the roses, we'll think of the spirit of the bird, just like the spirit of the food we eat lives through us, and the spirits of people live through their children and family. She was a bit concerned about that one, asking if I was going to die soon. I told her that I didn't expect to, but that maybe Grandma might.

'She's been calling the plant her "roses bird", and keeps asking when we'll have the roses that look like birds. I'm not sure how much a four-year-old really understands, but I feel I'm giving her some positive associations about death, more positive than the ones I'd received. I know I'm learning more about the Death card through it. The question from our homework, "What are you transforming?", is appropriate for my situation. I'm also using the affirmation, "Life brings death and death brings life", to help me along those lines.'

*'You're so right, Mara,' I said. 'Our childhood impressions tend to remain with us throughout our lives. As we learned with the Empress card, change is the result of imagination. Alter the image and the impression and you have an excellent chance of altering the result. The Qabalists call the Death card the Imaginative Intelligence. By consciously imagining ways to give your daughter some different impressions from those you received about death as a child, you are working with an aspect of this Intelligence.'*

## Suggestions for Application and Integration of Death

Now it is time to die and be reborn. The exercises which follow are the chance for you to become more able to accept death as part of life, perceive the seed of the new within the old, allow yourself to fully mourn a loss, allay the fears of the newness which follows transformation, move forward at the appropriate moment and look forward to the regeneration that follows death.

1  Draw or colour the Death card with your Higher Self as Death, a reminder that it is your own Self which chooses your death, no matter whether it is the death of a destructive way of behaving or the disintegration of the physical body.

2  Set the card in a visible place as a reminder to your conscious and subconscious minds to use and absorb its teachings to let go of an untenable way of relating, give in to something that you might not like but that is for the greater good, or become more accepting of death as you are surrounded by it daily.

3  Dream on Death.

4  Play the note G natural on a musical instrument. Intone IAO or hum along with the music. Now meditate on the card for a few minutes. As you do so, contemplate what in your life is dying or passing away in order for there to be some type of rebirth and renewal. What death or transformation can you see or feel yourself starting to experience? Then contemplate what attachment needs severing – what you might be clinging too long to, or what requires work with the six phases of death: Denial, Anger, Bargaining, Depression, Acceptance and Mourning.

Experiment with imagining your own death and funeral as a way of facing death's inevitability. Contemplate what you would most like to be remembered for, then imagine how you will realise these goals in your life. Next, request that the card's teachings guide you to this end. Or if you are faced with a worrisome situation, event or problem, such as acceptance of the passing on of some relationship, ability or physical attribute such as youth, imagine how Death might approach it. If it seems workable, do it. I was aware of the Death card when? Before/during/after . . .

5   Go out into the world and enact the teachings of Death. For example, I remembered the card's teachings as I was deciding whether or not to take in an old and sick stray cat. After a few heart-wrenching hours, I decided that the cat was definitely dying, and even though I might prolong the process for a while, I already had two healthy cats who could possibly get what the sick cat had, and because they are territorial animals, would certainly give the stranger a hard time. I made up my mind to let death take its natural course or let someone else in the neighbourhood intervene, which is what happened. I enacted the teachings of Death and this is what happened . . .

6   The Rerun. After having an experience and realising in retrospect how the Death card's teachings might have inspired you to let go of a dead or obsolete pattern, habit or unproductive course of action, shown that you are more than just your physical body, facilitated a rebirth or transformation in your attitudes or made you feel hopeful in the face of some type of death, mentally relive the situation, *including* your insights. This will help the behaviour become more automatic next time. If possible, actually rerun the situation in real life with this new attitude or behaviour.

7   Ask yourself the following questions:

'What do I desire to transform or eliminate?' 'Where am I afraid to let go or move forward?' 'How might I direct my sexuality or creative energies in new ways?' 'Where could I be crying over spilled milk?' 'What death am I denying?' 'What do I need to mourn?' 'How and what might I cut back in order to regenerate and have more energy available for more important projects?' 'What might I sublimate rather than suppress?' 'How am I about to let go of a dead way of relating?' 'What transformation am I preparing for?' 'What part of my life or another's is dying in order to be reborn?' 'How might I propagate the idea that death is not the end of life, but a natural continuation of my soul's journey?' 'What do I most wish to be remembered for after I die and what am I doing towards this end?' What are some of the things I fear most about my own death?'

'What Gateway of Life am I in or developing through in the previous question?' Indicate: Childhood, Adolescence, Adulthood or Wisdom. Why?

'What do I need to do in order to develop the above further?' I need to . . .

'What step(s) do I want to take towards this goal and how can the Death card guide me?'

8   Use a personal statement regarding the presence of the Death card in your life at this time: 'I prosper from the transformations in my life.' 'I weed the garden of my life, so I have room to plant the flowers.' 'Death, in the form of my body's metabolic processes, keeps my body alive and healthy.' 'I know that the darkness of death precedes the light of life.'

9   Inspirational words and quotes:

'Your fear of death is but the trembling of the shepherd when he stands before the king whose hand is to be laid upon him in honour.'                                 Kahlil Gibran, *The Prophet*

'In the midst of life we are in death.'        *Book of Common Prayer*

'We begin to die as soon as we are born, and the end is linked to the beginning.'                                   Manilius

10   What symbols stand out in the card? What do they say to you? How might they be useful in daily living? Bring the symbol(s) into your life in some way so as to integrate the card's teachings. Death's scythe reminds me that I cannot stop time, but make the most of each moment.

11   Wear and surround yourself with the Death card's colour, blue-green, to remind you of the card's teachings when needed, such as turning away from an untenable situation, relinquishing a particular behaviour, or recalling that the same divine spirit guides us in life and in death. Notice how you are affected.

12 The Death card's astrological correspondence is to the sign of Scorpio, governing the functions and traits of reproduction, elimination, argumentativeness, power, desire, regeneration and transformational abilities. Practise getting what you desire by seeking your Higher Self through what you desire. Surrender to your greater need to eliminate or transform an unwieldy situation rather than to cling unproductively to its present form. View sexuality in a new way, perhaps as Goddesses and Gods mating. Bring something new from the ashes of the past as does the Phoenix, symbol of Scorpio. Be more perceptive and objective about a desire, as is the Eagle, another symbol of Scorpio. Be aware where you are stinging like the Scorpion. Notice what happens: your thoughts and feelings and the outcome.

13 Remember that Death's Hebrew name, *Nun*, means both 'fish' and 'to grow'. How can this remind you of the card's meaning or help in your life process? The fish reminds me that when I find myself swimming too hard against life's tide, I either rest a bit, try another strategy, or become cold-blooded (non-emotional) like the fish and surrender to what is.

14 Try a few drops of the scent opoponax associated with Death as a reminder to integrate the card's teachings.

15 Have a cup of tea made from the herb elder. Sit quietly as you drink and consider the herb's ability to induce sweating and remove putrefying matter from the bloodstream; act as a laxative, antiseptic and stimulant; and assist the process of composting; then consider the like qualities of the Death card.

## *Part Four*

### THE GATEWAY OF
### ADULTHOOD

The following cards portray the Fool-adult's progressive maturation and continued individuation through their adult years towards old age, or Wisdom. Of course, this transition may occur at any chronological age.

Being an adult means you become increasingly able to consciously direct and redirect your mind, body and emotions, rather than have them direct you. You are more proficient at not being led by erroneous and obsolete thought patterns, destructive emotional impulses and your senses. Death, like the Chariot, is a double Gateway marking the passage of the adolescent into adulthood. You enter tentative about your abilities and exit with confidence. Upon reaching maturity, the fully developed adult – a person skilled at attending to their physical, mental and emotional needs – somehow perceives that 'something is missing' and becomes naturally drawn to focus on the development of his/her spiritual identity to fill this gap.

Entry into the next Gateway, Wisdom, will depend upon how skilfully you confront and deal with the suppressed and repressed aspects of your personality lying dormant in the subconscious from the previous Gateways of Childhood and Adolescence. Through unrelenting desire, deliberate effort, conscientious and diligent action, you now (in adulthood) use the Rules and Tools gathered from prior cards and Gateways (initially used for survival and pure ego-gratification alone) to refine yourself. In other words, the same laws, principles and helpers must be consistently called upon to bring you to the last lap of your chosen path and up to the mountain-top. Spiritual practice means practising until you are perfect.

Increased ability gives way to increased duties and moral obligations. Consequently, the Gateway from Adulthood to Wisdom poses many new demands. The aim is for the life traveller to welcome the added responsibilities as signs of the liberation to come at the Gateway of Wisdom, not feel oppressed and burdened. Remember, you and the Wiseones are faced with the identical tasks of 'chopping wood and drawing water' in your everyday lives. What differs is how you engage with such.

14     **TEMPERANCE**     ס

# CHAPTER 18

# Temperance

## General Information and Symbolism

The Archangel Michael, whose name translates from Hebrew to mean, 'Who is like God', reigns over Temperance. Edgar Cayce's trance readings state that Michael is the archangel who hovers before the throne of the Most High and is, in fact, the intermediary between God/dess and humanity, or the 'Way to God'. This is depicted on the Tree of Life where Michael stands at the entrance to the sphere of Beauty, *Tiphareth*, the Christ Consciousness. Cayce's reading further states that 'Michael is the lord of the guard of change that comes to every soul that seeks the way'. In other words, what happens in our lives comes from the divine, the Higher Self, whose work is bringing the soul home. This is given additional credence by the fact that the Angel (as does the Fool) wears the Most High's Hebrew name, the *Tetragrammaton – Yod, Heh, Vav, Heh –* above his heart.

Michael also wears a seven-pointed star, symbol of mastery, over his heart. (If you try drawing it, you will find that unlike the five or six pointed star, it demands a very steady or master's hand.) Because it has no precise formula, its execution is a question of personal ability. This suggests the truth that there are guidelines, but no precise formulas for spiritual growth. Aspirants follow general guidelines that are watched over by the Archangel Michael, referred to in Qabalah as the Holy Guardian or Guiding Angel, who has our best interests at heart. He guides but does not direct, as your particular path to self-mastery is dictated by your own heart of hearts.

The rainbow over the Angel's head refers to the practice of alchemy, traditionally defined as the transformation of lead into gold. However, those trained in esoteric alchemy are aware that this is a metaphor for the transformation of an ordinary person into an enlightened one via divine guidance (the Angel) and the *Athanor*. The *Athanor*, or 'furnace', is an alchemical term referring to the various 'firing processes' or metabolic and chemical changes within the alchemist's body that accompany and precede the refinement, elevation and transmutation of personal consciousness. These alterations, or 'temperings', enable the aspirant to withstand the increased levels of stress and strain inherent in the attainment of higher states of awareness. The word 'temperance' refers to the refining procedures employed in metallurgy. When metals are tempered or tested, they are heated and cooled to purify and strengthen them. This process is beautifully portrayed by the Archangel pouring water on the Lion – symbol of the fixed Fire sign, Leo, associated with courage, pride and ego – as he holds a burning torch over the Eagle, symbol of the highest evolution of the fixed Water sign, Scorpio, associated with the ability to be more objective about wants and needs, passion and desires, to bring forth personal transformation. This illustrates the alchemy of courageously tempering or cooling the aspirant's immature tendencies, while firing up the passionate desire to seek the highest when meeting life's challenges. In turn, such attitudes and behaviour facilitate further integration of the teachings put forth to this point. Temperance addresses the importance of applying the teaching of truth to everyday life. This provides feedback as to how skilled you have become in their application as well as refines and improves your skill with these essential tools to develop your consciousness further. To summarise, the aspirant is having his 'metal tested'.

The Qabalistic function linked with Temperance is Wrath. During times of intense personal transformation – when we feel that we are 'on fire', or 'in the fire' – we may feel enraged or that the Wrath of the Most High is upon us. We may alleviate our misery simply by not fighting it. The harder our ego wrestles with our Higher Self, in the guise of the Archangel Michael, the more likely our discomfort will continue to increase. The solution is to surrender to the refiner's fire, as it always wins. As soon as you give in to the divine force that is aiming only to assist you, the heat is turned down.

Iris was the Greek goddess of the rainbow who, according to myth, personified the bridge between heaven and earth. The rainbow's spectrum contains the colours of the seven inner centres or *Chakras*, whose activation and alignment (one of the goals of spiritual alchemy) is a pathway to inner peace and enlightenment (the 'pot of gold' at the rainbow's end). The native American tradition has a tale called 'Warriors of the Rainbow' that tells of peoples of all colours unifying to strive for world peace. This may be compared to the way the alignment of our inner rainbow functions to bring peace within.

The Angel's stance, one foot on the earth, the material world, and one in the water, the spiritual world, shows you that by the daily integration of the Rules and Tools of the Game of Life, balance and wholeness occur. It is by engaging with life in a balanced way that you progress beyond the extremes of either living a completely worldly life – without thought of its spiritual purpose, or totally withdrawing into spiritual realms – without thought of spirits' worldly purpose. Wholeness is experiencing the spirituality of the material world while simultaneously recognising that material things and daily situations are spiritual instruments.

With Temperance, an interdependent working relationship between the self-conscious and subconscious aspects of the personality is evident. The need for differentiation between these parts of the personality depicted in the Lovers is gradually decreasing, as there is now conscious recognition that both stem from the same Source. Therefore, the card is sometimes known as the Consummation, or Alchemical Marriage, the blending and refining of opposing elements within the human personality to make a new more integrated individual. As in alchemy, we must 'slough off' who we are not to get to who we are. Finally, alchemists often speak of finding the secret elixir of longevity. When the advanced practitioner gains the direct knowledge that their soul is deathless or eternal, they have discovered the elixir.

A golden path leads from the pool's edge up to the mountains, above which a sun beams down. The sun resembles the Crown or Source, *Kether*, shining down upon and through the masculine and feminine pillars of Mercy and Severity on the Tree of Life, symbolising that once you commence climbing the spiritual path, the journey's end is within sight. Those on this High-way recognise that everything that happens is the 'Way to God'.

The Archangel Michael, often called the 'Archangel of the Sun', reigns over the southern quadrant of heaven and the element of Fire and displays a solar disk on his forehead. He is the fire of the soul that enlivens, purifies and transforms the human mind and emotions. Michael is the 'dispeller of fear'. The Bible says, 'Michael rid heaven of the Dragon', (Satan and his demons) as he helps to slay the dragons within each aspirant. Progress in our daily lives and spiritual work depends upon our ability and willingness to seek divine guidance when our demons come out. Michael is the divine guide we learn to turn to at such times.

The colour of the Temperance card is blue, its musical note is G#

and its herb is echinacea. *Samekh* is the Hebrew name for Temperance and means 'a support, or foundation'. The teachings of truth are there to support us at *all* times. At this point, the foundations for the next stage of 'house' (*Beth*, the Magician) or personality building have been laid. To complete the job means taking what has been accomplished from the previous stages of work and employing it as a support, while continuing to build. If, however, the foundation is weak or incomplete, the personality, like the house, will be unprepared to bear the demands of the superstructure above it. Remember, when you construct your life – your thoughts, words, actions and interactions – upon the secure foundation of Eternal Being, you will not fail.

Sagittarius is the mutable (adaptable, combining the qualities of cardinal or initiating energies with fixed or stable energies) Fire sign associated with Temperance and rules the hips, thighs, femur, coccygeal and sacral vertebrae, sciatic nerves and muscular system. As a dual sign, its half-human half-animal symbol, the centaur archer, has the head, arms and trunk of the human and legs of a horse. Much like Michael's fire and water combine to make steam or spirit, this symbol represents how reconciling our animal and human selves brings us wholeness.

The bow of the archer, Sagittarius, is signified by the rainbow over the Angel's head. It intimates the goal of our efforts to complete the next stage of life work, the 'pot of gold' at the rainbow's end. The Hebrew word, *kavanah*, means 'a feeling of concentration and devotion'. *Kavanah* stems from the root, *kaven*, meaning 'to aim'. Therefore, just as an archer aims at a target, *kavanah* may denote lovingly aiming consciousness towards a certain end, which in the case of Temperance is self-healing and enlightenment. The Sagittarian personality says: I'm determined, jovial, adventurous, open-minded and philosophical and I pursue my inner promptings. I verify, test and examine by trying things out for myself. Sagittarians tend to be visionaries with a passion for life who love to explore and conquer new realms. Ruled by the planet Jupiter – called Guru in Indian astrology – one of the Sagittarian's major lessons is to be attuned philosophically and spiritually while tasting and trying life; in other words, to view what is happening in your life from the greater as well as the mundane perspective.

Sagittarius is the sign opposing Gemini, wherein the dual aspects of the personality (self-consciousness and subconsciousness) are blessed by the Archangel Raphael and set out on a journey to mend their differences and become one. This underscores why Temperance is alternatively known as the Alchemical Marriage.

It is through the deliberate, loving and often painful practice of a skill that you master it. Paul Foster Case said that 'The only failure is the failure not to try.' Inherent in mastery is the ability to create a perfect product. In view of this, Aleister Crowley named this card Art. Mastery may be either the art of living a fully conscious life, or of producing a perfect product by mixing creativity, proper planning and the most perfect ingredients available in precise ratios at the right time with a certain measure of flexibility, passion, wilfulness, endurance and trust.

With Temperance comes the heartfelt acknowledgement that the fruits of your actions, whatever they are, make you a better person. This is the major prerequisite for initiation into more advanced states of awareness. Today, there is a general tendency to think of initiation as the recitation of mystical *mantras*, versicles and formulas in semi-darkened rooms filled with exotic scents and holy symbols. Yes, it may take that form, but for the most part, it is having conscious responses to ordinary living. Essentially, it is the performance of your job that determines your readiness for promotion. This may be perceived also through Temperance's number, 14. Your willingness to 'see' what behaviour is genuinely required (the Magician and Emperor cards respectively) strengthens and activates your inner-knowing that help from above is always available, number five (the Hierophant, the sum of one and four).

In the Qabalah, Temperance is the Intelligence of Testing and Trying. In the process of perfecting a product, it is tested to get the bugs out of it. A test is also a diagnostic tool used to determine what one knows and also to improve knowledge. Consider this Intelligence in terms of life's stresses, strains, tests and trials, which inevitably cause you to master the teachings of truth and become happier and more complete.

### Gateway of Life: Adulthood

Temperance represents the renewed sense of purpose that follows the ego's death experienced with the Death card. With Temperance, the goal of Wisdom and self-mastery looms ahead. In the refinement and redirection of human awareness, the personality slowly grows from the unconsciousness of the Lovers, to the consciousness of Temperance, to the superconsciousness of the World card. The steps from Temperance onwards refine and transform the personality further. If you could put this into a mathematical formula, it might look like this:

will + loving desire + patience + persistence = ongoing refinement of your immature personality traits

Here you must take what you have learned from previous cards and passionately and deliberately apply it. As a result, attitudes and behaviour are enhanced, modified or dissolved. Uncomfortable as the heating and cooling process of tempering may be, it serves to slowly mature the individual into greater states of awareness.

Experiencing Temperance at any of the Four Gateways of Life may bring forth certain experiences. CHILDHOOD: A woman is ignorant of the fact that her illness may actually benefit her health, because it demands that she take better care of her body; ADOLESCENCE: A hot-headed man finds that he must cool down before acting on his impulses, otherwise he will regret it afterwards; ADULTHOOD: A beautiful woman realises that in order to lead a fuller life she must develop her mind as well as her body; WISDOM: In a televised debate, 'Right to Life' and 'Pro-Choice' advocates agree that they have some common goals.

## Divinatory Questions for Temperance

*Upright:* What is being tempered, integrated or tested? What seemingly inharmonious ingredients are you attempting to blend? Might present difficulties be preparing you for the next stage of development in your work, relationships, etc.? What are you willing to go all out to achieve? How are you blending and balancing your spiritual and material lives? What support are you seeking? What are you synthesising? Why have you been feeling fired up? Are you bringing together winning combinations? Might you need to cool off? What foundations are being strengthened? What theories or philosophies are you testing out? In what area of your life are you seeking the 'pot of gold'? What test or trial are you passing or gaining insight from? Might you be reconciling your differences with another? How has your fire been stoked? What goal is becoming more attainable? What physical transformation or healing might you be engaged in? How have you been turning lead into gold? Are you beginning to consider living an art? In what area are you balancing your intellectual and intuitive sides? Where in your life might a more moderate attitude be helpful? How have you surrendered and stopped wrestling with the angel? How are you connected with your guardian angel?

*Reversed:* What are you slowly reconciling yourself to? What might you be trying to temper too quickly? Are you overly hot (emotional) or cool (intellectual)? In what areas have you resisted perceiving daily life as a spiritual journey? Which part of your life – spiritual or material – could do with more attention? What incongruous elements are you attempting to force together? What stresses and strains have been getting to you? What supports have you avoided using? How has the fire of life been put out – where have you lost your drive or motivation? Where has your foundation been shaken? What have you been attempting to temper? In what area of your personal or professional life have you been 'in the fire'? Are you worried that you'll never reach your spiritual goals? Might you be fighting a battle you know you will not win?

## Personal Experience

Ordinarily, I make the connection between each Tarot card's Hebrew name and its meaning easily, yet I was initially stymied when associating *Samekh*, meaning 'a support or foundation', to Temperance. But knowing that the cards have a distinct way of working on the subconscious mind, I relaxed. And although I may sometimes consciously forget them, I believe they are working subliminally to instruct, strengthen and purify me. Such was the case when I tacked the Temperance card up on the wall next to my bed.

During this time of my life, I was slowly discovering how frequently I would wear a smile when I honestly was unhappy or angry inside, or when I acted accepting and loving towards another although I actually felt very much the opposite. I relate to this as my 'pseudo-angelic' period. Looking back, I can see now that I was coming to grips with my old patterns of repressing and suppressing my feelings out of guilt, low self-esteem and fear of abandonment, loss and reprisal. The following is how a friendship became the arena for understanding this aspect of my personality and the Temperance card better.

On the surface, the relationship appeared to be an unlikely one, since my friend was single, very rich, exceptionally career-minded and quite spoiled, whereas I was a single parent without great professional aspirations and had to work incredibly hard for every gain I made in life. Yet, despite our differences, this woman and I shared some deep spiritual interests and yearnings. Now, my friend was in the habit of being behind in her schedule most of the time. But instead of paying attention to my gut-level discomfort at being kept waiting, and wanting to appear completely loving and accepting (what, for me, meant being very spiritual at the time), I unconsciously made excuses for her tardiness and pretended that everything was fine. She, in turn, unconsciously rewarded and reinforced my behaviour by telling me what a 'dear and patient friend' I was when she finally did show up or was ready to relate to me.

Then, for some unknown reason, one of these waits caused my genuine feelings to surface. It was an exceptionally hot summer afternoon and as I waited for her for well over an hour, I felt a great surge of anger (my inner fire). Unable to suppress it, I reached the undeniable conclusion that I had been angry with her every time she was late. Much to my surprise, I greeted her by letting her know how miserable it was for me to sit in the broiling heat for so long. I am the first to admit my words were powerful, since they were fuelled by my new awareness, plus a backlog of freshly liberated emotion. Yet I was careful not to attack her character, just to tell her the problem her behaviour caused me. But because she had never heard even the slightest hint of a complaint from me, she became hurt, defensive and claimed I had attacked her. Strangely enough, I didn't feel the least bit guilty while explaining my actions nor afterwards. She continued to resist my communications for weeks and proceeded to get sick, intimating that my negativity was responsible for her illness. Unfortunately, we grew farther and farther apart.

It took a while to digest what had happened, but one morning several months later, I awoke from a disturbing dream about her looking right at the Archangel Michael in the Temperance card. Through this I finally understood what had actually occurred between us. I recognised that the foundation (*Samekh*) of our relationship was unstable because it was based upon dishonesty. As part of my Higher Self's (the Angel in Temperance) efforts to mature me by pointing out where my personality needed refinement, the weakness in our friendship and my personality surfaced to shake up my already shaky foundation. Examining my anger, I recalled that Wrath, the Qabalistic function connected with Temperance, can be a catalyst when properly employed. My anger was a genuine attempt at curing the relationship of its dishonesty.

With time, I realised how my untruthfulness had contributed to the problem, not only in that friendship, but in others, too. I also became cognisant that my friend and I had worked *together* to

the relationship through my fear, denial and avoidance, and
attery and inability to accept either criticism or take
sibility for her tardiness. Yet, on the spiritual level, we were
working towards building better foundations for future relationships. True, I had lost a friend, but gained an invaluable lesson. I
learned that good friendships are vehicles for increasing self-
awareness and self-love. And it is only by laying honest and
trustworthy foundations that they are able to withstand the test of
life's dramas – everyday relating.

Since then, I have seen myself grow from a fearful and insecure
child in this aspect of my personality into more of an adult.
Becoming appropriately open and honest about my thoughts,
feelings and needs has been painful and sometimes frightening for
me in the short run, but over time my 'true' friendships have
deepened, reinforcing this behaviour, while those built on less
substantial ground have naturally fallen away. The following
affirmation was of considerable help throughout this refinement
process: 'I look upon each and every relationship in my life as a
means through which my Higher Self guides, purifies and
strengthens my soul.'

## Student Experiences

❖ Rick, a retired policeman, husband and father of two teenage
sons, shared his experience of becoming the Archangel Michael
during meditation: 'For homework, you keep insisting we meditate
on the cards and apply the symbols in them to our lives. I haven't
been too good at doing this until the Temperance card came along. I
meditated and became the Angel and found that by doing so, I could
look at my personality somewhat objectively. I think it worked,
because I've been connected with the Archangel Michael from
attending church as a boy.

'Standing with one foot on the land and the other in the water, he
showed me I am no longer dominated by my intellect. My feet were
planted in two worlds, the world of my mind and the world of my
feelings. I've been slowly opening up emotionally. I've been so
"mental" most of my life that being aware of my feelings is somewhat
new to me. I mean me, an ex-cop, being an angel in meditation is
really something! I find I'm enjoying this change and probably
wouldn't have seen it so clearly if I hadn't done my homework.'

'*The dictionary defines temperance as the proper mixture or proportion of elements or qualities,*' I said. '*Being human is synonymous with the tendency to be out-of-balance in some area of your personality or life. And whether you're correcting an imbalance between being either too materially oriented or not material enough, realigning your intellect and emotions as Rick is, or moderating the tendency to be excessively outgoing or indrawn. There is almost always the need to temper yourself in some way. In reality then, your imbalances or misalignments are opportunities to become aware of what element or quality is needed in order for you to become more tempered and whole.*'

❖  'I'm a love addict, plain and simple,' began Ali. 'For as long as I can remember, I've needed others to make me feel complete, to take care of me emotionally, to validate me, because I haven't been able to do so myself. Like you, I've had a weak foundation in the area of relationships. Over the past year or so, I've been working on letting go of or cooling down my needy child ego, and with it has come the firing up of my courage and a desire to take better care of myself. This goes along with the Eagle and the Lion symbolism. I want to be more objective about my sexuality and emotions. I want to stop being overly dependent on others for love.

'I'm learning – and it sure isn't easy – to put my Higher Self first. Classes like this one and membership in an ongoing support group for people with the same problem have been incredibly helpful. So the neglected child in me who must have lots of love, who behaves desperately and compulsively in order to get satiated, is finally growing up. Studying the Temperance card brings home how much I'm connecting with my Guardian Angel, rather than having it personified in someone else. I'm using the card to remind me not to yield to the temptation of getting involved in a relationship before I'm absolutely ready. Loving *me* is my top priority. Being able to look at what's honestly important and not fight it, I'm putting the teachings from the Tarot and my twelve-step programme support group to work when I make decisions that are best for me, those that realign me with the spiritual teachings I'm so immersed in.

'I want to be initiated into a higher level of consciousness in this area. For me, that initiation takes the form of developing into a person who's in a healthy love relationship with myself first; then I'll attract someone who's similarly evolved. My goal is making me put the teachings to the test of life, almost forcing me to become more integrated. The Angel's feet make me remember this: one foot in my inner work, building a loving relationship with my Higher Self, the foot in the water; the other foot in my outer work, testing out what I've learned in relationships with others, the foot on the land.'

*'Not "fighting it" is wise, Ali,' I assured him. 'If you were to fight with the Angel, you would be fighting only your Self and things would become more difficult. Our studies of the Gateways of Life tell us that Temperance is the juncture at which life without a spiritual connection is dissatisfying. You're responding to this by valiantly and lovingly calling up your passion and willpower to bring you a new kind of satisfaction.'*

❖  'I know you all felt the earthquake early on Sunday morning, but let me tell you, it didn't compare in magnitude to the one at my house later on,' shared Marilyn. 'My husband and son had a terrible fight. I knew something had happened the minute I walked into the house after going to the spa. Before I could even open my mouth to ask, my husband poured the whole thing out. Both he and my son are so level-headed, it was pretty serious for them to have come to blows.

'God, you should have seen them. They were like two wild beasts, all scratched and still growling mad. It was awful just being in the same room with them. At first I couldn't help but get emotional. It reminded me so much of the many frightening physical confrontations I'd had with my own parents. I felt my husband and son's anguish and mine very acutely. My husband saw what was happening to me and pleaded with me not to let my emotions get to me. I instantly knew he was right and checked myself. I took some "time out" to figure the best way to help them.

'So I sat down in my meditation corner, and there was the Temperance card. I took a good long look at it and figured out that in order to heal the situation, my son and husband would have to want to let go of their excessive pride, ego and animalistic behaviour, which was still seething right beneath the surface in them both. I could help by not getting emotionally involved and by remaining detached from their melodrama. I also understood that I needed to let my feelings out, but at a more fitting time, when I wouldn't be adding to the confusion.

'Sitting there, I admitted that the situation has been heading in this direction for a long while. I felt comforted by the Angel's presence, reminding me that the Self is always working, even when things are upside down and crazy. What a comfort that is to know! What happened between my husband and son had been building up beneath the superficial niceness of their relationship for a long while, and like the earthquake earlier that morning, released the tensions by bringing matters out into the open. Again, the Self at work. I felt relieved, almost like I'd passed a test or something. Yes, testing relates to Temperance's teachings, too. I guess I did pass a test, since I stopped myself from freaking out. With their permission, I ended up phoning our family counsellor for an emergency appointment to help sort things out with someone objective.'

*'You successfully sublimated or elevated your impulse to "freak out" into something very constructive,' I told Marilyn. 'Figuring out what was really happening extricated you from your own emotional trap. It gave you access to this energy in a different way. It provided you with the energy to find out what to do in order to help your son and husband. I believe you actually lived Temperance's number, 14, which reduces to 5, taking action from your quiet all-knowing centre rather than from your initial reactive impulse.'*

❖   'I'm slow to learn. I've been in another resistant state. Yet I've been doing my homework and asking to know my Guardian Angel, and I've met someone who could easily be her,' began Barb. 'I've been feeling sick during the past few months since I opened my new business. But instead of taking time off, I "stuff" how I feel and continue to put all of my energy into the business. That's really almost all I think about. Finally, my partner nearly forced me to call her doctor.

'The doctor took some blood tests and confirmed what I already "knew"; I'm anaemic. It's a tendency I've had since adolescence. I should know enough to automatically take iron supplements when I get run down, and around my periods. But I don't take them. She told me it's a wonder I'm not feeling worse. When I told her I'm a vegetarian and the thought of eating all that bloody stuff for iron makes me nauseous, she put me on a great diet high in non-animal sources. I'm also supposed to be in bed by 10:00 pm every night until my next blood test in three weeks. And she suggested I nap during the day. I'll tell you, I walked out of her office feeling frustrated that my activities were being curtailed, although as far as doctors go, she's a prize. She's like having a mom, making me do what's good for me. She's like the Guardian Angel in Temperance, making me take my medicine.

'So I've been taking short snoozes for energy rather than having my usual three o'clock coffee. And yesterday I found myself more clear-headed than I've been in weeks. I think I'm getting into some healthy new habits. I guess it's curative and preventative medicine in one. You know, she's the first doctor who's treated me with something more than iron pills and the strong recommendation to eat red meat. Did you know that you can increase your iron intake by cooking in iron pots? I'm excited! Of course, I have to cook, something I don't ordinarily take time to do. Everyone at home is on a different schedule and takes care of their own meals except on weekends, when we may go out to eat together.

'I started off telling you that I did my homework, that I'm integrating Temperance. Browsing through the list of homework questions, "Where is the stress and strain of making you a better, healthier, stronger person?" jumped out at me. I realised that the stress and strain, the hard work and frustration of integrating my work and family with nurturing myself will ultimately make me a stronger, healthier and more balanced person. It actually is already beginning to. I'm going to become more and more like the Angel, balanced between both worlds, the world of work and family and the world of caring for myself. Because if I don't, there won't be anyone to cash my paycheck. I've been wearing more blue (Temperance's colour) to help me remember this, too.'

*'By finding ways to combine the seemingly conflicting elements of your work and health situations, you're doing a great job with the Temperance card, Barb,' I told her. 'Are you aware that you're putting the Hebrew letter, Samekh, to work too? You're seeking support by calling forth your skills and knowledge from the previous cards, such as: the will to focus in on your problem (the Magician); activating the Empress's nurturance; reaching for the Hermit's "helpers and tools"; and relating to the concept of having Temperance's Guardian Angel guide you through this time of stress and strain. Finally the Intelligence of Testing and Trying of the Temperance card is encouraging you to get in there and exercise the means at your disposal for coping.'*

## Suggestion for Application and Integration of Temperance

The teachings of the Temperance card may inspire you to fire up your desire and cool down your ego to move forward on your life path and reach for the pot o' gold at the rainbow's end. The following exercises offer ways in which to understand that coping in a conscious manner with life events leads to higher consciousness. Feel encouraged about your spiritual pursuits, verify or test a belief or theory and combine conflicting elements in your multifaceted life.

1  Colour or draw your own version of the Temperance card with your Higher Self as the Archangel.

2  Set Temperance in a visible place as a reminder to your conscious and subconscious minds to use and absorb its teachings to create a bridge between your spiritual and everyday worlds, remain true to your spiritual path despite its incessant tests and trials, or become more cognisant of the alchemical process going on in your life.

3  Dream on Temperance.

4  Play the note G$^{\#}$ on a musical instrument. Intone IAO or hum along with the music. Now contemplate the card for a few minutes. While doing this, think of the Archangel Michael as your Guardian Angel. Request that he make his presence known in your life. Ask that he stand by when you or another are in need to serve as a reminder that you are God/dess's child. Contemplate how you might already feel under the Angel's protective wings, have the need to call upon his presence or feel that you are wrestling with him. Or request that Temperance's teachings guide you through a particular situation, such as the need to cool down an immature personality trait or ignite your passion in order to grow, gain the courage and will to put the Rules and Tools of the Game of Life into conscious daily use, achieve a better balance between your intellect and feelings or spiritual and everyday activities, or feel more trusting of the processes of spiritual alchemy. Imagine how the teachings of Temperance can enable you to achieve this. Jot down the times when you became aware of Temperance in your interactions. I was aware of Temperance, my Guardian Angel when? Before/during/after . . .

5  Go out into the world and enact the teaching of the Temperance card. I enacted the teachings of Temperance and this is what took place . . .

6  The Rerun. After having an experience and realising in retrospect how Temperance's teachings might have bridged some gap between your Self and another, reconciled feelings and reason, improved coping skills and provided the recognition that your worldly activities are very much a part of your spiritual path home, helped perfect a skill or made you aware that your Guardian Angel was testing or strengthening you, mentally relive

the situation, *including* your insight. This will help the behaviour become more automatic next time. If possible, actually rerun the situation in real life with this attitude or behaviour.

7   Ask yourself the following questions:

'What foundations are weakening or already weak?' 'What test have I just passed or failed?' 'In what situation(s) am I feeling like I am "on fire", or have been doused with water?' 'Where am I being supported and guided without realising it?' 'Why am I feeling angry or frustrated with a situation, and how can I constructively redirect my energies?' 'What skill am I looking forward to mastering?' 'In what situation(s) am I perceiving the spirituality of the material world?' 'What strain am I holding up or giving way under?' 'What conflicting elements am I synthesising?' 'In what area of my personal or professional life might I derive success by relying upon and applying the teachings of truth or the Rules and Tools of the Game of Life?' 'How has my concept of failure changed to one of nearing success?' 'What foundations are supporting me?' 'How are stress and strain making me more reliant upon my Guardian Angel?' 'What test do I wish to retake?' 'In what ways is spiritual alchemy being activated in my life at this time?' 'Where are my foundations weakening?' 'How is a strained relationship, or the stress and strain of daily life, encouraging me to find better ways to cope?' 'How is Michael helping to slay my inner dragons?' 'What initiation have I experienced?' 'What new thing or concept is it important for me to test out?' 'How is your "metal" being tested?'

'What Gateway of Life am I in or developing through in the above?' Indicate: Childhood, Adolescence, Adulthood or Wisdom. Why?

'What do I need to do in order to develop the above further?' I need to . . .

'What step(s) do I want to take towards this goal and how can Temperance guide me?'

8   Use a personal statement regarding the presence of Temperance in your life at this time, such as: 'Engaging with my problems makes me wiser and stronger.' 'Right understanding of the events of my life builds the foundations for success.' 'Picking up my

tools, I become a master; letting them lie, they gather dust.' My personal statement or affirmation is . . .

9  Inspirational words and quotes:

'If God is for us, who is against us?'                    ROMANS 8:31

'The essential thing about following the road to Enlightenment is to avoid being caught and entangled in any extreme; keep to the middle path.'

'I rest my life, from day to day upon the sure Foundation of Eternal Being.'                    Paul Foster Case

10  What symbols stand out in the card? What do they say to you? How might they be useful in daily living? Bring the symbol(s) into your life in some way so as to integrate the card's teachings. The rainbow reminds me both to be hopeful when I feel overwhelmed and that I'm never given more than I can handle, even if the 'handling' means asking for help. I hung a rainbow-emitting crystal in my bedroom as a reminder of this.

11  Wear and surround yourself with Temperance's colour, blue, to remind you of the card's teachings when needed, such as remembering your Guardian Angel's presence, mustering up the courage to put a theory to the test of life or re-engaging with something you previously did not master. Notice how you are affected.

12  Temperance's astrological correspondent, Sagittarius, governs traits and functions such as adventurousness, verification, distant journeys, open-mindedness, philosophical beliefs and improve spacing determination. Use the card to inspire you to continue your lifelong adventure down the path back to Eden, or to experience something new while employing your belief system to help determine its validity and usefulness. Note what happens: your thoughts and feelings and the outcome.

13  Remember that Temperance's Hebrew name, *Samekh*, means 'a support or foundation'. How might this remind you of the card's meaning or help in your life process, such as deriving support from the spiritual tools you have available or feeling propped up by the Holy Guardian Angel?

14 Try a few drops of the scent of dill associated with Temperance as a reminder to integrate the card's teachings.

15 Have a cup of tea made from the herb echinacea. Sit quietly as you drink and consider the herb's properties as a blood purifier, antiseptic and digestive aid. It also is excellent for expelling toxins and poisons (the native Americans used it to treat blood poisoning and snake bite) and like penicillin, it tempers excessive heat. Contemplate the similarities between echinacea and Temperance.

**15 THE DEVIL ♈**

CHAPTER 19

## The Devil

**General Information and Symbolism**

The monstrous red-eyed, horned, winged and clawed Devil, composite of all that the human mind imagines him to be, perches upon his throne holding an inverted torch. The upside-down torch portrays what is involved in conjuring up the Devil. First, when excessive egotism directs you to believe that you act alone, and that your personal actions are separate from the One Will, you abuse and misdirect the life force within you. Second, you are motivated to act *only* for the purpose of self-aggrandisement. Third, you impose your will upon others unnecessarily and/or without their consent. Fourth, because of narrow-mindedness, you misuse your powers of observation by thinking that there is nothing more to people, places and things than what is readily apparent and that there is nothing more to life than the material world and sense pleasures. The Devil has one male and one female breast illustrating it can be of either sex. It has goat-like horns and a beard, intimating that he/she is the 'horny old goat', entrapped by an unwholesome obsession with sex. This is depicted by the eagle's legs, signifying Scorpio, and in this case, the misuse of sexual energies or the life force. The bird's talons further indicate how, when we cling to Self-defeating ideas and behaviours, we are in the Devil's clutches. Finally, the torch alludes to those who struggle against their Self. These individuals may refuse to take responsibility for their weaknesses and 'scapegoat' or project their own shortcomings on others. Or due to their lust for power, try to 'get someone's goat' because of feelings of inferiority which create an uncontrollable need to do anything to feel superior.

The Devil, however, is in reality the Archangel Uriel, whose name translates from the Hebrew to mean 'Light of God'. Uriel has dominion over the northern quadrant of heaven and the element of Earth. How can the Devil, symbol of all that is evil, be an archangel? Please take a few minutes to consider how often wisdom or enlightenment may be the end result of dark times, in addition to the esoteric concept that everything, animate and inanimate, carries the light of the God/dess within. How, then, can the Devil, considered by the Qabalists to be the 'Shadow of God', be excluded? It is not accidental that Lucifer, one of the Devil's many names, means 'Light Bearer'.

The personality is the vehicle through which we return to Eden, symbolised by the Devil card's similarity to the Lovers. Every human being has both light and dark sides, which are part of the same Self. The concept of the Devil, the demonic or dark side, is universal. Hindus claim the *Rakshasas*, Hebrews the *Shedim*, Tibetans have a *Tulpa*, the ancient Greeks, Pan, and even the Space Age 'Trekkies' identify their troublemakers in the form of 'Klingons'. The word 'Devil' comes from the Greek *diabolus*, meaning 'to discredit or slander'. It is by exorcising the ways in which we discredit ourselves, our shame and guilt about who we are in totality, that we purge our devils. In truth, we have both dark and light – unevolved and evolved – qualities. I find it fascinating that in the Balinese culture the dark demons of fear, envy, greed and the like are ritualistically fed as are the spirits of light. It is impossible to become properly motivated when caught up in self-hatred, since it turns you into your own enemy. Acceptance magically enables the bound humans in the card to face their immaturities with compassion so that they may lift off their chains and get on with their lives.

Bondage is by choice, not chance, although sometimes you may be unaware that you are bound. The two human figures wear loose chains stating this. It is by acknowledging your freedom of choice and that the consequences of your actions educate you, that you become motivated to handle problem areas as they arise and thus free yourself from bondage. It does no good to dwell endlessly on your shortcomings or punish yourself for being human and possessing undeveloped personality traits. Some people do this by berating themselves mercilessly, making their life a living hell, while others opt for the physical route of substance abuse, another more subtle form of corporeal punishment. Both are tools of self-torture that turn oneself into a scapegoat. It is imperative that you forgive and accept your humanness in the form of your foibles and frailties while welcoming each as opportunities to grow. Allowing these qualities to own or 'bedevil' you, rather than rising up and taking charge of them, is what is being 'possessed' by the Devil actually means. Consistent with this concept is the belief that the ancient practice of Satanism was actually the act of acknowledging and accepting the dark and disowned side of the personality. To conclude, the first step in freeing ourselves from bondage is to acknowledge that we are bound. Remember, the chains are loose and therefore may be removed at any time.

The words 'devil' and 'divinity' grew from the same root, the Indo-European Devi (Goddess) or Deva (God). [1] Other definitions of the word 'devil' are: the personification of something evil or undesirable; a subordinate evil spirit; the opposite of truth, an error, a lie; an individual who disregards the rights of others; an unfortunate person; an undesirable adversary; something that is 'thrown across' one's path.

When travelling the spiritual path, the contrast between light and dark behaviour is bound to become more pronounced as you become more conscious. Inherent in new-found awareness is that it occasionally gives way to shame and the tendency to conceal further discomfort, rather than bringing it into the light. You may, however, perceive this as just another devil 'thrown across your path', to test your sincerity. Exoteric religion fails to teach that the Devil is instrumental in launching you on your quest for wholeness, God/desshood. Once again, all things and experiences are set in motion by the Most High. The Serpent or Devil foretells of this catalytic process in the Garden of Eden when Adam and Eve are promised they 'shall not surely die', but 'will have their eyes opened and become wise'.

The presence of Adam and Eve in the Devil card restates their potential to move out of the darkness, their own shame, guilt, fear and ignorance, and to once and for all cease being dominated by their animalistic selves, shown by their tails and hoofs. Both the Tree of Knowledge and Tree of Life depicted in the Lovers now comprise Adam and Eve's tails. These symbols indicate that the ability to discern between right from wrong (Eve – the subconscious), and the conscious will to live and learn via interactions with daily life and ascend the Tree of Life (Adam, selfconsciousness), have been severely impaired by the terror of engaging with the dark or unknown parts of one's Self. This is reiterated by the Devil's bat wings, which signify that he is a creature of darkness that is unable to see the light.

With the Devil card, remnants of your limited early training arise

1 Barbara G. Walker, *The Women's Encyclopedia of Myths and Secrets*, Harper & Row, San Francisco, 1983, p. 225.

to plague you and those around you, suggested by the Devil's half-cube throne and by the inverted pentagram, or five-pointed star, over his head. In contrast to the all-knowing and all-seeing Priestess and Emperor who sit on cubes, the donkey-eared Devil sits on a half-cube denoting his half-assed perceptions. The upright pentagram has long been used by the ancients and practitioners of Hermetic magic as a healing and protective talisman and to sanctify a particular space. It further symbolises evolving human awareness and actually depicts the well-grounded human embracing life and reaching up to heaven. ☆

Conversely, the inverted pentagram worn on top of the Devil's head indicates a welcome haven for evil spirits and entities and the workings of black magic, wherein individuals deny (or are ignorant of) the spiritual origins of their everyday world. It signifies dominance by the ego's immature personality traits, such as extreme selfishness, uncontrollable anger, stubbornness, inflexibility, bondage to material and sensual pleasures, the need to dominate and manipulate others and the like. The reversed pentagram also puts the genitals on top, symbolising thinking and acting solely from instinct and the desire for sensual gratification.

The word 'devil' is 'evil' with a *d* in front of it. It is also the word 'lived' spelled backward, suggesting that living with the Devil is existing, not living. We cannot deny the existence of evil, the conscious intent to do harm. Some say Hitler was the Devil incarnate. Perhaps so, yet what allowed his evil to propagate is the horrendous truth that little was done to curtail him until it was too late. In essence, the lack of widespread protest and action actually helped him to do his work. Hitler may be likened to an unconscious child whose actions ask that he be stopped. In allowing others to go unchecked, we inadvertently hurt ourselves. We are morally obligated to place limits upon our children's behaviour, both for their own and others' safety and well-being. We have the same duty to protect ourselves, others and the planet from acts of evil. Please note that I also use the word 'evil' as a synonym for immaturity. Having an adult body does not necessarily mean you are mature. If you are *genuinely* mature, you will not behave in such ways. To conclude, the Devil may be perceived as the adversity needed to help us grow both individually and as a race. In reality, change and maturity come through both desperation and inspiration. When enveloped in the darkness and despair of the Devil, bear in mind the truth that in time darkness actually inspires us to seek the light.

Remember the childhood game of 'Pin the Tail on the Donkey'? The Devil has the ears of a donkey, long regarded as a synonym for stupidity. This asserts that we should not take ourselves too seriously, but be able to laugh at our own and others' brainless and asinine behaviour. Consider all the money and effort spent on providing comic relief: joke books, comic books, movies, all sorts of gadgets, television sitcoms, clowns and comedians (especially 'black' humorists), all attempting to relieve some of our dark feelings by giving us a chuckle at ourselves and the ironies and incongruities of daily life. I recall listening to humorist Lenny Bruce and for the first time being able to laugh at the social, political and religious atrocities so prevalent in today's world, rather than being only frustrated, infuriated and immobilised by them. Laughter somehow weakened their grip on me. It's useless to spend your energies hating; instead, take the appropriate measures to work towards whatever changes are necessary. It is not surprising, then, to learn that Mirth is the Qabalistic function associated with the Devil. Esoteric traditions prescribe cultivating the ability to see the world with a sense of humour. Who knows? It just might inspire someone else to do likewise.

As you come to terms with your human failings, you take increased responsibility for the Devil's existence. The Devil is a product of the human mind, portrayed by his having a navel. The navel is represented by the symbol for Mercury, significator of the human mind in astrology. This is also corroborated in the Aquarian Deck for the New Age, in which the Devil is entitled 'The Thinker'.

Qabalists associate the card's number, 15, with the word *Jah*, an abbreviation for 'wisdom' and *Jehovah*, God of the Hebrews. Fifteen also combines one, the Magician, giving your personal attention to five, linking up with your conscience and Higher Self, the Hierophant, which brings wise discrimination, healing and harmony, and six, the Lovers, the sum of one and five (take a look at the similarities between the Devil, the Hierophant and the Lovers).

The Devil card is associated with the musical note A, the colour blue-violet (indigo) and the herb lobelia. The Hebrew name for the Devil is *Ayin*, meaning the human eye as an organ of sight. You see what you have been trained to see. Unless you turn your head or consciousness to adjust your perspective, your sphere of perception is limited. This infers the change of view needed to examine people, places and things in their entirety, going beyond the narrowness of the axiom so often associated with the Devil, 'All you see is all there is', signified by the Devil's uplifted right hand that bears the glyph for Saturn. You are taught how to interpret the images of daily living and may easily come to believe in them, no matter how erroneous they are. One of the major goals of Tarot study is to cultivate your ability to perceive yourself and circumstances via the Greater Reality, to take a more objective or unhabituated perspective on life. Here is an example of my first awareness of how mistaken it can be to take things at face value.

Because I was raised in a racially segregated neighbourhood in the early 1950s, I was taught, both consciously and unconsciously, to be prejudiced towards people of colour, especially African-Americans. When I had to travel to junior high school in a racially mixed neighbourhood, I felt extremely uncomfortable when first attending classes. However, after getting to know my classmates, I began to understand my racist conditioning and started to overcome it.

The cardinal (initiating and of foremost importance) Earth sign Capricorn, governing the knees and all other joints, skin, teeth and skeletal system, is associated with the Devil. Capricorn is ruled by Saturn, planet of discipline, structure and limitation, and has been dubbed the 'Greater Malefic' by those who resist, fear, or do not understand the value of these qualities. On the other hand, Saturn also signifies crystallisation, a hardening process that eliminates flexibility. The Capricorn personality says: I achieve, apply, use, control, persevere, limit and rule. I'm determined, disciplined, prudent, powerful, narrow-minded, dutiful, reserved, ambitious, stable, authoritative and resourceful. Like its symbol the mountain goat (the Devil has goat's horns), Capricorns may ascend to positions of power and spiritual prominence. They can benefit from building dreams and ambitions in an assertive, prudent and flexible fashion, while maintaining or developing a sense of humour. Developed Capricorns have had enough repercussions from being small-minded, controlling and humourless, for them now to desire to free themselves from such. Essentially, they are on the road up the mountain, and the business of admitting and confronting their humanity and limitations allows them to get out of their own way. Like their symbol, the mountain goat, the Capricorn will reach the greatest heights of success when they focus on controlling themselves rather than others.

In the Qabalah, the Devil is known as the Renewing Intelligence. Renewal is the act of restoring oneself or some object to a state of newness. This Intelligence addresses the renewal gained from converting a narrow perspective of life to a larger more expansive view. Once you give yourself permission to confront, find humour in and accept as normal your fears, human frailties and immaturities, you are restored as is your outlook on life.

## Gateway of Life: Adulthood

Here you glimpse the dark, unevolved, disowned, repressed and suppressed parts of your personality, exposing what you have long feared, ignored, denied, or been oblivious to. Qabalists term this the Dweller on the Threshold, and state it is the sum total of all the unresolved personality conflicts which stand between your Higher Self and your personality. The Devil proffers the opportunity to face your hidden agenda. This means admitting that you have problems – that you feel powerless over certain behaviours, etc., and consequently have work to do. In other words, when you stop running from your demons, they stop chasing you. Those in Twelve-Step Programmes say this is the first step on the road to 'Recovery' and means you are 'out of denial'. It is having the insight that you have given up your power to a substance, individual, group or to your own emotions (the rage-aholic), that you were never properly empowered, and therefore your life has become unmanageable.

The initial stages of spiritual work can be torturous, as the job of lovingly confronting your shadow does not abound with inspirational role models. What may be of service here are reminders from the Fool and High Priestess: there is nothing but God/dess; all life comes from the dark womb of this Source.

The Devil lies within and without. You imprison and alienate yourself with the chains of fear, shame, envy, greed, laziness, guilt, ignorance, hatred, and stubbornness plus the racial and social biases learned, consciously and unconsciously, from family, peers, culture and society. At this juncture, as an aspiring adult you are ready to widen your perspective of both yourself and the world around you. The chance to courageously examine immature and erroneous patterns of relating is available. Here, too, is the tendency to sweep what is found back under the rug due to guilt, and the twin sisters shame and fear.

Living this card at the Four Gateways of Life may give expression to certain attitudes and behaviour. CHILDHOOD: An athlete takes cocaine, fails a random drug test and then claims someone set him up; ADOLESCENCE: A woman wrongfully accuses another of trying to lure her lover away from her, and even after being shown that the other woman was not to blame, stubbornly refuses to retract her accusations; ADULTHOOD: A man faces up to the fact that he was molested as a child; WISDOM: A man signs up for a remedial reading programme instead of continuing to be ashamed of his illiteracy.

## Divinatory Questions for the Devil

*Upright*: In what area of your personal or professional life are you feeling bound, limited or imprisoned? Why have you been feeling sinful, ashamed or guilty? Where are you seeking to exert undue control or manipulate circumstances on your behalf? How are you fearing your own or another's humanity? Is it possible that a combination of fear and lack of information is immobilising you? How have you not been your best Self? What are you obsessed or bedevilled with? Where could it prove helpful to admit you are sorry or don't know something? When do you think you'll realise that you can cut yourself or another loose at any time? Who are you envious of? Why are you reacting negatively to constructive criticism? What illusion are you trying to maintain? What have you taken only at face value? How are you behaving more like an animal than a human? Is it possible that you are being unduly stubborn and inflexible – acting like a donkey? Which disowned aspects of your personality are you refusing to acknowledge? How do you think you got yourself into your present dilemma? What fears or hidden things from your past have been demanding you take another look at them? Are you blaming or projecting your shortcomings on others? How might you be supporting evil by not acting to stop it?

*Reversed*: Are you slowly overcoming a deep-rooted fear? How have you exorcised a worn-out or ignorant belief? What fear is founded upon a lack of knowledge, rather than on reality? Are you sharing some long hidden thoughts and feelings? Are you involved in re-envisioning your life? How have you expanded your perspective of a difficult situation or person? How have you liberated yourself from possible mental, emotional or physical enslavement? How has despair motivated you to seek the light? Could you be growing less fearful of the unknown? Where might some comic relief lighten up a tense or stressful relationship or circumstance? How have you disarmed an old devil or obsession? Have you recently gained wisdom from an untenable situation in your personal or professional life? How might you expand your perceptions? How has developing a sense of humour about your demons and weaknesses helped? How are you working with your feelings of envy – of not being or having enough? How have you been thinking yourself into a less fearful state? Where might your honesty and willingness to accept yourself in totality inspire another to do likewise?

## Personal Experience

The Devil is often called the Prince of Darkness. Why do people fear the dark? We fear it because we cannot see. In fear-provoking situations, we become like the child whose jump-rope is transformed into a venomous snake coiled on the darkened closet floor. Instead of reasoning out the impossibility (turning on the lights) of a serpent's presence in the midst of winter in an apartment in New York City, the immature mind reacts from fear and fantasy. Another instance of this might be taking another's upset personally without questioning the person about how they are behaving. Interpreting life from this narrow perspective, without benefit of rational thought and conscious communication, is hellish. Statements such as, 'Is something bothering you?' or 'Did I do anything to hurt you?' are an initiation into adult behaviour and lead the way to wisdom. This type of reasoning turns on the light to discern fact from fiction, reality from paranoia.

In spite of much resistance, I have found the Devil to symbolise my childish, unevolved personality traits, known by many schools of thought as one's dark side or shadow. Typing the first draft of this chapter, I summed up the situation in a single word when I mistakenly typed 'unloved' when I thought I had written 'unevolved'. These unloved characteristics are part of being human, bestowed upon us by our own Higher Self as part of our life's work. By confronting my fears and lurking self-images, I have been able to demystify them. Instead of fearfully denying their existence (which causes them only to loom larger than ever), I bring them out into the open, greatly reducing their potency. Bringing my problems, shortcomings and immaturities into the light makes them feel less threatening and more manageable.

When I re-entered college at the age of thirty-five, I had a very paternalistic professor who I was sure gave me dirty looks and who also reminded me of the worst traits of my father. I was punctual, participated in class discussion, handed in my papers and did well on exams. But no matter what I did, his behaviour towards me persisted. Finally, things became so unbearable for me that I migrated from the front row of the lecture hall to the last. Eventually (I'm not sure why I waited so long), I became so bothered I did a Tarot reading. When the Devil turned up in the position of 'Overall Perspective on the Situation', I recognised the card's link with the Hebrew noun *Ayin*, meaning 'eye', and accepted that my perspective of the situation was limited, just as is the eye's peripheral vision.

I decided to continue my search by 'dreaming on' the card. That night I awoke after dreaming that I was sunbathing nude on a campus bench. I interpreted this to mean that I needed to put aside my fears of the unknown (the Devil), look my professor in the eye and bring my concerns out into the open.

Following final exams, I mustered up enough nerve to visit the professor during his office hours. I put on my indigo blue jeans and sweater (the Devil's colour) as a reminder of my purpose to ask questions and express my concerns, and headed off to campus. I took several deep breaths before entering his office, thought of the Devil card for a moment to reinforce my mission, and eased my way into the crowded cubicle. I waited until we were alone, looked at him directly and asked if I had done anything to bother him during the semester, explaining my perception of what was going on between us. He became thoughtful and then answered, 'My daughter is also a red-head. Of course, I like you.' I immediately understood that I was a painful reminder of his daughter, whom he had mentioned briefly but emotionally in one of his lectures regarding the misuse of consciousness-expanding drugs. Without 'turning the lights on' – minus this essential piece of information – I had misinterpreted his pain and sadness to mean disapproval of me. I thanked him, wished him a good vacation and with great relief went on my way.

I mulled over the experience while driving home and recognised that it had given me the chance to experience the metaphysical principle of the Devil being opportunity in disguise. I had taken a chance and expressed my fears instead of allowing them to continue playing devilish tricks with my mind and I had gained the opportunity for some genuine emotional management. Yes, the Tarot had again proven correct. My perspectives were narrowed by old fears of my father disapproving of me, no matter how well I thought I was behaving. What I sometimes humorously refer to as my dark, lurking self-image had again appeared to taunt me. Only this time, I had turned the lights on!

**Student Experiences**

❖ Nat, a recently divorced middle-aged woman, shared her experience of self-exploration through the Devil card: 'I've had a lifelong string of painful relationships with both men and women, and after this last divorce, I'll admit I've been locked into blame and withdrawal from everyone except my birds. I know you've all noticed how infrequently I talk in class. Sometimes I think it's miraculous I'm even here at all. But the question from our homework, "What have you been seeing from a limited perspective?" prodded me to think about my stuff with relationships more deeply.

'I think I'm ready to face the fact that I've been contributing to the problem in some eye-opening ways – there's your Hebrew word *Ayin* at work. I'm coming to acknowledge that some part of me, some part of my personality, is attracted to these miserable relationships, that I'm not just the innocent victim I believed I was. It's almost really funny, but I'm not quite ready to laugh.

'While meditating on the Devil card, I saw it was the opposite of the Emperor. He sits on his cube of many-sided thinking and reasoning and, of course, sees what is there rather than what he wants to see. The Devil is perched on a two-sided throne, showing his and my limited perspective. Things are either black or white for me. Do you know I had a dream in which my teeth were breaking off? Afterwards, I remembered that the Devil's sign Capricorn rules the teeth, bones, limits and structure. My old structures are breaking down.

'I think that the Devil is the part of me that's afraid to tell others what I need and expect from a relationship. When I don't do this, I get hurt and angry and feel rejected, and of course don't communicate my feelings, other than by withdrawing. Yet, if I let people know what I need, I may also be disappointed and feel rejected if they don't come across. I'm trying to decide what's best. I think my first step is to accept that I've been blinded by blaming others for my suffering. I stayed in those relationships until I was literally nearly dead. What a chance this is to use the teachings to help me change. But for right now, I'm working on not hating myself for taking so long to see.'

*'You might also work with a personal statement or two to help break the mental stress – loops of self-hatred,' I told her. 'Something as simple as, "I'm doing the best that I can", works amazingly well. If you find that you're having a hard time believing you are in fact doing your best, you*

*might consider this to be an opportunity to do some of the "clean-up" work I suggested earlier on. You're learning one of the Devil's most important teachings, how to stop slandering yourself and others – keep in mind how the Slanderer is one of the Devil's many names. And by doing this you're removing your chains, not only from Eve (you as woman and your subconscious patterns), but from Adam, your conscious mind and others of the opposite sex, too.'*

❖   'I was standing at the bus stop on my way home from work, when I saw a woman yelling and hitting a little girl of about three,' began David. 'I'm not sure if it was her child or not. Somehow, I felt she didn't belong with her. Anyhow, people were just standing there ignoring the whole affair, reading their newspapers or talking; teenagers were fooling around, some looking at the sky and at other passers-by. I almost remained one of them until I remembered what you said about us being morally obligated to intervene in evil doings; otherwise, we're condoning them.'

   'It wasn't easy, but I went up to the woman and said the first thing that popped into my mind: "Pick on somebody your own size." It was a childish thing to say, but I'll admit I'm a bit childish in this way. And that's where I was coming from, that part of me that has been abused and battered. Well, she turned her anger on me and screamed for me to, "Mind my own damn business!" But she turned her anger away from the child and stopped hitting the poor little creature. My intervention also helped attract some nonverbal support from the crowd, who paid attention to the goings-on once I stepped in.'

*It seems that by doing his 'homework', David opened the door to more mature behaviour in this area of his personality. He stopped that woman from using her child as a scapegoat, something which parents or people in positions of power unfortunately tend to do. It is great David remembered that not speaking out actually gives people permission to continue their behaviour!*

❖   'You suggested we try meditating on accepting the dark, unevolved and unloved parts of ourselves, to open up our hearts and accept the shadow side of our Self,' began Jan. 'It's something I'd never dreamed of doing, since I'm always so busy denying those parts of me even exist. Well, you got me. I've been doing it several times a day and it's amazing. I imagine myself at various points in my life in difficult and embarrassing situations, being my most unlovable self, and then opening up my heart to that person, me. I look at myself as a best friend would or like I'd look at some disabled person or one of my kids. Anyhow, it's working in some subtle ways. I'm actually feeling less judgmental. I've turned the Devil card upside down to show my Self that I'm reversing my habits, and I'm using the personal statement, "I love all of me".'

*To progress spiritually, it's essential to work with our subconscious or shadow side, as Carl Jung termed it, and not against it. The Devil's raised hand has the Saturn symbol on it, reminding us of the limitations of being human. Part of our work as spiritual aspirants is not to feel guilty (one of the Devil's tools) about our shortcomings, but to face up to them with love and understanding and then do what we can to develop them.*

❖  'I tend to keep negatives hidden inside. I don't like sharing them because it magnifies my imperfections ever so much more,' said Vincent, a computer engineer. 'If I don't talk about it, it's not there. Only I know the deep, dark truth about me.

'We have a new hot-shot supervisor at work, and he gave me my annual evaluation several weeks ago. Boy, did he do a job on me! I've been depressed and angry ever since. I'm so bothered, I've been waking in the middle of the night hearing his comments running through my mind.

'We've been discussing bringing our fears, worries and our hidden side into the light with the work on the Devil. So I've been entertaining the thought of sharing my evaluation with a couple of co-workers. I have a feeling my supervisor has treated others the way he treated me, and they're not talking, either. I grew up in a family of superachievers and had to be on top of everything all the time. So when I'm not, I keep it hidden. I try not to look at my faults. But they're not really hidden, because they eat me up inside. Here I am, sharing this and feeling better already. "Standing naked with it", as you would say. It's almost laughable that I have to be so letter-perfect. I'm trying not to do the same thing to my kids. I think it's important to talk with others at the office. I'll bet they're hiding things, too.'

*'Vincent, you're lifting off the chain, breaking your bondage from childhood, and righting the pentacle all at once,' I said. 'That reversed pentacle is your own excessive ego working against your Self. Your early training made you your own adversary, made your immaturities and imperfections the "Devil",*

*or enemy, and by doing so, stifled your growth in these areas. Your courage and willingness to look at your situation is really gifting you with some tremendous movement in this part of your personality. Congratulations!'*

❖   Mary, a mother of three, shared this: 'I'm ashamed of my body and have been all of my life, and it's time I came to terms with it. My mother was a Hollywood-type beauty, with blonde hair, big green cat's eyes and a perfect figure. She was so obsessed with keeping her weight the same as it was when she was in high school that she hardly ate. When I took after my father's side of the family, big-boned and very peasant looking, she didn't hide her disappointment. I had my nose fixed for my Sweet Sixteen present and was always told how much better I'd look if I'd only lose weight. (I know I eat to suppress feeling hateful and guilty for being ugly.) She'd also tell me that I'd be more attractive if I didn't have my father's horse laugh. What awful things to say to a young girl!

'Now when people tell me I look good, I think to myself, "You don't see my hips and thighs. Look closer at my wrinkles." I'm hurting my Self with this kind of attitude. Slandering was the word you used – I could sue myself for slander. When I meditated on the card, I felt like Eve. Here I am still bound to what my mother wanted me to be and she's been dead almost a dozen years now. But Eve's chains are loose and I'm going to start taking them off. You asked the question, "What do you want to free yourself from?" Why should I be ashamed of what I am? I'm the Goddess. There's a class being offered next month at the YWCA on "Body Image and Self-Esteem" and I'm enrolling. It's time to lift off those chains. Forty-five isn't too late. My mother died wearing them. I won't. Who knows? I could live to be ninety.'

*'It looks as if you're actively engaged in going deeper into the meaning of yourself as a woman,' I told Mary. 'Passing up what the Hindus term* maya, *or illusion, what the Devil signs with his upraised right hand. Here, the self-conscious mind has become so attentive to the superficial appearance of things, it believes that nothing besides what the five senses report either matters or exists. Your mom was raised with those beliefs and passed them on to you. The Devil, however, is the first step in spiritual advancement, wherein individuals realise that there is a great deal more to both themselves and the life they lead than the superficial point of view they've become accustomed to and, in most instances, been trained to believe.'*

**Suggestions for Application and Integration of the Devil**

Is it time to look at your dark side? Time to face what is bedevilling or obsessing you, take off your chains of bondage, and perhaps have a good laugh at both yourself and life's incongruities? If so, proceed. If not, return to page one of this chapter and start over again.

1 Colour or draw your own version of the Devil card with yourself as any of the figures.

2 Set the Devil card in a visible place as a reminder to your conscious and subconscious minds to use and recall its teachings to know that there is more to life that what your five senses indicate, to frighten the Devil away with humour, knowledge and understanding, or to focus on extricating yourself from a detrimental situation.

3 Dream on the Devil, bearing in mind that he or she is in reality the Archangel Uriel.

4 Play the note A on a musical instrument. Intone IAO or hum along with the music. Now meditate on the card for a few minutes and try the following: Imagine yourself at various points of your life, in different settings, being your most unlovable (unevolved) Self, doing the things you are now ashamed of, embarrassed by, feel guilty about and hate yourself for. Next, open your heart to yourself as you are – to your dark, unevolved, unloved side. Have compassion towards that part of your Self as you would for some poor wretch. Please note: the purpose of this meditation is to help you to know this behaviour as part of your whole Self, not reinforce it. Acceptance is one of the first steps on the road to change.

   Or if you are faced with a fearful, guilt-provoking or embarrassing situation, event or problem, such as feeling chained to a desire, situation or person, or trying to control, bully or manipulate another because you feel powerless, frustrated or inferior, imagine how the Devil's teachings might help lift off your chains of bondage. If it seems appropriate, give it a try. Jot down the times when you became aware of the Devil in your interactions. I was aware of the Devil when? Before/during/after . . .

5 Go out into the world and enact the teachings of the Devil card to help liberate yourself or another through laughter. Or

consider a situation in which you have felt a moral obligation to intervene. Consider what you believe to be right action, and what intervention strategy might best be enacted to achieve it.

6   The Rerun. After having an experience and realising in retrospect how the Devil's teachings might have made things different – freed you from some restrictive, inflexible or stubborn behaviour, injected humour, helped you to have been more honest about who you are and what you genuinely think and feel, or helped you accept criticism in a less defensive manner – mentally relive the situation, *including* your insight. This will help the behaviour become more automatic next time. If possible, actually rerun the situation in real life with this new attitude or behaviour.

7   Ask yourself the following questions:

'What have I been seeing from a limited perspective?' 'What am I hiding or hiding from?' 'Where and why do I feel trapped?' 'Where have I been discrediting myself or another?' 'In what situation(s) have you stopped condoning evil behaviour?' 'Where in my personal or professional life do I feel out of control, powerless?' 'What unconscious bond am I removing?' 'How is rigidity damaging me or another?' 'Where have shame, guilt, fear or ignorance been victimising me and holding back my enjoyment of life?' 'How are shame, guilt, fear or ignorance actually serving to make me grow?' 'How am I being prejudiced towards another person or group?' 'Why have I blamed my shortcomings on another person or group?' 'Could it be that laughter might prove useful in a somewhat serious setting?' 'Am I becoming more willing to face my dark side?' 'In what situation have I been acting like an ass?' 'What wisdom might I gain from an adverse situation?' 'Whom or what have I been trying my best to manipulate?' 'How might accepting myself in totality inspire another to do likewise?' 'What obsession am I facing?'

'What Gateway of Life am I in or developing through in the above?' Indicate: Childhood, Adolescence, Adulthood or Wisdom. Why?

'What do I need to do in order to develop the above further?' I need to . . .

'What step(s) do I want to take towards this goal and how can the Devil card guide me?'

8  Use a personal statement regarding the presence of the Devil in your life at this time, such as: 'I love all of me.' 'My shadow is my Self.' 'There's more to people and situations than first meets my eye.' My personal statement is . . .

9  Inspirational words and quotes:

'No one can insult me, unless I give them my permission.'

Eleanor Roosevelt

'Humour is the source of all wisdom.'

'Knowledge is power.'                        Old Spanish Maxim

'The only thing we have to fear is fear itself.'

Franklin D. Roosevelt

10  What symbols stand out in the card? What do they say to you? How might they be useful in daily living? Bring the symbol(s) into your life in some way so as to integrate the card's teachings. The reversed pentagram reminds me that when I feel emotionally overwhelmed, I can use the adversity as an opportunity to find my Self, not lose it.

11  Wear and surround yourself with the Devil's colour, blue-violet (indigo), to remind you of the card's teachings when needed, such as when you wish to remember that the darkness in your life may be helping you grow, to be less stubborn or controlling, to expand your perspective on a situation or maintain a sense of humour. Notice how you are affected.

12  The Devil's astrological correspondence, Capricorn, governs achievement, perseverance, stability, resourcefulness, discipline, prudence and dominion. Practise using the card to expand your ability to be resourceful and persevering in achieving a goal, while disciplining yourself to be prudent not to go overboard in your efforts. Or if you tend to be overly restrictive and are desirous of control, use the card to help you relax and laugh a bit. Note what happens: your thoughts and feelings and the outcome.

13  Remember that the Devil's Hebrew name, *Ayin*, means 'the eye as an organ by which to see'. How can this remind you of the card's meaning or help in your life process?

14  Try a few drops of the scent nutmeg associated with the Devil as a reminder to integrate the card's teachings.

15 Have a cup of tea made from the herb lobelia. Sit quietly as you drink and consider the herb's properties as an anti-inflammatory, expectorant, emetic and diuretic and consider the teachings of the Devil card. Caution: this herb must be used sparingly as too much will cause illness and, in some cases, death.

16 | THE TOWER | ⟡

# CHAPTER 20

# The Tower

## General Information and Symbolism

The besieged Tower depicts the consequences of running from reality. A tower may function to protect and aid observation. But when protection and observation turn into fear-riddled or elitist behaviour – to hide, isolate, dominate or to tower over others – God/dess intervenes. We may deny or suppress what is true so as not to lose face, maintain the status quo, become powerful or materially successful and the like, but at the cost of genuine Self-worth. Of course, there is often tremendous pressure and reinforcement to conform to society's and other's needs and expectations. Consequently, under certain circumstances, learning to acquiesce or be a 'good child' is a survival skill that in time becomes counter-productive. When this type of behaviour corrupts and undermines (a reference to the Tower's weak underpinnings) your relationship with your Self, nervous breakdowns, job loss, illness, accidents, turmoil, anger, rage and anxiety will eventually ensue.

As explained in the Lovers and other cards, nudity signifies openness, honesty, truth and reality. Therefore, the clothed people being thrust from the Tower portray the dislodgement of dishonest, unrealistic, unconscious, immature, narrow-minded, supremacist, Self-abnegating attitudes and behaviours. Such are expressed by stating things such as, 'I'm comfortable as is. I don't want to see. I'd rather be right than happy. I don't like change. I'm better than everyone else.' This comes as the end result of being dominated by either too much ego or intellect (the falling male), or an unmanageable amount of emotion (the falling female). The three flaming windows allude to the burning off of such attitudes and behaviour, as they signify the supernal triangle, or three top *Sephiroth* on the Tree of Life – the Crown, Wisdom and Understanding. When other means fail, Wisdom and Understanding are brought about by the Divine Force. Simply, if a child will not listen and is hurting themselves or others, it is their parents' job to step in.

The Tower shows that some basic law of life is either unknown, ignored or violated. When an offender is unable or unwilling to pay attention (one, the Magician) to an error in their ways, act in accord with what is most loving, make amends or be more discriminating (six, the Lovers), the law is enforced from above (seven, the Chariot, the sum of one and six). Lightning is an ancient cross-cultural symbol for the descent of divine energies into the physical world. Thus the lightning bolt, knocking the crown of immaturity, misunderstanding and mock wisdom from the Tower, indicates this action. In reality, the lightning serves to both 'enlighten' and 'lighten-up' your karmic load. On a final note, number 16 suggests that when you can get your ego out of the way and perceive the Tower's activities as ultimately loving, you are victorious.

In the final analysis, the Tower asks you to accept that the destruction of your unsound and hazardous mental and emotional constructs and behaviours is a gift, indicated by the twenty-two sparks of golden light in the form of the Hebrew letter *Yod*. Again, *Yod* symbolises the hand of God/dess reaching down to humanity, and our hands reaching up to this Source for help. Since all comes from God/dess, why is it so difficult to recognise the Tower as the handiwork of God/dess? This is reiterated by the group of 12 falling *Yods* shaped like the figure eight over the Magician and Strength, stating 'As above, so below'. The other grouping of ten *Yods* forms the Tree of Life, suggesting that life teaches us what is best for us.

It is a spiritual misconception to think that the only way to become closer to your Self and God/dess is through catastrophic events and suffering. Such things are usually encountered only *after* other means have gone unheeded. But this premise is often difficult to acknowledge owing to the ego-crushing shame, the uprooting of what is safe and secure, the disruption, pain, privation, fear and loss accompanying catastrophes and tragedies. Under these circumstances, it is useful to ask yourself, 'Mustn't the old be torn down to make room for the new?' 'Doesn't dawn always follow darkness?' Perhaps events such as the Holocaust and Hiroshima are God/dess's way of forcefully assisting humanity to create a more compassionate and peaceful world.

The Tower's eroded foundation indicates that a life built upon unconsciousness and behaviours that demean and alienate you from your Self. The Tower itself represents the human being, who, in the words of revolutionary therapist Wilhelm Reich, must at some point 'tremble and scream for health'. Although traditional yogic philosophy advocates the transcendence of this mode of expression, in some sects it is celebrated as the *Kundalini* energy rising up from the Second *Chakra* or Reproductive Centre (which the Tower represents), the part of your physical body that contains the life force's power to procreate, initiate action, transform and disintegrate, up to the Throat Centre, or Fifth *Chakra*, your creative Self-expression. Yes, the card shows a structure breaking down; however, when outmoded ways of expressing yourself are destroyed (even when done against your personal will, as in the case of the Tower), you are actually in the process of discovering how to express yourself more constructively. Remember, an organism is actually *rebuilt* by its metabolism – anabolism builds after catabolism destroys. When you learn how to ventilate damaging thoughts and feelings, but not attack others in the process (although in certain instances we must beat pillows, yell, cry and cuss up a storm), the tendency to turn such into acts of real violence upon yourself and others dissipates.

The Devil card brings forth an awareness of our dark and disowned side, whereas the Tower illustrates the necessity to face this side in order to evolve further. There is a natural point in the evolutionary process when karmic cleansing is directed at cleaning out wounds – old hurts and angers. Anger that has been stored becomes rage. We can repress and suppress only so much before we explode or implode. The Tower depicts the release of internalised oppression by drawing up and out the rage stored from years of surviving untenable (dysfunctional) life situations, i.e. abusive, alcoholic or drug-addicted parents, mates or other significant persons. When children feel powerless and the like, they become hurt and angry. However, when parents or caretakers respond to their child's feelings by inflicting more pain and anger, children learn to turn their feelings in upon themselves, and/or inappropriately displace them on to others – siblings, peers, animals, or the world at large.

As with other types of behaviour, we must be taught, preferably as children, how to use anger constructively – as an impetus for change. During times when political, social and economic pressures – joblessness, homelessness, illness and the lack of adequate health care or a malfunctioning political system – compound with religious intolerance and one's own survival issues, people, like the Tower, 'blow their tops'. This may explain why so much anger in the form of violence keeps erupting throughout the world.

The colour of the Tower is red, its musical note is C (these are the same as the Emperor, or Aries, ruled by Martian energy) and its herb is garlic. The Hebrew name for the Tower is *Peh*, meaning 'the mouth as a vehicle for speech and communication'. The Tower has 22 levels of masonry, the number of letters in the Hebrew alphabet. Your words have the potential to build or destroy things, yourself and others. A variation on an old rhyme reminds us of this, 'Sticks and stones can break your bones, but words can break your heart.' You empower prayers and affirmations to alter your fate and smooth out life's wrinkles. The shaman's healing chant or curse may determine life or death. Qabalistic Words of Power and Buddhist and Hindu *mantras* have been used for countless generations to heal and quell both internal and external chaos.

The word mantra translates from the Sanskrit to mean 'thinking power'. Yogis define it as 'the language of the Gods and Goddesses', saying that it is not only an assemblage of letters and syllables, but an inner vibration that pulses at the mind's root. It is said that to have the knowledge and use of the right mantra is to know your Self. The ancient Sanskrit *mantra*, *Om Namah Shivaya*, (pronounced, *ohm-na-ma-she-vi-uh*) states that all occurrences are initiated by God/dess. In this belief system, the god Shiva is assigned responsibility for change and transformation. Inner and outer life can be tumultuous, but these words can breed acceptance, understanding and homeostasis in their midst.

The Tower is further connected to communication by its traditional link with the Tower of Babel. At the time of the Bible tale, all humanity supposedly spoke the same language, but abused the gift by conspiring to build a tower to heaven in an effort to challenge God's supremacy. In response to this arrogance, the Most High struck the tower down, and as further insurance against such trespasses, everyone was made to speak or 'babble' a different tongue. Now look back at the Hebrew letter *Peh* and see how it resembles a mouth with a tongue sticking out of it. The Tower has often been linked to the Greek word *hubris*, connoting disrespectful behaviour, overstepping proper boundaries and the erroneous evaluation of one's place in the scheme of things. It draws its origin from incidents in which humans tried to be better than their gods and goddesses – stuck their tongues out at them. The deities' response to such arrogance was to put such persons in their rightful place, as the Most High did at the Tower of 'Babble'. The Tower tells us that we must surrender to the fact that we are not in total control.

Communication is a powerful tool that breaks down or creates barriers in the blink of an eye. In their quest for enlightenment, many aspirants cease speaking in order to be rid of habitually detrimental ways of expressing themselves, and to gain a new perspective on life. The Tower advocates taking maximum responsibility for what you say; not faulting others for their words or opinions; listening; putting aside the need to be 'right' for the sake of understanding; trying out another's language or style of communicating (known as style-shifting in Linguistics); these positive practices are all excellent means of enhancing communication.

Mars, God of War, is associated with the Tower card. This Roman deity appeared red, not only because of his planet's reddish colour, but because of his association with the new year's blood sacrifices, which he presided over. Mars goes hand in hand with courage, nervous energy, assertive and aggressive behaviour and physical action, taking form as fierce bursts of initiating energy to transform and disintegrate whatever obstructs its path. Facing Mars in the form of internal and external upsets, you often feel as if war has been declared on you – it is not surprising that the sphere of severity is linked with Mars on the Tree of Life. Yet the flashes of truth indicated by the lightning bolt are elicited by your own conscious and unconscious needs to shed worn-out attitudes and behaviours. Mars is the force that gets stagnant energy moving. Because the planet is linked with the reproductive organs, it also symbolises sexual energy and physical desire. In a natal chart, the placement of Mars indicates how actively one seeks to gratify one's desires. Mars may forcefully act to eliminate or activate desires, so that you may get to the truth about what you have a passion to achieve in life.

In the Hindu trinity, the functions of Mars are represented by the God *Shiva* and his consort, the Goddess *Kali* (who in this pantheon is more assertive than the god-energy). Consisting of *Brahman* the Creator, *Vishnu* the Preserver and *Shiva* the Destroyer-Transformer, the trinity is very much a part of Indian life. *Shiva-Kali* prepare the way for *Brahman* by cleaning up when *Vishnu's* works are past: the monsoon drenches the parched earth so that the next harvest may grow. Hindus term our present era of time the *Kali Yuga* – Age of *Kali*, the dark goddess – during which destruction and explosive

transformation will precede the next era, the *Satya Yuga* – Age of
Truth and Enlightenment. This is a hidden yet fundamental aspect of
the Tower card.

  In the Qabalah, the Tower is called the Exciting or Arousing
Intelligence. In physics, when you excite a substance, you raise it to a
higher energy level. This Intelligence is the cathartic influence from
the hand of God/dess that descends to disrupt and eliminate
apathetic, unconscious, immature and outmoded feelings and
behaviours, to raise you to a higher level of awareness and clears the
way for you to lead a better and fuller life. The Arousing Intelligence
is a true cosmic alarm clock that awakens us from inertia and sloth.

## Gateway of Life: Adulthood

After the Devil asks you to confront your shadow, the Tower is about
your own Higher Self purging you and allowing you a glimpse of the
process's higher purposes: to end stagnation, increase wisdom and
understanding, cleanse false pride and open our eyes to reality. Like
it or not, the Tower brings you to terms with the lurking self-images
uncovered by the Devil. If this is not done voluntarily, the Self has an
uncanny way of foisting it upon you for the sole purpose of guiding
the seeker to higher states of awareness. In this sense, the Tower may
be viewed as the ultimate lesson in constructive criticism. For those
following a Twelve-Step format, the Tower card speaks of having
the realisation that a power greater than yourself can restore you to
sanity.

  At this stage of your development, you are cautioned against being
intolerant of others' rights to live as they believe, often manifested
by taking rigid stands on moral and spiritual behaviour ('holier than
thou' attitudes and behaviours) for yourself and others. This is
exceptionally dangerous, since you can deceive yourself into
believing you are developing spiritually, when you are actually
isolating yourself – propagating and supporting immaturity through
bogus spirituality. Here you may also come to terms with such
concepts as the fraud of being celibate while harbouring fears of sex
and intimacy; the ridiculousness of practising vegetarianism while
still craving steak; or the hypocrisy of turning the other cheek when
anger demands to be expressed. All are damaging to the body, mind
and spirit. There was a study completed at Johns Hopkins University
on breast cancer patients which seems to support this concept.
Women who were 'good adjusters', defined as those who were
cheerful, not terribly upset by the loss of their breasts, easy to

manage and eager to jump back into living, experienced a higher rate of recurrence than the 'bad' patients, who were angry, sad, frightened and often difficult to manage. Might it be that some unresolved issues still plagued the 'good' girls, while the 'bad' girls had healed themselves by expressing their pain and negative feelings?

Individuals living through the Tower at the Four Gateways of Life may exhibit certain attitudes and behaviour. CHILDHOOD: A man is told he has a predisposition for skin cancer, yet develops it because he does not bother to take proper precautions; ADOLESCENCE: A woman begins to recognise the incongruity of being 'Pro-Life' while avidly supporting the death penalty; ADULTHOOD: Hot oil is carelessly splattered, touching off a raging fire in a restaurant's kitchen, but because the cook keeps a full fire extinguisher within arm's reach, the fire is put out with a minimum of damage; WISDOM: Acknowledging that he has been living in a hurt, angry and frustrated state after his divorce, a man fears he may get sick or injured because he's been so distracted with his problems. So he immediately begins venting his pent-up feelings by writing poetry and talking with friends, joins a sweat lodge and begins a programme of cathartic Yoga breathing several times daily.

## Divinatory Questions for the Tower

*Upright:* What dream has crumbled? What insight have you received? Where might your overly emotional or intellectual approach to things cause disruption? How have you felt God/dess's hand in your life? What misconception have you been flattered or cajoled into supporting? What have your words or actions inadvertently destroyed? What trouble signals have you denied or avoided? How has your ego been crushed? What worn-out way of relating or thinking must be replaced? What unstable construct has finally borne its bitter fruit? How have your efforts to run the show failed? How has excessive pride brought you to where you are now? How has self-protection become isolation and/or elitist behaviour? What feelings are demanding to be expressed? What beliefs have proved false? Whom or what have you been at war with? Have you been expressing a lot of old rage? How have you struggled to maintain the status quo? How are you using anger constructively – as an impetus for positive change? How have you displaced your angry feelings? Whom or what have you tried to dominate? What have you given up or surrendered to under duress? What is no longer inert?

*Reverse:* What dire situation has passed? What are you slowly rebuilding? What shake-up did you see coming so that you took steps to reduce its impact? Why have you been resisting constructive criticism? How has venting your feelings served to restore and deepen a relationship? How has foresight helped to avert a tragedy? What efforts to manipulate you have you recognised for what they are? What has been shaken loose before it fell down on you? How have you braved a disaster? In what area of your personal or professional life has being honest reduced your anxiety? What immaturity are you glad has been crushed? Why isn't this a good time for impulsive decision-making or actions? How are you attempting to make up for your own or another's harsh words or actions? How has God/dess behaved like the loving parent intervening when you, the child, are out of bounds and cannot monitor yourself? How has rage or anger been cleansing?

## Personal Experience

Because I meditate for many hours on each card as I write this book, their principles become especially active in my life. Reaching the Tower, considered to be the deck's cataclysmic yet catalytic omen, I took a deep breath and asked myself, 'Oh, oh, what's going to happen next?' It was, as it turned out, one of the last deep breaths I took for several days to follow.

Now, the background against which this book was written, as I have indicated, was life to the nth degree: teaching classes weekends and evenings; helping care for my dying father-in-law; relating with my two teenagers, mother, friends and husband; plus swimming and meditating regularly to keep myself balanced. In view of this, it was often a terrific struggle sandwiching in writing time daily, and I sometimes felt quite overwhelmed by my project. So when people asked me how the book was going, I often responded by sighing, 'It's like being ten months pregnant.'

I was only one day into writing about the Tower card when it became active in my life, presenting itself in the form of a phone call reporting that one of my sons had cut school for the week, after vehemently insisting I drive him there daily. What ensued was an intense, definitely Tower-like confrontation which concluded with many of his gripes about school being aired, and his being punished for lying.

The next morning I awoke feeling drained, only to find that our slightly leaky hot water heater had become a geyser overnight, turning the back hall into a veritable wading pool. The plumber had told me that they sometimes reseal themselves, so I had ignored its slight but continual leakage. Now I was paying the price for my denial and avoidance – I had simply failed to read the road signs.

During the course of the day, I attempted to sit down to write, but was unable to concentrate – jittery Martian Tower energy. When I finally did begin to organise my thoughts, around 1:00 pm, the phone rang, bringing an anxious plea from my other son to bring some dry clothing to school because he had just fallen into a mud puddle and was soaked to the skin.

Desiring to return to writing as soon as possible, I got a speeding ticket on my way to bring the clothes (talk about not reading the road signs). By dinnertime I realised I had not written a word in two days and felt besieged by the Tower's harsh influence.

The next day of allotted writing time was committed to preparing for an upcoming talk at a local community college. Still no progress on the book. That evening, I unconsciously dressed in red (the Tower's colour) and coincidentally (Ha!) taught the Tower card to my beginning-level class. I explained that it meant not only the potential to view traumatic experiences as God/dess's handiwork and the development of our ability to surrender and learn life strategies that are better for us, but that these occurrences are often a response to our avoidance behaviour, unconsciousness, excessive pride, laziness and emotion.

In the wee hours of the next morning, I was jolted awake from a restless sleep with my heart pounding in my ears. Lying in bed, struggling to calm down, I was again confronted by the reality that I was, like the Tower, being struck by lightning, or the will of God/dess it symbolises. With that I understood that I had been so preoccupied with the business of life and feeling frustrated at not being able to write, I needed to be roused and reminded to catch my breath and recentre. I was so busy poisoning my mind by dwelling on angry, frustrated self-talk and scenarios, I had succeeded in disrupting my body's equilibrium. I immediately recalled reading the latest research in the field of psychoneuroimmunology, which stated that this type of inner dialogue reduces normal immune system response and escalates anxiety. The message was clear: Pay attention to my stress signals and watch my inner dialogue.

Next on my agenda: some supportive affirmations and a real day off. The Tower let me know in no uncertain terms that the book would be finished in God/dess's own time. I eased up and surrendered to the Tower's truth telling – to go with the flow.

**Student Experiences**

❖ 'I can't believe it. I really can't believe it. Here we are studying the Tower, and I get an eviction notice. Thrown out of my house just like the people in the card,' began Fran, a jeweller. 'When I rented my place, I arranged to get a reduced rate by doing all the yard work. But I've found my landlord's standards and mine to be quite different. The truth is I hate gardening and yard work. I love working with my hands on my jewellery, but not in the dirt. Also, the rent's been a couple of days late for a few months now because I've had some trouble getting my debtors to pay me on time. I've explained the situation to the landlord and I thought he understood, but on top of the condition of the yard, I guess it was too much for him.

'He's an older, retired businessman and comes by once in a while to check things out. I always make him tea and cookies and think everything is fine, although he always mentions the state of the garden somewhere in our conversation. I think I've been going on a false sense of security. I've assumed, since we have this nice personal relationship, that everything else is okay. Well, evidently it isn't. It's time to face up to the fact that I've been deceiving myself.

'I get so busy with filling jewellery orders and my spiritual studies, time just slips away. Looks like my chickens have come home to roost. The truth's out. I'd better restructure my Tower to put these material considerations in a place of greater importance. Keeping to my agreement is as important as my spiritual studies. In fact, I think it's an extension of it. I think the Universe has pulled me up short over my dishonesty.'

*Fran is absolutely correct, keeping agreements is an important part of integrating spiritual work. Separating your everyday life from your spiritual life is asking for your Tower to come tumbling down. Sometimes it's much easier to separate the two, but when the discrepancies become too great, Tower-like situations arise. It looks as though Fran's approaching a new Gateway in this area. 'Maybe you're making the transition from Childhood to Adolescence, because of your naiveté, about this interrelationship,' I suggested. 'The important thing is that you realised the teachings quickly, which will help you lessen or avoid the same type of pattern again.'*

❖ Dan shared a terrifying and sobering experience. 'I had a terrible fight with my woman friend on Saturday night. Our relationship is highly explosive, like the Tower. We always seem to be blowing up at each other for one thing or another. But Saturday night I was so angry at her, I couldn't get away fast enough. I jumped into my truck and actually burned rubber as I pulled away from her apartment. I was so distracted, I almost hit a kid riding right next to me on a bike. I didn't even know he was there. It was dark and he was wearing dark-coloured clothing. It was a hell of an experience for me. It woke me up to what's important. Just like the lightning flash striking the Tower, I was stunned by the message. I consider myself lucky, although my heart nearly stopped. I don't want to hurt somebody else just because I'm angry and hurt. I think the message is to stay off the road when I feel like I did the other night. Take a walk and cool down before getting behind the wheel. I'm going to pay attention so I don't have to live though a worse Tower, like vehicular manslaughter.'

*'When you allow your emotions and physical appetites to distract and victimise you, the Tower acts to refocus your attention on what's really important,' I told him. 'In other words, it finally "hits us", as is happening to the people in the card. We often think we act independently, but by almost hitting that cyclist, you had immediate feedback as to how your actions and attitudes affect those around you. You experienced yet another facet of the Tower's teachings.'*

❖ 'The question, "What has come up that you've been avoiding?" was all too appropriate for me,' said Shirl. 'I've been avoiding getting enough exercise. It's income tax time again and I'm in my workaholic mode from dawn to almost midnight. All I do when I work for those hours is sit, sit, sit. One appointment after the next. I mean, I've taken enough Yoga and stress-management classes to know a few exercises to do easily at the office, but I just go on automatic. I've been saying, "Tomorrow I'll exercise," for weeks now. And here I am, miserable. Usually I have a massage every couple of weeks, but when I looked back in my book, I found it's been nearly six weeks since I've had an appointment. It's hard to believe the synchronicity of pulling my back out and studying the Tower card.

'Being honest, it isn't. I've been asking for it. I hope those upside-down people don't mean I'll have to be in traction again, but rather that I'll reverse my ways. You told us last week, "When you resist doing something you must do for yourself, it gets done for you." Well, here I am, getting it done for me.'

*'Your back is like the Tower's weak foundation, so you might use this symbol as a reminder to continually shore it up,' I told Shirl. 'That way you won't wind up with that surprised look the people being thrown from the Tower have, because your back went out. The Tower tells us that by ignoring the road signs, we take the chance of getting lost, having an accident, or getting forcibly stopped by some authority figure. Looks as if you might have got a ticket for speeding! When altering an old pattern or adopting something new, it's best to begin when we have the desire and will-power to nurture it along, not when we're worn down, rushed or on "automatic". This enables us to have it there when we need it.'*

❖ 'I went to see the movie *Broken Rainbow* with my husband last weekend,' said Karen. 'Talk about arousal and awakening! Did it wake me up! The film is about the forced relocation of the Navajo Indians from the Big Mountain Reservation. There's supposed to be trouble between them and the Hopis, but in reality the land is uranium-rich and our dear government wants it back. Anyhow, I've been politically asleep since Reagan's election, and this was the shock I needed to bring me around. Let me tell you, it was absolutely appalling, not only to me, but to others in the audience. You could hear people gasping and crying throughout the showing.

'So I made a donation for supplies and then went home to write a pile of letters to Washington to tell the government to stop forcing the Indians out of their homes – like the people being thrown out of their Tower. It seems like an incredible injustice. But it moved me and maybe a lot of others to action. I just can't stand there on the sidelines and watch the terrible Tower-like destruction going on there. I can see why the Tower card is called the Exciting Intelligence, it stirs up change. As in the case of Big Mountain, it excites people to act and help transform things. Perhaps situations such as these are God's way of getting those of us who are asleep to be awake and active. I've been trying the statement, "The hand of God is in everything" to remind me of this.'

*'This situation is clearly arousing your passion and desire, associated with the Martian aspect of the Tower,' I said. 'Unlike the Navajos, the people in the Tower card are being relocated because they've violated some important law of life. If anything, it looks as if our government is breaking the law. It's certainly a pitiful situation. It might, however, also be useful to look at the Navajo as "survivors". Their tribe was in existence long before we came to this country and for decades has been struggling long and hard with this*

*government's policies. What I'm trying to say is that we are all, in one sense or another, "survivors" of the various Towers in our lives. And as seen in concentration camp inmates, dire circumstances may sometimes bring out the best in people. Please don't misunderstand – I'm not telling you not to act; quite the contrary: the support, intervention and political clout of people such as yourself are exactly what is needed to help turn things around. Maybe this is showing you that next time you have a personal Tower, perceive yourself as a survivor as well, and again call up your own Mars energies to do all in your power to thrive.*

*'And finally, for those of us who are able to act socially and politically, but not interpersonally, I believe these situations are models through which to learn how to do this. This aspect of the Tower shows how disasters are often the result of our own self-defeating behaviours, and how we will in time learn to overcome both our fear and its consequence, the failure to act.'*

❖ 'I learned about two aspects of the Tower card this week: communication and misuse of spiritual tools and teachings,' shared Gloria. 'I'm pretty positive that's what went on between a friend and me the night after our last Tarot class. My friend has some unusual Tarot cards and offered to do a reading for me. When we sat down to do it, he instructed me exactly how to shuffle the cards. But I didn't do it, because his method didn't feel right. He got so angry when I wouldn't comply, he ran off without so much as giving me a second chance or even talking about it. I felt controlled, and I guess he felt rejected. Come to think of it, I felt rejected and I believe he felt controlled by me.

'I can see now that I could have asked him first if it was okay to shuffle the cards my own way, not just go ahead and do it. The ritual was important to him, and he was the person giving me the reading. I really didn't honour that. He, on the other hand, could have told me the rules without getting so peeved about what I did. He took it as a personal affront instead of seeing it as something I needed to do to feel right about what we were doing. I think we're both guilty of poor communication and spiritual one-upmanship. Here was the opportunity to share something meaningful between us, and our egos got out of hand and ruined it, just as excessive ego obliterates the Tower.'

'*Gloria's evaluation of the situation is aligned with what we discussed about intolerance of others' beliefs at this card's Gateway of Life. As she learned, discounting others sometimes begs that things blow up in our faces. One way or another, power trips beget power trips. Gloria certainly got instant feedback when her friend gave her the same type of treatment. They were like two children sticking their tongues out at each other. I hope Gloria and her friend can get together and talk about what happened.*'

## Suggestions for Application and Integration of the Tower

The following is geared to help you persist and learn from uprooting or hair-raising (also consciousness-raising) Tower-type experiences. These exercises may provide the opportunity for you to become more cognisant of danger signals, to hold a better attitude while enduring feedback from misidentification of truth and immature or unconscious behaviours. They might also remind you not to overpower others and to rebuild what has been lost on a firmer foundation.

1   Colour or draw your own version of the Tower, with yourself as either or both of the figures.

2   Set the Tower in a visible place as a reminder to your conscious and subconscious minds to use and recall its teachings to see the hand of God/dess in life's upheavals, to increase your abilities to handle personal cataclysms, or to avoid being flattered or manipulated into wrong action.

3   Dream on the Tower.

4   Play the note C on a musical instrument. Intone IAO or hum along with the music and concentrate on your reproductive centre (Second *Chakra*) while you do this (you might feel a slight warmth or tingling in this area). Now meditate on the card for a few minutes. Think about a situation in your life in which you might not be heeding signs of danger. Next, experience the initiating power and drive present in your Second *Chakra*, move it up into your heart and transform it into a courageous desire to pay attention to and engage with these signals. Try to perceive them not just as threats to your ego, but as indications that you have endangered yourself or another by overstepping, or not respecting, some important boundary. Ask that the Tower's teachings guide you through this situation. Or if you are faced

with a worrisome situation, event or problem, such as thinking that you're 'better' or more 'advanced' than others, needing to be more than just a 'survivor', or being stuck in the habit of isolating yourself, imagine how the Tower's wisdom might help you handle it. If it seems appropriate, do it. Jot down the times when you recognise the card's presence in your interactions. I was aware of the Tower when? Before/ during/after . . .

5 Go out into the world and apply the Tower's teachings. I enacted the Tower and this is what occurred . . .

6 The Rerun. After having an experience and realising in retrospect how the Tower's teachings might have helped you or another come to terms with conflict sooner or more easily, provided insight to a shake-up in your personal or professional life, or helped you stop towering over others, mentally relive the situation, *including* your insight. This will help the behaviour become more automatic next time. If possible, actually rerun the situation in real life with your new attitude or behaviour.

7 Ask yourself the following questions:

'What fear-provoking situation can I no longer deny and avoid dealing with?' 'Am I handling my anger effectively?' 'In what situations do I think I am better than others?' 'What deep-seated belief or fear has been uprooted?' 'Where am I experiencing a loss of self-esteem?' 'Where have I lacked humility (exhibited *hubris*), and what has been damaged or destroyed because of it?' 'What am I holding on to, despite my own better judgment?' 'How might I have "saved face", yet sacrificed Self respect?' 'How am I lightening up?' 'Where and why have I been misled or allowed myself to see a lie as truth?' 'What idea or belief has proved to be erroneous?' 'How might an offering of constructive criticism be of value?' 'What has shocked me into awareness?' 'What series of events is about to be set off due to my immaturity, excessive emotionality or ego?' 'How has my false pride been crushed?' 'How can I come out of isolation?' 'What unpleasant realisation must I now confront?' 'Where might humility function to alter the repercussions my actions have had upon myself or another?' 'What idea, problem, or habit pattern needs to be broken down so that something better might be built up?' 'What dream has crumbled to make room for something new?'

'What Gateway of Life am I in or developing through in the above?' Indicate: Childhood, Adolescence, Adulthood or Wisdom. Why?'

'What do I need to do in order to develop the above further?' I need to . . .

'What step(s) do I want to take towards this and how can the Tower guide me?'

8    Use a personal statement regarding the presence of the Tower in your life at this time, such as: 'The hand of God/dess is everywhere.' 'Shake-ups are wake-ups.' 'God/dess frees me from what is no longer useful.' My personal statement is . . .

9    Inspirational words and quotes:

'*Om Namah Shivaya*, (pronounced Ohm-Na-ma-she-vi-uh) – All events are the work of God/dess.'

'Remember, the difference between comedy and tragedy is that in comedy the characters figure out reality in time to do something about it!'

10   What symbols stand out in the card? What do they say to you? How might they be useful in daily living? Bring the symbol(s) into your life in some way so as to integrate the card's teachings. The Tower reminds me not to isolate myself from new ideas, because in doing so, I fall behind in my personal and professional development.

11   Wear and surround yourself with the Tower's colour, red, to remind you of the card's teachings when needed, such as having the courage to face a tumultuous situation, express hurt, anger and frustration constructively, work effectively with the catastrophic results of an unconscious decision, cease over-protecting yourself or let go of spiritual elitism. Notice how you are affected.

12   The Tower is astrologically conjoined with Mars, ruling physical action, courage, internal and external shake-ups, initiating and nervous energy, consciousness and hair-raising experiences. Is there some facet of your life in which you anticipate this type of intervention? If so, don't wait until it happens to you; instead,

bravely take it upon yourself to initiate handling things (even if this means asking for help) before they blow up. Note what happens: your thoughts and feelings and the outcome.

13 Remember that the Tower's Hebrew name, *Peh*, means 'mouth as a vehicle for speech and communication'. Where might this remind you of the card's meaning or help in your life process? Spend a few minutes a day being aware of your inner and outer dialogues. Ask yourself how silence might be advantageous. Or if someone reacts negatively to your communication, stop and examine the intention and energy, the tone, behind your words, not just the words themselves.

14 Try a few drops of the scent pepper associated with the Tower as a reminder to integrate the card's teachings. Caution: it might make you sneeze or burn sensitive skin.

15 Add garlic, the herb associated with the Tower, to your food. While eating, think about its need to be crushed before it's potency is fully activated, plus its properties as a stimulant, cathartic, antiseptic and expectorant and consider the like qualities of the Tower.

17　　THE STAR

# The Star

## General Information and Symbolism

The Star is the natural outgrowth of the Tower's upheaval – the calm after the storm, the cleansed and vacant feeling following catharsis. It is simply our turning over a new leaf. Once our obsolete behaviours are shaken or purged by the Tower's fall, we accept that not living in accordance with the truth causes mishaps, and realise that we must either live in closer alignment with the universal laws and principles and nature, or regress to old patterns that will lead to further cataclysms.

The Goddess gazes into the water, connoting a self-imposed period of reflection and soul-searching. Through this, you not only fill the void, but gain the opportunity to transform your problems and immaturities into challenges to be met instead of a backlog of mental and emotional garbage waiting to tumble down upon you. Towers will continue to fall (being human means dealing with mental and emotional management), but inspirational practices will help you become more aware of their impending presence, rendering them fewer and farther apart, and improve your coping skills. By tapping into the teachings of truth as symbolised by the card's introspective mood, you will discover how to proceed.

To bring about the best relationship between your spiritual and material worlds, you must take charge, lovingly yet firmly, of your mind, body and emotions. The nude Goddess of Truth – Isis unveiled – shown balancing between land and water, demonstrates how, when the veils of illusion are pulled back, you realise that mind, body, emotions and the two worlds are in reality inseparable and interdependent.

The Goddess rests one foot upon the water's surface, illustrating the miracle of understanding – revelation and discovery – derived from concentration (the Qabalistic function of this card is Concentration/Meditation) on introspective and inspirational practices.

The pool's ripples state not only that contact with the Self has been made, but suggest the long-term implications evolving from this contact – actions always create some type of reaction – the Wheel of Fortune's 'wheels within wheels'. The ripples also represent the potential to be more objective about the Tower's cycle of destruction, and life cycles in general.

Water flows into the pool from the vessel, symbol of the human body, in the Goddess's right (conscious) hand, signifying that it is your conscious choice to engage in these Self-sustaining activities. In addition, this symbolises the aspirant pouring the insights and inspirations gleaned from Self-reflection back into the collective unconscious to become available to influence and transform others.

Appealing to God/dess for guidance and direction is the process of opening your mind and heart through prayer and meditative practices. Like the Goddess's nakedness, these divest you of illusions to bring out truth. Prayer is the act of beseeching your Higher Self for guidance. Her knees are bent, signifying the practice of falling to one's knees, physically or symbolically, to request help from on high. Her body forms the glyph for Saturn, showing that she recognises her limitations and now asks for the guidance to go beyond them. Saturn further suggests the discipline and self-control needed to spiritually practice while simultaneously surrendering control of the outcome. Meditation, the act of focusing and clarifying your thoughts and feelings, is primarily accomplished by a deep desire 'to know', symbolised by the female figure. Meditation, as we learned with the Hierophant, is the act of becoming quiet and observant enough to hear, see, smell, feel or even taste our solutions, shown by the five streams flowing from the Goddess's left-hand pitcher. The Goddess pours water on to the earth with her left (subconscious) hand, communicating how the cleansing and healing aspects of prayer and meditation clarify and transform our automatic responses to what our senses present us with.

The contents of a pitcher take on the shape of the container, just as we as vessels shape, and take the shape of, what is in our mind. The pitchers are decorated with ovals bound by four bars. This represents how the Life Force, the oval or Fool's zero, expresses itself through the four worlds and elements, the four bars binding it in place. The four Qabalistic worlds function to direct and hold formlessness in form. Both in the creation of life and meditation, the limitless Life Force is consciously drawn through and into limited form, our physical body. This occurs so that we can be the conduit for bringing the energies of God/dess out into the world.

The planet Mercury is associated with clearly directed attention, an essential prerequisite for both worldly and spiritual success. The Ibis, a great fishing bird, symbol of concentration and attention and sanctified by Mercury, indicates this. The bird's angular beak shows that it sustains itself by fishing, in much the same way we sustain ourselves by angling in the waters of higher consciousness. Focusing your attention upon the Greater Truths affects all levels of being – physical, mental, emotional and spiritual. The act of stilling your mind and emotions gradually moves the *Kundalini* or Holy Spirit up your spine through the *chakras*, indicated by the seven smaller stars, to elevate your awareness. The seven small stars represent the seven mythic Pillars of Wisdom and the Seven Prophetic Priestesses, implying that wisdom and prophetic powers are created by the proper alignment of the seven internal luminaries, or *chakras*. The Ibis, perched on one leg atop the tree (or human head) further symbolises this procedure.

As mentioned previously, in Tarot and Qabalah, trees are likened to humans – your body is the roots and trunk, the foliage your head and brain. According to legend, the Buddha sat under a tree and meditated until he reached enlightenment, just as you remain under the dominion of your physical body and world until you aspire to more objective states of awareness. The act of summoning one's God/dess Self through concentrated effort and loving desire (prayer and meditative practices) slowly draws your life force (*Kundalini*, *Chi*, *Ki* or the Holy Spirit) up from the base of your spine (sometimes termed the 'Root' *Chakra*) to the pineal and pituitary glands, centres of higher consciousness within the brain. Scientific research demonstrates that prayer and meditation stimulate these glands to release chemical substances which induce certain physiological changes, balancing the body and clarifying the mind and emotions. The induction of such states, coupled with the use of spiritual teachings in daily life, lead to Self-realisation and union with one's God/dess Self within. Please note that you must use *both* ingredients of this 'recipe', otherwise what you are preparing will be incomplete.

The dictionary defines meditation as 'contemplation and honest reflection', conveyed by the nude Goddess gazing into the pool. Qabalists regard meditation to be a magic mirror through which you may discover and behold God/dess within and without. It is the 'mirror of prophecy' often associated with the ancient Hebrew meditation practices. Looking into this mirror leads you out of bewilderment – the 'wilderness' within. *Time Magazine*, in a cover story on stress management, defined meditation as 'The use of various techniques to develop a temporarily passive awareness of the outside world which sets the mind and body at ease'.[1] Meditation aims to develop the witness consciousness studied in the Wheel of Fortune and other cards. The great yogi, Paramahansa Yogananada, called meditation 'the longing of the soul for the infinite'. The word itself is derived from the Sanskrit word *medha*, meaning 'wisdom'. The Hebrews have several words which relate to the meditative state: *hagah*, *hitboneuth* and *hitbodeuth*. *Hagah* is a verb which means 'the repetition of words in a sweet or passionate manner', as in prayer. *Hitboneuth* indicates 'self-understanding', the goal of meditative practice. Meditation is also considered to be the practice of isolating the Self from the personality, and *hitbodeuth* means 'seclusion' or 'self-isolation'. This tells you that meditation is a means through which you may temporarily bypass obsolete ways of thinking and feeling in order to generate new ideas, find truth, peace and inspiration, and make contact with your inner Self, or intuition. It may also empower you to remain centred on what you want to think when you want to think it.

As the teachings of the Tarot become integrated into your daily experiences, it becomes a form of meditation. That is, not only do you become increasingly conscious and able to witness your behaviour when taking 'time out' from life to meditate and also while engaged in ordinary chores and activities. For those who are Self-realised (have experienced God/dess within), all actions are performed in this highly focused state. In other words, every task is carried out with total awareness, or in a fully awakened state. In time, this combination of living and sitting meditation leads to *samadhi*, *satori*, or enlightenment, the complete union of the individual with the Source, as depicted by the World card. This type of consciousness makes life's mountains into molehills as shown by the shrinking mountains in the card's background. This symbol also tells us that no problem is unsurmountable.

The large Star represents the Star of Bethlehem which appeared to announce the birth of Jesus. The Christ was one saviour who brought hope to a troubled world. In the same way, hope, depicted as stars glimmering in the darkness, may be our saviour in dark times. This Star also suggests the act of receiving sustenance from the Source of Life while meditating. (A student aptly likened it to 'suckling at the breast of the Cosmic Mother'.) In the Thoth deck,

1 *Time Magazine*, 3 June 1984.

the Goddess pours fluid from the great waters over herself, suggesting how meditation nourishes both ourselves *and* our environment. This Source may actually be seen during meditation as a Star, eye or luminous blue pearl. Yogis, alchemists and metaphysicians alike describe meditation as the opening of the Eye of Truth. Plato states, 'There is an eye of the soul which is more precious than ten thousand bodily eyes; by it alone Truth is seen.' The one large star underscores the fact that there is only one truth. Duality disappears by aligning our personal reality with the greater impersonal reality through inspirational practices. Finally, it is valuable to remember that just as all of us are enlivened by the one Life Force, the smaller stars are enlivened by the one great star, as it symbolises that Force emanating through the Crown, *Kether*, on the Tree of Life.

The number eight again appears, since there are eight eight-pointed stars shimmering in the sky, representing new possibilities after the Tower's fall. Eight reiterates the interconnectedness of matter and spirit, the inner and outer worlds, which comes from meditation. It also indicates the unfolding of complete human potential by embracing the interconnection of heaven and earth. The Star is number 17, consciously aligning and unifying the focusing powers of the personal and divine will; the Magician (one) helps the Charioteer to victory on his or her journey through life (seven). Seventeen adds up to eight, further emphasising the idea of unifying and balancing the material and spiritual worlds via the Star's teachings. It is of interest to note that 17 is a prime number. This means it has itself and unity as its only factors.

The colour of the Star is violet, its musical tone is A$^{\#}$ and its herb is skullcap. *Tzaddi*, the Hebrew name for the Star, means 'fishhook'. Look at the letter and notice its resemblance to this implement. Just as a well-baited hook lures a fish up out of its waters, the desire and intent to know entices new ideas and inspiration from the waters of consciousness through you.

The Star is associated with the fixed (stable, nonvolatile) Air sign of Aquarius the Water Bearer, which influences the lower legs and ankles. Saturn (the World) and Uranus (the Fool) share the rulership of Aquarius, indicating that by fixing your attention, you open up to divine inspiration and become more able to deal with worldly limitations. The Aquarian personality says: I know, invent, detach and lead. I'm individualistic, idealistic, intuitive, friendly, open-minded, a visionary who envisions unconventional solutions to problems, and derives satisfaction from philanthropic and humanitarian works. Aquarius is symbolised by a human, implying that the Aquarian Age will be a time when the heartfelt humanitarian ideals of peace, generosity and equality will work in harmony with mindful scientific technology, in order to heal the earth and her people. In this age, your conscience becomes your guide. Examples of this can be found in the stand taken against continuing to support the Contras in Nicaragua, the refusal to confirm an alleged racist and sexist to the Supreme Court and the re-unification of Germany. On a final note, because the Aquarian can be overly detached and impersonal, the evolved native loves not only humanity, but has learned to embrace people on an individual basis as well.

In the Qabalah, the Star is known as the Natural Intelligence. The natural consequence of your request for divine guidance is the knowledge of the true nature of yourself. This Intelligence will in time direct your innate natural powers to transform your worn-out responses, plus remind you to ascribe the highest possible meaning to mundane living.

## Gateway of Life: Adulthood

The Star is the light of hope at the end of a dark tunnel. Humbled by the events of the Tower, the aspiring adult is stripped of yet another layer of false pride and immaturity, and in your nakedness you discover that all you really have is your Self. Peace and joy stem from within. Consequently, you decide to accept and befriend who you are. You actively seek out contact with your inner Self, the voice of the Hierophant heard in childhood, but which then went unrecognised, unappreciated or was conditioned out by others and/ or your need to survive. At this time, you reconnect with your conscience and allow it to be your guide. You now have the option to rebuild your life with the objective of living honestly. Qabalists say you seek to build your life on the sure foundation of eternal being. When you are attuned with your Self, you shine like a star. You vigorously pursue living in accordance with the greater truths and apply the Rules and Tools of the Game of Life daily. Spiritual aspirants find that prayer and meditation teach you to *live* in a meditative state and that all activities may be considered spiritual practice. With increased frequency, ordinary interactions become metaphors for spiritual growth. You become focused, disciplined, increasingly objective and hopeful.

In Twelve-Step philosophy, the Star suggests: the decision to turn your will and life over to the care of the Most High; admitting the exact nature of your errors and immaturities; humbly asking God/dess to remove all defects of character; and seeking through prayer and meditation to improve your conscious contact with God/dess as you understand Him/Her, praying only for knowledge of His/Her will for you and the power to carry it out. Stars are distant suns; the closer we get to them, the brighter the light. This symbolises the hope one begins to feel at this stage of one's recovery.

Living this card at the Four Gateways of Life may bring about the following attitudes and behaviours. CHILDHOOD: You are attracted to introspective practices because you have read that various psychic phenomena sometimes accompany them; ADOLESCENCE: You seek out intuitive guidance only when deeply troubled; ADULTHOOD: Because a doctor goes about her work in a clear and focused state, she grows increasingly capable of tuning into the best healing procedures for each of her patients; WISDOM: A spiritual teacher lives what he or she teaches.

## Divinatory Questions for the Star

*Upright:* How are you shining? What truths are you searching for? What truth do you wish to know no matter what it may be? How are you attuning yourself to higher consciousness? What insight have you received? Could this be a time to be especially honest with yourself or another? What veils have been pulled back? Are you feeling more hopeful, centred and present than in a long time? What are you discovering about your preconditioned self? Is this a time for Self-reflection? How have your perceptions been clarified? What insight into the possible future implications of your current actions have you received? Have you gained some important recognition? Are you tapping into some abundant new resource? Have you begun following your own star? Are you seeking to bring meditative awareness into your daily life?

*Reversed:* Do you feel as if new awareness and consciousness are slowly dawning? Have you been frustrated in gaining recognition? Have you been engaged in excessive soul-searching? Are you fearful of unleashing some new potential? What truth have you tried to avoid seeing or feeling? How might you better star in your own life? Could meditation and prayer be mediums through which you might attain more physical and mental serenity? What attitude or situation has been reshaped owing to prayer, meditation and spiritual practice?

## Personal Experience

Whoever said, 'When you wish upon a star, your dreams come true,' was right. While earnestly studying the Star card, I wished for an honest love relationship, and within a few weeks, there it was. After knowing my new friend only briefly, I found him admirably truthful when he invited me to his best friend's birthday dance, casually mentioning that both his ex-wife and a woman he was intermittently dating would be present. Jarred, but not surprised by his honesty, I cringed inside as I thanked him for the invitation, while in contrast I lied about having other plans. Having previously gone through many distressing situations in which I was accused of being 'overly attached' when I objected to my lovers being intimate with other women, I doubted my ability to remain detached and centred enough to enjoy the party. Because I was embarrassed to admit my feelings, things were left where I could arrive up until 2:00 am if I felt like dancing.

The night of the party, I made up my mind to reserve my final judgement until after I had taken a relaxing bath and had meditated. In my studies of the Star card, I had learned about its associations with the revelation of truth, and decided to meditate on it to find out the best way to handle the upcoming evening.

Still uneasy in spite of the bath, I lit my favourite incense and sat down with the Star to request divine guidance. With an open heart and mind, I asked the Goddess to indicate the best way for me to approach the situation for my greatest good. Immediately, my mind was flooded with vivid memories of past hurts and jealousies, and after some tears came the astounding reality, 'I am a totally unique and special person.' The Natural Intelligence of the card also revealed to me that feeling pained when someone you love is unfaithful, is natural behaviour. Suddenly, I no longer felt ashamed of my feelings. I was so moved by the accuracy of these insights that I became determined to give the party a try. Putting on my best dress, which just happened to be a violet velvet – the exact colour of the Star – I slipped into my dancin' shoes and was out the door before I knew it.

Driving through crosstown traffic, I bolstered my courage by repeating the Star's potent truth, 'I am a totally unique and special person,' and walked into the party feeling confident and happy. I enjoyed dancing with my friend, alone, and with others throughout the evening. Once or twice I caught sight of him talking with other women and I felt twinges of fear and jealousy. Yet as soon as I reminded myself of the truth in the form of my affirmation, these feelings dissipated. As to the relationship? It deepened, and we have been together over twenty-five years.

## Student Experiences

❖ 'I've known for aeons how important it is for me to be conscious of what I do daily,' professed Kim. 'When we discussed the Star last week, I remembered studying Zen Buddhist meditation years ago and found that many of the principles were the same. But I wasn't ready to practise meditation regularly. Since working with the Star card, I think I'm finally there.

'I'm aware that it's important to do whatever I do with as much consciousness as possible. This week, I experimented with being present and aware while doing my routine activities. It definitely takes a strong will to do that. But I feel so inspired by the woman in the card, I genuinely want to live my life with as much focus as I'm able to. I'm in the habit of going around wishing I were doing something other than what I'm doing while I'm doing it. You know, living in the future, or never-never land. But being present while I do each thing as I'm doing it, whether it's grocery shopping, working on the computer or pumping gas into my car, makes a tremendous difference in my life. It seems to make the time go by faster and makes me feel as if I'm not wasting my precious hours as I work and do household chores.

'I've also been using the affirmation, "Everything I do is spiritual". I even went to the import store and bought some lovely Japanese incense to put me more in the mood to stay present while I cook dinner and do other such chores.'

*'I love your statement,' I told Kim, 'and it sounds like you're definitely putting the card to good use. I think in time you'll find yourself to be just like the Ibis on the treetop, viewing life's events from an elevated or altered state.'*

❖ Judith, a feminist and writer, told this story: 'Last Saturday, my family went to a *Bat Mitzvah*, a Jewish girl's initiation into womanhood, similar to the Christian confirmation ceremony. I was raised in the Jewish faith, but left it behind years ago because I felt a genuine lack of recognition of the woman's power. I perceived women to be treated with much less importance than men. Well, at first I thought I'd pass up the invitation, but at the last minute I decided to go because I wanted to be there for our daughter – it was her friend's ceremony.

'What an awful experience! Throughout the ceremony, which, unbelievably, had remained unchanged since I was a child, were constant references to God our Father and Lord. Unfortunately, I wasn't able to refrain from adding several "our Goddess, our Mother" comments. Then came the part of the service where the *Torah*, the holy scriptures, are given to the child, symbolic of passing down the tradition to the next generation. I became absolutely enraged as the father passed it to his daughter, while the mother sat smiling stupidly from the sidelines. To me, this was a blatant denial of the Goddess living within that young girl as well as her connection with her mother's lineage. I got so infuriated that I heatedly whispered to my husband, "This is a travesty. It's the mother's place to do that, not the father's."

'By this time, my husband had become quite disturbed by sitting next to my hostile energies and loudly replied, "Go tell the family about it. You chose to be here. Shut up!" I nearly choked on my anger and embarrassment. Almost immediately after the ceremony, I fled to take a run and regroup.

'As I fell into a good pace, I thought about the Star card and real spirituality. I thought of her being the Goddess of Truth, and automatically my mind went back to the *Bat Mitzvah*. Yes, I had spoken the truth as I saw it, and I felt good doing so, but I was still upset by my husband's comments. Running for a while, it finally dawned on me that he'd also spoken the truth. I had in fact chosen to attend. I knew what I was getting myself into, and although I was hurt, angry and embarrassed by his reaction to me, he was right. What took place was also the truth for the *Bat Mitzvah* girl and her family. I flushed with embarrassment right then and there. My behaviour was so adolescent, I barely could stand myself!

'I slowly understood that my ego had been excessive and my outbursts definitely out of place. I'd asked to be silenced. And then, instead of spending my day sulking as I usually do when I'm hurt and angry, I shared my revelation with my husband – pretty mature behaviour for an adolescent. We had a good laugh on me. I thank the Goddess of Truth for this potent insight.'

*Judith experienced the 'Revelation' aspect of the Star, and it moved her forward into more adult behaviour. The process of revelation offers us the chance to decide between staying with present behaviour, as inappropriate or ineffective as it may be, or cutting our Self loose. Judith's running meditation clarified her perception of the situation – the five streams flowing from the goddess's vase.*

❖ 'I'm in the middle of getting ready to take a long trip,' began Peggy, a Yoga instructor and practitioner. 'I'll be gone for three to four months. Things have been so busy, I feel as if I'll never be finished with it all in time. You know, issues like, who's going to live in my house while I'm gone? Where will I live when I return? What about my animals? What clothes to pack and which to put into a trunk for storage? I've been taking the Star into my body by doing some of the Yoga balancing postures I usually tend to avoid. I've been inspired by the symbol of the Ibis. It's been wonderful. I definitely feel recentred and balanced. It's a neat form of meditation for me to be doing at this time.'

*'It's great when you can use the "medicine" you prescribe for others on yourself,' I told Peggy. 'There you are, a Yoga teacher doing your Yoga in a time of need. This works especially well because of all the energy we've empowered our various tools and medicines with. It also adds credibility to our work. So when we teach it to others in the future, we also subtly communicate, "This really works." I believe this long-term result is symbolised in the card by the pond rippling out from its centre.'*

❖ 'I do lots of extra work and don't ask to be paid for it, and I never get so much as a thank you,' protested Jane, a medical assistant. 'I guess you could say my boss is a pretty thankless creature. This past week I put in so much overtime, I decided to ask for an extra $50. He shocked me by responding to my request with a flat-out, "No." I mean, not even, "I'll think about it." And to make matters worse, he added that I could have done it in less time! I was furious and angrily confronted him with what I'd been doing for free. When he answered, "Nobody's asking you to do that," I was absolutely stymied.

'I practically ran out of the office and couldn't wait to crawl into my bed and cry. After a few hours of feeling sorry for myself, I caught sight of the Star card peeking out at me from my open notebook. So I decided, enough of this and pulled out the homework questions. "What recognition am I searching for?" nearly jumped off the page at me. I definitely needed to re-evaluate my need for recognition at work.

'Thinking about it (I guess I was actually meditating on it without realising it for a day or so), it came to me that I do things the way my mom does. When she does something for someone, it's always with an unspoken, "This is what I want back." Now I see that I need to be more direct. If I want recognition and appreciation, I must ask to be paid for what I do. It's how people are compensated for their time and energy in the world of business. If this can't happen, either I shouldn't do the extra work, or I should look for another job. Great question! Thanks.'

*'The large golden Star in the card depicts how we all need to be "stars" at one time or another in one way or another,' I said. 'It's very important that we learn how to gain recognition, whether it's from others or ourselves. One way we can accomplish this is by giving ourselves time to evaluate truthfully and reflect on the question or issue, as the Goddess in the card does. If we learn that a specific need is indeed valid, then we may seek ways to fulfil it by repeating the inquiry process.'*

❖   'By now you all know that I work for a pharmaceutical company,' Monica told us. 'Lately, business has been steadily getting worse because several of our best-selling drugs are being manufactured generically. And of course, in response to the decline in business, morale around our sales office is unspeakably bad. Thank goodness, the company officers scheduled a meeting the other day to discuss the problem. Since then, spirits seem to have lifted. Actually, there's almost a feeling of hope in the air.

'I've been keeping the Star card next to my bed as a positive and hopeful reminder when I awaken in the early morning hours worried about my future. The symbol of the waters being stirred is comforting to me because it reminds me that honing in on the problem will generate some sort of solution. I've been meditating and asking for God's guidance more regularly lately. And somehow, I have the distinct feeling that something positive will come from all this, even if it's just me becoming a calmer person in times of distress.'

*'You certainly have the right idea, Monica,' I said. 'When you request divine guidance, you're also inadvertently asking for your sensory perceptions – the five streams pouring from the Goddess's pitcher – to be sharper so that you will become more knowledgeable about what direction to follow. The card teaches us to be awake and aware while going about our everyday lives. Perhaps you'll benefit from paying careful attention to what your senses tell you. Don't discount the article you're reading, the radio talk*

*show you accidentally turn on while driving to work, even the experience a
family member tells you about. Any one of these may provide important
ideas and information. Be like the Goddess, open yet discriminating.'*

## Suggestions for Application and Integration of the Star

It's now time for you to become a Star. These exercises suggest ways
in which you can become more aware of the meditative aspect of
mundane life; evaluate yourself and your life circumstances more
honestly; look to the Divine for insight and inspiration; open up to
new energies; feel more calm, peaceful and Self-centred; be a Star;
renew hope after a disappointment; or discover how to proceed with
a problem in alignment with your greatest good.

1 Colour or draw your own version of the Star with yourself as the
   Goddess. If you are male, identify her as your inner Self.

2 Set the Star in a visible place as a reminder to your conscious and
   subconscious minds to use and absorb its teachings, to recall the
   value of doing centring or meditation exercises and prayer, look
   to the Source within for sustenance, or renew hope after having
   your dream or plan shattered.

3 Dream on the Star.

4 Play the note A# on a musical instrument. Intone IAO or hum
   along with the music. Meditate on the card for a few minutes. If
   you're faced with a worrisome situation, event or problem, or are
   at a crossroads and don't know how to proceed, try the following.
   Caution: unless you genuinely want to know the answer, *stop here*.

   Now approach the Goddess with an open heart and mind and
   humbly request that she help you to discover what you need to
   know or do in order to handle the situation for your greatest
   good. Ask that the teachings of truth guide your quest. It is
   *essential* to repeat this ritual with as much desire, feeling and
   willingness to know as possible, until your answer presents itself.
   Remain alert and open to your response. Remember, it may not
   reveal itself during this procedure, but as you go about your daily
   activities. Jot down the times when you recognise the card's
   presence in your interactions. I was aware of the Star when?
   Before/during/after . . .

5 Go out into life and enact the Star's teachings. I enacted the Star
   and this is what took place . . .

6 The Rerun. After having an experience and realising in retrospect how the Star's teachings might have guided you to focus on a situation more effectively, opened you to divine inspiration or direction, let you see life as a meditation or enhanced your sensory perceptions, mentally relive the situation, *including* your insight. This will help the situation become more automatic next time. If possible, actually rerun the situation in real life with this attitude or behaviour.

7 Ask yourself the following questions:

'Where am I experiencing new-found peace?' 'What have I unexpectedly discovered?' 'What new energies or resources am I open to?' 'What truth do I wish to know, no matter what it turns out to be?' 'In what situation have I fallen to my knees to ask for guidance?' 'How am I carrying what I focus on in formal periods of meditation out into my life and ordinary interactions?' 'Why am I fearing or avoiding prayer and meditation?' 'What recognition am I searching for?' 'Where am I feeling overwhelmed by new ideas and energies?' 'How is my spiritual practice guiding me to sense people, places and things differently?' 'Where would I like to be the centre of attention or avoid attention?' 'What area of service to humanity or what consciousness-raising group or event would I like to participate in?' 'What am I no longer ashamed of?' 'Where might I be a better friend to myself or another?' 'What do I wish or pray would come to pass?' 'In what area of my personal or professional life could a period of Self-reflection be fruitful?' 'What fulfilment do I feel worthy of receiving?'

'What Gateway of Life am I in or developing through in the above?' Indicate: Childhood, Adolescence, Adulthood or Wisdom. Why?

'What do I need to do in order to develop the above further?' I need to . . .

'What step(s) do I want to take towards this and how can the Star help me?'

8 Use a personal statement regarding the presence of the Star in your life at this time, such as: 'I shine like a star.' 'Everything I do is spiritual.' 'I grow increasingly hopeful about the future of the planet and humanity.' My personal statement is . . .

9 Inspirational words and quotes:

> 'God forgets His or Her own real nature and seeks God.
> God prays and meditates on God. God adores God.
> And God is seeking to find God.
> It is God who inquires and God who replies.'

'There is an eye of the soul which is more precious than ten thousand bodily eyes; by it alone Truth is seen.'                Plato

10 What symbols stand out in the card? What do they say to you? How might they be useful in daily living? Bring the symbol(s) into your life in some way so as to integrate the card's teachings.

11 Wear and surround yourself with the Star's colour, violet, to remind you of the card's teachings when needed, such as a reminder to keep to your daily spiritual practice, to feel more hopeful, pursue truth in a situation no matter how uncomfortable this might be. Notice how you are affected.

12 The Star's astrological correspondence is Aquarius, governing traits such as friendship, leadership, humanitarianism, broad-mindedness, intuition, inventiveness and detachment. Where might you intuitively enact these to be of service to others, your Self and/or the planet? Note what happens: your thoughts and feelings and the outcome.

13 Remember that the Star's Hebrew name, *Tzaddi*, means 'fishhook'. How might this remind you of the card's meaning or help in your life process?

14 Try a few drops of the scent bergamot associated with the Star as a reminder to integrate the card's teachings.

15 Have a cup of tea made from the herb skullcap. This herb is high in calcium, potassium and magnesium and is therefore used to aid alcohol and drug withdrawal. Sit quietly as you drink and consider the herb's properties to quiet, calm (an antispasmodic and nervine), tone and strengthen the nerves, reduce internal inflammation and the like qualities of the Star card.

**18**     **THE MOON**

# CHAPTER 22

# The Moon

## General Information and Symbolism

The moon has been worshipped since antiquity. Its human face tells us that humanity must somehow identify with what they deify. It further intimates how societies sometimes ascribe human characteristics (anthropomorphise) to non-human beings, objects and natural phenomena to make them more comprehensible. All phases of the Moon are visible, symbolising how you must develop through all levels of consciousness before achieving Self-realisation of God/desshood. Trying to avoid this natural course of events is both impossible and a denial of the process of spiritual evolution. The full, waxing and waning moons also show the three aspects of the Goddess: maiden, mother and crone. This underscores the futility of fighting the natural cycles of life – ebb and flow, flux and reflux.

The wolf and dog baying at the Moon illustrate the transformation of your unconscious or untamed thoughts, feelings and actions – the wolf, into conscious tamed ones – the dog. This is achieved by a combination of will, desire and discipline that is motivated by love. These symbols also suggest our potential to make magic and co-create miracles. Turning a wolf into a dog implies the ability to shift the shape of our lives. Although the dog is a modification of the wolf, the animals are basically the same, demonstrating the importance of accepting both the evolved and unevolved aspects of the personality as they stem from the same source. The animals stand side by side, signifying the value of staying in touch with your instincts while domesticating and educating the animal self. The message is clear: to ascend to the highest, you must move beyond life's dualities, the twin towers, to blend your wild, instinctive feeling self with your domesticated, intellectual thinking self, and accept that all is One. The creatures on the path portray humanity's physical and spiritual evolution, that of coming forth from the watery womb where all life originates. The crayfish emerges from the water symbolising the most primordial levels of being. This act tells us that eventually each of us reaches a point in our development when we stop living in the watery subconscious realm of worn-out automatic habit patterns and reactions. The grey stones suggest the wisdom gained in adapting to the world and evolving through our animal nature to walk the path to Self and God/dess hood (I have always imagined a trail of footsteps on the path up the mountain). Plant life springs up to show yet another of the five developmental steps in the evolutionary process: mineral, vegetable, animal, human and superhuman (those who stand on the mountain-top lighting our way). The Moon and undulating path itself represent how the refinement process operates – waxing and waning, rising and falling. Comfort lies in recalling a principle from the Wheel of Fortune – because the spiritual path spirals, we never return to the same place again.

For the better part of the past 2,000 years, the Piscean Age, much time and energy has been directed towards suppressing and rejecting our physical appetites and emotions as a means of invoking the spirit. With the onset of the Aquarian Age and the evolution of consciousness, self-abnegation is on the wane. The human mind is slowly becoming aware that, just as the Moon reflects the Sun, we reflect the Divine. Our body is not only a spiritual instrument, but both it and the physical world around us mirror the world of the spirit. The unfolding of higher consciousness occurs in and through the physical body and environment. This accounts for the increasing amount of attention being paid in the Western world to good health, preventative medicine and personal and planetary healing, more than at any time during the last 2,000 years. Thus, the present emphasis on physical fitness and health may be seen as preparing and maintaining the body for its daily tasks, which are in reality service to the Self.

The path leads up through the mountains above to its Source. Conversely, the pool, the Source of the path below, stems from the very same heights. These symbols are added reminders of the Moon's reflective quality and again reiterate, 'As above, so below; as below, so above.' Your spiritual path is 'revealed' by searching the *depths* of your heart, mind and soul, indicated by the path's beginning at the water's edge. The path is clear, yet guarded by animals and watchtowers. The number 18 suggests that the Moon card calls for the application of attention and will in order to transform your primal energies and passions with loving determination – the

Magician and Strength cards respectively. Eighteen adds up to nine, indicating that the Hermit (number nine) offers the tools with which to accomplish this. The way home is illuminated by the Moon, which, owing to its changeability, produces varying degrees of light and darkness. This reminds the seeker that the way has its share of joys and sorrows. It also cautions you against dwelling too long on past hurts, errors or immaturities. Self-reflection is essential, but prolonging it has the potential to immobilise the seeker with fear of repetition and can delay getting on with life. The falling *Yods*, or hands, recommend that you view your past as the assistance from God/dess which has brought you to where you presently are in life. Finally, because the number 18 means *Chai* or 'life' in Hebrew, the 18 *Yods* reiterate that life and light descend from above to help you out of the darkness when you are ready to reach for it.

The colour associated with the Moon is violet-red, the musical note is B natural and the herb is lemon balm. *Qoph* is the Hebrew name for the Moon and means 'back of the head'. This knot-like portion of the brain, sometimes referred to as the 'brain stem', contains the cerebellum and medulla oblongata. This is where reflexive thinking and automatic bodily functions, such as equilibrium, heartbeat, blood circulation and respiration rate originate. Messages from the brain's frontal lobes to set the body in action are received in this area. If, for example, you are faced with an anxiety-provoking situation, a message interpreting the situation as such is relayed from the forebrain to the hindbrain for arousal. The 'flight or fight' response is then engendered, unless a message to negate this process follows. This locale also transmits information required for healing to the rest of the organism.

Healing may be defined as reflecting upon (possibly re-experiencing) and relinquishing damaging memories and events, then repeatedly replacing such with a restored association or neural imprint. Here it is of interest to note that the Qabalistic function of the Moon is Sleep wherein new ideas and attitudes become absorbed into the mind and body. Now, for an example of how this process operates. A woman dreams that her body is being invaded by a large green blob. Soon afterwards, she turns up with a life-threatening illness. Subsequent to exploring some deep long-standing worries, she learns how to combine the power of mental imagery, prayer, meditation and affirmation to alter her emotional responses and improve her health habits, thereby repeatedly replacing her sick and dying image (and condition) with a healthy one. Please understand that this does not always work this well, as other elements must be considered, such as the fact that we are co-creators, and that the final outcome is up to God/dess.

It takes an unspecified amount of time for the body to convert a neural imprint into a physical reality. That is, the mind can take charge of the body, but it takes a while for the body to catch on. The bodily intelligence must be able to cooperate by producing whatever chemical alterations are needed for homeostasis, repair and healing. There is also the matter of clearing karmic debts, which takes precedence over all else. The process of being sick and dying in many cases turns out to be what is called for to heal an individual's spiritual afflictions. In these instances, the body is sacrificed for the sake of spiritual growth.

The Moon is associated with the dualistic birth sign, Pisces. This mutable (combines the qualities of cardinal energies with fixed energies. Adaptable and changeable energy that can either move or remain still.) Water sign, ruling the feet and lymphatic system, is depicted by two fish swimming in opposite directions. Pisces is the last sign of the zodiac, and inherent in this placement is the impetus to complete your worldly business. From this may arise the conflict between self-acceptance and self-denial, or the desire to perfect and transcend your lower nature and immaturities while still having karmic knots (another reference to the Hebrew letter *Qoph*) to undo. The Piscean personality says: I believe, sacrifice, hide, self-abnegate, dwell in other worlds, heal and transcend. I'm devoted, changeable, understanding, subject to guilt and feelings of inferiority, sensitive, kind and compassionate. Owing to the Piscean tendency to be excessively sensitive and compassionate, the unevolved native tends to assume the world's burdens, becoming in some cases immobilised by guilt and chronic depression instead of understanding that we are all being guided, step by step (Pisces rules the feet), along the path depicted in the Moon card, homeward. In their quest for higher consciousness, the evolving Pisces must be sure to honour their physical body, surroundings and feelings rather than seeking to deny or transcend them as a quicker route home. The goal is simply to dissolve attachments without losing the ability to feel.

What occurs in the final phases of personality development can enslave you as easily as free you. Here your conscious purpose and hidden agenda is examined and aligned. By this phase of the journey you know what must be done in order to live more responsibly, yet because of your own immaturities and humanity, you are not always able to comply. Being human is synonymous with having certain patterns and *samskaras* (past life imprints) to contend with. The towers serve as a gateway to the next world, suggesting that one may wander in the wastelands beyond, or follow the path to the mountain-top – the greater reality. In truth, some wandering may be needed, as it is the final exploration and excavation of old memories, pain, fear and self-denial – the dark or hidden side of your persona – symbolised by the dark side of the Moon. (Please note, if you react to your remaining imperfections with self-destructive behaviour, including internalising your feelings, becoming severely judgmental and indulging in food and/or substance abuse, therapeutic intervention is more than likely needed to help you complete the process.) The journey through the remaining darkness is an important means of becoming self-accepting. With this attitude, you find that pain and suffering are the pangs of giving birth to your Self, rather than the throes of death. Your humanity is something to be learned from, because in reality every act eventually leads to the heights of wisdom and understanding.

However, if the conflict between who you are and who you wish to be is ignored, it may foster internal strife, the state I call 'transcendental schizophrenia'. Here the desire for liberation becomes so intense (often because life is so painful) that, instead of patiently evolving through your immaturities, you attempt to transcend (in reality, avoid and deny) the worldly work required to achieve this state. At this point, the personality may become immersed in such a love-hate conflict that it becomes unable to resolve its dispute, and in extreme instances can lose contact with the immediate environment, reality and the world at large.

As you travel along your path, the spiritual energy (*Kundalini*) rises through the body via the practices initiated and instilled by the other Tarot cards (another reference to the 18 descending *yods*). While passing through the *Chakras* below the heart, known as the seat of animal consciousness, primitive instincts may be roused, resulting in some unusual side effects. On the Tree of Life, Foundation, *Yesod* (Sphere of the Moon), is the seat of your primal instincts and subconscious awareness. Practitioners of particular forms of meditation and spiritual exercises such as Siddha Yoga and *Subud*, an Indonesian discipline that expresses these energies via a spiritual practice called *latihan*, sometimes experience animal-like behaviour suddenly being expressed through their bodies. It is not unusual for them to hiss and slither like a snake, howl like a dog or wolf, or even roar like a lion. These individuals should be properly forewarned that such events signal the rising of their spiritual energies; otherwise, they may believe they are going mad.

Tradition associates the Moon with lunacy and psychism, and there are other events which might cause you to feel you are alternately mad and spiritually aware: dreams, visions or premonitions about the future; access to past-life memories; suddenly seeing auras; and communicating with the dead and other non-physical or non-human entities such as *devas* (nature spirits) or demons. Over-involvement in such phenomena can cause problems, since they are only *signs* of spiritual evolution, *not* the evolution itself, and may prove very distracting from the real work at hand, your spiritual progress. They are the sideshows, *not* the main event!

Also, at this stage of the path depicted by the Moon card, you may experience unusual physical complaints, illnesses, mood swings, sleeplessness, exhaustion and the sounds of strange music and voices. Unexplained anxiety and the feeling you are intoxicated or on a hallucinogenic drug are not uncommon. In his book, *Kundalini: Psychosis or Transcendence?* Dr Lee Sanella advises reassurance – the support of family, friends and educated and informed professionals if need be. He goes on to state that, 'Although confused, fearful and disoriented, they are undergoing a therapy from within far superior to any we yet know how to administer from without.'[1] Experiences of this type are referred to in some groups as Karmic Clearing, the removal of various blockages, which results in increased liberation and well-being. All of these phenomena are by-products of engaging in the disciplines prescribed by the Tarot, or for that matter, any spiritual path or study. A word of warning! Be wary of practices which bring on these experiences prematurely, rather than allowing them to evolve naturally. Such often result in a great deal of disorientation, fear and confusion and in the end prove to be less advantageous than those practices which operate more slowly, but naturally.

In the Qabalah, the Moon card is called the Corporeal or Bodily Intelligence. This Intelligence relates to the teachings of truth (the

1 Lee Sanella, MD, *Kundalini: Psychosis or Transcendence?*, Lee Sanella, MD, San Francisco, 1976, p. 61.

previous Tarot cards) that have become incorporated into the mind and body. It is what has become second nature and is then spontaneously reflected back into your everyday actions and interactions, helping you bring heaven to earth and earth to heaven. In other words, by repeatedly desiring to live in accord with the greater truths you, in time, automatically do so.

## Gateway of Life: Adulthood to Wisdom

The Moon reflects tangible evidence of physical, mental, emotional and spiritual changes initiated by the previous cards. Renewal after disaster or illness, attainment of a long-sought goal and the release of deep-rooted resentments and forgiveness exemplify a few aspects of this developmental stage. On the brink of Wisdom (the Moon is a double Gateway, as are the Chariot and Death cards), you now have at your disposal everything needed to negotiate your way through life to attain higher consciousness. At this juncture, you might become acutely sensitised to your body as a living house for the Divine. Qabalists refer to this phenomenon as *Adonai Ha Eretz*, 'The Most High on Earth'. As a well-developed seeker, you acknowledge your Self to be a reflection of God/dess and care for both your inner Self and outer body reverently. Consequently, you have become so finely attuned that you are ready to move on to Wisdom. The possibilities discussed in the Magician are embodied in the Moon. You are able to apply the higher powers and the Rules and Tools to lovingly control and direct your visible (physical) and invisible (mental, emotional) worlds. This takes the form of practical application of these abilities and tools to all facets of your life. Occasionally, you will still fall asleep and lose your way. The point here is not to punish yourself, but to concede that you are doing the best job possible, and that the highway home has many ups and downs.

Finally, you become able to look back at the path you have taken through life and to accept, and perhaps even express gratitude for, what has occurred. You have complete faith that what you experienced was what it took to bring you to where you now stand, simply the phases necessary to motivate your growth and development. According to the Twelve-Steps, you are taking a searching and fearless moral inventory of all persons you have harmed, including yourself, then admit your wrongs and make amends. You recognise that the karmic knots, or lessons, of this lifetime contain the potential to bring you to higher consciousness.

Furthermore, you become able to healthfully detach yourself and acknowledge the 'parts played' by those who harmed you. This does not suggest that physical, mental, emotional, sexual or substance abuse is a good thing. It means you reach a point in your evolutionary process (a.k.a. 'recovery') when you stop permitting these things to run and to ruin your life. We all have various types of unpleasant karmic knots to untie in our lifetime, in every lifetime. When undone, these bring wisdom in their wake. Finally, new behaviours start becoming second nature and are reflected, like the moon, back into your daily actions and interactions. Now when you feel out of sorts, instead of taking a drink or popping a pill and the like, you *automatically* take out your journal to write, call your sponsor for support and feedback, or even turn over a Tarot card to help you to focus on the truth about what is afflicting you.

Living the Moon card at the Four Gateways of Life may cause certain attitudes and behaviours. CHILDHOOD: During a week-long spiritual retreat, a man has numerous psychic experiences and becomes so excited that when he returns home, he spends most of his time trying to duplicate them, severely neglecting his family, friends and business; ADOLESCENCE: A woman on the spiritual path feels wonderful when she feels 'in touch' (the path's ups), but becomes guilty, hateful and despondent when she feels 'out of touch' (the path's downs); ADULTHOOD: Membership in a group geared to support and help adult children of alcoholics enables a woman to forgive her parents for their weakness, and as a result she goes on her way to leading a happier alcohol-free life; WISDOM: A Jewish woman is faced with a situation in which her boss is unconsciously making derogatory remarks about Judaism. But rather than call him names in return (the way in which she handled this type of remark as a girl), she knows automatically that this response is unproductive. Instead, she takes him aside after working hours and expresses herself in a way that makes him gently aware of his unconscious attitude.

## Divinatory Questions for the Moon

*Upright*: What fears might be keeping you from achieving an important goal? What could you mistakenly be depriving yourself of? Have you stopped to count your blessings lately? Is an old wound finally healing? What could be distracting you from your spiritual work? What desires, thoughts or feelings would you like to be rid of? What instincts have been refined? Is it time to experiment with lucid dreaming? How do you perceive yourself evolving? Have your psychic powers been on the rise? Might psychotherapy be useful in order to help you stop wandering in the wasteland of your past? What painful feelings are you finally allowing yourself to experience? Are you becoming more aware of the natural ups and downs of the spiritual path? What desirable new attitude or behaviour has become automatic? How has forgiveness opened the way for you? What are you in the process of domesticating or letting go wild? What old unconscious habit pattern are you emerging from? What fears might be keeping you from achieving an important goal?

*Reversed*: What unusual experience have you undergone? How have you been warned to be careful of getting distracted by psychic phenomena? What are you hesitating to discipline, train or domesticate? What is becoming second nature? Why are you resisting self-healing or healing in general? How are you slowly overcoming your inclination to feel guilty about who you are or what you've done? What wisdom does your body hold? Where has the repetition of certain thoughts and actions borne fruit? What have you inappropriately attempted to transcend? Are you engrossed in overcoming psychic distractions from your spiritual work? Have you become less fearful of what you don't know? What situation has become a blessing in disguise? How might an acceleration of your spiritual journey be counter-indicated? What incident from the past could you be dwelling too long upon?

## Personal Experience

'Watch out, I have eyes in the back of my head,' seemed to come out of nowhere while I was meditating on the Moon card's Hebrew name, *Qoph*, which means 'back of the head'. I could clearly recall my mother standing, hands on hips, as she menacingly delivered her message to my younger brother and me before leaving us unsupervised. This statement was her way of letting us know that, although she was not going to be around to watch us, she would know what we were up to, so we'd better be good. Reflecting back, I decided that her scare tactics worked to keep us safe and obedient for much of our early childhood. Yet when her words surfaced after so many years, I couldn't help but believe that there was some important connection between them and the Moon card. Despite my efforts, however, I was unable to figure out what it was. I was left to trust in the metaphysical guideline which states, 'If you meditate on something long enough, its meaning and purpose will be revealed.'

During this same period, I was deeply committed to overcoming an irrational and destructive cycle of self-denial, guilt and over-compensating behaviour because I wasn't earning as much money as my husband. The cycle went something like this: first, I had a slump in my work; second, I invalidated myself because of guilt about my decreased income; third, I began silently deferring to my mate because 'he earns more; thus I should compensate by doing more at home.' Finally, I would get upset with myself and him (although he definitely didn't have problems with my economic fluctuations) for my behaviour. This pattern intermittently wreaked havoc in my marriage, and so I desperately wanted to put an end to it.

Interestingly, self-denial, guilt and overcompensating behaviour are among the immature personality traits associated with my birth sign, Pisces, linked with the Moon card.

Normally, Bernard and I help each other with our respective chores and responsibilities. However, there always seemed to be a fine line for me to tread between what I had time to do and what my guilt and conflict about money dictated I do. So when my work got slow, which happened to me more frequently than to him, I would have to choose how available I wanted to be. There were times when I would work so hard at using my head – my forebrain and reasoning – to help me undo this karmic knot that my neck and shoulders were knotted and aching by the time I reached a decision. It was tiring, yet I was slowly working on it. I knew that changing deep-seated behaviour takes time and that I was using my tools as best I could to guide me.

Then, at the beginning of a week when my work appeared to be light, Bernard asked if I would help him out by screening tenants for a small rental property. After carefully checking the situation out, I agreed. As it happened, the phone rang incessantly for the next three days, owing to an acute housing shortage in our city. Needless to say, I was relieved to find a reliable tenant and get back to my own work, which by then had been piling up.

I was just getting settled into my routine when Bernard then asked if I would mind purchasing some appliances for the new tenant. Up to this point I would have had to struggle amid a morass of conflicting thoughts and feelings, but without a moment's hesitation, I told him it would definitely be bothersome, especially in view of the last few days of disruption. As soon as the words were out of my mouth, I realised that I didn't have to think about my response, which meant that for the first time the work I had been doing had finally been absorbed and internalised. I had actually achieved some of the karmic unknotting I had been labouring over!

The next evening, I reviewed several Tarot cards, including the Moon, noticing that the Qabalists call the Moon the Corporeal or Bodily Intelligence. Recalling this Intelligence to be the attitudes and behaviours that have become incorporated into my automatic awareness, I then remembered how I had tried to connect my mom's warning, 'I have eyes in the back of my head,' to the Moon card some time before, and within a few minutes of meditation knew that it was directly related to the interchange I had had with Bernard the previous morning.

I no longer had to work so hard at supervising that particular pattern, because the decision of how to behave, to speak my mind and say, 'No', without reproaching myself, was now part of my automatic consciousness – the eyes in the back of my head. True, it was different from what my mother had meant (I, rather than another, was in charge), yet it was perfect for where I stood on my life path (and for my personal assimilation of the Moon card). I had finally seen in an important new way, using the part of my brain which reflexively relays messages to my body and mind, and by doing so had undone a considerable piece of an old karmic knot.

## Student Experiences

❖ 'All the women in my family, back to my great-great grandmother, have had babies before they turned twenty,' shared Julie, mother of three teenagers. 'And I've been afraid that my only daughter may unwittingly do the same, even though at 18 she has access to birth control, something which I didn't, and says she knows right from wrong.

'The homework question, "What memories are haunting me?" made me take a good long inventory. One of my biggest fears is that she is going to ruin her life, like I did, in a way. I know I really can't stop her from doing what she wants. I can only love and educate her. And I realise that if I don't start trusting her and stop projecting so much fear and worry, she may get pregnant just to spite me – justifying, or better yet, fulfilling my fears. I must stop looking for problems. I've done my best. I think it starts with my letting go of my past, and realising that we each have our own karma. I need to believe her when she says that finishing school and becoming a professional means a lot to her.

'In meditation, I got the idea to visualise us walking down different paths to the mountain, not the same path. I need to see her as a separate person and think that she's got enough smarts and self-love not to be sidetracked. I guess it comes down to my not trusting her boyfriend. He's so in love with her, and so insecure. He wants to get engaged when she graduates from high school, and to me that says marriage and babies aren't far behind.

'She insists she won't get married until she's done with college, but I think he's going to pressure her, since she's planning to go to school out of state. Nope, it's up to her. It's her life and her path, and she'll surely do what she needs to do. Her inner Self is guiding her. I want to start treating her like the adult she is, because she's more likely to act that way if I do.'

*'You're on the right track,' I said. 'People can only be where they are on their path through life. At most we can offer them information and the wisdom of our experiences, but unless they're ready to take them in, it's of little use. You're experiencing how our children travel their own path. What's that great line from* The Prophet? *He says that our children come through us, but not from us. And although we house their bodies, we can't house their souls. Or as you so accurately stated, you each have your own path to follow. When children leave home, it's as if they and their parents pass through the Moon's gatelike towers into the unknown. This card's another double Gateway, and its number, one plus eight, may provide clues to what's coming. Remember how the Woman in Strength had to work with the Lion? Perhaps you may be consoled by paying attention to how well your daughter has learned from life so far and trust that you've done your best to prepare her for what may lie ahead.'*

❖ 'Meditating on the Moon card, I identified with both the dog and wolf,' said Ellen, a secretary and mother of two grown children. 'I have this wild woman living inside me who unpredictably appears every so often. I've lived such a boring and domesticated life, but I'm usually frightened of the unknown. It's embarrassing, but I'm quite doglike. I know that my present work is to become less so, to break free a bit. I'm slowly learning about bringing more of my instincts – my wolf woman – out, through things such as the Tarot.

'I'll admit I get scared because I both want and fear loss of control. I'm like those Pisces fish swimming in two directions at once. Yet I'm also at the place where I think I'm enough in touch with my Goddess that I won't do anything really harmful.

'The Moon has fascinated me since I was a child, when I would spend hours trying to see its face. My husband laughed after I read to him from Anais Nin's journal about how she took moon baths, but I slept out on my back porch during the next full moon. A new friend has asked me to attend a Harvest Moon Ritual and Celebration next month. It's no coincidence I was invited at this time. I definitely plan to go, to mark my commitment to bringing out more of my intuition. Who knows? I just might love it.'

*'It's great that you accepted rather than denied those feelings,' I said. 'It's like pointing those Piscean fish in the same direction to avert inner conflict and guilt. You're activating one of the most evolved Piscean qualities, that of honouring your Self.'*

❖    'I've been haunted by my childhood and family as long as I can remember,' began Candace, a university student. 'For some reason, I've been thinking about all of it again over the last few months; thinking that if I hadn't had such a miserable childhood, I'd be farther along on my spiritual path; feeling sorry for myself because I really didn't have a female role model – my mom died when I was six. Wishing we'd had more money when I was growing up so I could have had some fun. I might have learned to ski, taken dancing lessons, or gone to a better school.

'So our discussion on the Moon card made me look at what's really been going on. You said we'll do better in life if we accept and even appreciate our past because it's brought us to where we now are on our path. That made some things clearer for me. I'm a good person and I have a pretty happy life. I actually consider my childhood to be partially responsible for my spiritual awakening, because of what was said in class. I realised, hey, that's my background and it's made me what I am today.

'And the strangest things have been happening. I remembered some of the good times I had growing up for the first time in ages. Summer visits with my grandma and grandpa and feeling grateful for the good job my father did raising me. I mean, he could have remarried someone I might have hated, as happened to some of my friends. But I know that would have brought me to where I am, too. I had a lot of time alone and I was lonely, but I listened to music and made all my own clothes. I read lots of good books and wrote poems. The more I thought about it, the more accepting I became. It was also the best thing I could do to move forward spiritually. I've had some problems: my self-esteem has been really low at times. But who doesn't have something to deal with? I have dwelled on what I was cheated out of long enough. I accept that it's made me who I am now. You know, it's looking better and better to me.'

*'You're taking the symbol of the falling yods from the Moon card to help integrate the card's teachings, Candace. You're counting your blessings, which is going to enhance your spiritual progress. The card shows us that dwelling too long on lost dreams and disappointments won't help. Accepting our lives to be a reflection (as is the Moon) of who we are and what we need is usually the best thing we can do. And as we become increasingly aware of and responsible for our co-creative powers, our life is bound to reflect our progress.'*

## Suggestions for Application and Integration of the Moon

Would you like to travel your life path with greater effectiveness, let go of past hurts, reduce guilt, increase your ability to heal yourself, and start to accept your true feelings, increase compassion towards yourself and others, and reduce anxiety about heading into unknown territory, among other things? If so, begin the following exercises:

1   Draw or colour your own version of the Moon card with your face as the luminary.

2   Set the card in a visible place as a reminder to your conscious and subconscious minds to use and absorb its teachings such as feeling confident to go forward into the unknown, having your dog and wolf natures peacefully coexist, remaining humble about signs of spiritual development and honouring the physical as spiritual.

3   Dream on the Moon.

4   Play the note B on a musical instrument. Intone IAO or hum along with the music. Now concentrate fully on the card for a few minutes. Imagine yourself heading down the path towards the mountains; now look behind you and see how far you've progressed, noting the various ups and downs. Now look forward to the ups and downs to come. Although you're not sure what you will next encounter, your past experiences have taken you to where you now are. Take a minute to count your blessings and to appreciate your progress. Now you might request that the Moon's teachings guide you through an upcoming event. Or if you are faced with a worrisome situation, event or problem, such

as fears of expressing or domesticating your animal tendencies without thinking that you're mad; feeling guilty and despondent about conditions in the world; or explaining some strange experiences you had; imagine how the card's teachings might help you handle it. If it seems feasible, give it a try. Jot down the times that you were aware of the Moon in your interactions. I was aware of the Moon when? Before/during/after . . .

5 Go out into the world and enact the teachings of the Moon card in order to progress down your life path more competently. I enacted the Moon card and this is what happened . . .

6 Take a moon bath, walk, dance, ski, swim or play in the moonlight. Remember the teachings of the Moon card while doing so.

7 The Rerun. After having an experience and realising in retrospect how the Moon's teachings might have inspired you or another to let go of past fears, hurts, and guilts (remember these may be perceived as helpers encouraging you to make necessary changes), move forward on your path without being immobilised by irrationality or be more respectful of your physical body, mentally relive the situation, *including* your insight. This will help the behaviour become more automatic next time. If possible, actually rerun the situation in real life with this attitude or behaviour.

8 Ask yourself the following questions:

'In what situation(s) might I forgive myself or another in order to progress spiritually?' 'Why am I feeling guilty?' 'What memories are haunting me?' 'Where might I be dwelling too long on past injuries, errors or immaturities?' 'What cycle is ebbing or flowing?' 'What karmic knots are slowly being untied?' 'Where is instability (mine or another's) causing dissension?' 'Of what have I healed myself?' 'In what area of my life am I venturing out into new domains?' 'Where might self-denial be harming me or another?' 'Why am I swimming in more than one direction at once?' 'In what area of my personal or professional life are my powers waxing or waning?' 'What message, teaching or behaviour has suddenly become automatic?' 'How has my desire worked to tame a wolf?' 'What hidden thoughts and feelings am I expressing with increasing clarity?' 'How might my wolf and dog natures cooperate to do some magic or co-create a small miracle?' 'What cycle have I become sensitised or desensitised to?' 'Where is my path taking me?' 'How am I better accepting my wild side?'

'What Gateway of Life am I in or developing through in the previous question?' Indicate: Childhood, Adolescence, Adulthood or Wisdom. Why?

'What do I need to do in order to develop the above further?' I need to . . .

'What step(s) do I want to take towards this goal and how can the Moon card guide me?'

9  Use a personal statement regarding the presence of the Moon in your life at this time: 'I lovingly bring my hidden side into the light.' 'My life path brings me increasing amounts of spiritual satisfaction.' 'My body's ability to heal itself gets stronger and stronger.' My personal statement or affirmation is . . .

10  Inspirational words and quotes:

'You will forget your misery; you will remember it as waters that have passed away.'                                                    JOB 11:16

'To err is human, to forgive, divine.'          Pope, *Essay on Criticism*

11  What symbols stand out in the card? What do they say to you? How might these be useful in daily living? Bring the symbol(s) into your life in some way so as to integrate the card's teachings. The *yods* falling from the Moon and over the path remind me that despite my initial fears, something blessed may always be found within what befalls me on my path through life.

12  Wear and surround yourself with the colour violet-red (fuchsia) to remind you of the card's teachings when needed, such as a reminder to honour your body's divinity, wanting to be in a healing or healthful frame of mind, being more accepting of an unknown situation or desiring to forgive yourself or another. Notice how you are affected.

13  The Moon card's astrological correspondence is to the sign of Pisces, governing traits such as understanding, transcendence, sensitivity, self-acceptance and self-denial. Call upon your understanding and sensitivity to accept a personality characteristic

or physical trait within yourself or another which you would rather deny having or have been overly sensitive about. Notice what happens: your thoughts, feelings and the outcome.

14  Remember that the Moon's Hebrew name, *Qoph*, means 'back of the head'. How can this remind you of the card's meaning or help in your life process? It has helped me to recall that looking at the traumas hidden in the back of my mind is essential, but prolonging the process has the potential to immobilise me with fear of repetition and can delay my getting on with life.

15  Try a few drops of the scent violet associated with the Moon as a reminder to integrate the card's teachings.

16  Have a cup of tea made from the herb lemon balm. Sit quietly as you drink and consider the herb's ability to induce sleep, ease mental fatigue and lift and rejuvenate the spirits – melancholy and moodiness – and consider the similar qualities of the Moon card.

# *Part Five*

## The Gateway
## of Wisdom

This last group of cards delineates the passage of the Fool into Wisdom, the perfection of the personality leading to Self-realisation and God/desshood. In the Qabalistic tradition, these states may be equated to how the aspirant enters the Gateway of Wisdom as a physically, mentally and emotionally balanced Adept, *Adeptus Minor*, and exists as a karma-free Exempt Adept, *Adeptus Exemptus*. Again, as in other Gateways, it may be nearly impossible to have all facets of the personality in one Gateway at a time, especially this one. If you were fully liberated from your physical, mental and emotional needs, there would be no desire whatsoever for the pleasures of ego gratification, and the workings of life would be unnecessary. In other words, such drives are part and parcel of the human condition and inherent in having a human body. Without these, life in the body would cease and the blending of individual self-consciousness, the personality, with universal or superconsciousness (depicted by the World card) would occur spontaneously.

The Moon, like the Chariot and Death, is a double Gateway, marking the passage of the adult into old age or Wisdom. The focal point of this final Gateway is to permanently repair the breach between the subconscious and self-conscious minds. Here, everyday life is lived in a meditative or completely clear state of awareness. Fully individuated, you are no longer held hostage by your past experiences and childhood conditioning. The stranglehold of obsolete social and cultural indoctrination is broken as well.

With diligent application of the Rules and Tools begun in the Gateway of Adulthood, you have now progressed far enough along your path to be able to serve God/dess, your Self, humanity, the planet and its non-human inhabitants with great love. In the simplest of terms, you are thriving! Life becomes a joyous event giving you the opportunity to know, perceive and be God/dess simultaneously. You are now the beneficiary of complete guidance from your Higher Self and you unfailingly apply what you receive to the challenges of daily living.

19    **THE SUN**

# CHAPTER 23

# The Sun

## General Information and Symbolism

Then the Most High said, 'Let there be light: and there was light,' and from this light life on earth was created. Two children frolic naked in the sunshine of light and life, while the Sun beams down approvingly from above. The children's nudity signifies the return to a more realistic, authentic and open-hearted state of being. Their hands are joined suggesting that they are proficient at genuine intimacy, both personally, with the joining of their subconscious and conscious minds, and interpersonally. Adam and Eve are about to blossom into full spiritual maturity as shown by their pubescent state.

As in the Chariot card, there is a wall or boundary in the background, indicating that each child's boundaries are well defined. The aspirants now know where they begin and end. The Death card is implied by thirteen *Yods* descending above the wall. These underscore the demise of any remaining barriers to conscious thinking, feeling and being. Notice how six *Yods* fall on each side while the thirteenth hangs between them. This arrangement states that the higher level of unity sought in the sixth card, the Lovers, has been achieved. Furthermore, thirteen is the value of the Hebrew word *achad*, meaning 'unity', indicating that the death of separation brings unity.

Qabalists have long taught that the Sun is a living reflection of our true Self and that every human being is a miniature solar system – microcosm mirrors macrocosm. Similarly, those in the scientific community who subscribe to the 'Gaia' theory that the earth is a living, breathing entity believe the same of the sun. It is not strange, then, that from time immemorial cultures throughout the world have portrayed the Sun with a face. The Sun demonstrates its aliveness in others ways as well. It sends out straight and wavy radiations, indicating that light is both passive and active in its particle and wave states. In addition, there are eight (remember the figure eight over the Magician and Strength) of each type of ray, symbolising the reciprocation of energy. Just as we derive life from the sun, it derives life from us. This concept clearly reiterates, 'As above, So below, As below, So above.'

The sun, astrologically linked to the Sun card, is associated with the Heart *Chakra*, signifying it is the heart of hearts that continually fills us with light and life. The sun is situated in the middle or heart of the Tree of Life, Beauty or *Tiphareth*, the centre associated with the beginning of Christ or Buddha consciousness. When one's heart is open, individuals seem to glow from within and radiate outwards like the sun. Inherent in this state of consciousness is participation. You become obliged to bring your spiritual understandings, or inner teacher, out into daily living, illustrated by how the children's feet bridge both circles or worlds. Each child's inside foot is firmly planted in spirit, telling us that when we are grounded in spirit, it is safe to venture out into the world. In the words of Maharishi Mahesh Yogi, 'Established in spirit, perform action'. Finally, because they live from the centre of their being they are their true selves.

A wall, symbol of the material world and its limitations, indicates that the restrictions of living through your unconscious conditioning have been surpassed. You are tolerant and accepting, meaning that you do not unfairly label or categorise people, places or things, nor are you overly attached to the fruits of your labours. As an open-hearted person, you view the world and yourself from a loving vantage point. In conclusion, it is interesting to note that the wall has eight layers, reminding us both that the finite originates in the infinite and that the veil of matter originates in spirit.

Sunflowers, known to follow the sun's path, rise above the wall, symbolising how all the earth's creatures depend on the sun and the universal life force it represents for sustenance. In this sense, the Sun's light is truly manna from heaven. Because the ancients deified the Sun, it is said that the original Holy Trinity was Dawn, Noon and Sunset and, according to some, Maiden, Mother and Crone. Four of the flowers turn to the children, one reaches for the Sun. These represent the mineral, vegetable, animal and human kingdoms that spiritualised humanity (the fifth sunflower) is entrusted to care for. They face the children acknowledging that the reborn Adam and Eve have returned to the Garden of Eden ready to fulfil their original task, that of preserving, protecting and restoring the earth and her creatures.

The sun can be relied upon to nurture and support all forms of life in this solar system. It is, in fact, the centre of our world, but owing to modern industry and technology, this is no longer as evident as it was in pre-industrialised times. Although overshadowed by such inventions as 'Gro Lights' and tanning booths, the sun is responsible for all life in this solar system. All living and non-living forms (including 'Gro Lights' and tanning booth components) are its by-products. The sun produces our heat, light (both day and night), food and fuel, as well as the constituent parts of our shelter, transportation and clothing. It is understandable, then, how the Qabalists liken the sun to parents who lovingly provide for their child.

Now that we have discussed the life-giving aspects and properties of solar energy, it would be one-sided not to mention its destructive aspects as well: misuse of nuclear energy and the admission of too much sunlight via the enlarging holes in the earth's ozone layer, causing a sizeable increase in the number of skin cancers, head my list. I am certain you can add others to it. Depending upon how the solar force is harnessed, the sun has the potential to maintain or destroy life on earth, as well as in this entire solar system.

The colour of the Sun card is orange, its note is D (like the sunshine vitamin) and its herbal correlations are angelica and bay laurel. It is not surprising that the Hebrew name for the Sun card is *Resh*, meaning 'the human head and face'. In traditional Chinese medicine, an aspect of the system called Differential Diagnosis is focused on the face. By 'reading' one's face (lines, etc.), an expert may determine the entire body's strengths and weaknesses. In addition, our thoughts, feelings, attitudes and experiences are etched into our faces. It is fascinating to observe how the most beautiful people can become ugly when their attitudes and behaviour are so, while an irregularly featured face appears beautiful when that person's inner nature and thoughts are likewise. The card's association with the face also asserts that at this point in the Tarot's progression, you have 'seen the light' and face life with an illuminated outlook. You know that your energy and power come from the Source of life, represented here by the Sun.

As previously mentioned, the Sun card's astrological association is the sun itself. The sun is the regenerative force behind the whole solar system and without it all life would cease to exist. Similarly, the Greek god of the sun, Apollo, ruled over miraculous healing and medicine and prophetic visions. As noted, on the Tree of Life, the Sun is seated in Beauty, *Tiphareth*, the conscious personality, through which the Crown, *Kether's* (the Higher Self's), influence descends to earth, while it also conveys Kingdom or *Malkuth's* (the lower Self's) aspirations up to heaven. The sun's placement in the natal horoscope chart is a key one because it indicates the potential brought to focus in one's lifetime. The sun sign suggests the native's basic temperament, the group of traits, attitudes and habits distinguishing individuality and personal vitality. The works of Copernicus maintain that our universe is heliocentric (sun-centred) rather than geocentric (earth-centred), as previously put forth by Ptolemaic theory.[1] This may be likened to the spiritual precept that the 'little I àm', or earthbound ego, with maturity surrenders to the 'Big I Am', the great heavenly Ego. Or, as asserted by the Magician card, you are meant to appreciate and celebrate your individuality, yet remember that it comes from the One. Each of our personalities reflects universal consciousness in its own particular way, while at the same time, each is interrelated with every other. The Great Mother and sun goddess of the Hindu pantheon, *Aditi*, mothered twelve zodiacal children. This myth seems to be beautifully portrayed in the Thoth deck's Sun card, wherein all the signs of the zodiac radiate out from the centre of the sun.

The Qabalah and modern biology are getting closer to agreeing that no personality can be altered without influencing others. Substantiating this are the scientific studies of Rupert Sheldrake. To paraphrase and summarise his writings on the topic of *Morphic resonance and behaviour: an experimental test:*[2] If a number of animals, say rats, learn a new trick which rats have never performed before, then other rats of the same, or a similar species, worldwide should be able to learn the same trick more easily, even in the absence of any known kind of connection or communication. Transformations of this nature have occurred and continue to occur. Applying this concept to human behaviour implies that when you aim to liberate yourself, you are aiming to free the rest of humanity as well. This occurs by tuning into and adding your personal input to the Collective Unconscious which we all share. When we develop the seed ideas given or drawn to us by virtue of our individual personality, such contribute to and influence the entire Collective Mind. Simply, we make deposits in the Bank of the Collective Unconscious from which others who are similarly attuned may

1 Copernicus was severely persecuted for his assertion.
2 Rupert Sheldrake, A *New Science of Life: The Hypothesis of Formative Causation*, J. P. Tarcher, Inc., Los Angeles (distributed by Houghton Mifflin Company, Boston) 1981, p. 185–91.

come along and take out a loan (here it may be of interest to know that the Sun card's Qabalistic Intelligence is the Collective Intelligence).

Research is continually uncovering new information underscoring how essential light is for health and well-being. Life on earth evolved under the full spectrum of natural sunlight. Recent studies have demonstrated that there are specific endocrine responses, through photoreceptor mechanisms in both the skin and retinas, to narrow bands of wavelengths within the electromagnetic spectrum, not only to the difference between light and dark as previously believed. Such things as sunblocks, windows, windshields, fluorescent lighting, industrial smog, tinted contact lenses, etc., inadvertently prevent the complete spectrum from entering our bodies, causing many of us to become light-deficient. Deficiencies manifest in a whole array of symptoms ranging from visual maladies and learning disabilities to headaches, sleeplessness and depression. In response to this, Dr John Ott has developed neurophotonic therapy, in which imbalances are supplemented by exposure to those colours or 'rays' diagnosed as deficient.

Qabalists state that God/dess, or the life force, is the Source of all, and is thus responsible for the existence of the planets and luminaries. Again, this is clearly stated in the first lines of the Book of Genesis. Living in a world composed of solar by-products, everything is light. This offers a new understanding of the terms 'illumination', 'enlightenment' and 'seeing the light', implying awareness of this all-pervasive presence, the light of God/dess, the Divine Sun in everything.

Many astronomers believe there is an enormous black hole in the centre of our galaxy that is surrounded by swirling streams of electrically charged gases spinning at speeds ranging from 100 to 400,000 miles per hour. Could it merely be coincidental that Qabalists, like scientists, describe the life force, God/dess, the 'Sun behind the sun', the Crown on the Tree of Life, *Kether*, in similar terms – 'The Beginning of the Swirlings?'

The card's number, 19, is a combination of the concentration and will of the Magician (one) on the Hermit's (nine) light (the various resources, tools and teachings), empowering you to ride the roller-coaster of life – the Wheel of Fortune (one + nine = ten) with ever-increasing ease and detachment. Finally, the Wheel reminds you of the importance of jumping in and putting your shoulder to the wheel of daily life, to do your part for the benefit of humanity.

The number 10 is a combination of one and zero, suggesting increased strength of character and vitality due to personal alignment (the Magician, one) with the energies of the life force, symbolised by the Fool (zero). On a final note, numerologists claim that 19 is the most blessed of vibrational patterns as it contains both the first (one) and last (nine) of the single digit numbers.

In the Qabalah, the Sun, known as the Collective Intelligence, aids your personality in collecting, retaining and synthesising information and teachings to recollect who you truly are. Then you can radiate that true Self out into everyday life. This Intelligence helps you live by the wisdom of the experiences you collect consciously and unconsciously, on a day-to-day basis, in order to co-exist more peacefully with your Self, others and the planet earth.

### Gateway of Life: Wisdom

The children face away from the wall (beyond what is known) as did the Charioteer, illustrating that another stage of growth has been attained. As previously noted, the seat of the sun on the Tree of Life, Beauty or *Tiphareth*, is also called the centre of Christ Consciousness, the Messiah or Redeemer existing within each human being. Following the purification of the Moon card, you have, in the words of Jesus, 'become as little children'. This, of course, does not mean regressing to immature behaviour, but having the openness of the child with the wisdom of your adult years behind you. You are no longer just surviving, but thriving! Having absorbed the teachings of truth and the Rules and Tools of the Game of Life via their experiences, persons of this stature exert a benevolent influence over their life and surroundings. Remember, the children's feet span the inner and outer worlds, emphasising how, at this stage of development, it is essential to take the inner spiritual teachings out into the material world. Such people are the dedicated participants and leaders in everyday life, those who teach by example but do not proselytise or make others feel wrong for their beliefs and practices. Consequently, people and creatures feel loved and accepted just being near them. Because their thoughts, words and deeds are aligned with higher truth, these individuals naturally master whatever they do. In essence, the inner teacher is taken out into daily life. Of course, there is also the possibility of alienating others with too much light and enthusiasm, or burning out by not taking care to regenerate.

In Twelve-Step programmes, the Sun speaks of continuing to take personal inventory and when wrong promptly admitting so. You are becoming healed and independent of, rather than dependent upon, destructive substances and relationships. You are healthfully inter-dependent and Self-reliant. The two children hold hands, illustrating how you continually put yourself in the company of others who do likewise. At this point in your 'recovery', you have healed your precious inner child, and by doing so are able to extend the light of recovery to others. (When the Qabalist Jesus of Nazareth said, 'Become ye as little children,' this is probably what he meant. The ancient teachings of the Tarot and Qabalah have offered the tools with which to reclaim and heal the 'Inner Child' since its inception.) Your heart is open. You unconditionally accept and enjoy your life and who you are.

Certain behaviour and attitudes may result from living the Sun card at the Four Gateways of Life. Childhood: A high-energy person will go, go, go until he or she either gets sick or drops from exhaustion; Adolescence: A man tries to outshine his business partner by telling prospective clients, 'I've taught him everything he knows.'; Adulthood: A woman initiates a community action lawsuit to stop a freeway project from entering a poverty-stricken neighbourhood until there is a proper relocation plan for the residents; Wisdom: To exhibit her support and confidence in a young actress, a world-famous performer insists that one of her new movie's most important scenes be filmed predominately focusing on her shy co-star.

## Divinatory Questions for the Sun

*Upright:* How have you been re-energised? What wall or obstacle are you surmounting? Are you feeling energised by the life force? What important person has approved of, or is enthusiastic about, you or your work? Are you becoming more open and tolerant? How might you be developing your own special creative dreams and ideas? What has your heart opened to? What are you feeling enthusiastic about? What are you willing to face? What higher level of unity have you achieved? What has come to light? Have you been appreciating yourself as a source or resource for others? What teachings or experiences are enabling you to move into a new phase of life? In what ways are you living more authentically? Have you been working well with others? Has your child-like enthusiasm and enjoyment increased? How has your vitality and health improved? Is greater intimacy with yourself resulting in greater intimacy with others? Are you reawakening to the beauties of life?

*Reversed:* What are you unwilling to face? Where have you lost energy and enthusiasm? Are you no longer missing what you have left behind? Where have you insisted on giving unsolicited help or advice? How have you felt burned out, exhausted? Do you feel as if your creative energies have dried up? What walls have you put up? How have you pressured others to see things from your point of view? Why have you been turning your back on an important source or resource? Is this not your time to shine? Might it be wise to let another shine instead? Do you desire to live more authentically? Could you be too open and accepting? Would you benefit from a good dose of fresh air and sunshine? Why have you been thriving less lately? How have you turned your back on your creative gifts? What are you hesitant about bringing out into the world? To whom could you be closing your heart? What new state of awareness are you slowly opening up to? Might you be feeling a lack of intimacy in your life?

## Personal Experience

When I first began practising Hatha Yoga, meditation, fasting and vegetarianism, I felt so healthy and full of life I wanted everyone I knew and cared about to benefit from these practices. Every chance I got, I talked about how great I felt and why. At the height of my excitement, I planned a visit to my parents on the East Coast to share my new self. Armed with books, recipes and a great surge of energy, I headed to New York City with the intention of bettering my family's health and well-being.

But things didn't work out as planned. Instead of being interested in what I had to offer, family members responded by switching the subject or arguing against the practicality of my various practices and philosophies. My mom made comments like, 'You'll get anaemic if you don't eat meat,' when I gave her a gourmet vegetarian cookbook. My dad's response to Yoga and fasting was, 'I get enough exercise from the work I do. The idea of eating raw foods and nuts and fasting is ridiculous. I need my strength.' In effect, my family was satisfied with things as they were. The visit left me feeling frustrated and invalidated, though I could also see that my family felt threatened by my desire to change their lifestyle.

I returned home to California feeling pained, and after several days of feeling miserable, sought out the Tarot's guidance. Asking for insight about my visit to my family, I drew the Sun card from the pack. Yes, helping my family had been my aim, but was the antithesis of what had occurred. Acknowledging that there was some message I wasn't getting, I decided to leave the card out for a while (something I do when I do not immediately get a card's significance). Carefully placing the Sun card near my Yoga mat and meditation corner, I went on about my day. Starting the next day with Hatha Yoga and meditation as usual, I came up out of a posture which is coincidentally called *Suryanamaskar* – Salutation to the Sun – caught sight of the Sun card shining out at me and nearly lost my balance as I realised what it meant. I had used my visit to my family as a means of sharing the light of spirituality and good health, but primarily to validate who I had become and my new lifestyle. There I was, for the first time ever, in love with my body and happy as could be, yet this went unnoticed because I had overwhelmed my family with insights and information they had not asked for. Of course they were turned off! I had presented myself with so much intensity that I had, in fact, scorched them.

I felt so awful, I wanted to hide. From this experience, I quickly learned the value and importance of waiting until others ask me for help and information, rather than dispensing it unsolicited. Who I am is enough of an advertisement for what I do. Explanations are unnecessary unless others request them or otherwise indicate in some way that they are ready to receive what I have to give.

### Student Experiences

❖ 'Talk about climbing the walls! I work with an obnoxious man who drives me nuts with his sexist and racist remarks and attitudes,' said Laurie, a clerk in the police department. 'And he's a born bully, to boot. I've spoken with our supervisor about the problem and he's acted as mediator for us a few times when communication has been impossible. We just seem to clash all the time now. It's almost become a kid's game of "I'm gonna get you first". The situation is so intolerable now that I've thought about quitting. But, after carefully considering it, I realised that this job is an important stepping-stone to where I want to be in my field. So why should I let him spoil it for me? I'm determined to stick with it.

'After meditating on the Sun card, I thought about him and how your suggestion to climb over a wall applied to my situation. It occurred to me that I have the power to stop playing this game with him. I can ignore him, rather than locking horns with him all the time (I'm sure he's a Capricorn like me). It could be worse. I could be his wife or daughter; thank the Goddess that I'll be rid of him when I move up sometime next year. But in the meantime, this isn't any way to live. I'm going to experiment with "lightening up" and ignoring him, keeping in mind that I'm climbing over the wall and out of the rut I'm in each time I do.'

*'I'd agree; you're playing a child's game, Laurie, and by calling up your power to stop playing it, you are moving into another Gateway of Life. By calling a halt to your immature behaviour, you're surrendering to what you know is right action, giving up your little ego to your Higher Self. To quote what you just said, you're "lightening up" and by doing so you're definitely taking a more "enlightened" approach to the situation.'*

❖ 'The thought that the person who has attained the Sun's powers enjoys his life has stuck with me all this week,' shared Sally, an assistant manager in a large computer firm. 'Not only have I been trying to enjoy my life more, but I've been making it a point to pay attention to others enjoying theirs. The other day I took my children to the beach, and it was delightful just watching them play. It made me see how sadly out of practice I am. It seems to me that our culture encourages decadent freakouts, but not genuine joy.

'Now, our company is running an ad for a new graphics person and today we got a truly wonderful résumé. Rather than sending in the traditional pile of paper, this man sent us a genuine work of art, beautifully expressing the Sun child who enjoys life.

'He artfully arranged his business cards from his last ten years of employment on a sheet of fine vellum. I wanted to hire him immediately. I wanted to yell out, "This is just what we need around here!" The ultra-conservative bosses were stirred, but in a very different way. They acted as if it were an insult. Can you believe that? Probably the most creative person we've had apply in years, and they were insulted!

'We need more people like that man in the all-too-serious world of business. I thought it was such a refreshing change that I stuck my neck out and voiced my opinion. I even considered calling the man up and telling him what a unique and highly creative idea his résumé was.'

*When we lose the joy of living, we have trouble relating to it in others. People like Sally's bosses wind up judging such behaviour in others as improper, disrespectful or even childish. And as another consequence of being cut off, people such as these must then go to real extremes to feel pleasure, or even feel. The Sun card is about having a child's heart in an adult's body, a lesson we can all benefit from.*

❖ 'I've been living the Sun card in Reverse,' Diane, an executive secretary, told us. 'I've been the picture of ill health for months now and I started getting sick again, this time right in the middle of our weekly office meeting. My boss kept looking at me as I sat there getting more and more stuffed up. He took me aside afterwards and told me that he was concerned because I've been sick every few weeks for almost a year. Now, if that doesn't say something about the Sun's burnout, I don't know what does! When he asked me if I'd had a good physical, I took the initiative and told him straight out, "If you don't want me sick, get me the help I need so I can relieve some of my stress."

'I'll tell you, I'm usually pretty reserved, and he was definitely shocked by my directness. But guess what? He agreed with me and promised to get one of the new clerks to start helping out at the beginning of next month. I hope he follows through. Actually, I can make sure he keeps his word. You know, I felt so much better. And my cold didn't get as bad as it was promising to do. I'm sure that expressing my feelings helped a lot. I think the Sun card made me see I could do something about my situation.'

*A case of exhaustion and burn-out like Diane's forces us to seek out health and healing. In the long run, situations like hers can rejoin us with the world of duties and obligations in a new way. It took courage for her to speak up and take the chance of getting a 'No'. Going beyond the wall of our own 'what if's', we live like Sun children, who are true to their Selves and use the card's energies in their lives.*

❖ 'The homework question, "How can I create a healthier, more enjoyable life?" was exactly what I needed,' offered Carla, a freelance writer. 'I've decided I need to spend at least an hour a day out in the fresh air and sunshine. I recently read this study in *Prevention Magazine* about people who get depressed when they don't get enough sunlight, and I'm pretty sure I'm one of those people. I'm a true child of the sun! Look at my Mediterranean complexion! I thrive on the sun! But I get so busy working, most days I don't go outside until it's almost dark! I mean, it's crazy; I've turned into a night person. I also feel even more depressed in the wintertime when there's less sunlight available. It's actually all quite predictable. Now I'm determined to go out every day, no matter how busy I am. Maybe I can even do some of my proofreading sitting outside.'

'Light deprivation is a very real yet subtle phenomenon,' I told her. 'Perhaps the symbol of the sunflowers that naturally pursue the sun's path can somehow help you to change your pattern, Carla. Maybe putting a poster of Van Gogh's Sunflowers somewhere could remind you that, by getting enough light and feeling good, you're not only following the Sun, but the renewing spiritual "light" it represents.'

❖ 'I lived the Sun card this week by being supportive to a co-worker,' shared Nicole, a programme coordinator at a nearby college. 'You mentioned that being supportive to others – shining your light and inspiring them with positive feedback – is an aspect of the Sun card. You also said that not doing so is a disservice to your Self and the world at large. Well, there's this young woman at work who's very, very bright and equally ambitious. She could well be the person to take my job when I retire. Quite honestly, I've been feeling threatened by her. It's almost as if she's waiting for me to drop in my tracks. That's a terrible way to feel about someone. But after the comment about being supportive to others, I thought about the mentors I've had and decided it's my turn to put out some support and encouragement. Thinking about it, I also responded to our assignment to "Climb over some wall", or "Open your heart to another".'

'So, wearing my scarf covered with bright orange marigolds (because orange is the Sun's colour), I made an appointment to have lunch with this woman. I planned to offer my services as a consultant on a new project she's been assigned. You should have seen her face when I asked her. It showed me how distant and unfriendly I've been. But I know that opening my heart to her (the Sun card is linked to the Heart *Chakra*) will warm her up, as well as myself. I'm using the affirmation, "Helping and promoting others is helping my Self". '

*Orange is a special colour in Eastern spiritual traditions. In the order of* Shankaracharya, *the oldest monastic order in the Hindu tradition, the renunciates wear orange robes, symbolising that they have given up their small personal lives and pleasures for the joys of the larger impersonal life. Like the individual at the Gateway of Wisdom, these people are completely devoted to serving God/dess. By appropriately helping and promoting others, we may become like the sun giving off the light of the Self.*

**Suggestions for Application and Integration of the Sun**

The following are means through which you may open your heart, regenerate your physical, mental and emotional energies, increase vitality and enthusiasm, overcome walls or blockages, and be more like the sun in your world and shine.

1   Colour or draw your own version of the Sun card with yourself as one of the children, the Sun, or both.

2   Set the Sun card in a visible place as a reminder to your conscious and subconscious minds to absorb its teachings to appreciate the physical sun as a representation of the light of God/dess; let your own light shine or encourage another to do so; and seek out and follow the Source of life for genuine well-being and sustenance.

3   Dream on the Sun.

4   Play the note D on a musical instrument. Intone IAO or hum along with the music and concentrate on your Heart *Chakra* in the middle of your chest as you do so (you might feel it warm up or tingle as you do). Now meditate on the card for a few minutes. While meditating, ask that the Sun's teachings guide you through a particular situation. Or if you are faced with a worrisome situation, event or problem, such as feeling 'burned-out', heavy or closed-hearted, or unwilling to go over your mental and emotional walls to deal with a difficult person or situation, imagine how the child (either male or female) would tackle it. If it seems feasible, do it. Jot down the times when you became aware of the Sun in your interactions. I was aware of the Sun when? Before/during/after . . .

5   Try this meditation: Sense yourself immersed in sunshine; feel its warmth and intensity. Then, just as a car fills up with fuel, fill yourself up with the sun's life-giving powers. Imagine it regenerating your body, mind and spirit. Then, when you feel 'full', sense yourself as the sun itself, radiating light and energy out into your daily work and interactions; your immediate environment, family, friends, and acquaintances; and to the rest of humanity (even those you are at odds with), the world's other creatures and the planet herself. Please note that if you are ill or exhausted, you might want to use all the fuel for yourself until you feel well again.

6   Go out into the world and pretend you are the Sun or one of the children. Let the card remind you to love yourself or another unconditionally. Initiate some service to help heal the planet such as recycling, signing a petition that is pro-environment, or refusing to purchase food served in plastic containers that cannot be recycled. Try out the card as a hint to climb over some wall, to overcome some obstacle which has been standing in the way of your being more trusting, authentic or intimate.

7   The Rerun. After having an experience and realising in retrospect how the Sun's teachings might have enabled you to face a situation with a brighter outlook, shine without attachments or expectations, conserve your energies where appropriate, or be more supportive and encouraging, mentally relive the situation, *including* your insight. This will help the behaviour become more automatic next time. If possible, actually rerun the situation in real life with this attitude or behaviour.

8   Ask yourself the following questions:

'What accomplishment would I like to bask in?' 'In what relationship(s) have I become capable of, or fear, being more intimate?' 'In what ways might I bring my inner teacher out into the world?' 'In what aspect of my life can being too energetic or enthusiastic be a hindrance?' 'Why am I feeling burned-out and what can I do about it?' 'How can I be a more effective source of light?' 'In what situation is my heart opening?' 'What person or project can I be more supportive of?' 'How might I create a healthier, happier, more enjoyable life?' 'How am I seeing "the light" in all?' 'What obstacle do I finally want to overcome?' 'Where might I bring enthusiasm and energy without making others feel wrong for their attitudes and beliefs?' 'In what ways am I allowing the sun to be my teacher by shining without attachments or expectations?' 'In what ways may I shine in service to another or my community?' 'How might I express more acceptance and appreciation of my own or others' similarities *and* differences?' 'Where in my personal or professional life might I benefit from working collectively?'

'What Gateway of Life am I in or developing through in the above?' Indicate: Childhood, Adolescence, Adulthood or Wisdom. Why?

'What do I need to do in order to develop the above further?' I need to . . .

'What step(s) do I want to take towards this goal and how can the Sun card guide me?'

9 Use a personal statement regarding the presence of the Sun in your life at this time, such as: 'The Sun's benevolent energy moves through every cell and muscle of my body, regenerating me and activating my participation in life.' 'I work effectively with others who are different from myself.' My personal statement is . . .

10 Inspirational words and quotes:

'And God will supply your every need.'                    PHILIPPIANS 4:19

'When deeds exceed learning, learning endures, but when learning exceeds deeds, it does not endure.'

Rabbi Chanina Ben Dosa

'A merry heart maketh a cheerful countenance.'    PROVERBS 15:13

'Established in spirit, perform action.'    Maharishi Mahesh Yogi

11 What symbols stand out in the card? What do they say to you? How might they be useful in daily living? Bring the symbol(s) into your life in some way so as to integrate the card's teachings.

12 Wear and surround yourself with the Sun's colour, orange, to remind you of the card's teachings when needed, such as increasing your joy and enthusiasm; opening your heart to support and encourage others' creativity; helping to heal and restore the planet; working with others in a more cooperative spirit; or remembering to 'look to the light'. Notice how you are affected.

13 The Sun's astrological correspondence is to the sun, presiding over your basic temperament or personality, the group of traits distinguishing your individuality and personal vitality from those belonging to another. The sun also refers to where and how your 'little I am' will eventually surrender to your 'Big I Am', or Higher Self. Call upon your 'Big I Am' to help you set the sun on an undesirable attitude or a personality trait you associate with your 'little I am'. Note what happens: your thoughts and feelings and the outcome.

14 Remember that the Sun's Hebrew name, *Resh*, means 'the head and face'. How can this remind you of the card's meaning or help in your life process? When I feel down, *Resh* reminds me to offer someone a smile or do some good deed. Doing this creates a new energy circuit, since I believe that what I put out has a way of coming back to me in one form or another.

15 Try a few drops of the scent cinnamon associated with the Sun as an olfactory reminder to integrate the card's teachings.

16 Have a cup of tea made from the herb angelica, associated with the Sun. Sit quietly as you drink and consider its properties as a tonic (it is an American cousin to ginseng), heart strengthener, aromatic, eye brightener and improver of circulation and consider the qualities of the Sun card. Or burn bay laurel, once used by the ancient priestesses of the Sun God, Apollo, for purification and protection and to induce prophetic dreams and visions. Bay laurel is also made into victory wreaths.

20 JUDGEMENT

# CHAPTER 24

# Judgement

## General Information and Symbolism

The Archangel Gabriel, meaning 'Messenger of God', presides over Judgement and the western quadrant of heaven. Because the sun sets in the west, Gabriel is recognised as the 'Angel of Completion'. Also known as the 'Fire of Water', Gabriel is in charge of the final purification and blending of the fire of the mind and the water of the emotions to make steam, or the completely spiritual person. Like Joshua, he sounds his trumpet to bring down the walls of unreality. Gabriel stands in eternity delivering those in the temporal world below from the great illusion. He sends out the message that, although the nature of the physical world and the body is transitory and mortal, there is an eternal and immortal quality to both life and the human soul. Qabalistic writings say of this, 'All souls exist before the formation of the body in the suprasensible world, being united in the course of time with their respective bodies. The descent of the soul into the body is necessitated by the finite nature of the former: it is bound to unite with the body in order to take its part in the universe, to contemplate the spectacle of creation, to become conscious of itself and its origin, and finally, to return, after having completed its tasks in life, to the inexhaustible fountain of light and life – God.'[1] This understanding (often accompanied by an experience which gives it validity) blows away the human ego to the point where we are finally redeemed from all small-mindedness and over-attachments to the physical world. We are able to view ourselves and life, even if momentarily, from the spiritual or eternal perspective.

The breath, voice or Word of the Most High is channelled down through Gabriel's trumpet. Qabalists say that the Word of God/dess

---

1 *The Jewish Encyclopedia*, Cabala, p. 476.

is a message encoded in a vibration. It is the final sounding of the cosmic alarm clock awakening those who can hear to the message of truth and greater understanding (the call to consciousness is always being broadcast, but only those who are attuned hear it). Seven rays emanate from the trumpet, corresponding to the seven musical tones which vibrate at the same sound frequencies as the seven *chakras*, serving to align and harmonise them. Vibratory attunement allows one to hear both the 'music of the spheres' and the voice of one's inner teacher. This symbolism underscores the importance of internal balance when making accurate judgements. Both the four-armed cross and the Angel's four-sided banner refer to the Emperor (number four) and another type of balance and stability. Good judgement, considered to be the highest level of reason, is balanced because it is motivated by the dispassionate desire to do what is for the greatest good. The cross implies the resurrection that occurs from this type of action as well as reaching the crossroads where one can no longer deny truth, no matter how uncomfortable it may be. Finally, each of the four quadrants created by the cross represents one of the four basic elements, and therefore the mental and emotional resources necessary to achieve judgement both in decision-making and as a state of transpersonal awareness. These are: Fire – inspiration; Water – imagination and emotion; Air – discrimination and mental planning; and Earth – manifestation – physical action and finished products.

The people are naked, indicating that they are unashamed of who and what they are, the true Self. They are confident that they have, and are, doing the best job possible for their level of development. When the body drops away, or you mentally and emotionally progress beyond your immature personality traits, that which was, is and will be appears different than when seen through the eyes of an embodied individual. We are shocked to find that it is we who 'judge' ourselves. Seeing with the eyes of your true Self (from the Fool's perspective) you are unencumbered by personal bias. Consequently, it is said that Gabriel represents your own Self who, through time and experience, learns how to save you.

Many religious groups prepare us for this final judgement with set periods of atonement (at-one-ment) and confession. Fasting, prayer and meditation set the scene for self-reflection during the Jew's Holy Day of *Yom Kippur*, the Moslem's month-long *Ramadan*, and prior to the Catholic's Holy Communion. At such times, individuals reflect on their deeds and decide how to best improve their judgement and forthcoming actions. One is absolved of misdeeds and immaturities by resolving to change attitudes and behaviours. In the name of personal growth and human progress, we must be willing to periodically re-evaluate our life and life systems. If this is not done, both we and the systems will stagnate and die.

The Child with arms spread to the heavens has its back to us, denoting that in order to fully embrace the state of consciousness depicted by Judgement, you must turn your back on the world as you have known it. This is the only Tarot card in the Major Arcana in which both the Woman (subconsciousness) and the Man (self-consciousness) turn to heaven, confirming that their dualistic nature has finally been unified and neutralised through time and the evolution of consciousness that it brings. The people are traditionally grey, the colour of neutrality and wisdom. Grey not only comes from blending the polarities of black and white, but is also the product of mixing all colours – distinctions of separateness – together. This suggests assimilation of the teachings of all the preceding cards, and intimates that at this level of development, you are at peace with your Self (your own male-female, anima-animus) and humanity at large. This concept is again expressed by the Child, universal symbol of regeneration and the blending of opposites – the conscious and subconscious selves.

Icebergs float in the card's background, alluding to how, with true Judgement, the mind becomes not only crystal clear and stable, but that such a mind reflects the Self within. The icebergs also tell us that Judgement is the consolidation of knowledge and experience via appropriate control and direction of feelings and imagination – the watery side of the personality. This is substantiated by the card's number, 20, the High Priestess (two) and Fool (zero) cards respectively. These cards state that the automatic ability to employ the universal teachings or the Fool's eternal point of view has been attained. Number 20 reduces to two, implying that the light has come to the dark, hidden or unknown side of the personality, bringing wholeness and transforming it into a true mirror of the Divine. Finally, the journey is over, the stream first seen in the High Priestess (two) card has become the ocean.

People rise from ocean-borne coffins, symbolising their 'arising from the depths' and coming into the light – a complete meta-morphosis of the subconscious mind. The ability to come out of a 'box' suggests resurrection because the people break free from their limited understanding of who they are and what life is really about. All forms of shame, Self-depreciation, mental and emotional disabilities and instabilities, and even the fear of death, vanish. Accompanying this level of release is often the power to create physical forms, or 'apports' as they are referred to in metaphysics, at will, whether a basket of fruit, loaves and fishes or an actual human body. Instances of the ability to both manifest and resurrect physical forms are not unique to Jesus. A contemporary example is that of Sri Yukteshwar, guru of the world-renowned Indian Yogi, Paramahansa Yogananda. The following account explains the phenomenon of Sri Yukteshwar's post-death appearance to a grieving Yogananda in a Bombay hotel room in 1936:

> 'But it is you, Master, the same Lion of God. Are you wearing the same body like the one I buried beneath the cruel Puri sands?'
>
> 'Yes, my child, I am the same. This is the same flesh and blood body. Though it is ethereal, to your sight it's physical. From cosmic atoms, I created an entirely new body, exactly like that cosmic dream body which you laid beneath the dream sands at Puri in your dream world. I am in truth resurrected.'[2]

Such persons may uplift others not only figuratively, as with the Sun card, but physically, too. Beings of this order may be born either in an exalted state or come into this life as unconscious as you or I, but possess an all-consuming passion, desire and will to attain full spiritual awareness during their lifetime, plus an abiding dedication to helping others do likewise. These persons are termed Self-realised in the yogic traditions, or *Adeptus Major* in the Qabalistic tradition. As mentioned previously, their superpowers are called *Siddhis* in India, and are tangible proof of spiritual attainment. Sathya Sai Baba, a contemporary Indian master dubbed 'Man of Miracles' by his devotees, materialises curative ash – *verbuti* – and protective amulets for followers on a daily basis, and has been said in very special instances to raise the dead.

Judgement's musical note is C, its colour is red and its herb is golden seal. The note and colour are the same as the Tower (Mars) card, denoting Pluto's status as the higher octave of Mars, sharing the common link of transformation via awakening. The Hebrew name for Judgement is *Shin*, meaning 'tooth' or 'fang'. Teeth are tools for assimilation and transformation. Nutritionists tell us that chewing

---

2  Paramahansa Yogananda, *Autobiography of a Yogi*, Self-Realisation Fellowship, Los Angeles, 1946, 1981, p. 475–6.

our food thoroughly is essential for good digestion and proper assimilation. This may be likened to a wise individual who chews over facts and information carefully before reaching a judgement. Taking this a step further intimates that decision-making at its finest involves the presentation of all facts, data, opinions and information to your Higher Self, then reaching a conclusion based upon universal truth. With this type of reasoning, the Serpent Power, or *Kundalini*, is fully ascended and balanced. This is probably what Jesus meant when he stated, 'Be ye as wise as serpents.' *Shin* also refers to consciously biting down upon, renouncing or restraining residual self-destructive impulses and immaturities, so that higher consciousness may enter and purify these patterns. This is illustrated by the body language of the Man and Woman in the card. He (self-consciousness) surrenders to the Angel, while the Woman (subconsciousness) opens up to the Higher Self or superconscious influence. Sound judgement may involve self-restraint, be painful, biting or stinging in the short run, but it will surely bring deliverance in the long term.

A brush with death is often the catalyst for accelerated spiritual development and wisdom. In the Eastern and Western traditions, there are innumerable accounts of Wiseones surviving poisonous snake bites (a reminder of *Shin*, the fang) or other types of accidents to find their consciousness elevated. In the East, dreams, visions and actual experiences of these creatures (poisonous snakes) are considered auspicious because they signify activation of the Holy Spirit, or serpentine *Kundalini*. It is customarily said of this that 'One has been bitten by God,' or, 'One is shedding the skin of the material world.'

On a final note, the association of retribution or karmic payback linked to this card may be understood as feeling the sting of one's conscience. This type of 'payback', or more truly *feedback*, is meant to motivate you to cease such behaviour, not immobilise you with fear. The goal is simply to forgive yourself (or another) and then move forward, doing your best not to get stung again.

Judgement is associated with the planet farthest from the sun, Pluto. Pluto is the Roman counterpart of the Greek Hades, God of the Dead and hidden worlds, and Persephone's consort during her time in the Underworld. The Plutonian experience tends to bring the personality into a life and death struggle for survival against the Higher Self as it arises from the depths to claim the soul. Pluto stands for those elements within the personality which have not yet been redeemed and integrated into the rest of the being. In other words, Pluto is 'the Deliverer' or Redeemer, who brings what is hidden into the light. Again, Pluto is the higher or more subtle octave of Mars. In contrast to Mars, where sudden, intense, forceful energy awakens you to God's presence, with Pluto the spiritual side of life is a given fact. Plutonian energy not only severs the final bonds of material attachment, but is responsible for escorting the spiritually aware individual or Adept through the final phases of development to become a completed spiritual vehicle. It may be insightful to learn that the Greek translation of Pluto is 'giver of wealth'.

Qabalists associate this aspect of the life force with Knowledge, *Daa'th*, the invisible *Sephirah*, situated below and between Wisdom and Understanding, on the Tree of Life. Knowledge functions much like the 'Wiseone's stick': the recipient initially experiences its blows (or bites, yet another reference to *Shin*) as painful; however, there is also the realisation that its purpose is both necessary and beneficial. This suggests that the cataclysmic encounters through which you are forced to experience your immortality bring wisdom, understanding and regeneration in their wake, as shown by how people report feeling resurrected or reborn, like the Child in Judgement. Finally, Pluto rules over volcanoes, making it easier to understand why Pluto is said to destroy with one hand as it builds with the other.

Pluto is also associated with the workings of group karma. In this sense, it relates to the reforming, destroying and transforming urges that are beneficial for the human race. As individuals attain more evolved states of consciousness, they act for the betterment of an entire social, political or religious group, not solely for their own purposes. Persons such as Moses, Christ, Gandhi, Che Guevara, Martin Luther King and Mother Teresa, to name but a few, align their personal destiny with the fate of a particular group.

In the Qabalah, the Judgement card is known as the Perpetual Intelligence. This Intelligence helps us to realise or 'know' the eternal, timeless, or perpetual aspect of ourselves – the Self within – personally. The Perpetual Intelligence is the everlasting, ever-available teachings of truth (the Rules and Tools of the Game of Life) that connect us with the eternal aspect of ourselves, others and all daily experience.

### Gateway of Life: Wisdom

Judgement may be defined as: the final judgement of humanity by the Most High, the formal utterance of an authoritative opinion or the administration of a decision such as having a judgement against your name. Yet with the Judgement card come still other meanings. You have reached the pinnacle of life, wisdom, and live in the eternal and temporal worlds simultaneously. Living in the eternal time frame means that you are able to transcend ordinary time. You live in the state of timelessness – what Qabalists term Fourth Dimensional consciousness. Viewing life from the greater point of view, you know that there is enough time, in divine time, to accomplish everything.

You have achieved good judgement by employing the teachings of truth as reference points in all mundane acts. The ancient metaphysical dictum, 'Know thy Self', has been realised. Having 'realised' the Higher Self within, you hear only its call. Released from your need for approval (and fear of disapproval), you are objective enough about your personality and actions to evaluate yourself wisely. Simply, you have attained such a level of clarity that you can get out of your own way and be your Self.

Judgement illustrates such fully matured individuals as the master or mistress of their body, mind and emotions, ruling themselves in ways that are dedicated to what is truly for the highest good. Furthermore, as living examples of those who have attained complete Self-knowledge, they serve to exemplify the teachings of truth. Such Wiseones offer others the environment, tools and models necessary for transformation, yet with the inherent knowledge that personal change cannot be pushed upon anyone.

Judgement is the passageway to Self-realisation and/or sainthood, just prior to God/desshood, wherein the individual consciousness may be reabsorbed back into the Source at will (Yogis call this latter state *maha samadhi*). It is subsequently the final reckoning with your immaturities, or the shedding of your last skin. At this juncture, the *Kundalini* is fully awakened and you experience what Eastern religions term *nirvakulpa samadhi*, or meditative union with the Self. But as this is a lesser state of union than the final or *maha samadhi*, you continue to live in the world as an example for others to follow.

The journey back to Eden has been long and often strenuous. And as you learned from the Hermit, support and inspiration are mandatory along the way. Judgement is living proof that enlightenment is not only possible, but has been attained at some, if not all, levels. Judgement depicts those who know that their human weaknesses have helped deliver them to higher consciousness. These are the Wiseones who have put aside the discomfort of personal evaluation and constructive criticism to know truth. Through concerted will, desire and action, they have earned their elevated status.

In the Twelve-Step model, you have learned to automatically make evaluations based upon the eternal teachings and big picture, rather than on what is socially expedient or geared solely for momentary gratification. In addition, you no longer confuse your Self with your experiences. You embody the last line of the Serenity Prayer:

> God grant me the serenity to accept the things
> I cannot change,
> The courage to change the things I can,
> And the wisdom to know the difference.

Individuals at the Four Gateways of Life may exhibit certain attitudes and behaviour. CHILDHOOD: At this stage you may act purely from instinct, and although consequences are often unpleasant, do nothing to change your behaviour; ADOLESCENCE: Vegetarian parents are excessively judgemental when their eight-year-old child wants to eat hamburgers at school like the other children; ADULTHOOD: An executive is able to receive employee feedback as an opportunity to look at and improve his managerial skills; WISDOM: Although in strained disagreement with a friend who is getting married, a woman attends the wedding after 'judging' that not doing so is spiritually incorrect.

### Divinatory Questions for Judgement

*Upright*: Have you successfully 'bitten down on' your immature ego in order to make a good judgement? Do you have a profound sense of being reborn? Could you be experiencing a regeneration as a result of tuning in to your Higher Self? What worldly concern have you released yourself from? Might it be advisable to first be what you want others to be? Is some part of you reawakening? What are you being delivered from? What skin are you finally shedding? What has become clarified? What have you finally seen from the eternal point of view? Might you be your own best critic and judge? Is your ability to evaluate and give constructive feedback improving? What rite of passage are you celebrating? How might you be atoning for an immature judgement? Is a significant transition into higher consciousness taking place at this time? Have you 'realised' who and what you truly are? How is loving control of your mind, body and emotions helping you move into a new phase of life? Are you involved in some social or political action that aims to clean up society's karma?

*Reversed*: Are you feeling fearful of upcoming changes? What reality has been permanently altered? Have you been excessively judgemental of yourself or another? What have you finally come to terms with? In what situation might you be better off by putting aside your pride and asking for feedback? How might guilt be immobilising you rather than serving you to use better judgement? Are you resisting hearing or listening to your Higher Self? In what situation might a change in attitude or behaviour help absolve you of a past transgression? Are you blowing your own horn too loudly, believing that only you have the best judgement? Why have you wanted revenge? Might confessing to immature behaviour be in order? Are you feeling judged? What judgement have you worked to remove? What view of life do you wish to be delivered from? Where are you slowly starting to perceive life from the eternal or timeless point of view? What attitude or behaviour is changing due to assimilation of new facts and information? What is getting slowly clarified or realised? What resurrection do you wish to experience? How are you defrosting the frozen parts of yourself?

## Personal Experience

In the early 1970s, I decided that the attainment of Self-realisation and God/desshood, or deliverance from worldly life, were my foremost goals; so I aggressively (and quite obsessively) directed my energies towards these pursuits. To keep myself focused, I read an unending procession of inspirational books about the lives of saints and masters from the Eastern and Western spiritual traditions, studied Tarot and spent time with various teachers and gurus from the then-emerging Human Potential Movement. This mindset also led me to seek out ways of resolving the relationship with my ex-husband with as much understanding as possible.

Now, in order to be satisfied that I know a Tarot card, I need to feel or experience it in my everyday life. Yet when it came to the Judgement card, I was at a loss to live out what it represented to me. Those at the Judgement stage of development, wisdom, live everyday life from the eternal versus temporal point of view. I had experienced this momentarily only once, when as a young child I nearly drowned. In spite of repeated meditations, intense study and efforts to 'dream on' the card, my knowledge remained purely intellectual.

However, in the process of finding the means through which to handle my difficulties with my ex-husband, an acquaintance suggested some work with her mother, who did past-life readings. Instantaneously, I was sure this would be what was lacking in my picture of the situation and quickly set up an appointment. Little did I know that this encounter would provide me with the key to assimilate (assimilation being one of the functions of the Judgement card) the relationship with my ex, the Judgement card and my obsessive pursuit of spirituality all at one time.

After the reader explained that I might not be given the exact past-life situation between my husband and myself, but would certainly be given a metaphor through which I would gain insight, she proceeded. The reading proved remarkably helpful, adding the missing dimension (Judgement is linked with fourth dimensional consciousness) to the difficulties I was having in achieving closure to the relationship with my ex-husband. Afterwards I headed for the woods to contemplate the information I had been given. While walking for several hours, I had many insights, the most important of which turned out to be the certainty that the spirit is deathless. The reading provided additional proof of my having lived before, personally reinforcing the knowledge that, although my body is mortal, my spirit is immortal. Yes, I had lived in the past, was living now, and until I earned my graduation from the school of life, would live on in future bodies and circumstances. It was just a matter of stepping beyond my limited perception of who I am and my environment to perceive the eternal Self within. The reading actually helped me to *experience* the truth that there is a spiritual purpose behind *every* physical act. In essence, I had had a quick glimpse of the state depicted by the Judgement card, deliverance from my mundane perspective of life into an eternal one, what Qabalists term the Fourth Dimension.

I considered this powerful event for many weeks, and as time passed, my sense of urgency about achieving Self-realisation and God/desshood strangely dissipated. At first I felt somewhat panicky, thinking that my desire was gone. But the longer I thought about what had happened, the clearer things became. The encounter with my previous lifetime had enabled me to experience my own eternal nature, and by doing so I recognised that I have all the time in the world (eternity) to complete the work required to reach my goals. This was evident by how I was presently rectifying the errors made in the past with regard to my husband. When I am able to judge my present life in terms of the greater life – life in the timeless eternal world – ordinary time does not exert its usual pressure upon me, explaining my decreased fervour and anxiety.

From these insights also developed the awareness that the weakness of much of the Human Potential Movement was that people were 'doing business'. The eternal truths were being imparted without the principle of timelessness to accompany them. Many teachers and techniques promised improbable shortcuts to higher consciousness, such as enlightenment in a week or weekend seminar. What it came down to was that Self-realisation and God/desshood had mistakenly become commodities and were being equated with the quick acquisition of some new material possession.

My search for greater understanding of my relationship, combined with my desire to live the Judgement card, inadvertently freed me from some erroneous beliefs about spirituality. I found that Self-realisation, the state represented by the wisdom aspect of the Judgement card, occurs only in divine time. I must, in fact, ripen in accord with nature's cycles; seeking speedy shortcuts creates little more than obsessive behaviour and discord.

## Student Experiences

❖ Tim, a counsellor, shared his experience of Judgement: ' I have a client whom I dated a few times after she had resolved her counselling issues. But recently she's had another crisis and wants to resume our professional relationship. I felt terribly torn about the situation. First, I thought, "It isn't a good idea to switch roles again." Then I remembered that my business is slow right now and that I can honestly use a few more clients.

'After our class on Judgement, I contemplated my circumstances and my conscience helped me "judge" that it would be best for both of us if she saw another counsellor. It was clear that our relationship can't become therapeutic once again. Do you really want to hear something? The very next morning after I made my judgement, the phone rang and I got two new clients. If that isn't cosmic confirmation, I don't know what is.'

*'Taking what we believe to be the best course of action always has its rewards,' I said to Tim, 'but whether they are immediate or come somewhere down the line isn't predictable. Religion teaches that we must wait until death or Judgement Day for our "final reward". We often don't see that our reward is the raising of our consciousness, which occurs by*

*taking right action at the time. By examining your situation from its various angles and then stepping beyond your personal attachments, you lived Judgement's teachings. I would also say that you stepped into the Gateway of Wisdom in the area of client-patient relationships.'*

❖ 'Seeing Gabriel blowing his horn made me realise that I've been holding my breath,' began Michelle, a college re-entry student and single parent. 'Also, that homework question, "What rite of passage are you facing?" addressed my situation. Since I returned to school, I live only for the future: getting my BA, going to grad school, doing my internship and so on. I'm so much there that I'm not here. I don't appreciate how much I've accomplished and am accomplishing. So I want to celebrate now, not wait until graduation next January, or when I pass my boards, five years from now. Who knows? With all the chaos going on in the world, next year may never come and I could lose out on a good time! I've been using Gabriel to remind me to breathe, to be here in my life and body now. The card reminds me that in many ways, all I have is the moment. So I may as well enjoy my life as it is, not wish it away as I've been doing. I think I want to wear more scarlet (Judgement's colour), the colour of life and vitality, too. Yes, I think my judgement is getting better.'

*'Holding your breath is like being dead to the "now", and in many ways the present is all there is. Seeing your life from the bigger picture, Michelle, rather than just this little segment, is living the Judgement card. Remember back to the Magician's pointing finger? When I'm worked up about something, I focus and ask myself, "How important is this in the whole scheme of my life?" It lets me take time out to re-evaluate things and see if my greater judgement tells me to behave in a different and healthier way, just as you're now doing.'*

❖ 'Last class you briefly mentioned Judgement's connection to atonement and "at-one-ment" which sparked a lot of thought for me,' shared Judith. 'Being raised Jewish, I had to think about atonement yearly when, on *Yom Kippur*, we Jews fast and ask God to forgive our sins from the previous year. I dreaded the holiday – no, not because I couldn't eat, but because I had to say I was a sinner. And I didn't feel like one! Sure, I had hit my sister a few times, cheated on a spelling test or two and "borrowed" change from my mom's purse, but that didn't make me feel like I had to repent. Thinking about the Tarot's teachings, particularly Judgement, I gained a new perspective on sin. Those so-called "sins" were and are in actuality my immature behaviour. I finally understood that it's okay to ask for the guidance to be wiser, more mature, and increasingly "at-one" with my Self in the future. It's so simple, I wish somebody had explained it to me that way when I was a kid.'

*'It looks as if the Judgement card has changed your judgement of your childhood religious training,' I said. 'You've applied the card's Hebrew letter,* Shin, *the idea of chewing or mulling things over thoroughly, to help in your life process, as the homework suggests. And it's worked to help you reassimilate the teachings of the Jewish tradition.'*

❖ 'Those homework questions are always so relevant for me. This time, the one on spiritual and religious awakening pertained directly to what happened to me at church last Sunday,' began Joanna. 'I don't have much affinity for Catholicism since I started balancing my rigid religious upbringing with New Age spirituality. I still go to church with my parents on holidays – it makes us seem like more of a family. But they're very set in their ways and can't understand the new practices I'm involved with. Last week was Easter and dutifully I went off to church again. However, this time something truly uplifting happened to me. Somehow I tuned out the priest and tuned in to Jesus.

'I've associated pain and suffering with holiness ever since I first saw Jesus bleeding through his crown of thorns and wounds in the painting on my mother's bedroom wall when I was about three or four years old. As my surfer son would say, "It was awesome!" But sitting there in the pew, looking at Jesus on the cross this past Sunday, I went beyond this concept to see that I don't have to be crucified – suffer through life – to know God. That was meant for another time, another age. My mind wandered to thoughts of the Christ Child and then to the Child in Judgement. It became apparent that the reborn Child in the card is the little child Jesus referred to when he said, "Become ye as little children." I know I can enjoy life and find God at the same time. The New Age teachings say this over and over. However, I never actually felt it until now.

'It also occurred to me that I could enjoy my life so much more if I dropped some of my heavy judgements of others. The scriptural quote, "Judge not, that ye be not judged," came to mind. I'm trying out the quote as my personal statement for the Judgement card. When I looked back at Jesus after thinking this all through, I swear he smiled down at me. As I lined up for Holy Communion, I realised that I had already had Holy Communion through my experience. By the time Mass was over, I felt as if I was the one who was raised from the dead. I felt like the Child in Judgement. I've kept the card in sight this week to keep my experience alive.'

*'Deliverance, meaning the act of liberation and unburdening, is another name for the Judgement card,' I said. 'Millions believe Christ was the Messiah. New Age messianic consciousness teaches that it's up to us to evolve to the point where we can deliver and resurrect ourselves. In other words, we may be inspired by messianic figures such as Jesus, Krishna and Buddha, but we are our own Messiahs. It sounds as if you were inspired to rise above some old dead attitudes. As you discovered, experiences like these can give us a new lease on life.'*

❖ 'In the Tarot deck I used before taking this class, the Judgement card is called the "Knower",' Jane, a writer and editor, told us. 'It's a great match, in my opinion, because to me real judgement is a sense of knowing in your heart and soul that something is aligned with spiritual principles. My roommate and I have been discussing our plans for the upcoming weekend before I leave on holiday. I've been planning my trip for months, and now that it's almost here, there's so much to be done before leaving, it's incredible. Well, we were really unconscious about how we discussed things – we yelled back and forth between the kitchen and living room. As it turned out, she had invited guests for the weekend before I leave without talking with me first. I flew off the handle. Here I am, trying to get everything done, and there are people to entertain!

'After a lot of ranting and raving, I grabbed the dog and went for a walk, hoping to cool down. I was on fire! Do you know what happened just as I was on my way out the door? As I passed my desk, I caught sight of both the Judgement and Knower cards that I'd left standing side by side as a reminder for me to use the card's teachings. Immediately, I knew our judgement was off, mine for exploding and hers for not communicating with me before making plans.

'Walking along, I tried your idea of rerunning a situation mentally to get a different slant on it. I came up with a line of questioning that would lead to her admitting she'd been inconsiderate to invite company, without my jumping down her throat.

'I wanted to try the questions out, so before bed I asked her to run through the conversation again with me. She was very resistant, saying that I'd made my point earlier. But she relented, and by the time we were done, both of us felt a lot better.

'We agreed that guests from Friday to Saturday would be fine, but that I needed to have my Sunday completely open to finish packing. She promised to take our guests out for breakfast early on Sunday and say goodbye to them after that.

'The Judgement card made me face the fact that my judgement was off. My "Knower" acted unconsciously. But I'm working on it.'

*'I think Jane put the renewal, resurrection and Self-knowing facets of Pluto to work for her. First off, she knew that she had behaved unconsciously. Next, she knew that in order for things to change or be resurrected, she had to consciously re-evaluate what had been said and done, and then "rerun" the conversation. From all of this came a new beginning and a resurrection in her relationship.'*

## Suggestions for Application and Integration of Judgement

The following is designed to help you use better judgement, be more Self-knowing, liberate your eternal point of view, enjoy spiritual, mental and/or emotional redemption, set a better example and discover how you can be the best judge of your Self.

1   Colour or draw the Judgement card with yourself as any or all of the figures.

2   Set the Judgement card in a visible place as a reminder to your conscious and subconscious minds to apply and absorb its teachings.

3   Dream on Judgement.

4   Play the note C on a musical instrument. Intone IAO or hum along with the music. Focus on the card for a few minutes and, as you do so, contemplate how your judgement of yourself and others may be like living in a coffin of incomplete understanding. Ask your Self how the teachings of the Judgement card might liberate your judgement, appraisal or knowledge of a situation, person or thing to a higher level of awareness – to transform your mundane point of view into an eternal one. Or if you are faced with a worrisome situation, event or problem, such as the desire that someone be different than they are; the need to restrain your immature ego so that your Higher Self may come through; or

deliver yourself from small-mindedness and an obsession with material things, ask that the card's teachings guide you or imagine how the Archangel Gabriel in Judgement would handle it. If it seems appropriate, give it a try. Jot down the times when you became aware of the Judgement card in your interactions. I was aware of Judgement when? Before/during/after . . .

5   Go out into the world and enact the teachings of Judgement. I enacted the Judgement card and this is what happened . . .

6   The Rerun. After having an experience and realising in retrospect how Judgement's teachings might have inspired you to labour and examine all possibilities before reaching a judgement; experience a resurrection; save yourself from yourself; feel less judged or transform your tendency to be judgemental into better judgement, relive the situation, including your insight. This will help the behaviour become more automatic next time. If possible, actually rerun the situation in real life with your new attitude or behaviour.

7   Ask yourself the following questions:

'Where might my judgement of myself and others be detrimental?' 'In what area of my personal or professional life am I realising my full potential?' 'What is causing me to formulate more mature evaluations of people, places or things?' 'What religious or spiritual awakening am I having or fearing?' 'What worn out and excessively materialistic attitudes and behaviour am I finally willing to shed?' 'How are others' judgements and evaluations exerting a positive or negative influence over me?' 'What am I longer "boxed-in" by?' 'In what situation or relationship might biting down on old tendencies or habits help me attain greater awareness?' 'Where might a self-imposed period of at-one-ment be useful?' 'What promotion, initiation or rite of passage am I facing or avoiding?' 'What new realisation have I opened to receiving?' 'How might I absolve myself from a past immaturity?' 'How might I experience God/dess's perpetual presence in my everyday life?' 'What would it be beneficial to atone for?' 'In what situation(s) has your judgement become so clear that you are able to act without caring what others think?' 'What old dead way of thinking or behaving have I risen above?'

'What Gateway of Life am I in or developing through in the previous question?' Indicate: Childhood, Adolescence, Adulthood or Wisdom. Why?

'What do I need to do in order to develop the above further?' I need to . . .

'What step(s) do I want to take towards this goal and how can the Judgement card guide me?'

8 Use a personal statement regarding the presence of the Judgement card in your life at this time. 'I can effect change in others only by being what I want them to be.' 'My experiences are delivering me to wiser decision-making.' 'I am immortal.' My personal statement is . . .

9 Inspirational words and quotes:

'Let not the wise disturb the mind of the unwise with their work. Let him, working with devotion, show them the joy of good work.'                                    BHAGAVAD-BITA

'So then you are no longer strangers and sojourners, but you are fellow citizens with the saints and members of the household of God.'                                    EPHESIANS 2:19

'Let me say at the risk of seeming ridiculous that the true revolutionary is guided by great feelings of love.'  CHE GUEVARA

10 What symbols stand out in the card? What do they say to you? How might they be useful in daily living? Bring the symbol(s) into your life in some way so as to integrate the card's teachings.

11 Wear and surround yourself with Judgement's colour, red, to remind you of the card's teachings when needed, such as taking a more eternal or wholistic point of view; setting a good example; helping promote or sustain uplifting feelings; becoming better at scrutinising and synthesising data; or feeling more at ease with personal examination and constructive criticism. Notice how you are affected.

12 Judgement's astrological correspondence is to the planet Pluto, governing such things as evaluation, integration, the assimilation and synthesis of information and experiences to promote better judgement, the power struggle between the personality and Higher Self, resurrection and deliverance from misjudgement to

wisdom and Self-knowledge. Use the Judgement card to remind you to open your heart and mind up to evaluating some aspect of your personal or professional life in which you have been prejudiced, one-sided, intolerant or unreasonable, so that you may improve your evaluation skills and judgement, and empower your Higher Self. Note what happens: your thoughts and feelings and the outcome.

13 Remember that Judgement's Hebrew name, *Shin*, means both 'fang' and 'tooth'. How can this remind you of the card's meaning or help in your life process?

14 Try a few drops of the scent basil associated with the Judgement card as a reminder to integrate the card's teachings.

15 Use golden seal, the herb associated with Judgement internally or externally as a digestive aid, liver tonic, laxative or antiseptic for open sores. Although it is a very bitter-tasting herb, it acts to usher in the sweetness of healing. Consider golden seal's properties and those of the Judgement card. Please note: this herb should be avoided during pregnancy as it stimulates involuntary muscle contractions.

21 **THE WORLD**

# CHAPTER 25

# The World

## General Information and Symbolism

This card is named both the World and the Universe to indicate the interdependence of the two spheres. The Dancer is enclosed within a wreath, suggesting the physical world, or planet Earth, floating within the universe (the surrounding space). This symbolises that the material world – its events and activities – are supported by the limitless or greater universe. It also shows that the mature person, the Dancer, is his or her own authority. Persons such as this may live in the world, but are not of it – they affected the world but are no longer affected by the world. There is simply no longer any need for self-gratification, except what is needed to sustain the human body. Such individuals are considered 'volunteers' as they have chosen to incarnate for the sole purpose of serving God/dess by assisting humanity.

Although the Dancer has been interchangeably called an androgyne and a hermaphrodite, I feel the need to clarify these terms, and to assert that the Dancer is androgynous. The prime difference between the two is that one is an external physical manifestation – the hermaphrodite has both male and female sex organs – while the androgyne's characteristics are psychological and spiritual in nature (this is not to say that the hermaphrodite cannot internalise androgynous characteristics). It is important to differentiate, because if one *must* be a hermaphrodite in order to reach the level of awareness depicted by the World card, the likelihood of the occurrence diminishes radically. On the other hand, if the Dancer is androgynous, we *all* have the potential to blend our male and female character traits into a whole being.

There are two wreaths; one is worn, while the other surrounds the Dancer. A wreath is a human product, symbolising that it is time to celebrate the victories that its maker laboured to create. The larger wreath is composed of 22 clusters, denoting the Dancer's evolution through and assimilation of the 22 states of consciousness depicted by the Tarot. The smaller wreath signifies victory over personal trials and tribulations – life's ups and downs. The horizontal figure eights over the head of the Magician and Strength reappear in this card entwined around the large wreath's top and bottom. These tell us the principle 'As above, so below' is being lived. As a result of passionate attention and the passage of time, one has graduated from the school of life.

The Dancer holds wands, symbols of will and the fire of divine inspiration, in both hands. These are shown as spirals wound in clockwise and counter-clockwise directions (right and left hands respectively), illustrating the outer and inner cycles of work required to become the Dancer. The wands function like antennae to draw down and send out – receive and transmit – our creative energies. Qabalists say the wands depict the absolute balance of male and female forces – solar and lunar *Kundalini* currents – within the Dancer. The former may also be seen in the ancient Minoan[1] snake goddess who bears a flailing serpent in each hand. In many Eastern Traditions, the individual who is freed from physical attachments is likened to the snake, which sloughs its skin and leaves it behind in a lifeless heap. Finally, the wands reiterate the necessity of paying attention to your true origin, the One Will, while choreographing and performing the routine dance of daily living.

The Dancer is surrounded by the Guardians of the four corners of the universe,[2] Lion, Eagle, Human and Bull, which correspond to the four basic elements, Fire, Water, Air and Earth, and to the Magician's tools: the Wand – inspiration; the Cup – imagination and emotion; the Sword – discrimination and mental planning; and the Pentacle – physical action and finished products. By way of the Dancer's mastery of the tools of practical magic, the world and its elements are ready to do the Master's bidding. In other words, when you are aligned with your Self, the elements and tools become your allies. If you compare the Four Guardians here to those on the Wheel of Fortune, you will see that the Ox/Bull, a creature representing earthly desires, now turns towards the infinite world of spirit. The Bull is meant to remind us of the Fool, *Aleph*, the Bull and

---

1 The advanced Bronze Age culture that flourished in Crete from about 3000 to 1100 BC.
2 For further information about the four Cornerstones or Guardians, please refer back to the chapter on the Wheel of Fortune card.

Spirit of Life. It's action illustrates how someone at this level of development is not only intent upon serving the greater world, but lives in the superconscious state of the Fool while in a physical body.

The Dancer is perfectly poised on one foot, illustrating the centred state wherein body, mind and emotions operate in complete accord. This stance reaffirms the importance of being balanced and centred in order to perform the ever-changing dance of life to your maximum ability. Dancing is an art and skill which demands that participants discipline their steps to harmonise with a musical background. Similarly, life asks you to discipline your actions to harmonise with the background of everyday events. If you are attuned to the music and the background, and are adept in your movements, both dancing and life may be ecstatic. The Dancer's eyes are closed, to represent this state. This attitude may be seen in the Sufi's Divine Dances, which give an exquisite rhythmical form to spiritual consciousness, as well as by the whirling dervish whose movements spiral like the dancer's wands and the cosmic energy they represent.

The World card shows the fully balanced and integrated human as the Wiseone pictured in the Hermit card. Wiseones are those human beings who have married their Selves and become fully unified, visible, living, flesh and blood manifestations of the Divine presence, described in the Qabalah as the *Shekinah*, derived from the Hebrew verb, *shakhan*, 'to dwell'. Persons of this stature live on the earth, yet are validated by and depend upon the greater world (the universe) alone, shown by the fact that they are supported by and dance on air (another reference to the Fool and spirit). They continually turn inward and upward to their God/dess Self and the Source, while turning outward and downward to the work of the everyday world at hand. Wiseones embody the concept, 'trust in the universe and it will support you!'

The musical note associated with this card is A, its colour is blue-violet (indigo) and its herb is comfrey. The musical note and colour are the same as for the Devil card, hinting at their common connection, the principles of limitation and materiality. With the Devil, however, you are limited by materiality, whereas in the World card you become liberated by understanding the true nature of physical limitation. The World also represents the First or Root *Chakra*, the seat of the sleeping *Kundalini* at the base of the spine. This centre contains the karmic patterns (seeds or *samskaras*) that we bring into this life, our lifetime obligations, or 'work'. This centre is often referred to as the 'survival centre', hinting that the only way to release these patterns and do more than survive, or thrive, is through the dedicated application and integration of the universal and natural laws and principles – be it through the Tarot or any other spiritual discipline. Meeting your responsibilities has the potential to bring karmic fulfilment and unify the material and spiritual worlds to the point where enlightenment is spontaneous. You become free simply by confronting and working with and through your limitations.

The Hebrew name for the World card is *Tav*, meaning 'a sign or mark of finality or agreement'. When something is signed, it means you accept responsibility for it. This concept in its most developed state is about assuming complete, yet *non-attached* (remember the card's connection to the Wheel of Fortune and the witness state of the sphinx), responsibility for yourself, others and the planet. Furthermore, the World card marks the completion of the Fool's journey and the commitments you have 'signed on' for. It *marks* your fully conscious or superconscious return to the Source from whence you came.

The World is associated with the planet of the Roman earth god who 'sowed the seed' (a reference to the First *Chakra*), Saturn. Saturn is regarded as the last personal planet, and as such functions to help the personality bridge the final gap between the personal and transpersonal – the outer planets of Uranus, Neptune and Pluto – so that individuation is completed. Therefore, Saturn is called the 'Tester' who strives to perfect the personality through ongoing challenges. Saturn governs sobriety, pensiveness, melancholia, discipline, structure, hard work, absorption, time limitations and freedom. Saturn, Father of the Gods, ate or absorbed his children back into himself. Stretching this analogy a bit, it may be interpreted as the aspect of our divine parents who lovingly discipline us into absorbing our lessons and the Rules and Tools of the Game of Life upon which they are based. Furthermore, it may speak of the ability to parent and direct ourselves, which naturally follows genuine maturity. The individuation process is now complete!

The works of Thomas Carlyle speak of the golden age of Saturn in which 'a new social order is brought to the world'. Saturn operates to 'take out the old and bring in the new', hence the planet's connection with 'Father Time'. Saturn takes about 29½ years to return to the astrological sign it was in at the time of your birth. For many, the 'Saturn Return' is a time of soul searching and re-evaluation, suggesting, as does the World card, the need to disengage from external authorities in order to become fully self-regulating and encounter your Self. Here you may temporarily or permanently break with outer supports and authority figures, such as parents and peers, to feel more independent (another reference to how the card's central figure dances on air) and/or seriously address the need to re-parent yourself. Changes in job, career, relationships and locale may occur at this time of life, to demonstrate your independence and leadership abilities.

Such behaviour is the result of either passing up an earlier period of self-evaluation and rebelliousness because of fear of the unknown or of others; the desire to be a 'good child'; or simply being out of touch with your need to step out of your prescribed role and take stock of yourself, events, etc. For many in their Saturn Return, it is essential to know whether life is happening by choice or chance. The main purpose of this period is to go deeper than the unrest and dissatisfaction you initially feel in order to create a life of conscious choice as opposed to demonstrating unconscious or emotionally-motivated reactions to external influences. At this point, a lifetime goal or ambition may become evident, plus the recognition that hard work and self-discipline are essential to any achievement. To conclude, because Saturn relates to both structure and time, we must remember to keep our structures flexible so they will withstand the tests of time.

You are conditioned to think that you came into this world through your parents alone, but in reality, birth is much more than a biological fact. This is symbolised by the elliptical or womb-like wreath surrounding the Dancer, reminiscent of zero, the Fool, the Spirit of Life. With the World card, you recall not only your true origin, but in the most advanced states, you find that you are actually divinity incarnate. This is implied by the card being numbered 21, which blends the *yin* or femininity of the High Priestess (two) with the *yang* or masculinity of the Magician (one). The reunion of those polarities, which are unconsciously joined in the child but then programmed out, now owing to much time, will, patience, loving discipline and desire, recurs when you become completely aware and clear. Finally, two + one = three, the Empress, *Daleth* the Door, suggesting entry into a new world.

The Dancer is draped with a swirling scarf which forms the Hebrew letter *Kaph*, the 'grasping hand', associated with the Wheel of Fortune, symbolising that the individual has completely grasped or mastered the teachings of the Tarot, the Rules and Tools of the Game of Life. As a full-fledged Wiseone, this individual is an embodiment of the teachings. A Buddhist student likened this to what is known in Buddhism as 'Taking Refuge'. In other words, by unequivocally embracing the teachings of the Buddha, one becomes the Buddha.

In the Qabalah, the World card is known as the Administrative Intelligence. Since an administrator is in charge of carrying out company policy, this Intelligence refers to those individuals who have earned the right to represent their company – the cosmic governing body. Representatives have the honour and duty of implementing its policies – the teachings of truth – wherever and whenever called for. Their task is to help make the world a better place by applying the universal teachings to worldly matters. They are, in a sense, the ultimate social, political and spiritual activist.

## Gateway of Life: Wisdom

The Wise Fool completes the journey. As in all fairy tales and myths, the hero or heroine returns home victorious. At this stage of development you are completely adept at controlling and directing your responses to life events. As a student wisely noted, 'You are your own experiences.' Deep insight into what occurs around you is normal. This intimates why liberated individuals become capable of liberating others and will do everything in their power to mitigate a particular individual's or group's karma. Qabalistic tradition calls these persons *Exempt Adepts*, exempt in that they are rewarded for completing their worldly work (karma) with the option of not needing to go through another physical life cycle. In the end, it all comes down to the desire. When all desires naturally dissolve, especially the desires to perpetuate individual consciousness and assist the enlightenment of others, then one is liberated from the bonds of birth, death, rebirth and redeath. You become free to get off the wheel of *samsara*, a Sanskrit term meaning the 'ever-flowing cycles of birth and death'. Persons of this stature may either take *Maha samadhi*, and be reabsorbed back into the Source, or may come and go between earth and heaven at will in order to perform service.

Functioning in the realms of greater human possibility, Exempt Adepts handle the limits of everyday life in unlimited ways, while refraining from taking personal credit for their accomplishments – 'the Self, God/dess did it'. Everything that takes place is regarded as the working of the Most High. Having passed the final rite of passage into perfect wisdom, they are at one with the greater world or universe, Source of all life. The Wiseone is completely united with his or her God/dess Self, known in the Hindu tradition as an *Avatar*, divinity incarnate.

In terms of the Twelve-Step and recovery programmes, the work is done. 'Having had a complete spiritual awakening as a result of working the other eleven steps, you carry the message to others and practice the principles in all your affairs.' And from another point of view, you have successfully wrapped up the process of re–parenting yourself!

Experiencing the World at the Four Gateways of Life, an individual may encounter certain behaviour and attitudes. CHILDHOOD: A woman is financially independent, but because she leads a sheltered and isolated life, cannot understand how others can be homeless and hungry; ADOLESCENCE: After twenty years of marriage, a woman takes her first steps towardss personal autonomy by spending time with her friends on a regular basis; ADULTHOOD: Early on in life, a couple decide that they desire union with their God/dess Selves more than anything else. Yet, rather than give up commitments to work, community, family and friends, they pursue their goal by applying spiritual concepts to their daily lives; WISDOM: A person acts and interacts from a perfectly centred state with others and everyday life situations at all times.

## Divinatory Questions for the World

*Upright:* What have you completed with almost superhuman effort? Have you been feeling as if the world is yours for the taking? How have you been dealing with authority figures? What has discipline brought forth? Have you become more self-regulating? Are you handling 'the system' or bureaucracy well? How are you re–parenting yourself? How are you finding freedom and enjoyment within the restrictions of your daily routine? What cycle of life have you become liberated from? What mastery or finished labour calls for celebration? What have you become more responsible for, yet also more detached from? Are you feeling that your female and male selves are more balanced and attuned to each other? What humanitarian service are you selflessly performing? How do you experience the spirit of life supporting you?

*Reversed:* Have you been feeling unable to move about freely within the boundaries of your life and personality? Are you slowly learning how to regulate yourself? What transition are you hesitant about? Has your world turned upside down? What cycle(s) are you feeling tied to? Are you slowly absorbing the fact that your everyday work is also your spiritual work? Are you feeling stressed and overwhelmed by the world's demands – work, community obligations, relationships and family? How might you take refuge from the storms of life? How might a combination of hard work and non-attachment liberate you or another? Are you resistant to the demand that you play both male and female roles in life? What powers and tools are you afraid to employ? What tools and powers are slowly becoming your allies?

## Personal Experience

The week my husband and co-parent went to Hawaii for some rest and relaxation, I was sole parent-in-charge, a role I had not had in some years. The first few days coincided with the long weekend before our sons had to take their final exams for the autumn semester of high school. So when my fifteen-year-old told me he wanted to sleep over at his best friend's home and then go to San Francisco the following day, I decided he could do one, but not both. He responded to my limit by insisting he could handle it all. In spite of his protests, I remained firm and very 'in charge'. After storming off into his room for some time, he emerged to reluctantly choose the sleepover, promising to be home by eleven o'clock the next morning to study.

By noon the following day, he had not returned, so I called his friend, only to learn from his sister that both boys had taken off for San Francisco at 6:00 am. Needless to say, I was hurt and angry that he had broken our agreement. I spent the rest of the day inter-mittently storming, crying and figuring out my response to his behaviour.

When he finally sauntered in at almost 8:00 that evening, his first words as he stepped through the door were, 'You'll see, I can handle my exams.' I talked to him for the better part of the next hour about the importance of keeping his agreements, and how hurt and angry I was with him for defying me. I ended my tirade by grounding him after school for the entire next month. His response to this was to tell me, 'We didn't have an agreement. You forced me into making one.'

The situation haunted me for the next several days, and when I sat down to teach the World card at the end of the week, I rapidly got another sense of what had occurred. The first awareness started creeping up on me while explaining *Tav*, the card's Hebrew name, which means 'the signing of an agreement'. My understanding deepened when explaining the parental aspects of Saturn (the planet associated with the World card). It was Saturn that helped me become cognisant of how strictly I had been controlling the household since my husband went on holiday, and how the mature person, the Dancer, is developed enough to be his own authority and set his own limits. I was so moved by the time class was over, I remained to meditate on the card for quite some time.

Yes, I had raised my son to be self-regulating, and he was doing just that. I could now recognise that he was asking for more freedom by telling me he could place the needed restrictions upon himself so as to pass his exams and be with his friends, too. Next, I contemplated my reasons for not empowering him and came up with some old concepts about parenting that indicated I was holding on too tight and using more discipline than was appropriate. With this in mind, I decided to discuss the situation further with him.

After sharing my realisation, he apologised for lying, and said it was impossible for him not to do what he knew he could do. He also claimed that it was more important for him to agree with his Self than to agree with me, confessing that it was so essential he was willing to deal with the consequences of his actions, whatever they might be. He finished up by telling me he knew I would understand, but not right away.

As I sat there paying close attention to his words, body language and general presence, I realised he was no longer a boy but a young man. It was definitely time for me to cut some more of those apron strings. I acknowledged this by letting him know I could understand his need to be more independent and responsible for himself (like the Dancer in the World card), and if his grades turned out okay, I would feel he could handle himself during exam time without my interference. I added that I would rescind his punishment if he would guarantee not to break his agreements with me again. He said that in the business class he was taking in school, he had learned that both parties had to agree on the terms of a contract before it was binding. Again, the Hebrew letter, *Tav*, entered the picture. It was uncomfortable, yet I could admit that although I came from a place of loving motherly concern, I had been overprotective and insensitive. On the Tree of Life, the Mother (*Binah*, or Understanding) is the sphere of the planet Saturn. I simply went overboard in my role of 'parent-in-charge'. Thanks to the World card, my son and I shook hands and moved into a new, more adult phase of our relationship.

**Student Experiences**

❖ 'I'm getting initiated into a new world and I love it,' began Mary, a longtime metaphysician and businesswoman. 'My husband and I married young and so much of our energy went into being sexy with each other that we hardly talked. Well, that resulted in our four kids. Then there was always so much to do and talk about in regard to raising them that we had to learn how to communicate (we had family therapy on and off for several years to help). Meanwhile, the family took so much of our juice that our sex life became almost nonexistent. It's strange, but at the time neither my husband nor I had a chance to miss it.

'Now my youngest daughter is gone and I should feel "the empty nest". Actually I did, for about a week. But what's happened instead is that my husband and I are rediscovering each other sexually. And I think what makes it so great between us is that we have developed a wonderful communication from all our years of dealing with the family. So it's not just an act of passion, it's something on a higher level. A true union. Time has severed the limitations and responsibilities of being parents, and now we're stepping into this whole new world.'

*'Yes, Father Time takes out the old to bring in the new, Mary. Also, you're experiencing an often-undisclosed aspect of the World card, that of the Dancer's body and senses being enhanced by increasing awareness, not lost or transcended as you might think. The Dancer sees and knows the world for what it is, God/dess's play, and from this point of view enjoys each moment and sensual pleasure to its fullest. Have fun!'*

❖ 'You've suggested using the Hebrew letters, and I finally tried it out with the World card. *Tav*, the "signature", applied to my signing the final decree for my divorce,' said Willow, a physician's assistant. 'It's almost spooky the way the card came into my life at this time. I feel such a mixture of emotions, I almost can't stand it. One minute I'm crying because I'm sad, and the next because I'm happy. I was very childish in the relationship with my husband. He took care of me from the first day we met. And I let him. I wanted that. Then when I got my first job, things began to change fast. I liked taking more responsibility for myself, paying my bills and being able to take classes. But being more independent in the context of our relationship was a terrible strain because of how we'd set things up. We tried to adjust, but basically my new attitudes put him out of a job. He couldn't handle my not being dependent on him for everything. He sulked, was insulting and nasty, while I cried a lot.

'Finally, I opted to move out, and now I'm ready for our divorce. He's so lost and sad, I feel really sorry for him. He's a "caretaker" and will probably find another woman to take care of, fast. But maybe he'll finally direct some of his caretaking towards himself, instead. I certainly hope so, because I'm his third wife.

'I used both the *Tav* and the World card to remind me that signing that piece of paper is like signing my Emancipation Proclamation. It's a formal recognition of my maturity at long last. It's strange, since we separated I have gained twelve pounds. My breasts have been growing, and I started menstruating regularly for the first time in my life. I guess, I'm finally becoming a full-grown woman.'

*'You've spoken about an important aspect of the World card, Willow,' I told her. 'Maturation leading to self-regulation. When we unexpectedly become more in charge of ourselves, sometimes others can't switch gears. You've gone through a great deal of pain and "testing", both Saturnian facets of the World card, and have emerged a more mature person. I'd say you've come into the Gateway of Adulthood.'*

❖ 'I've been a beautician since 1951, but when I first started going to school again at the age of fifty-three, I fantasised about becoming a TV anchorwoman,' said Zia. 'I got married the same year I finished beauty school and have been home raising my kids and being a housewife ever since. I worked in a salon for a short time. But after the kids were born, I started doing hair appointments at home, and I'm still there. Well, you should have heard my husband when I mentioned the idea of being on TV while we were watching the late news one night. He told me flat out I'd never do such a thing because one, he wouldn't stand for it, and two, I'm too old. He's very old-fashioned and extremely possessive and feels that women belong at home.

'I'll tell you, I was so angry at his attitude, I considered leaving him. But our relationship and family are very important to me. I love him and I don't want a divorce. Meditating with the World card helped make things even clearer. That Dancer dancing in the middle of the victory wreath helped me decide that I could be victorious in the middle of my situation. I'm that Dancer, and even though the floor space is small, I can still dance.

'So last week, when the head of the Women's Re-Entry Programme at school asked me to be interviewed on local radio and TV, I was thrilled. I'm going to talk about how wonderful it is to be out of the house and in the world, how stimulating it is to be going to college at my age and with my background. This is really all I want. I want to be out in the world learning and exchanging with others. That's what the World card means to me. Surrendering to this has made me freer to enjoy what I have and not feel bad about what I've missed. Every time I go off to school, I feel as if I'm the Dancer in the card, dancing on air.'

*'Facing up to your restrictions and limits and enjoying yourself anyhow! Now that's what I call really living the World card!'*

❖  'It's difficult to be a woman in today's world,' shared Liza, a graphic artist. 'I worked so hard to get liberated and now I find that society doesn't support my efforts. I worked my way through school and even extricated myself from my relationship with my chauvinistic husband during my Saturn Return. I've been raising my daughter alone ever since. But lately, I feel burdened by a lack of money. I guess that's Saturn too. The basics are so expensive that paying for extras like this class is a struggle. The idea of getting "equal pay for equal work" is still only a concept. I know I must surround myself with good people and spiritual teachings that support me. That's what the wreath in the World card means to me. But sometimes it's hard to do.

'The main message I got from meditating on the World is that I can love. I'm not sure how it fits into the card, but there it is. There are so many people in this world who have everything materially, yet can't love. I know the ideal is to have both, and I'm working through this karma of mine. But for right now, I need to celebrate my gift. I counted my blessings all week and have felt less oppressed and less depressed. I have a wonderful daughter and great friends who care.

'Just looking at my plants shows me what love can do. I've even been loving stray animals on the street and smiling at people in the supermarket. I suppose I'm applying the homework assignment of using my limits to get me past them. For so long I've been bitter about having my ideals dashed. But that's the state of the social and political world now, and being bitter isn't going to make things any different. Appreciating what I have, taking charge of my thoughts and feelings and working towards change in time just might.'

*Liza is definitely being challenged to appreciate herself from within and co-create her own reality, two of the main teachings of the World card. A principle of the Wheel of Fortune suggests that once we stop fighting and surrender to things as they are, they begin to change. Then we begin to get off the Wheel. I wonder if this might not be what Liza's already doing? Of course, we never do know just how long it's going to take to complete our karmic cycle, only that changing our responses will ultimately change the results.'*

## Suggestions for Application and Integration of the World

Would you like to feel as if the world is in the palm of your hand? The following are to help you be more worldly while at the same time spiritual; find freedom within the obligations and limitations of your daily life; remind you that your Self is 'in charge' at all times; and enjoy the benefits of self-regulation, among other things.

1  Colour or draw the World card with yourself as the Dancer.

2  Set the World card in a visible place as a reminder to your conscious and subconscious minds to use and absorb its teachings on how to meet your mundane obligations with an expanded sense of what they are truly about; lovingly discipline yourself to complete a cycle; and recall that, when you are aligned with your Self, the tools of life are at your command.

3  Dream on the World.

4  Play the note A on a musical instrument. Intone IAO or hum along with the music and concentrate on your Root *Chakra* at the base of your spine as you do so (you might experience it tingling or feeling slightly warm while doing this). Now direct your full attention to the World card. Think about some of the restrictions you are now experiencing in your work, relationships, spiritual development, etc. Next, consider how you might make the best of things despite these limits. Imagine yourself as the Dancer dancing freely within a restricted area, so that the very act of enjoying yourself might carry you beyond your feelings. Ask that the card's teachings guide you through a particular situation in which you feel crunched or suffocated. Or if you are faced with a worrisome circumstance, event or problem, such as feeling that the world is too much for you; stressed or overwhelmed by your responsibilities; wanting to be more self-regulating; or wishing to

triumph over a personal trial or tribulation, imagine how the Dancer might handle these things. If it seems feasible, do it. I was aware of the World when? Before/during/after . . .

5    Go out into the world and enact the teachings of the World. I enacted the World and this is what happened . . .

6    The Rerun. After having an experience and realising in retrospect how the World's teachings might have inspired you or another to meet an obligation with more acceptance; deal more effectively with red tape; perform masterfully; or see that you can control and direct what is going on around you by adjusting your inner awareness, mentally relive the situation, *including* your insight. This will help the behaviour become more automatic next time. If possible, actually rerun the situation in real life with this attitude or behaviour.

7    Ask yourself the following questions:

'Where might I apply the universal teachings to some worldly circumstance and thereby increase my level of Self-mastery?' 'How are self-discipline, organisation and flexibility freeing me in the midst of my responsibilities?' 'How can I best utilise the resources available?' 'How am I honouring the demands of the physical world in order to meet my spiritual obligations?' 'In what ways are the events around me mirroring my inner state?' 'Where would it be beneficial to place limits on my personal or professional relationships?' 'Where might taking charge of my responses to a situation or person help things turn out better than expected?' 'How have I successfully re-parented myself?' 'What old behaviour or idea is being taken out to bring in the new?' 'What would I like to absorb or surrender to?' 'In what ways am I becoming a better receiver and transmitter of cosmic energy?' 'What contract or agreement am I about to finalise?' 'Where have I achieved mastery?' 'As a challenge is the necessary prerequisite for victory, what has been conquered?' 'Where am I dancing amid restrictions?' 'What red-tape or bureaucratic b.s. have I over-come?' 'Where am I letting go and letting God/dess do it?'

'What Gateway of Life am I in or developing through in the previous questions?' Indicate: Childhood, Adolescence, Adulthood or Wisdom. Why?

'What do I need to do in order to develop the above further?' I need to . . .

'What step(s) do I want to take towards this goal and how can the World card guide me?'

8   Use a personal statement regarding the presence of the World card in your life at this time: 'I am liberated through my obligations and responsibilities.' 'My Self always supports and nourishes me.' 'As I live in the world, the universe is at my disposal.' My personal statement is . . .

9   Inspirational words and quotes:

'You will know the truth and the truth will make you free.'

JOHN 8:32

'You are not required to complete the work, but neither are you at liberty to abstain from it.'                     Rabbi Farfon

'For as long as space endures, and for as long as living things remain, until then may I, too, abide to dispel the misery of the world.'                     Tenzin Gyatso, 14th Dalai Lama

10   What symbols stand out in the card? What do they say to you? How might they be useful in daily living? Bring the symbol(s) into your life in some way so as to integrate the card's teachings.

11   Wear and surround yourself with the World's colour, blue-violet (indigo), to remind you of the card's teachings when needed, such as to recall that your Self is 'in charge', not to be intimidated by authority figures and be a better receiver and transmitter of cosmic energy in order to get a job done. Notice how you are affected.

12   The World's astrological correspondence is to the planet Saturn, governing discipline, self-regulation, self-parenting, inflexibility, detaching from or severing ties with external authorities that try to overpower you and accepting worldly obligations and responsibilities as spiritual work. Apply discipline and self-regulation to handle any of the above. Note what happens: your thoughts and feelings and the outcome.

13   Remember that the World's Hebrew name, *Tav*, means 'a mark of completion'. How can this remind you of the card's meaning or help in your life process?

14 Try a few drops of the scent cypress associated with the World card as a reminder to integrate the card's teachings.

15 Have a cup of tea made from the herb comfrey, sometimes called 'The Miracle Herb'. Sit quietly as you drink and consider the herb's properties as a tonic, skin renewer (when the leaves are applied externally), anti-inflammatory and healer of broken bones and consider the teachings of the World card. Caution: Because comfrey has been found to contain carcinogens or cancer-producing agents, it should only be ingested in very small amounts.

## *Instructions for Colouring*

**O – The Fool**

| | |
|---|---|
| Yellow | Background; circles on garment (but not flame in top circle); shoes. |
| Green | Trefoils surrounding circles on outer garment and other tendril-like figures (not belt); leaves on rose; wreath around head. |
| Violet | Mountains (use a somewhat pale colour because they are distant mountains; the peaks are snowcapped, so do not colour where snow is to be.) |
| Brown | Eagle on wallet; precipice in foreground upon which the Fool stands. |
| White | Sun; inner garment; dog; rose; eye on flap of wallet; mountain peaks. |
| Flesh | Hands and face (since it is obvious where flesh colour should be used, we shall not indicate it hereafter; see exceptions on Cards six and twenty.) Remember there are many races besides the Caucasian. |
| Blonde | Fool's hair is traditionally this colour, variations are definitely acceptable. |
| Citrine | Fool's hose (citrine is a yellowish-green made by a mixture of orange and green.) |
| Gold | Star on shoulder; girdle; knob on staff. |
| Silver | Moon on shoulder. |
| Red | Feather; spokes of wheels, flame on top circle and lining of sleeves in outer garment; wallet (except eagle and eye). |

**1 – The Magician**

| | |
|---|---|
| Yellow | Background; spearhead; lily stamens. |
| Green | Foliage. |
| Black | Hair (optional). |
| Blue-Green | Girdle (serpent). |

| Brown | Table. |
| White | Inner garment; headband; spear shaft; uplifted wand; lily petals. |
| Gold | Pentacle (or coin) on table; sword hilt; circle at end of spear shaft. |
| Silver | Cup. |
| Steel | Sword blade (mix a little blue with grey). |
| Red | Outer garment; roses. |

## 2 – High Priestess

| Yellow | Left foreground. |
| Green | Palms on veil (not centres). |
| Blue | Background; robe (should have white in it also where it shimmers down in front and out of the picture to represent flowing water). |
| Grey | Throne; veil background. |
| White | Inner garment; cross on breast; head drapery; right pillar; centres of palms; Hebrew letter on left pillar. |
| Silver | Crown. |
| Brown | Scroll (paler to look like parchment). |
| Red | Pomegranates (seeds deeper than skins). |

## 3 – The Empress

| Yellow | Background; shoes; staff of sceptre. |
| Green | Foliage; grass; wreath on head; robe (except cuffs, girdle, collar edging and panel); ball on sceptre (not bar and cross). |
| Blonde | Hair (optional); wheat ears. |
| Blue | Stream and waterfall. |
| Brown | Tree-trunks; ground area beside waterfall. |
| Grey | Stone bench. |
| Gold | Stars; collar edging; girdle; cross and bar on sceptre. |
| Silver | Crescent. |
| Copper | Shield (except dove; mix red and brown to create copper colour). |
| White | Pearls; panel in dress; cuffs of dress; dove; highlights in waterfall. |
| Red | Roses; triangle on breast. |

## 4 – The Emperor

| | |
|---|---|
| Yellow | T-cross and circle in right hand. |
| Green | Foreground. |
| Blue | Stream at base of cliff. |
| Grey | Stone cube (except ram's head). |
| Violet | Belt and flaps on tunic (not borders nor medallion on left shoulder). |
| White | Borders of tunic flaps and belt; medallion; ram's head; beard and hair (traditionally this colour to show ancient wisdom); border only of inverted T on globe in left hand; sleeves. |
| Gold | Inverted T and cross on globe; framework and points on helmet. |
| Brown | Slopes from height in foreground to stream's edge. |
| Orange | Background above mountains. |
| Steel | Leg armour and breastplate. |
| Red | Globe in left hand (not inverted T or cross); helmet (except borders and points); entire mountain. |

## 5 – The Hierophant

| | |
|---|---|
| Yellow | Crown (not trefoils, crossbars or circle at top); yoke behind ears (except fringe); staff in left hand; orphreys (Y's) on vestments of kneeling priests; lily stamens. |
| Green | Garments of figures in foreground (except collars, sleeve edges, flowers and orphreys). |
| Violet | Fringe on yoke. |
| Grey | Background (light); pillars (dark); throne (darker). |
| Gold | Crown ornaments; key pointing right (except dots in circle). |
| Silver | Crescent at throat; key pointing to left (except dots in circle). |
| Blue | Undergarment showing at bottom. |
| Blue-Green | Scarf or border of outer robe. |
| White | Undergarment at throat, navel and sleeves; shoes; collars and sleeve edgings of chasubles; dots in key circles; lilies on chasubles at right. Alternate squares at base of throne. |
| Red-Orange | Outer garment (not scarf or border); dais (Mix equal parts red and orange). |
| Red | Roses on chasuble at left. |

## 6 – The Lovers

Yellow
: In every case, except the sun, the yellow in this card is used beside red or red and green. The five fruits on the tree behind the woman are yellow with red cheeks. The flames behind the man are yellow with red at the base, after the manner of the blue and yellow in a flame from an old-fashioned gas jet. The angel's flesh is yellow, but pale so as to give the appearance of flesh.

Blue
: Background (but not above angel's head).

Green
: Foreground and foliage; serpent around the tree; angel's hair (with yellow and red).

Violet
: Angel's garment; mountain (paler in colour).

Gold
: Sun and background above angel.

White
: Clouds.

Blonde
: Woman's hair (optional).

Brown
: Tree-trunk behind woman.

Red
: Angel's wings (see note under yellow).

## 7 – The Chariot

Yellow
: Background; chariot wheels.

Green
: Trees and grass; wreath under rider's crown.

Blue
: Stream; moon faces on shoulders (faces only, not crescents); deeper blue on canopy and panel behind charioteer (but not stars) and on wings on front of chariot (not disc between them).

Grey
: Chariot and chariot pillars; wall before city (both sides of chariot).

Gold
: Crown; belt (not figures); collar edging; ornament in square on breastplate; disc between wings; sceptre in right hand (except crescent at top of sceptre).

Silver
: Crescents on shoulders and on sceptre; stars on canopy and back panel.

White
: Cuffs; castles in city (not rooftops); shield on chariot; white sphinx and stripes on headdresses of both sphinxes; design on skirt of rider.

Steel
: Armour on arms or rider.

Brass
: Breastplate (greenish-yellow to simulate brass).

Blonde
: Hair (optional).

Red
: Rooftops; symbol on shield on front of chariot.

## 8 – Strength

| | |
|---|---|
| Yellow | Background; lion's eye. |
| Green | Foliage, rose leaves, leaves in woman's hair; foreground (but do not extend all the way in right foreground, because the mountain range carries over to the right). |
| Violet | Mountain (both sides of background). |
| White | Woman's dress; lion's teeth. |
| Blonde | Woman's hair (optional). |
| Red | Roses; lion; flowers in hair of woman. |

## 9 – The Hermit

| | |
|---|---|
| Yellow | Lantern rays between black lines. |
| Blue | Hermit's cap. |
| Brown | Staff; shoe. |
| Grey | Robe (not right sleeve of undergarment); foreground (not peaks). |
| White | Hair; beard (to show ancient wisdom); right sleeve; mountain peaks. |
| Gold | Star. |
| Indigo | Background (indigo is a deep blue-violet and black, indicating a night sky, but may be substituted with black). |

## 10 – The Wheel of Fortune

| | |
|---|---|
| Yellow | Serpent; eagle's eye; lion's eyes. |
| Blue | Background; sphinx (not headdress). |
| Brown | Animals (lion should be tawny, a mixture of brown and yellow). |
| Orange | Entire wheel in centre. |
| Gold | Sword hilt. |
| Steel | Sword blade. |
| Grey | Clouds (but they are grey on white, storm clouds). |
| Blonde | Man's hair (optional) eagle's beak (upper and lower). |
| White | In headdress of sphinx; clouds as stated above; bull's horns; eye of Hermanubis (jackal-headed figure). |
| Red | Hermanubis (except eye); eagle's tongue. |

## 11 – Justice

| | |
|---|---|
| Yellow | Between curtains in background. |
| Green | Surrounding square on crown; cape over shoulders. |
| Blue | Sleeves (same shade as canopy of Chariot in card seven). |
| Indigo | T on chest (may be substituted with black). |
| Violet | Curtains (not ropes, tassels and fringe); oval around neck; veil connecting pillars of throne (lighter violet for this veil). |
| Grey | Throne and dais. |
| Gold | Balances; sword hilt; rings holding ropes on curtains; outline and peaks of crown. |
| Steel | Sword blade. |
| White | Shoe; square on crown; panels beside T on chest. |
| Blonde | Hair (optional). |
| Red | Circle in square on crown; garment (not cape or sleeves); rope, tassels and fringes on curtains. |

## 12 – The Hanged Man

| | |
|---|---|
| Yellow | Slippers; halo around head. |
| Blue | Coat (not crescents, buttons, belt or stripe down front and around neck) same shade as canopy in card seven. |
| Green | Grass. |
| Brown | Scaffold; hill slopes. |
| Grey | Background. |
| Silver | Crescents, belt, buttons and front stripe. |
| White | Hair (to show link with ancient wisdom); rope. |
| Red | Hose. |

## 13 – Death

| | |
|---|---|
| Yellow | Sun; band on man's crown. |
| Green | Leaves and rosebush (not rose). |
| Blue | Stream. |
| Brown | Scythe handle. |
| Steel | Scythe blade. |
| White | Skeleton; rose; cuff on hand in centre; leave the seed in upper left corner uncoloured. |
| Blonde | Woman's hair (optional). |
| Gold | Points on man's crown. |
| Red | Background. |

## 14 – Temperance

| | |
|---|---|
| Yellow | Crown over mountain peaks; *Yods* over eagle; torch flame (interspersed with red to represent flames); lion's eyes; path up to mountains. |
| Brown | Lion (see card ten); eagle (except beak and legs); torch handle. |
| Blue | Pool; stream from vase. |
| Green | Grass. |
| Orange | Ornament on head of angel; vase. |
| Violet | Mountains in background (paler colour). |
| Gold | Background; star on breast. |
| White | Dress. |
| Blonde | Angel's hair (optional); beak; legs and talons of eagle. |
| Red | Angel's wings (these are highlighted with blue). |
| Rainbow | Rainbow is a succession of bands of colour, beginning on upper left side of arc with violet and applying in succession blue, green, yellow, orange and red. |

## 15 – The Devil

| | |
|---|---|
| Yellow | Insignia above cross below navel of devil; hair of the male and female figures (optional), the torch flame and the tail of the male figure are yellow shot with red. |
| Green | Tail of female figure. |
| Brown | Feathers, legs and horns of devil; torch handle; foreground; body and wings of devil (more effective if a little grey is mixed with pale brown to give a dull, earthy colour). |
| White | Star; beard (again to show link with ancient wisdom); horns of male and female figures. |
| Steel | Chains; ring on pedestal. |
| Red | Fruit on tail of female figure; cross on devil's body; devil's eyes; note also what is said under yellow. |

## 16 – The Tower

| | |
|---|---|
| Yellow | Two rope-like bands on crown; crown of woman; *Yods* (with tongue of red in right corner of each); flames (with preponderance of red to make realistic); Solar disc, except gold edges around triangular rays. |
| Blue | Dress of woman; hose of man. |

| Gold | Crown (except yellow parts); lightning flash; point around Solar disc. |
| Grey | Tower; clouds (heavy storm clouds as in card ten). |
| Brown | Cliff (top of cliff lighter brown). |
| Blonde | Woman's hair (optional). |
| Red | Boots and coat of man; shoes of woman; see also under yellow. |

## 17 – The Star

| Yellow | Central Star. |
| Green | Grass; tree leaves. |
| Blue | Background; pool; water from vases; deeper blue for ovals on vases and stripes around their necks. |
| Violet | Mountains (note there are rising hills before the peak). |
| Orange | Vases (except stripes designated otherwise, ovals and handles). |
| White | Smaller stars; vase handles and stripes across ovals not indicated red; highlights on water. |
| Brown | Tree-trunk. |
| Blonde | Hair (optional). |
| Red | Top band over oval in vase at left of card; lower band over oval in vase at right of card; remainder of both vases; bird on the tree. |

## 18 – The Moon

| Yellow | Moon and rays; path; *Yods* same as in card sixteen. |
| Green | Grass in foreground (note this does not reach towers). |
| Blue | Background; pool. |
| Grey | Towers; wolf; stones around pool. |
| Violet | Crayfish; mountains (paler shade). |
| Brown | Dog; plains between grass and mountains. |
| White | Tower windows; highlights on pool; wolf's fang. |

## 19 – The Sun

| Yellow | Sun and rays; sunflower petals. |
| Green | Grass (circle should be darker than rest of grass); leaves. |
| Blue | Background (this should encircle the rays extending from the sun, with blue projections similar to those on the face of the sun in the card extending inward slightly from the blue circle towards the sun.) |

Brown      Sunflower centres.
Grey       Wall.
Orange     *Yods*.
Blonde     Hair of both children (optional).

## 20 – Judgement

Yellow     Bell of trumpet; rays from clouds.
Blue       Background; water; angel's dress (darker blue).
Grey       Bodies of human figures; coffins (dark grey).
White      Clouds; banner (not cross); icebergs (with delicate blue highlights); collar edging on angel's dress.
Gold       Trumpet.
Blonde     Hair on woman, child and angel (optional).
Red        Angel's wings; cross on banner.

## 21 – The World

Green      Wreath (except binding top and bottom).
Blue       Background (leave blank ellipses around spirals in hands).
Brown      Animals (as in card ten).
White      Clouds as in card ten; colour rays from ellipses around spirals extending into the blue of the background.
Blonde     Hair on man and dancer (optional); beak of eagle.
Violet     Veil around dancer.
Red        Binding at top and bottom of wreath; wreath on head of dancing figure.

*Table of Attributions*

| Name | Hebrew Letter/Name Hebrew Numerical Value | Card Number | Colour | Musical Note |
|---|---|---|---|---|
| The Fool | A/*Aleph* (Ox or Bull) 1/1,000 as a final letter | 0 | Pale-Yellow | E |
| The Magician | B/*Beth* (House) 2 | 1 | Yellow | E |
| The High Priestess | G/GH/*Gimel* (Camel) 3 | 2 | Blue | G# |
| The Empress | D/DH/*Daleth* (Door) 4 | 3 | Green | F# |
| The Emperor | H/E/*Heh* (Window) 5 | 4 | Red | C |
| The Hierophant | U/V/W/*Vav* (Hook or Nail) 6 | 5 | Red-Orange | C# |
| The Lovers | Z/*Zain* (Sword) 7 | 6 | Orange | D |
| The Chariot | CH/*Cheth* (Fence) 8 | 7 | Yellow-Orange | D# |
| Strength | T/*Teth* (Snake) 9 | 8 | Yellow | E |
| The Hermit | Y,I,J/*Yod* (Open Hand) 10 | 9 | Yellow-Green | F |
| The Wheel of Fortune | C,K/*Kaph* (Grasping hand) 20/500 as a final letter | 10 | Violet | A# |
| Justice | L/*Lamed* (Ox-goad/to teach) 30 | 11 | Green | F# |
| The Hanged Man | M/*Mem* (Water) 40/600 as a final letter | 12 | Blue | G# |
| Death | N/*Nun* (Fish/to sprout or grow) 50/700 as a final letter | 13 | Blue-Green | G |
| Temperance | S/*Samekh* (Prop, peg or support) 60 | 14 | Blue | G# |
| The Devil | O/*Ayin* (Eye) 70 | 15 | Blue-Violet | A |
| The Tower | P, Ph,F/*Peh* (Mouth) 80/800 as a final letter | 16 | Red | C |
| The Star | Ts/Tz/Cz/*Tzaddi* (Fishhook) 90/900 as a final letter | 17 | Violet | A# |
| The Moon | Q/*Ooph* (Back of the Head) 100 | 18 | Violet-Red | B |
| The Sun | R/*Resh* (Head and face of man) 200 | 19 | Orange | D |
| Judgement | Sh,Sch/*Shin* (Tooth or serpent's fang) 300 | 20 | Red | C |
| The World | Th/*Tav* (signature or cross) 400 | 21 | Blue-Violet | A |

| Herb | Astrological Sign or Planet | Chakra | Element or Metal | Scent | Qabalistic Intelligence |
|---|---|---|---|---|---|
| Ginseng[1]<br>[see footnote on p. 426] | Uranus | — | Uranium | Galbanum | Fiery |
| Astragalus | Mercury | Seventh (Crown) | Mercury | Mastic | Transparent |
| Cramp | Moon | Sixth (Third Eye) | Silver | Camphor | Uniting |
| Dong Quai | Venus | Fifth (Throat) | Brass or copper | Myrtle | Luminous |
| Ginger | Aries | — | Cardinal Fire | Pine | Constituting |
| Sage | Taurus | — | Fixed Earth | Vanilla | Eternal |
| Parsley | Gemini | — | Mutable Air | Worm-wood | Disposing |
| Dandelion | Cancer | — | Cardinal Water | Sandal-wood | House of Influence |
| Cayenne | Leo | — | Fixed Fire | Frankin-cense | Secret of All Spiritual Activities |
| Liquorice | Virgo | — | Mutable Earth | Pettigrain | Will |
| Slippery Elm | Jupiter | Third (Solar plexus) | Aluminium | Balsam | Rewarding |
| Plantain | Libra | — | Cardinal Air | Pepper-mint | Faithful |
| Irish Moss or kelp | Neptune | — | — | Myrrh | Stable |
| Elder | Scorpio | — | Fixed Water | Opoponax | Imaginative |
| Echinacea | Sagittarius | — | Mutable Fire | Dill | Trial |
| Lobelia | Capricorn | — | Cardinal Earth | Nutmeg | Renewing |
| Garlic | Mars | Second (Reproductive organs) | Iron/steel | Pepper | Arousing |
| Skullcap | Aquarius | — | Fixed Air | Bergamot | Natural |
| Lemon Balm | Pisces | — | Mutable Water | Violet | Corporeal |
| Bay Laurel or Angelica | Sun | Fourth (Heart) | Gold | Cinnamon | Collective |
| Golden Seal | Pluto | — | — | Basil | Perpetual |
| Comfrey | Saturn | First (Root) | Lead | Cypress | Administrative |

| Name | Function | Direction | Opposites |
|---|---|---|---|
| The Fool | — | — | — |
| The Magician | — | Above | Life/Death |
| The High Priestess | — | Below | Peace/Strife |
| The Empress | Feelings and Clairsentience | East | Wisdom/Folly |
| The Emperor | Sight and Clairvoyance | North-East | — |
| The Hierophant | Hearing and Clairaudience | South-East | — |
| The Lovers | Smell | East-Above | — |
| The Chariot | Speech | East-Below | — |
| Strength | Digestion | North-Above | — |
| The Hermit | Coition | North-Below | — |
| The Wheel of Fortune | — | West | Wealth/Poverty |
| Justice | Work/Action | North-West | — |
| The Hanged Man | — | East to West | — |
| Death | Motion | South-West | — |
| Temperance | Wrath | West-Above | — |
| The Devil | Mirth | West-Below | — |
| The Tower | — | North | Beauty/Ugliness |
| The Star | Concentration/ Meditation | South-Above | — |
| The Moon | Sleep | South-Below | — |
| The Sun | — | South | Fertility/Sterility |
| Judgement | — | North to South | — |
| The World | — | Centre | Dominion/ Slavery |

1 With the exceptions of cramp, ginger, dandelion and bay laurel, all herbal correlations are from *The Herbal Tarot*, by Michael Tierra and Candice Cantin, available through US Games Systems, Inc.

## About the author

Amber Jayanti, founder of the Santa Cruz School for Tarot and Qabalah study in 1975, is a practical mystic who has been living, studying, consulting with and teaching these subjects for over thirty years. She is the author of *Principles of the Qabalah* and the forthcoming *Living the Qabalah*. Amber is also a graduate of the Builders of the Adytum (BOTA), a Qabalistic Mystery School, and an honorary Grandmaster in the American Tarot Association.

## To contact the author

You may call her on (00 1) 831 423 9742
You may e-mail her on amber@practical-mystic.com
You may visit her website on www.practical-mystic.com